Critical Thinking and Communication
The Use of Reason in Argument

Third Edition

EDWARD S. INCH
Pacific Lutheran University

BARBARA WARNICK
University of Washington

Allyn and Bacon

BOSTON   LONDON   TORONTO   SYDNEY   TOKYO   SINGAPORE

Vice President, Humanities: Paul Smith
Series Editor: Karon Bowers
Series Editorial Assistant: Kathy Rubino
Marketing Manager: Kris Farnsworth
Composition and Prepress Buyer: Linda Cox
Manufacturing Buyer: Suzanne Lareau
Cover Administrator: Suzanne Harbison
Editorial-Production Service: York Production Services
Electronic Composition: Omegatype Typography, Inc.

Copyright © 1998, 1994, 1989 by Allyn and Bacon
A Simon & Schuster Company
Needham Heights, Massachusetts 02194

Internet: www.abacon.com
American Online: keyword: College Online

All rights reserved. No part of the material protected by this copyright notice may be reproduced or utilized in any form or by any means, electronic or mechanical, including photocopying, recording, or by any information storage and retrieval system, without the written permission of the copyright owner.

Library of Congress Cataloging-in-Publication Data

Inch, Edward S.
    Critical thinking and communication : the use of reason in argument / Edward S. Inch, Barbara Warnick. — 3rd ed.
      p.   cm.
    Warnick's name appears first on the earlier editions.
    Includes bibliographical references and index.
    ISBN 0-205-27293-2
      1. Reasoning. 2. Critical thinking. 3. Communication.
I. Warnick, Barbara, 1946– . II. Title.
BC177.W35 1997
168—dc21   97–16949
                                                           CIP

Printed in the United States of America.

10 9 8 7 6 5 4 3 2 1   02 01 00 99 98 97

To Pamela and Michael

CONTENTS

Preface — xi

SECTION ONE: CONCEPTUALIZING ARGUMENT — 1

Chapter 1: Arguments and Argumentation — 3
- Critical Thinking — 5
- Argumentation and Arguments — 7
- Perspectives on Argumentation — 11
- An Argument Model — 14
- Summary — 20
- Exercises — 21

Chapter 2: Contexts for Argument — 27
- Culture and Argumentation — 28
- Argumentation and Ethics — 37
- Summary — 41
- Exercises — 42

Chapter 3: Argument Occasions — 47
- Nature of Occasions — 49
  - Argument Spheres — 49
  - Argument Fields — 52
- Argument Situations — 56
- Summary — 58
- Exercises — 59

SECTION TWO: COMMUNICATING ARGUMENTS — 63

Chapter 4: Arguers, Recipients, and Argumentation — 65

- The Audience and Argumentation — 67
  - Selecting the Starting Points — 67
  - Supporting Reasoning — 69
  - Using Evidence — 70
  - Organizing Arguments — 71
  - Additional Concerns about Audience — 73
  - Analyzing the Audience — 74
- The Arguer and Argumentation — 75
  - Message Sources and Their Influence — 77
  - Enhancing Credibility through Argument — 79
- Fallacies Related to Audience — 82
  - *Ad Hominem* — 83
  - *Ad Populum* — 84
  - Appeal to Tradition — 85
  - Straw Arguments — 86
- Summary — 87
- Exercises — 89

Chapter 5: Language and Argument — 93

- The Nature of Language — 95
  - Language and Meaning — 96
  - Language and Abstraction — 98
  - Connotations and Denotations — 100
- Language in Argument — 103
  - Language, Thought, and Perception — 103
  - Functions of Language — 105
  - Using Language in Argument — 109
- Fallacies of Language — 113
  - Equivocation — 114
  - Amphiboly — 114

- Emotive Language 115
- Summary 116
- Exercises 118

SECTION THREE: PARSING ARGUMENTS 123

Chapter 6: Argument Claims and Propositions 125
- The Nature of Claims and Propositions 126
- Formulating a Proposition 131
  - Controversiality 131
  - Clarity 132
  - Balance 135
  - Challenge 136
- Types of Claims 137
  - Factual Claims 137
  - Value Claims 139
  - Policy Claims 140
- Continuum of Claims 140
- Summary 142
- Exercises 142

Chapter 7: Evidence: The Foundation for Arguments 147
- The Nature of Evidence 149
- Types of Evidence 150
- Evaluating Fact and Opinion Evidence 153
  - Reliability 153
  - Expertise 154
  - Objectivity 154
  - Consistency 155
  - Recency 156
  - Relevance 156
  - Access 157
  - Accuracy of Citation 157
- Evaluating Statistical Evidence 159

- Fallacies of Evidence 161
  - Begging the Question 162
  - *Non Sequitur* 162
- Research Strategies for Locating Evidence 163
  - Site Types 164
  - Source Types 168
- Summary 173
- Exercises 174

Chapter 8: Reasoning: Making Inferences **183**
- Formal Logic and Practical Reasoning 185
- Reasoning as Inference-Making 188
  - Quasilogical Arguments 189
  - Analogy 192
  - Generalization and Argument from Example 194
  - Cause 198
  - Coexistential Arguments 201
  - Dissociation 203
- Fallacies of Faulty Reasoning 205
  - False Analogy 205
  - Hasty Generalization 207
  - False Cause 208
  - Slippery Slope 209
- Summary 210
- Exercises 212

SECTION FOUR: ARGUING EXTENDED CASES **219**

Chapter 9: Case Construction: Arguing about Propositions of Fact **220**
- Arguing about Facts, Values, and Policies 223
- Relating Facts, Values, and Policies 224

- Principles of Case Construction 226
- Stock Issues in Fact-Based Cases 228
  - Definition 229
  - Threshold 229
  - Application 230
- Principles of Refutation 232
- The Issues Brief 234
- Summary 237
- Exercises 238

Chapter 10: Arguing about Values 245

- Values and Value Systems 247
- The Process of Value Change 249
- Values and Argumentation 250
- Stock Issues for Value Arguments 252
  - Definition 252
  - Field or Perspective 253
  - Criteria 254
  - Application 255
  - Hierarchies 255
- The Issues Brief 256
- Summary 259
- Exercises 259

Chapter 11: Arguing about Policies 265

- Policy Arguments and Policy Systems 267
  - Ill 270
  - Blame 272
  - Cure 273
  - Cost/Benefits 274
- Issues Brief 275
- Alternative Formats for Arguing Policies 280
  - Comparative-Advantages Case 280
  - Goals Case 283

- Alternative Formats for Refuting Policy Arguments ... 285
  - Strategy of Defense of the Present Policy System ... 285
  - Strategy of Defense of the Present Policy System with Minor Repairs ... 286
  - Strategy of Counterproposals ... 287
- Summary ... 288
- Exercises ... 289

SECTION FIVE: ANALYZING ARGUMENTS ... 293

Chapter 12: Argument Analysis and Criticism ... 295

- Benefits of Argument Analysis ... 296
- A General Model for Argument Analysis ... 297
  - Analysis of Simple Arguments ... 298
  - Analysis of Other Structural Patterns ... 302
  - An Application ... 307
- The Toulmin Model ... 310
  - The Nature and Background of the Toulmin Model ... 310
  - Six Parts of the Model ... 311
  - Difficulties in Applying the Model ... 315
  - Argument Chains and the Toulmin Model ... 317
- Comparison of the Two Models ... 318
- Summary ... 319
- Exercises ... 320

Appendix A: Intercollegiate Debate ... 327

Appendix B: Answers to Selected Exercises ... 341

Appendix C: Glossary ... 353

Appendix D: Fallacies ... 361

PREFACE

The changes we have made in the third edition of this textbook both reflect and anticipate changes that are occurring nationwide in the teaching of argumentation. While continuing to emphasize a rhetorical approach to the study of argument (in particular, the need to adapt to one's audience), we have expanded our treatment of reflective and critical thinking skills. These include being aware of differing points of view on a topic, avoiding personal prejudice, and being able to evaluate evidence, reasoning, and assumptions of one's own and others' arguments. We have also continued our emphasis on constructing argument cases in support of a central thesis or claim, which involves conducting research, identifying important issues that bear on the claim, and deciding on and defending one's position in a sustained argumentative case.

In Chapter 2, we have considered the relationship between culture and argument as manifest in various styles of argument, such as the presentational style and the analogical style. These two styles make use of a narrative logic that can complement the more traditional Western forms of informal logic. We have described these narrative forms in the belief that students in a multicultural society may need to work from a repertoire of argument styles and forms as they communicate with their audiences. Because of our emphasis on the critical thinking tradition, however, our book emphasizes the role of logical reasoning in argument.

Chapter 7 is sensitive to the tremendous changes in information access brought about by computer-mediated communication. This chapter includes suggestions for using computerized resources such as the World Wide Web, library databases, and CD-ROMs. For those who may not have access to such resources or who find traditional print-copy resources more efficient and easy to use, research strategies for print sources are described as well.

This book examines the forms of practical reasoning used in persuasive communication—speeches, conversations, essays, group deliberation, and other situations in which argument occurs. We believe that students learn by doing by analyzing topics for argument, conducting research, constructing cases, and analyzing and refuting others' arguments. We therefore emphasize examples and exercises that require active student involvement. Our view is that by producing and evaluating argumentation on topics of interest to them, students will effectively develop their critical thinking skills.

As in the first and second editions, we have produced a flexibly organized textbook. Section One, "Conceptualizing Argument," presents the basic theory of argument and argumentation that guides the remainder of the book. It provides for a discussion of the nature of argument, argumentation, and critical thinking—their function, contexts, ethical standards, and occasions. Section Two, "Communicating Arguments," presents an analysis of how arguers and recipients are interrelated. This section considers recipients, language use, sources, and forms of expression for argument. Section Three, "Parsing Arguments," considers argument components and how they work together. Specifically, this section considers the relationships and tests of claims, evidence, and forms of reasoning. The chapters in Sections Four and Five can then be read and studied in any order, depending on student needs and teaching interest. Section Four, "Arguing Extended Cases," focuses on the process for building extended arguments and examines how arguments of fact, value, and policy can be made. Section Five, "Analyzing Arguments," provides methods of analyzing and evaluating arguments.

We have also provided many study tools—lists of key concepts, an answer key, chapter summaries, a bibliography, and exercises that require students to apply chapter concepts. We have departed from previous editions in dividing the discussion of fallacies into the chapters to which the fallacy type is most relevant. However, the appendix on fallacies provides a typology that can be used to help students analyze argument strengths and weaknesses. The book's study aids should enable students to review for exams, do further reading, and have handy references when reading text material. We have used a variety of examples from law, education, ethics, business, and other fields to illustrate the argument concepts introduced.

The book treats topics that are standard in argumentation courses—reasoning types, fallacies, tests of reasoning and evidence, case construction, and, for courses including debate assignments, a debate appendix. The book focuses on argument in interactive and written communication as well as in speeches. It draws upon multiple argument models in Chapter 12 on argument analysis and criticism. These models were developed by philosophers Stephen Toulmin, Michael Scriven, and Irving Copi, and they have been highly useful to students in understanding how arguments work. Another feature of the book is its emphasis on argumentation about values. Chapter 10 provides extensive explanation of the aspects of value argument and the procedures for constructing cases on value issues.

We would like to conclude by thanking individuals who have helped us with the development of this textbook. We would especially like to thank Susan L. Kline of Ohio State University and Joseph W. Wenzel of the University of Illinois, whose assistance on the first and second editions of the book was extensive. We would also like to acknowledge the reviewers for the third edition, whose comments and suggestions were excellent: Beth M. Waggenspack, Virginia Tech University; Susan L. Kline, The Ohio State University; Jim Vickrey, Troy State University; Ronald O. Wastyn, James Madison University; Dale Herbeck, Boston College; Steven Schwarze, The University of Iowa; and Mark A. Pollock, Loyola University, Chicago.

E.S.I.
B.W.

SECTION ONE

Conceptualizing Argument

CHAPTER 1

Arguments and Argumentation

CHAPTER OUTLINE
- Critical Thinking
- Argumentation and Arguments
- Perspectives on Argumentation
- An Argument Model
- Summary
- Exercises

KEY CONCEPTS

critical thinking	evidence
argumentation	reasoning
argument	level of dispute
claim	argument chain

Three students—Kaidren, John, and Ramona—have selected Affirmative Action in college admissions as their topic for a group discussion for their speech class. They have completed most of their library research and are now deciding how to plan their discussion. Here is a segment from their group meeting[1]:

Kaidren: How about using the following question for our topic: "Does Affirmative Action promote unfair admissions practices?"

John: I think that would be a good way to state it. Affirmative Action assigns admissions spots to minorities that should be available to all applicants, and that's definitely unfair.

Ramona: Wait a minute, what do you mean by "fair"?

Kaidren: I mean treating all people in a way that is free of favoritism or bias. I mean practices that are impartial and equitable to everyone.

Ramona: So, in terms of admissions, what does that mean?

John: It means that students should be evaluated based strictly on merit, not on their race or other factors. It means not using quotas to admit people who shouldn't qualify for admission.

Kaidren: Yes, students' SAT scores, GPAs and other objectively measured achievements should be the only criteria used.

Ramona: Well, I think that if that is all "fair" means, then we shouldn't use the term. My *Webster's* defines "fair" as being "free from self interest, prejudice, or favoritism." Various studies have shown that standardized tests such as the SAT discriminate against minorities. Also, the factor that best predicts how students will score on standardized tests is their income. So I think SATs are biased against minorities and the poor and are themselves unfair!

John: What do you mean by "various studies"? Where did you get the information that the SAT discriminates?

Ramona: If SAT scores were used alone, the most selective colleges would admit practically no blacks. These colleges' average SAT scores for admitted students are above 600 in verbal and 650 in math. Since about five percent of whites and less than one percent of blacks score this high, blacks would be systematically excluded from these colleges. Also, the groups with the highest family income receive the highest average scores, and the score range goes down progressively right along with the income ranges. Just look at these charts from *The Case against the SAT* by James Cruse and Dale Trushein.[2]

John: Well, what about students' GPAs? I think that students who have worked hard in school and made good grades should be admitted. Affirmative Action quotas close out students whose record shows that they deserve to be admitted.

Ramona: Wait a minute! Quotas have been illegal since the *Bakke* decision, which ruled them illegal and at the same time approved the use of race (and gender) as a determining factor in college admissions. Today institutions use goals or target numbers that enable colleges and universities to promote diversity.

> John: Quotas, goals, targets—what's the difference? The effect is still the same. Students who are entitled to admission don't get in.
>
> Kaidren: Yes, John Kekes, professor of philosophy at the State University of New York in Albany, said in a 1995 *Congressional Quarterly Researcher* that "for every act of preferential treatment, somebody else is treated unjustly."[3] I don't think that's fair.
>
> Ramona: Look, admissions practices have never been "fair." Athletes, children of alumni, and other groups have often received preference in admission. It's often not what you know but who you know or what you can do for the institution that counts.
>
> Kaidren: Well, does that mean we should just ignore merit and admissions standards and begin admitting every person or group that has some special circumstance or condition that allows them special treatment? I think that would be chaotic!
>
> . . . And the discussion continues.

These three students are engaged in two processes that will be the focus of this book—critical thinking and argumentation. Critical thinking is a process in which a person tries to answer rationally those questions that cannot be easily or definitively answered and for which all the relevant information may not be available. Critical thinking requires judgment. Joanne Kurfiss defines critical thinking as *"an investigation whose purpose is to explore a situation, phenomenon, question, or problem to arrive at a hypothesis or conclusion about it that integrates all available information and that therefore can be convincingly justified."*[4] A person who has thought critically about an issue will not settle for the apparent or obvious solution but will suspend judgment while seeking out all relevant arguments, facts, and reasons that promote good decision-making.

While critical thinking does not necessarily involve communication, argumentation does. *Argumentation is the process of making arguments intended to justify beliefs, attitudes, and values so as to influence others.* We see argumentation in media ads for products, campaign ads for candidates, newspaper editorials, internet sites on public issues, business meetings where proposals are made, and in many other places. Argumentation occurs everywhere, and we deal with it as readers, listeners, writers, and speakers on a daily basis. This book is intended to help you improve your skills as a consumer and producer of argumentation.

CRITICAL THINKING

Critical thinking is regarded as a vital skill in today's society because it prevents people from making bad decisions and helps them to solve problems. As Richard W. Paul and Gerald M. Nosich recently observed:

> The kind of 'work' increasingly required in industry and business is 'intellectual,' that is, it requires workers to define goals and purposes clearly, seek out and organize relevant

data, conceptualize those data, consider alternative perspectives, adjust thinking to context, question assumptions, modify thinking in light of the continual flood of new information, and reason to legitimate conclusions. Furthermore, the intellectual work required must increasingly be coordinated with, and must profit from the critique of, fellow workers.[5]

Paul and Nosich go on to observe that supervisors and employers value workers who can reason well and express themselves clearly.

Good critical thinking is a prerequisite for all of these skills. What, exactly, is critical thinking? Many of its processes are shown in the discussion of affirmative action with which we began this chapter. Kaidren began that discussion by *clearly stating a question for discussion*. ("Does Affirmative Action promote unfair admissions practices?") As you will see when you read Chapter 6 of this book, discussions that are not based on clearly focused statements can often become confused or muddled because discussants lose sight of the points at issue.

Ramona almost immediately asked, "What do you mean by 'fair'?" Critical thinking requires *clarifying the meaning of terms* central to the discussion, and it is obvious that "fair" as a term will be central to any deliberation about the benefits and disadvantages of Affirmative Action. Does "fair" mean treating everyone strictly on the basis of merit, or does it mean eliminating factors that discriminate against minorities, or does it mean something else? It is not hard to imagine that this group will continue to be preoccupied by what "fair" means!

Good critical thinking also involves *developing and applying criteria for evaluation*. Does Affirmative Action actually promote fairness and equal treatment of minorities, or does it lead to further discrimination once they have been admitted? Does Affirmative Action actually enhance diversity in college classrooms? Does it benefit or damage other aspects of students' educations? All of these questions relate to whether Affirmative Action indeed fulfills the purposes for which it was intended. Answering them calls upon Kaidren, Ramona, and John to justify their own values and to present evidence about the actual performance of Affirmative Action as an admissions process.

Many other aspects of critical thinking are apparent in this brief discussion. John asked for the source of Ramona's claims about the SAT as part of the process of *evaluating the credibility of sources of information* used by the group. When Kaidren observed that extending Affirmative Action principles to all groups would result in admissions chaos, she was *pursuing the implications of the principles* behind the practice. When Ramona observed that admissions practices have never been "fair" because certain groups—alumni's children and athletes—have received special treatment, she was *comparing an analogous (comparable) situation* to shed new light on the question.

In addition to these examples, critical thinking involves many other processes such as:

- Refining generalizations and avoiding oversimplification
- Generating and assessing solutions to problems
- Comparing perspectives, interpretations, or theories
- Reading critically, seeking out information that disagrees with one's perspective
- Listening critically, seriously considering views with which one disagrees.[6]

The ability to apply these processes to a question or issue is what distinguishes the *novice* thinker from the *expert* thinker. Novice thinkers look for the easiest and most obvious solution, fail to consider possible objections and difficulties, read only sources that agree with their views, and are unable to identify what is wrong with faulty arguments. Expert thinkers thoroughly analyze problems before proposing solutions, read sources that disagree with their views, anticipate objections to their position, monitor their own effectiveness, and choose the most effective from a wide range of possible solutions and strategies.[7]

Thinkers who are truly "expert" will be prepared to deal with the "multilogical problems" of contemporary society—those problems that can be approached from many different and often competing perspectives.[8] These include, for example, environmental pollution, racial discrimination, governmental spending, overpopulation, and health care issues. Addressing such problems calls for people who are comfortable thinking across domains and disciplines and who can compare and evaluate competing perspectives, interpretations, and theories.

One of the central aims of this book is to assist you in becoming a more expert thinker. By selecting a thesis, identifying the central issues pertinent to it, conducting research, and constructing an extended argument, you will engage in a process of discovery that will enhance your critical thinking. But this is only half the story. Once you have developed a position, you will be required to communicate it to others through argumentation. Until you have anticipated your audience's values, beliefs, and objections, constructed your position in light of them, and responded to their objections, questions, and concerns, your development as a critical thinker will not be complete.

ARGUMENTATION AND ARGUMENTS

Argumentation as we have defined it at the beginning of the chapter is significant to the development and maintenance of a healthy society. It consists of the process of convincing others through sound reasoning and good evidence. Argumentation is only one part of the larger process of persuasion, which also includes factors related to the credibility (competence and trustworthiness) of the speaker or writer and also the use of style and emotional appeals. These other factors will be discussed in Chapters 4 and 5. For the most part, however, this book will focus more specifically on argumentation as a rhetorical/logical process.

Argumentation can occur only when people are interested in hearing or reading what others have to say and in seriously considering others' proposals. When parties engage in argumentation, they agree to certain conventions and tacit principles. They agree to rules for conducting the discussion, they make contributions as required, and they seek the approval of the other parties involved.[9] If people refuse even to listen to the other party, argumentation cannot occur. Instead of argumentation, the parties may agree to disagree and go their own ways, one party may simply force the other to comply, or there may be conflict between the parties.

Argumentation is a "macro-level" process. It involves the construction of cases or overall positions, such as the case for prosecution or defense in the law courts, a governmental proposal for a change in policy, a marketing campaign, or a business proposal.

Speeches, essays, group discussions, legislation, and political campaigns would all be examples of argumentation. Argumentation is composed of arguments that are its "micro-level" forms. *An argument is a set of statements in which a claim is made, support is offered for it, and there is an attempt to influence someone in a context of disagreement.* It is important to distinguish argument in this sense—a claim, plus support for it in the form of reasoning and/or evidence—from interpersonal arguments or disputes.[10] In this latter sense, "argument" is a kind of (usually unpleasant) interpersonal exchange, as when we say "John and Mary were having an argument." Sometimes described as "quarrels" or "squabbles," these kinds of arguments usually involve two or more persons engaged in extended overt disagreement with each other.

That is not the sort of "argument" with which this book is concerned. The "micro arguments" of the sort described here occur when we say something like, "John *made an argument* in support of his proposal for the new marketing plan." This view considers whether an argument is sound and effective; it emphasizes argument as a *reasoning process* and considers arguments as units rather than as interactive processes.

Arguments are only one kind of communication. When we greet someone ("Hello, how are you?"), issue commands ("Shut the door."), vent our emotions ("I hate it when you do that!"), make promises ("I'll return your book tomorrow."), and so forth, we do not produce arguments. To clarify the differences between arguments and other forms of communication, we will describe the important features of argument according to our definition.

First, to be considered an argument, a statement generally should make a claim. *A claim is an expressed opinion or a conclusion that the arguer wants accepted.* In the Affirmative Action discussion, some claims were:

- Students should be evaluated based strictly on merit.
- Students who have worked in school and made good grades should be admitted.
- Admissions policies have never been "fair."

Claims take on various forms in various contexts; they function as *claims* in relation to the support offered for them. As we will show in Chapter 6, claims of micro arguments may themselves function as forms of support for the "main claim" or thesis statement of an extended argument. Examples of "main claims" would include in criminal law the charge brought against the defendant by the prosecution, in the legislature the abbreviated version of a proposed bill or piece of legislation, and in medicine the diagnosis and recommended treatment regimen. In argumentation and debate, these "main claims" are often called *propositions* or *resolutions*.

When someone makes a claim, he or she is expected to offer further support for it in the form of reasons and information. If we issue a command or make a promise, we commit ourselves by making the statement, and no further proof is necessary.[11] Likewise, pure description ("The setting sun was reflected in a rosy haze."), small talk ("Things are so-so, could be better."), and other neutral statements generally do not make claims—they do not advance statements on which there is disagreement.

Sometimes, we can decide whether a statement is a claim only by considering its context. Arguers often leave their evidence, reasoning, or claim unstated. Do the following examples contain claims?

- When guns are outlawed, only outlaws will have guns.
- Coors Light, 'cause coffee's nasty after volleyball.
- Every time I'm nice to him, he ignores me.

If we know that the first statement is a bumper sticker displayed by an opponent of gun control, we can conclude that it is a claim. Spelled out, it would say that "making guns illegal means that only those who circumvent the law will have guns." Knowing that the second statement occurred in a Coors ad would indicate that the claim is "[Buy] Coors Light" and that the remainder is a good reason for doing so! It is ambiguous whether the third statement is a claim or not. Knowing more about the person's relationship to her friend would help us to determine whether it is a claim. Some claims can be recognized as claims only when we know about the speaker's intention, the claim's relation to the other statements made along with it, or the situational context in which a claim is made.

The second characteristic of an argument is that support is offered for the claim. Claims are supported by evidence and by the reasoning or inferences that connect the evidence to the claim. Evidence comes in many forms, but it always functions as the foundation for argument or the grounds on which argument is based.[12] When we make an argument, we move from statements we believe our receivers will accept (evidence) to statements that are disputable (claims). *Evidence consists of facts or conditions that are objectively observable, beliefs or statements generally accepted as true by the recipients or conclusions previously established.*

Evidence does not consist only of facts. From a *rhetorical* point of view (i.e., that arguers seek acceptance for their claims *from audiences*), it makes sense to regard any proposition or belief *accepted by everyone in the audience* as a starting point for argument. There are many statements ("A person is innocent until proven guilty." "One ought to keep one's promises.") that are *not* facts but that could function as evidence in relation to a claim.

In the Affirmative Action discussion at the beginning of this chapter, statements viewed as evidence by the speakers and taken as evidence by others count as evidence. Examples of such statements include:

Quotas have been illegal since the *Bakke* decision. (fact)

My *Webster's* defines "fair use" as being "free from self interest, prejudice, or favoritism." (dictionary definition)

Athletes, children of alumni, and other groups have often received preference in admission. (fact)

To be counted as evidence, statements should be generally accepted and viewed as relevant by all parties to the dispute or audiences to whom arguments are addressed. (If a statement is accepted by only one party—the arguer—then it is a *claim*, not evidence.) Kaidren and John must view *Webster's* as a credible source before they will accept Ramona's definition.

The arguer who begins establishing a claim on grounds that are not accepted will not get far. Furthermore, for evidence to provide reliable grounds for claims, it must conform to what actually is the case. If Kaidren and John could show that quotas have been upheld by courts since *Bakke*, Ramona's statement about the *Bakke* decision would not be able to function as evidence because it could not be considered "true."

Claims are also supported by the link that the arguer makes between the evidence and the claim. The part of the argument containing *reasoning* is frequently called the *inference*. Reasoning can take various forms. Those that occur most frequently will be described in Chapter 8, and you will become experienced at identifying them. *Reasoning constructs a rational link between the evidence and the claim and authorizes the step we make when we draw a conclusion.* Reasoning answers the question "How did you get from the evidence to the claim?"[13] It consists of general principles that say how the evidence and the claim are connected.

The study of argument is made all the more interesting because arguers often do not explicitly state their inferences. They provide evidence and make claims, but often one can only guess how the link between the two was made. For example, if we study the evidence presented by the three Affirmative Action discussants along with their claims, we will find that three of their inferences, all unstated, were functioning in the argument.

> Only use of objective measures, such as SAT scores and GPAs, will guarantee that all persons are treated fairly.
>
> People who have worked hard should be rewarded for their work.
>
> John Kekes is a qualified authority to speak on this topic.

Inferences usually make explicit a link (for example, between standardized test scores, "objectivity," and fairness) which enables the arguer to connect evidence with claims and thus construct an argument. Supplying unstated reasoning is difficult. To do it well, one must have a thorough knowledge of the structure and function of arguments and be able to interpret the argument accurately. We will discuss and illustrate various types of inferences and argument structures in Chapters 8 and 12.

The third and last characteristic of arguments is that they are *attempts to influence* someone in a context where people disagree with each other. The phrase "*attempts to influence*" is important because the arguer may or may not succeed. The recipient of the argument is free not to agree with the expressed opinion of the arguer. The person to whom the argument is addressed may accept the claim, reject it, or continue to express doubts about it.[14]

In the Affirmative Action discussion, Kaidren and John continued to reject Ramona's view that active consideration of certain groups was justifiable, but their continued skepticism does not mean that Ramona's claims were not an argument, because her aim was to *attempt* to influence Kaidren and John. In complex disputes, parties to an argument may also compromise, with each arguer accepting only a portion of the other's expressed opinions.[15]

To say that arguments are "attempts to *influence*" means that there must be a recipient, or "arguee," to whom the argument is addressed who is capable of responding to it. The arguee must be open-minded and able to change her beliefs or actions because of the argument. Furthermore, in choosing argument instead of command or coercion, the arguer recognizes that the process of argument is reciprocal—that initiative and control pass back and forth as the arguer states his viewpoints and the recipient weighs his support and decides whether to accept his argument.[16] As she listens to arguments, the recipient retains her option of challenging, questioning, criticizing, or countering the expressed opinions of the arguer.

The influence that arguments aim to bring about assumes many forms. Arguers may wish to cause recipients to become concerned about an issue on which they are ambivalent or neutral, to change favorable to unfavorable attitudes or vice versa, or to change behavior. Consequently, arguers often begin deciding how to phrase arguments by asking such questions as: What evidence will the other person accept? What are the beliefs, attitudes, and values of the recipient? What will gain attention? What authorities will be accepted? How much does the recipient know about argument? What response is being sought?

Arguments are attempts to influence *someone.* An argument may be addressed to oneself, to another person, to a small group, to an audience of individuals, or to multiple audiences. Arguments occur in writing, in conversation, in public speeches, and in all forms of communication. Argument is a complex phenomenon that occurs in numerous forms and media of communication and that is addressed to many different kinds of audiences.

Finally, to say that argument occurs only when there is disagreement or the potential for disagreement means that the topic addressed must be controversial, capable of inciting opposing opinions from the parties involved. For example, consider the following dialogue:

John:	Should we go to the movies this evening?
Mary:	Fine, what would you like to see?
John:	How about *Attack of the Killer Bees*?
Mary:	OK. Do you want to go to the 7 o'clock showing?
John:	Sure.

There is no argument here because there is no opposition. If Mary had rejected the whole idea of going to the movies, or if she had proposed another film and given reasons for preferring it, argumentation would have occurred. But as long as parties to a discussion agree with the opinions expressed, they will not produce arguments.

PERSPECTIVES ON ARGUMENTATION

Argumentation is a complex process with many dimensions. Scholars therefore disagree about how it should be described and explained. Some believe arguers have an obligation to determine truth through the use of true premises and sound reasoning.[17] Others argue that the "truth" frequently cannot be decisively determined and that argumentation should be studied as a means of influence in the social and political marketplace.[18] Still others, noting the tension between rational and nonrational factors of influence, have concluded that "a central focus of argumentation is on discovering and applying the general standards for determining what is true or reasonable."[19]

Joseph W. Wenzel summarized the various perspectives on argument and concluded that they could be put into three categories—*logical, dialectical,* and *rhetorical.*[20]

These are not three different kinds of argument; they are three different ways of looking at argumentation. Each perspective emphasizes a different set of functions and features of argumentation. They might best be understood if we examine the following argument from each of the three perspectives. This argument, which appeared in the conservation column of a wilderness organization's monthly newsletter, argues that the spotted owl, an endangered species that the U.S. Forest Service is mandated to protect, is being ill-served by Forest Service policies.

> The Forest Service wants to save only 1,000 acres per breeding pair, but scientists think they require an average of over 2,000 acres. The discrepancies between USFS acreage allowances and biologists' minimum recommended acreage has meant further study and a supplemental environmental impact statement to be issued sometime this summer. . . .
>
> Spacing of spotted owl management areas is also controversial. Scientists think they should be spaced from 1–6 miles apart, and the Forest Service plans to place them at the maximum of this range—6 miles apart, which will make it difficult for young owls to disperse from their original nest sites. . . .
>
> If scientists' recommendations and Forest Service plans are so disparate, perhaps there should be a moratorium placed on all harvest of spotted owl habitat. The burden of proof that harvest can continue without endangering the survival of the species should rest on the Forest Service.[21]

The author here presents two sets of evidence—Forest Service recommendations and scientists' findings regarding the spotted owl. She then shows that the two are not in agreement—that there are discrepancies that might affect the owls' well-being and even their survival. From this she concludes that a moratorium on habitat harvesting should be declared until the discrepancies can be resolved and there is agreement about what measures are needed to ensure the owls' survival.

The logical perspective asks, Is the argument sound? The dialectical perspective asks, Has the discussion been handled so as to achieve a candid and critical examination of all aspects of the issue in question? And the rhetorical perspective asks: Has the arguer constructed the argument so as to successfully influence a particular audience? All three perspectives are useful and necessary, and the significance of any one perspective at any time depends on the arguer's purpose and the situation in which the argument is made.

If we are to use a *logical* approach to this example, we will view it as a set of statements made up of premises and a claim or conclusion. The logical perspective emphasizes the accuracy of the premises and the correctness of the inferences linking premises and evidence to the claims they support. An argument favorably evaluated from the logical perspective will be based on correct evidence and will use reasoning that is sound according to the standards of logic. Dividing the preceding argument into its parts—claim, evidence, and inference—we might ask:

Is the evidence correct?
- Are scientists' recommendations accurately summarized?
- Do the recommendations reported cover all the studies that have been done?

Does the influence justify the move to the conclusion?

- Will maximum placement of the management areas actually interfere with dispersal?
- Will placing a moratorium resolve the discrepancy between the scientists' recommendations and the Forest Service's plans?

The logical perspective views argumentation as addressed to an audience of rational individuals well informed on the topic of the dispute.[22] It removes arguments from their situational contexts and considers them primarily as statements connected by logical inferences. The inferences are identified, classified, analyzed, and critiqued by comparing their structure and adequacy with prescriptions from logical theory.

Viewing the example from the *dialectical* perspective leads us to consider this argument as one move in an ongoing process of inquiry about policies concerning the spotted owl. By refraining from deciding on a position or course of action until all aspects of the question have been thoroughly explored, a dialectical approach to argumentation searches for significant issues, identifies alternatives, generates standards or criteria for selection, and uses them to test proposals. The dialectical perspective focuses on and enhances a candid, critical, and comprehensive examination of all positions relevant to the topic. It makes a concerted effort to seek out *all* points of view. In the spotted owl controversy, the arguer articulated the environmentalist position on the issue. A dialectical perspective on the argument would seek out the viewpoints of the scientific community, the Forest Service, and the timber industry. In regard to the argument in the example, we would be led to ask such questions as:

- What is the spotted owl's present situation? Is it in immediate danger? Is the decline in old growth forests the primary threat to the species, or are there other threats?
- What will be the impact of a harvest moratorium on the timber industry?
- Will the promised supplemental environmental impact statement provide information to resolve the disparity?
- Are there alternatives to the proposed moratorium?

Argumentation viewed from a dialectical perspective focuses primarily on the process of reaching the best conclusion. The assumption is that the "best" conclusion will be accepted if all points of view and issues have been carefully considered and discussed.

Viewing the example from a *rhetorical* perspective means that we see it as addressed to a particular audience in a social and political context in which recipients are to be influenced by the author's position. In the rhetorical perspective, arguments are viewed as appeals to an audience and we must take account of the circumstances in which the argument was made and the strategies used to influence its audience. Considering the argument this way might lead us to ask:

- Is the author aware of the interests and values of the newsletter's readers?
- What strategies does she use to structure and present the argument?

- Are there other arguments that might appeal to the readers' values and interests more successfully?
- Does the author appear knowledgeable and trustworthy? Will the readers believe her?

The rhetorical perspective on argument is important because of its emphasis on arguments as forms of communication. By taking account of the circumstances in which the argument was produced, the arguer's intent, and the beliefs and values of those to whom arguments are addressed, the rhetorical perspective enables one to interpret and evaluate the content of the arguments themselves.

Understanding that any argument can be viewed from any of these three perspectives is important. Each of the perspectives implies a different purpose and a different emphasis when one considers an argument. The logical perspective focuses on the structure of an argument and on its logical soundness when removed from a context. (This is the perspective of many courses in formal and informal logic.) The dialectical perspective considers especially the capacity of any given procedure for argumentation to contribute to reasoned and careful deliberation about an issue. The rhetorical perspective emphasizes the argument's *effectiveness* in persuading its audience. When individual arguments and argumentation are viewed from each of these three perspectives, different dimensions of the process of arguing are featured.

We will use all three of these perspectives—the logical, the dialectical, and the rhetorical—in various places in this book. For example, in Chapters 8 and 12 when we discuss forms of reasoning and argument analysis, we will focus on the logical perspective. In Chapters 9, 10, and 11, when we discuss analysis and the construction of argumentative cases, we will emphasize the dialectical perspective and its usefulness in discovering vital questions on a given topic. In Chapters 4 and 5, we will be particularly concerned with the kinds of questions raised by a rhetorical perspective, which is concerned with the arguer's relationship to other parties and with how arguments are expressed in everyday language.

AN ARGUMENT MODEL

An individual argument can be viewed as a set of connected statements; and individual arguments work with other arguments as part of a larger process of inquiry and proof or as a unit of persuasive communication addressed to an audience. When we seek to persuade people or work to advocate a particular position, we combine arguments to help make a persuasive case for our position.

Chapters 6 and 8 will examine how individual arguments work. In these chapters we will study how the inferences and logical patterns of arguments function to support a claim. However, it is important to remember that arguments do not occur in isolation but function as a whole to influence listeners. The content and interpretation of arguments, therefore, should be understood in terms of the predispositions and experiences of the recipients who hear and read them, the language in which they are expressed, and the context in which they arise.

One aspect of argument that is influenced by all these factors, but most particularly by the attitudes and beliefs of recipients, is the level of agreement that separates premises from claims and allows certain statements to be accepted by the audience without further support as evidence. For example, there is wide agreement that human life has developed and adapted itself to our planet. This we can accept as a premise. But the question of where human life originated can be much more controversial—some argue for evolution, others for creation, and yet others speculate that life began on another planet. These ideas are too controversial to be accepted as the evidence for a claim and are themselves argument claims that need to be proved.

To clarify the importance of this aspect in the conduct of argument, this section is devoted to developing a model of argument that illustrates the interrelationship of argument parts. Let us begin by considering the relationship of the three components of an argument that we have already defined. Visually represented, their relation can be seen in Figure 1–1.

An example will help illustrate how these three elements work together in an argument. In 1989, the Supreme Court decided *Texas v. Johnson,* a flag burning case.[23] The author of this case, Justice William Brennan, argued that respondent Johnson, who burned an American flag at the conclusion of a protest in Dallas against the policies of the Reagan administration and some Dallas-based corporations, could not be convicted of desecration of a venerated object [the flag] which would be a violation of Texas statute. Brennan began his opinion by observing that "we must first determine whether Johnson's burning of the flag constituted expressive conduct, permitting him to invoke the First Amendment in challenging his conviction."[24] To support his view that Johnson's act was indeed communicative, Brennan turned to the precedent of prior court opinions, observing that "The First Amendment literally forbids the abridgment only of 'speech,' but we have long recognized that its protection does not end at the spoken or written word."[25] Brennan notes that, in prior cases, the wearing of black armbands, the use of a sit-in by blacks in a "whites only" area, and picketing were all viewed as forms of "speech."

Using our argument model, the relationships among the parts of the argument could be displayed as in Figure 1–2. This is one example of several arguments that Brennan put forward in a lengthy argument supporting symbolic behavior as "speech" that deserved First Amendment protection. Each of the other arguments in Brennan's opinion

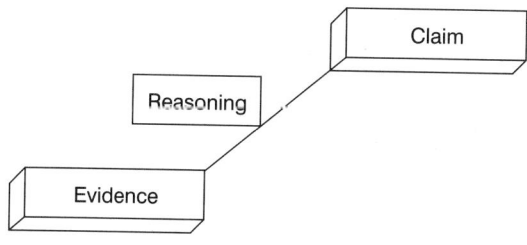

FIGURE 1–1 A Model of an Argument

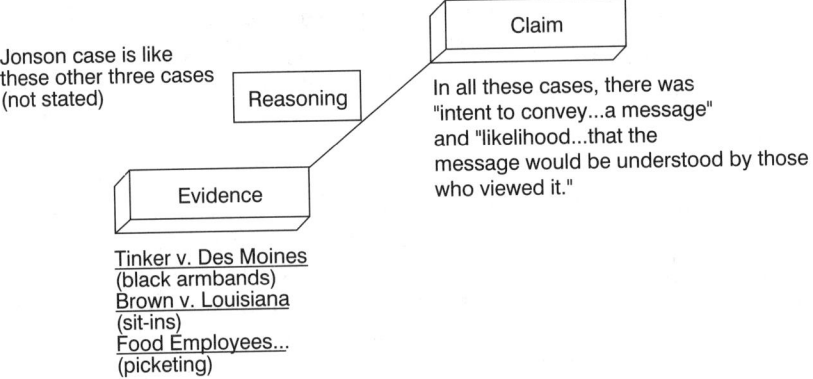

FIGURE 1-2 A Diagrammed Argument

could be diagrammed in the same manner, showing the relationship between evidence, reasoning, and claim in various micro arguments. It is important to remember that most often arguments do not function independently but rather in concert with several other arguments that work together in concert to present an extended argument case.

Diagramming makes it easier to see how the parts of an argument function in relation to each other and how they work together. As will be discussed in Chapter 12, diagramming is a critical step toward helping us to describe and evaluate arguments. Similarly, the other arguments Brennan used to support his claim can be diagrammed. Using this model to diagram his arguments makes it easier to see how the parts of the argument function.

Arguments occur in contexts that give rise to agreement and disagreement about the topic of the argument. Since arguments occur only when people disagree with each other, we can imagine a line that separates the statements of belief and value with which an audience agrees from those with which it disagrees. In other words, for any issue we can think of, there is a line that separates what we are willing to accept from what we are unwilling to accept initially. For instance, we might discuss the relative strengths of President Franklin D. Roosevelt and the four-term presidency. Even if you were a staunch political conservative and truly believed Roosevelt almost destroyed American freedoms through a strong centralized government, there is some aspect of Roosevelt's presidency you would accept. You might not agree with the arguer who says Roosevelt was the best president, but you would probably accept that he was president. You would also probably accept that he was elected for four terms and that under Roosevelt many government programs for economic reform were passed. While you might not accept the value of such programs you would probably agree with the facts of his administration (the WPA was established; the United States entered World War II). The point to be made here is that for any issue you can think of, there is a level of agreement on facts.

This level or imaginary line that separates what is accepted by the audience from what is not accepted we will call the level of dispute. Arguments that occur below the line are already accepted by the audience and those that occur above it are not accepted. The term *line* may be a little misleading here. We are not suggesting that all issues have clearly demarcated lines that all recipients of argument acknowledge. Such a position would fail to recognize that people do not have their minds made up on all issues. Rather, we can think of this line or level of dispute as a not clearly defined area in which people neither accept nor reject arguments immediately. Therefore, the level of dispute is the lowest common level that an audience is willing to accept. The claim of an argument must always fall above the level of dispute. Otherwise, the argument is already accepted.

Figure 1–3 helps to illustrate the role played by the level of dispute. Evidence in this model falls below the level of dispute because if evidence were disputed and fell above the line, then the evidence itself would need to be proved and anchored to the audience's accepted knowledge. In other words, the evidence would become the subject of an argument. The key is simply that arguments seek to move the audience from positions already accepted to new and different positions. An advocate, then, seeks to use acceptable evidence in order to reason with the audience to accept a new claim. For example, Brennan develops his argument by writing:

> In deciding whether particular conduct possesses sufficient communicative elements to bring the First Amendment into play, we have asked whether "[a]n intent to convey a particularized message was present, and [whether] the likelihood was great that the message would be understood by those who viewed it." 418 U.S., at 410–411. Hence, we have recognized the expressive nature of students' wearing of black armbands to protest American military involvement in Vietnam, *Tinker v. Des Moines Independent Community School Dist.*, 393 U.S. 503, 505 (1969); of a sit-in by blacks in a "whites only" area to protest segregation, *Brown v. Louisiana* 383 U.S. 131, 141–42 (1966) . . . and of picketing about a wide variety of causes, see, e.g. *Food Employees v. Logan Valley Plaza, Inc.*, 391 U.S. 308, 313–314 (1968); *United States v. Grace*, 461 U.S. 171, 176 (1983).[26]

In this argument, Brennan uses the U.S. Supreme Court cases he cites to support his claims. Since most of his reading audience is aware of these decisions or could quickly consult them, his citations would be firmly grounded below the level of dispute. Brennan uses these cases to establish that forms of symbolic behavior that are not explicitly "speech" have been held to be worthy of protection under the free speech guarantees of the First Amendment. By analogy, he thus argues that Johnson's action is sufficiently similar to the actions of protesters in the other cases to be worthy of free speech protection. His application of the prior cases to the one he is deciding thus falls above the level of dispute for his audience.

To be successful, Brennan needs to connect his claim, which is above the level of dispute, with the prior court cases (the evidence) which falls below. In other words, his

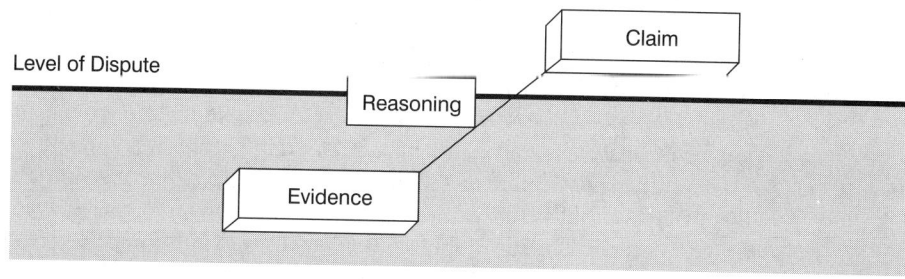

FIGURE 1–3 The Level of Dispute

goal is to connect what the recipients find reasonable and acceptable to a new claim that is unknown or unaccepted by the audience. He attempts to bridge the gap between the evidence and claim by offering reasons. His reasoning is that flag burning is a form of protest: "Johnson burned an American flag as part—indeed, as the culmination—of a political demonstration that coincided with the convening of the Republican Party and its renomination of Ronald Reagan for President. The expressive, overtly political nature of this conduct was both intentional and overwhelmingly apparent."[27]

Throughout his argument, Brennan drew upon commonly held assumptions about the nature of symbolic speech that were within his audience's knowledge and understanding and thus worked below the level of dispute. Audiences view communicative behavior as intentional, particularly when it is used in a context of protest. Brennan could use these assumptions about speech to draw the comparison and application to the Johnson case, and that application was what initially lay above the level of dispute.

What would happen to his argument if his evidence were not accepted as true by the audience? If the argument presented by Brennan was grounded in evidence that its readers were unaware of or disagreed with, he would have to establish that such incidents, court decisions, or examples actually happened or were reasonably acceptable to the audience. If the evidence is not accepted by the audience, it becomes an issue for dispute and will itself become a focus for argument.

The level of dispute exists and is drawn in the minds and perceptions of argument recipients. An arguer's objective is to adapt the evidence, reasoning, and claims to the recipient's understanding of the subject being argued. While this may appear to be a relatively straightforward task, it can become more complex as the number of listeners increases. Someone with a great deal of experience in one area may have a relatively high level of dispute. Someone with little knowledge of the area will have a relatively low level of dispute. When these two people are in the same audience, the arguer has the difficult task of adapting to the different levels of dispute of the different individuals. Often the result is argument directed toward the lowest common denominator that everyone in the audience can understand and agree with. While the lowest-common-denominator approach may appeal to some, it is just as likely to bore the other recipients.

The arguer chooses and adapts the level of dispute to the audience. This is a choice unique for each situation and audience. If an arguer receives feedback indicating confusion or disagreement, he or she may decide to raise or lower the level while arguing. For a critic examining the argument, understanding the level of dispute is important because its location implies the type of recipients assumed by the arguer and offers a better understanding of the argument context.

The third component of the argument, reasoning, connects the evidence and the claim. This is because reasoning serves as a logical and persuasive bridge between the two ends of an argument. By means of the inferences made, reasoning acts to draw a strong relationship between that which is known and accepted and that which is unknown or unaccepted. The reasoning inferred in Brennan's argument is that the *Johnson* case is sufficiently similar to the other cases cited to be treated in the same way. Once Brennan has established that the action is protected by free speech guarantees, then the issue to decide the case will be whether there are other government interests that outweigh free speech in this instance.

Once an argument is proven, what happens to the level of dispute? Logically, if the claim is proven and those to whom it is addressed accept it as a valid conclusion, then the level of dispute rises such that the claim now falls below the line. (See Figure 1–4.) This means that an advocate can now use a proven argument as evidence for another argument. The process of linking proven claims to unproved claims is called chaining, and is demonstrated in Figure 1–5. *An argument chain simply uses a proven argument as evidence for an unproved claim.* The argument advanced by Brennan helps to illustrate this concept. He wrote:

> Johnson was convicted for engaging in expressive conduct. The State's interest in preventing breaches of the peace does not support his conviction because Johnson's conduct did not threaten to disturb the peace. Nor does the State's interest in preserving

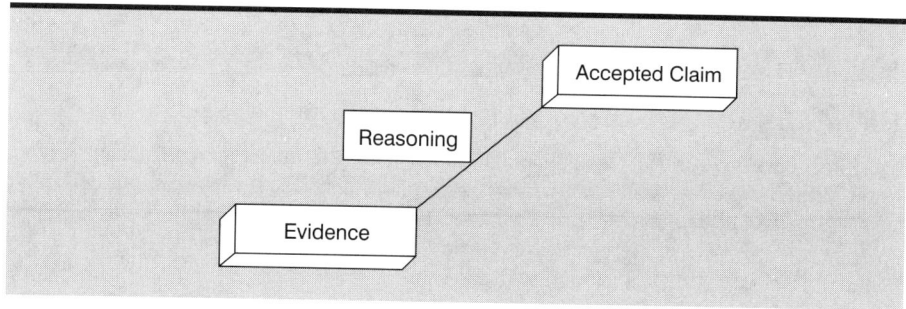

FIGURE 1–4 Level of Dispute in a Proven Argument

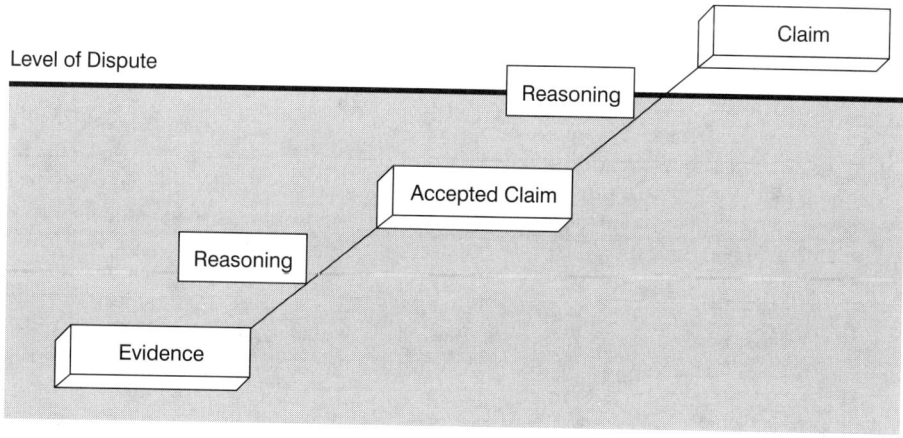

FIGURE 1–5 An Argument Chain

the flag as a symbol of nationhood and national unity justify his criminal conviction for engaging in political expression.[28]

In this passage, Brennan chains his argument. Having established early on that Johnson's action was entitled to protection as a form of protest and expression, Brennan here partially bases his final conclusion on the assumption that Johnson's action was "expressive conduct."

The concept of chained arguments holds many important implications for building *macro arguments,* or argumentative cases. For example, the arguer's central thesis or claim in a macro argument may lie far above the level of dispute and many preliminary claims may have to be established before the central claim is adequately supported. If the arguer begins with facts and premises accepted by everyone to whom the argument is addressed and builds arguments one step at a time, the level of dispute can be raised in increments until the central claim is proven. An extended example illustrating chained claims will be provided in Chapter 6.

SUMMARY

This book focuses on critical thinking and argumentation. Critical thinking, a vital skill in today's society, enables a person to investigate a situation, problem, question, or phenomenon to arrive at a viable hypothesis or conclusion. It includes such skills as clearly stating a question for discussion, clarifying the meaning of terms, developing and applying evaluative criteria, and evaluating the credibility of sources. Once you have gathered information on a topic and analyzed it using these processes, you must communicate your reasoning to others.

This process is called argumentation, which involves making arguments intended to justify beliefs, attitudes, and values so as to influence others. This is the second focus of this book. It involves constructing cases for or against a proposal. Argumentation occurs in law court cases, governmental legislation, marketing campaigns, and business proposals. Such extended cases are made up of individual arguments. An argument is a set of statements in which a claim is made, support is offered for it, and there is an attempt to influence someone in a context of disagreement. A person making a claim is expected to offer further support by using evidence and reasoning. Evidence consists of facts or conditions that are objectively observable, beliefs or statements generally accepted as true by the recipients, or conclusions previously established. Reasoning is frequently expressed in the form of inferences, constructs a rational link between the evidence and the claim, and authorizes the step we make when we draw a conclusion.

Argumentation can be viewed from three different but complementary perspectives, each of which emphasizes different aspects of argument. The logical perspective views an argument as a set of premises and a conclusion and is primarily concerned with whether the premises are true and the inference is correctly stated. The dialectical perspective describes argumentation as a process of discovering issues, generating alternatives, establishing standards for judgment, and withholding a decision until all viewpoints have been stated and tested. The rhetorical perspective emphasizes argumentation as a method of influence and considers whether arguers seem aware of the interests and values of the audience and state their arguments appropriately and effectively.

The chapter concludes with an argument model that was intended to illustrate the workings of individual arguments. Arguments are based on statements accepted by their recipients and for which no further support is needed. Because these statements provoke no disagreement, they fall below the level of dispute. When they are successively and successfully used to support new claims, the level of

CHAPTER ONE   Arguments and Argumentation

dispute rises and the formerly contested claim becomes a premise for a new argument. When a proven argument is used as evidence for an unproven claim, the result is an argument chain. The concept of a level of dispute is useful because it illustrates how the extent of the recipients' agreement with the arguer's claims may vary as the argument is being made.

EXERCISES (Please note: Throughout the book, exercise items marked with an asterisk have answers provided in Appendix B.)

Exercise 1 Can you distinguish a statement that is an argument from one that is not? Remember that an argument

   a. puts forth a claim

   b. offers support for it, and

   c. makes an attempt to influence someone.

Now, consider the following statement:

   If it rains tomorrow, I'm going home.

This is not an argument because the speaker offers neither a claim nor support for it. Rather, he merely states his intention, which does not depend on the other person's acceptance. Furthermore, the speaker does not explicitly try to influence anyone else but merely states what he himself intends to do. Consider the following statements, decide whether or not they are arguments, and explain the reasons for your decision. Remember that statements of one's emotional state or pure descriptions are not generally viewed as arguments.

* 1. Everyone who took up arms and participated in the disorders will be punished with all the severity of the law. All purveyors of fascist-communist ideas, who incited people to rebel, will also be made answerable in accordance with the law. There will be no more leniency to Communist-fascism in Russia.
       Boris Yeltsin, "Address to the Nation, 6 October 1993," *ITAR-TASS World Service in Russian:* online, Express Access Online Communications, Oct 6, 1993. soc.culture.soviet

   2. Fred: Why are you leaving so early for the meeting?
      Gale: Sue asked me to pick her up on the way. Are you going to watch that movie at 8 o'clock?
      Fred: Yeah. It lasts until 10 and then I thought I'd go to bed early.
      Gale: Fine. I'll see you in the morning.

   3. Twenty years ago, experts predicted that high-tech gadgets would leave us with too much time on our hands. We'd be living a life of leisure. Instead, cellular phones and laptop computers have made it possible for us to work anywhere, anytime. . . .
       Technology feeds our obsession with speed.
       Computers perform at rapid-fire pace. Rather than waiting for an operator to dial an overseas call, modems and fiber optic networks can link us with others around the world in a matter of seconds.
       Ellen Rosen, "Where Has All Our Leisure Time Gone?" *Seattle Times,* August 13, 1995, L2.

4. I try to remember when this rivalry between my daughter and me first began. I can't. It sometimes seems that we have always been this way with each other, that we have never gotten along any better or differently. I would like to make my daughter less miserable if I can, to help her be happier and much more pleased with herself, I don't know how.
   Joseph Heller, *Something Happened* (New York: Ballantine Books, 1974), 179.

* 5. [T]he data show that, if current trends continue, Social Security won't live to see another 60 years.

   The demographic trends that helped make Social Security so successful in its early years—plenty of workers paying in to support a few retirees—have started to work against it.

   In 1945, there were 42 workers for each Social Security beneficiary. Today, that figure is 3.3 workers. By 2030, it drops to two to one, according to the program's annual report.

   At current tax rates, Social Security starts to lose money by 2013—right around the time waves of baby boomers will start retiring.

   The deficits quickly mount. By 2070, annual Social Security shortfall will be more than $7 trillion.
   John Merline, "Should Social Security Retire? Public System Can't Stack Up to Market Returns," *Business Daily,* August 14, 1995, A1.

6. The good news is that students care deeply about the issues of the day, and they wish that politics gave them a way to act on their concerns. Colleges could help them by offering a different kind of political education—not just an education *about* politics but an education *for* politics, for the practice of democratic citizenship. For that to happen, colleges will have to broaden their definition of politics. Citizens have a larger role to play than voting and trying to influence their officials. We have to present political life in its larger dimensions so that students can find a variety of roles to play.
   David Mathews, "Why Students Hate Politics," *Chronicle of Higher Education,* July 7, 1993, A56.

7. The immense suffering by animals in connection with the fur industry is staggering and it pains me that so many men and women seem to be so totally indifferent to this fact. Maybe someday people will wake up and remember what Jesus said about the animals. "What you do unto them, you do unto me."
   Letter to the Editor, *Seattle Times,* December 29, 1985, A19

8. John: Should we figure the raises on a 3 percent cost of living increase plus merit?

   Judy: That will work as long as we have enough in the budget to cover it. How much is available to us?

   Dan: Well, we do have a reserve fund to cover any excesses. I think we should start out with what the staff ought to receive and concern ourselves with what's available later on.

   Judy: That sounds fine to me, as long as we have some excess.

CHAPTER ONE   Arguments and Argumentation   **23**

9. At our most basic level. we humans are animals; we have animal impulses and drives. We communicate, we eat, we relieve ourselves, we tire, we sleep—and we have sex. Ultimately, what makes us human is our ability to transcend our animal composition. What makes us human is our ability to channel and curb our God-given impulses in such a way that elevates the human spirit. Sexuality is one in a series of healthy life forces.
   Michael Gotlieb, "Sex and Sin: There Is a Difference," *New York Times,* December 20, 1994, A23.

*10. Nuclear power is uneconomical and unreliable, but above all nuclear power is unsafe. The chance of accident is unacceptably high, as demonstrated by Three Mile Island, Chernobyl, and the almost 30,000 mishaps reported by nuclear utilities over the past 10 years. The Nuclear Regulatory Commission, no foe of nuclear power, has estimated that the chance of a core-melt accident at the United States reactor may be as high as 45 percent over the next 20 years.
   Bill Magavern, "Safe Alternatives to Nuclear Power," *Christian Science Monitor,* January 11, 1989, 19.

Exercise 2 Following is the text of an "Op-Ed" article on mental health care by Keith Hoeller, Ph.D., Editor of the *Review of Existential Psychology and Psychiatry* published by Humanities Press. It appeared as "Search for 'Inner Child' Means Some Have No Medical Coverage," in the *Seattle Post-Intelligencer,* May 7, 1996, and is used by permission of the author.

After reading the entire article, apply the concepts in Chapter 1 by accomplishing the following objectives:

1. Locate all the claims, reasoning, and evidence in the article. Draw a line under each one and label it as claim, evidence, or reasoning.

2. Apply the standards for the logical, dialectical, and rhetorical perspectives to the article:

   - For the *logical* perspective, consider whether the evidence offered by the author appears to be accurate, whether his reasoning seems sound, and whether there are links established between his premises and his conclusions.

   - For the *dialectical* perspective, consider whether all aspects of the questions are thoroughly explored, whether all issues are considered, and whether standards for judgment are provided. Does this article contribute to public discussion about the viability and funding of mental health care in the United States?

   - For the *rhetorical* perspective, consider whether the article is adapted to the author's readership (newspaper readers in a large metropolitan area), and whether it addresses the circumstances and context relevant to the topic in our society.

3. What critical conclusions can you reach about the argument? Does it seem sound? How might Hoeller have improved the argument?

Although the American College of Physicians recently announced that 42 million Americans lack health insurance, the U.S. Senate unanimously passed a health insurance bill that would create a vast new entitlement program and would amount to the largest expansion of mental health insurance in our nation's history.

Because the House bill did not contain that provision, the matter now goes before a Senate-House Conference Committee. President Clinton is likely to sign the final bill. However, the lack of health insurance for millions is related directly to the increasing coverage of mental health treatments, as increasing coverage for some means rationing or eliminating coverage for others.

Indeed, if we were to abolish mental health insurance entirely, we could easily extend coverage to those Americans who don't have any health insurance—without any increased costs.

It is easy to see why the Association of Private and Welfare Pension Plans, an industry group, might estimate health insurance costs will rise 8 to 11 percent, and why the American Psychiatric Association would put the rise at a lower 3 to 4 percent. Businesses want to keep health costs down and psychiatrists want a new welfare program for themselves and other mental health professionals. Under heavy limitations by health maintenance organizations, psychotherapists of all stripes are seeing decreasing patient loads and incomes; the legislation might be better termed a "welfare for therapists" bill.

The Congressional Budget Office, which has zero expertise in the mental health field, has projected an unrealistic increase of only 1.6 percent. The CBO admits, however, that the figure assumes employers will react by eliminating other health insurance coverage or by dropping employee health insurance completely.

The actual increase is likely to be astronomically higher. Mental health treatment is already estimated to account for one-fifth of our total national health care dollars, $200 billion out of $1 trillion annually. Under the Senate bill, our annual national health care costs could be increased by 50 percent and still add to the millions of people who already are without any health insurance. . . .

[W]hile psychiatrists long argued that even psychotherapy should be done under a physician's supervision, psychologists were successful in establishing their right to practice therapy on their own. But soon after establishing their independence from psychiatrists, therapists now found they had to justify their existence—and their health insurance payments—by arguing that talking to people was beneficial to their health.

Not only do serious questions remain about whether and which psychotherapy "works," the whole idea that the mind can cause or cure disease remains doubtful at best. As Dr. Marcia Angell said in a review of the scientific research published in *The New England Journal of Medicine*, "the evidence for mental state as a cause and cure of today's scourges is not much better than it was for the afflictions of earlier centuries."

For in fact there is still *no* conclusive, scientifically reliable and valid evidence that any of the so-called mental illnesses is caused by physical disease, including, as many now claim, brain disease.

But there is an even more important danger in mental health insurance than just the waste of billions of dollars every year on pseudoscientific treatment of nondiseased people, and that is the very real and heavily documented threat to our civil liberties posed by the mental health movement. Although the media continue to refer to such groups as the American Psychiatric Association and the National Alliance for the Mentally Ill as "advocates for the mentally ill," that is a false moniker, for both groups have routinely supported legislation depriving Americans of the right to refuse mental health treatment.

While 42 million Americans are without any health insurance at all, our first goal should be to grant them a basic insurance package of legitimate health care, which is precisely what the Kennedy-Kassebaum bill was originally intended to do.

As long as any American has to go without basic insurance, we should not be paying for yuppies to talk to their therapists about their "inner child," or search for "repressed memories" of child abuse, or force Ritalin on their unruly 6-year-olds.

The $200 billion our nation currently pays for mental health care could go a long way to paying for legitimate health care for these Americans who are doing without. Presidents Reagan and Bush are still making us pay for their "Voodoo Economics." Let's hope that Congress will not make us pay for more "Voodoo Health Care."

NOTES

1. The substance of this discussion was adapted from a debate by Kaidren Winiecki and Ramona Hunter on December 7, 1995, in the University of Washington's argumentation course. Items from this debate are used by permission of the participants.
2. James Crouse and Dale Trusheim, *The Case against the SAT* (Chicago: University of Chicago Press, 1988), 91–92 and 125.
3. Cited in Kenneth Jost, "Rethinking Affirmative Action," *Congressional Quarterly Researcher* 5 (1995): 376.
4. Joanne Kurfiss, *Critical Thinking: Theory, Research, Practice, and Possibilities* (Washington, D.C.: Association for the Study of Higher Education, 1975), 2.
5. Richard W. Paul and Gerald M. Nosich, "A Model for the National Assessment of Higher Order Thinking," in A. J. A. Binker, ed., *Critical Thinking: What Every Person Needs to Survive in a Rapidly Changing World* (Santa Rosa, Calif.: Foundation for Critical Thinking, 1992), 87–88.
6. Paul and Nosich, 101; see also, James H. McMillan, "Enhancing College Students' Critical Thinking: A Review of Studies," *Research in Higher Education* 26 (1987): 3–29.
7. Kurfiss, 2–3.
8. Richard W. Paul, "The Critical Thinking Community," *The Center and Foundation for Critical Thinking,* 24 January 1996: online, Internet, 2 June 1996. <http://loki.sonoma.edu/Cthink/>.
9. H. P. Grice, "Logic and Conversation," in Peter Cole and Jerry L. Morgan, eds. *Syntax and Semantics: vol 3. Speech Acts* (New York: Academic Press, 1975), 45.
10. Daniel J. O'Keefe, "Two Concepts of Argument," *Journal of the American Forensic Association* 13 (1977): 121–8; and "The Concepts of Argument and Arguing," in J. Robert Cox and Charles Arthur Willard, eds., *Advances in Argumentation Theory and Research* (Carbondale, Ill.: Southern Illinois University Press, 1982), 3–23.
11. Frans H. van Eemeren and Rob Grootendorst, *Speech Acts in Argumentative Discussions* (Dordrecht, The Netherlands: Foris Publications, 1984), 97–108.
12. The term "grounds" is applied to the original data or evidence upon which an argument is based in Stephen Toulmin, Richard Rieke, and Allan Janik, *An Introduction to Reasoning,* 2nd ed. (New York: Macmillan, 1984), 37–44.
13. Stephen Toulmin, *The Uses of Argument* (Cambridge: Cambridge University Press, 1969), 98.
14. van Eemeren and Grootendorst, 79.
15. Douglas Ehninger and Wayne Brockriede, *Decision by Debate* (New York: Dodd, Mead, & Co., 1963), 7.
16. Ehninger, "Argument as Method: Its Nature, Its Limitations, and Its Uses," *Speech Monographs* 37 (1970): 102–3.
17. Glen E. Mills and Hugh G. Petrie, "The Role of Logic in Rhetoric," *Quarterly Journal of Speech* 54 (1968): 260–7; and Hugh G. Petrie, "Does Logic Have Any Relevance to Argumentation?" *Journal of the American Forensic Association* 6 (1969): 55–60.
18. Ray Lynn Anderson and C. David Mortenson, "Logic and Marketplace Argumentation," *Quarterly Journal of Speech* 53 (1967): 143–51.

19. George Ziegelmueller, Jack Kay, and Charles A. Dause, *Argumentation: Inquiry and Advocacy* (Englewood Cliffs, N.J.: Prentice-Hall, 1990), 3.
20. Joseph W. Wenzel, "Three Perspectives on Argument," in Robert Trapp and Janice Schuetz, eds., *Perspectives on Argumentation* (Prospect Heights, Ill.: Waveland Press, 1990), 9–26.
21. Joan Burton, "The Spotted Owl: A Victim of Forest Plans?" *The Mountaineer* 80, no. 7 (July 1986), 8.
22. Chaim Perelman and Lucie Olbrechts-Tyteca, *The New Rhetoric: A Treatise on Argumentation*, trans. J. Wilkinson and P. Weaver (Notre Dame, Ind.: University of Notre Dame Press, 1969), 34.
23. Texas v. Johnson 491 U.S. 397, US Supreme Court, 1988.
24. Texas v. Johnson, 403.
25. Texas v. Johnson, 404.
26. Texas v. Johnson, 404.
27. Texas v. Johnson, 406.
28. Texas v. Johnson, 420.

CHAPTER 2

Contexts for Argument

CHAPTER OUTLINE
- Culture and Argumentation
- Argumentation and Ethics
- Summary
- Exercises

KEY CONCEPTS
culture
argument style
quasilogical style
presentational style
analogical style
ethics

Argumentation is a practice that takes place between people who may or may not share a common set of experiences, cultural values, and standards for argument. Lack of understanding or consensus about how to interpret someone else's argument may lead to misunderstanding and even violence.

When we use arguments well, we can help our audiences think of alternatives they may never have considered and we might help them evaluate their decisions in better ways. At the same time, if we use arguments improperly or deceitfully, we have an equal opportunity for clouding issues, concealing the best choices, and leading our audiences to the wrong decisions.

The power of argumentation and its influence on people is considerable. We should not take our arguments for granted but should understand their effects. Given the contexts in which they are made, we should be able to evaluate whether our arguments are appropriate, reasonable, and ethical. Although these might seem like intuitive and obvious considerations for any arguer, the means for making reasonable and ethical arguments are not always apparent. Discovering the "right" arguments and still being able to make our points is often as difficult as constructing the arguments themselves. Furthermore, the appropriate argument is not always apparent and may change as our recipients change their attitudes, beliefs, values, and actions.

This chapter focuses on culture and ethics as two contexts in which arguments are made. The importance of these two elements of the argumentative situation was emphasized by Joseph Wenzel when he wrote that "In the course of social life, we pass through innumerable contexts in which arguing may occur. All of these are framed by the general matrix of our sociocultural system as well as by special features of each occasion."[1] The sociocultural system in which arguments occur incorporates certain values that play a role in making arguments and judging argument practices. Cultural values imply that arguments should be well supported, accurate, and intended to benefit their audience. Culture and ethics are therefore related to each other, and in this chapter we will show how values play a role in both.

CULTURE AND ARGUMENTATION

An American woman who was spending a study year in Greece went to the post office to pick up a package that had been mailed to her from home. The package was addressed to her in care of the Greek friend with whom she was staying. The postal clerk told the woman that he could not release the package to her because it was addressed to her friend and not to her. Her friend was out of town and, because she needed her package immediately, she began to try to persuade the clerk to give it to her. She pointed to her own name on the package label; she showed the clerk her passport to assure him of her identity; she reasoned with him, arguing that the package had her name on it and therefore must be hers. Regardless of what she said, the clerk continued to maintain that he could not give her the package because it was not addressed to her. Finally, he announced that it was his break and slammed the parcel pickup window shut, leaving her to storm out of the post office in disgust.[2]

Here we see a clear case of cross-cultural miscommunication that could be attributed to many causes. Perhaps the clerk felt that the woman was aggressive and insulting; perhaps he did not like Americans; or perhaps the woman did not speak Greek well enough to make her point. It's possible, however, that she used the wrong persuasive strategy. What else could she have done in this situation? She might have attempted to bribe the clerk, or told him a story about some other person who lost his job because he denied service to people, or returned to the post office later and refused to leave until she was given her package. The fact is that persuasive strategies and argument practices *vary across cultures.* By "culture" here, we do not necessarily mean some identifiable ethnic group such as a tribal culture or a national culture. Instead of being dependent on demographic or physical characteristics, a culture arises from shared experience, practices, and values. *Cultures are systems of shared meanings that are expressed through different symbolic forms such as rituals, stories, symbols, and myths that hold a group of people together.*[3]

This fairly complex definition requires some explanation. First, it implies that people who share a common culture enact the same communication patterns and practices. Members of some cultures use extensive nonverbal gestures when talking with each other, while others repeatedly show deference by nodding their heads or bowing to show respect. In some cultures, eye contact is avoided while in others it is valued. Second, cultures contain symbolic forms such as rituals, stories, and specialized language that provide a common framework so that people can understand one another.

The truthfulness of our cultural mythology is less important than that the members of a culture understand these stories and use them as part of a common experience that binds the membership together. For example, if asked who the first president of the United States was, a member of the United States' culture would probably respond, "George Washington." In fact, most of us may be able to recount a variety of stories about Washington: He told the truth about chopping down a cherry tree; he crossed the Delaware to attack the Hessians; and he threw a dollar across the Potomac River. Yet, there is fair evidence that some of these stories are not true. For instance, Washington was not really the first president of the United States. A man by the name of John Hanson from Maryland served as the first president of the United States under the Articles of Confederation. And, according to Tad Tuleja, author of *Fabulous Fallacies,* there were seven other presidents before Washington was elected.[4] Regardless of the historical accuracy of the traditional and commonly understood account, however, Washington serves as a cultural icon that represents a common thread of understanding for members of the United States' culture. All Americans identify with the myth, and that provides a common framework for understanding.

For an arguer, understanding the culture in which the argument is developed is important. Different cultures, with their different experiences and frameworks for interpretation, understand and evaluate arguments differently. In the United States, for instance, we are surrounded with arguments about whether abortion is right or wrong. Members of the pro-choice movement argue that women should have the right to choose and to control their own bodies and that abortion decisions should not be left to the government. On the other hand, members of the pro-life movement argue that human life begins with conception and that the choice to abort a pregnancy is tantamount to murder. While this remains a controversial issue decades after the Supreme Court handed down the *Roe v. Wade* decision that legalized abortion, few Americans would argue that abortion should be used as a preferred means of birth control.

While members of both sides of the issue might agree on this simple premise, the normative standards imposed by each movement's culture for evaluating arguments would be different. For example, cultural assumptions about when life begins would change the way arguments are evaluated in the context. If the cultural understanding is that life begins at conception, then the argument that abortion through the first trimester is warranted or justifiable would be equated with an argument for murder. Similarly, if the cultural understanding of life presumes that life does not begin until the fetus is viable outside the womb, then abortion could not be considered murder. Understanding and criticizing the two arguments depends on the cultural context in which they are placed.

Culture provides us with a framework for understanding and interpreting arguments and helps us evaluate their appropriateness. As people become adjusted to a culture, they learn the basic assumptions of that culture so that they can perform their roles and abide by its rules, values, and morality. When we make an argument, our recipients understand our basic cultural assumptions and use them as a framework for evaluating ideas and arguments.

The idea of a culture is not tied to a person's citizenship or ethnicity, but rather to those systems of shared meanings, common values, and basic assumptions. Within the American host culture, for example, there are many subcultures. African-American, Asian-American, Latino, and Native-American cultures are all members of the American host culture but have their own traditions, rituals, and norms that bind them together. Even a particular subculture can be further divided into additional subcultures with unique cultural characteristics. We can visualize the relationship between host cultures and subcultures as illustrated in Figure 2–1. In this figure, the larger circle represents the dominant, or national culture. Some of its basic assumptions (listed as A, B, and C) may be subscribed to by each of the smaller subcultures within it. Yet, the smaller subcultures have their independent traditions and institutions (shown with additional letters).

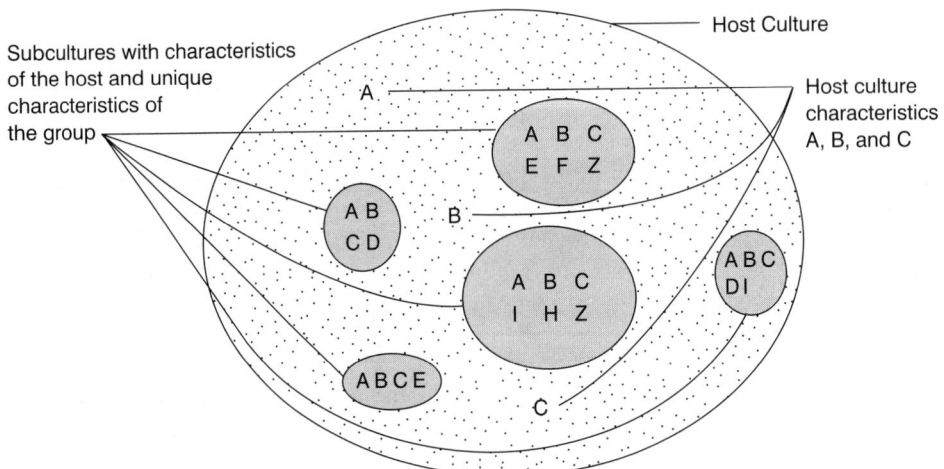

FIGURE 2–1 Within a dominant culture are subcultures with independent traditions and institutions.

For any of these subcultures within the United States, we could make the following statements about their membership:

1. We all share a common U.S. history and U.S. government.
2. We are all subject to the provisions of the Constitution, Bill of Rights, and other federal and state laws.

Of course, there are many other rules and conventions that members of our culture adhere to that are given to us from the host culture. At the same time, however, there are unique norms and rules that guide each of the subcultures. These might include:

- values and expectations for education, career, and social choices
- attitudes about government, law, or other cultures

The importance of culture and subculture in argument practices can be illustrated by reference to the civil rights movement of the 1960s and 1970s. African Americans during that period shared the belief that they were disadvantaged and discriminated against in housing, education, and individual rights. Differing subcultures formed around differing views about what was to be done about these conditions. Dr. Martin Luther King, Jr., and his followers believed in nonviolent protest and resistance to gain equal rights, while Stokely Carmichael and his followers were more militant.

Carmichael preached violence and separatism. He said:

> It seems to me that the institutions that function in this country are clearly racist, and that they're built upon racism.... How can we begin to build institutions that will allow people to relate with each other as human beings? This country has never done that.... Now several people have been upset because we've said that integration was irrelevant when initiated by blacks and that in fact it was a subterfuge, an insidious subterfuge for the maintenance of white supremacy. We maintain that in the past six years or so this country has been feeding us a thalidomide drug of integration, and that some Negroes have been walking down a dream street talking about sitting next to white people.... We were never fighting for the right to integrate, we were fighting against white supremacy.... We are tired of trying to explain to white people that we're not going to hurt them. We are concerned with getting the things we want, the things that we have to have to be able to function. The question is, can white people allow for that in this country?... If that does not happen, brothers and sisters, we have no choice, but to say very clearly, move on over, or we're going to move on over you.[5]

Carmichael appealed here to audience members who apparently believed that white people cannot be trusted, that promises of equality and integration are just a subterfuge, and that nonviolent protest will never succeed in obtaining the things that African Americans want and need to function. He felt that his audience would agree that confrontation and use of aggressive tactics might be the only way to achieve their ends.

Carmichael's statement can be contrasted with that of another African American, Barbara Jordan, who spoke as follows to the 1976 Democratic national convention:

> A lot of years have passed since [the Democratic Party first met], and during that time it would have been most unusual for any national political party to ask that a Barbara Jordan deliver a keynote address . . . but tonight here I am. And I feel that notwithstanding

the past that my presence here is one additional bit of evidence that the American Dream need not forever be deferred. . . .

We are a people in a quandary about the present. We are a people in search of our future. We are a people in search of a national community. We are a people trying not to solve the problems of the present—unemployment, inflation—but we are attempting on a larger scale to fulfill the promise of America. We are attempting to fulfill our national purpose: to create and sustain a society in which all of us are equal. . . .

As a first step, we must restore our belief in ourselves. We are a generous people so why can't we be generous with each other? We need to take to heart the words spoken by Thomas Jefferson: "Let us restore to social intercourse that harmony and affection without which liberty and even life are but dreary things. A nation is formed by the willingness of each of us to share in the responsibility for upholding the common good. A government is invigorated when each of us is willing to participate in shaping the future of this nation."[6]

While Carmichael believed that promises of integration and equality were a hoax perpetrated on African Americans by whites, Jordan believed that real equality between the races was possible, that progress had been made toward this goal, and that she (as a keynote speaker at a national convention) was living proof of that. Whereas Carmichael assumed that confrontation and protest were the only means of achieving basic civil rights for African Americans, Jordan felt that equality could best be achieved if all Americans—white and black—worked together for the common good.

The dramatic contrast between the arguments of these two speakers reveals the influence of two subcultures—one militant and the other nonviolent—within the African-American subculture at that time. This contrast also reveals the important role that values play in making arguments. As we will illustrate in Chapters 6 and 10, values can fulfill multiple functions whenever someone makes an argument. Some of the values used by Carmichael and Jordan include honesty, social justice, equality, and social harmony, and both speakers assumed a certain level of agreement by their audiences *that those values were important* and *that some were more important than others*. Each speaker, then, used agreement on values as a starting point or form of evidence for his or her arguments.

One important way that cultures differ, then, is in how they assign different levels of importance to different values. Some cultures value possessions and others value people. Some cultures value collectivism and relationships, whereas others value individualism. Some value progress and change, whereas others value tradition. The contrasting perspectives of different cultures even affect the ways in which their members value material objects. This was illustrated in a recent book written by Peter Menzel called *Material World: A Global Family Portrait*. His book considered thirty families and their possessions to see how values changed depending on culture and circumstance. His conclusions were:

Most valued possessions:

Namgay family of Bhutan (annual per capita income, $174)
    a book of Buddhist teachings
    school books
    jump rope

Thoroddsen family of Iceland (per capita income, $23,324)
> private airplane
>
> cello
>
> horse

Kalnazarov family of Uzbekistan (per capita income, $978)
> bicycles[7]

Differences such as these imply that arguers from one culture or subculture who seek to influence those from another culture or subculture should be aware of how values of their recipients are prioritized and should not assume that their own values, which may not be shared by the members of their audience, can be used as starting points or premises for arguments. Further suggestions for how one can make use of values in constructing arguments will be provided in Chapter 10.

In addition to different values, assumptions, and symbol systems, members of different cultures use different *styles* of argument. *Argument style refers to cultural preferences in the arrangement of arguments and the methods for developing extended arguments.* If it is true that a particular style that works in one culture may not be well received in another, that has important implications for how people should conduct themselves in cross-cultural situations. Clearly, the strategy used by the American woman who attempted to deal with the Greek postal clerk was unsuccessful! One person who has studied divergent argument styles as used in various cultures is Barbara Johnstone. In studying persuasive strategies used by Europeans, Arabs, and Asians, Johnstone identified at least three contrasting (and relatively incompatible) styles of argument.

The first style, preferred by North Americans and other Westerners, is the *quasilogical style. The quasi-logical style takes its model from formal logic, relates claims to each other deductively, and makes use of "logical connectives" such as "thus," "hence," and "therefore."* (We will say more about quasi-logical reasoning in Chapter 8.) For example, the American postal client argued that "this package has my name on it; I am the person in question; *therefore,* it is my package and I should have it." Johnstone makes the following observation about the quasilogical style:

> Quasi-logical persuasion is based on the notion that the key to the persuasiveness of an argument is the ideas that are expressed. If a claim is true, it is true no matter who states it or what sort of language is used. What is important about quasi-logical discourse is that its structure be orderly. . . . Once established via rational procedures, decisions are no longer negotiable, and they apply in any situation.[8]

Another aspect of this style of argument is its tendency to rely on "hard evidence" or physical reality for its premises. ("This here is my name on the package, and you can see it in writing.") At least partly because of Western culture's valuing of science and statistics, empirical forms of proof are considered more important and credible than personal experience or cultural values.

The quasi-logical style is most in line with the logical perspective as we explained it in Chapter 1. This approach to argument and the standards for argument practices it implies are very influential in this book, which was written for use in Western classrooms. Chapter 7 on evidence, Chapter 8 on reasoning, and Chapter 12 on argument

REPRESENTING CULTURE

This chapter attempts to describe the complexity of culture. Often it is difficult enough for the members of a culture to understand each other let alone understand the members of another culture. The following case study is an example of an attempt to introduce one culture (more accurately many cultures) to another. As you read the case study, ask yourself the following questions:

- What methods would I use to share my culture with another?
- What symbols, artifacts, sights, and sounds accurately depict my culture?
- If I could pick any ten things that would best share my culture with another, what would they be?
- Is the attempt at cultural introduction described in this case likely to work?

CASE STUDY
In 1977, the United States threw two bottles into the ocean—more accurately, the United States launched two probes into space. The probes, Voyager 1 and 2 were launched on September 5, 1977, and August 20, 1977, respectively. Inside each spacecraft, NASA placed an "Earth Time Capsule" intended to communicate to any interstellar spacefarers what life on Earth is like.

The contents of the time capsules were decided upon by a NASA committee which was chaired by Dr. Carl Sagan of Cornell University. The task of the Committee was to decide what to include in the spacecraft that would adequately introduce Earth and its variety of cultures to beings from another planet in another solar system. The challenge, as you might imagine, was enormous. What should be included? What artifacts, sounds, pictures, or drawings best represent what the planet Earth is like?

The Committee developed an etched metal plaque that was affixed to each spacecraft. On the plaque were drawings of a female and male human being, a map to our solar system and planet Earth, and a representation of a hydrogen atom (among some other images). The Committee also created a 12-inch, gold-plated, copper phonograph record on which were recorded in analogue form a variety of sights and sounds from Earth. Included with the record were a cartridge and needle with which to play it and pictorial instructions as to how to play the record.

The sights and sounds recorded on the record were diverse, and the Committee attempted to include representative samples from a variety of cultures. For example, the recording contains verbal greetings from Earth in 55 different languages (including some languages that no longer exist). It has several drawings and diagrams to help explain how things work. Included among these are drawings of DNA, each of the planets in our solar system, human anatomy, human conception, progression of evolution, and progression of human aging process. In addition, several photographs were included on the record. Among these were Malaysian father and daughter, group of children, family portrait, seashore, Snake River and Grand Tetons, sand dunes, fallen leaves, snowflakes over Sequoia, school of fish, Andean girls, Thailand craftsman, old man with beard and glasses in Turkey, and a supermarket in the United States. Finally, they included a variety of natural sounds, such as whales, birds, fire, tools, dogs, trains, tractors, heartbeats, sawing, and laughter.

> The contents of these two probes represent our attempt to introduce ourselves to beings from vastly different cultures. It will take about 40,000 years for these two probes to reach the nearest planet outside our solar system. If they are found, they will be found by beings with an advanced space flight ability. And while they may never be found and their capsules never opened, the hope is that one day these two spacecraft will successfully describe and portray our planet and its diversity to those of another.

analysis emphasize this approach. When communicating with people from non-Western cultures, however, you may find that one of the other two styles described by Johnstone is more prevalent.

The second style described by Johnstone is the *presentational* style. *The presentational style takes its model from poetry, sweeps the recipient along through a rhythmic flow of words and sounds, parallel clauses, and visual metaphors, and moves the audience through aesthetic appeal.* The presentational style aims to enhance the audience's awareness of something and makes use of terms such as "look," "see," or "behold." Johnstone notes that "In contrast to the dense, 'integrated' style of quasi-logical discourse, which calls on the audience's rational minds, presentational discourse creates 'involvement' in the way that good poetry does."[9] An excellent example of this process of visualization is in Dr. King's speech, "I Have a Dream:"

> I have a dream that one day this nation will rise up and live out the true meaning of its creed: 'We hold these truths to be self-evident; that all men are created equal.'
> I have a dream that one day on the red hills of Georgia the sons of former slaves and the sons of former slaveowners will be able to sit down together at the table of brotherhood;
> I have a dream . . . that my four little children will one day live in a nation where they will not be judged by the color of their skin but by the content of their character;
> I have a dream today.[10]

King's repetition of the phrase "I have a dream" encourages his audience to imagine a future where people live in true equality. He envisions scenes in which groups then separated by discrimination and segregation live together, and his use of metaphor ("table of brotherhood," "content of their character") makes his vision more immediate. This is a very fine example of the presentational style of persuasion. Johnstone notes that, in the presentational style, *people* are what is important and individuals make decisions for themselves. This style of argument occurs in Eastern cultures, in situations where truths are imminent rather than being subject to deliberation, and where "the persuader's task is to make a potentially available truth actually available—or present—in the audience's consciousness."[11]

The third style is the analogical style. *The analogical style makes its claims by calling to mind stories or fables known in the culture that imply principles and ideas favored by the arguer.* In Japanese culture, for example, the ceremony of tea is considered a model of appropriate behavior, and stories about the tea ceremony are often used to implicitly teach principles of behavior. Johnstone observes that the analogical style "persuades by teaching, reminding its audience of time-tested values by the indirect mode of story telling. Analogical arguers persuade by having their audiences make lateral . . . leaps between past events and current issues."[12] In the analogical style, *culture,* rather than institutions or individuals, is important, and the aim is to teach what is apt or appropriate in a given circumstance. An excellent example of this style is Christ's story of the good Samaritan:

> [A lawyer] seeking to justify himself said to Jesus, "And who is my neighbor?" Jesus replied, "A man was going down from Jerusalem to Jericho, and he fell among robbers, who stripped him and beat him, and departed, leaving him half-dead. Now by chance a priest was going down that road; and when he saw him he passed by on the other side. So likewise a Levite, when he came to the place and saw him, passed by on the other side. But a Samaritan, as he journeyed, came to where he was; and when he saw him, he had compassion, and went to him and bound up his wounds, pouring on oil and wine; then he set him on his own beast and brought him to an inn, and took care of him. And the next day he took out two denarii and gave them to the innkeeper saying, 'Take care of him; and whatever more you spend, I will repay you when I come back.' Which of these three, do you think, proved neighbor to the man who fell among the robbers?" [The lawyer] said, "The one who showed mercy on him" and Jesus said to him, "Go and do likewise."[13]

Many principles of value and behavior are succinctly communicated through this brief story. One's "neighbor" is not the person who lives next door. Samaritans were despised foreigners in Jesus's culture, yet it was the Samaritan, not the priest or the Levite, who helped the man. One's "neighbor" appears to be that person who has a certain quality—the quality of mercy for his fellow humans. And so it is implied that we should not treat only those we know or those who live next to us or share our lifestyle as neighbor. All humanity is potentially our "neighbor." Then, too, the character of the Samaritan himself reveals a model of behavior ("Go and do likewise.") This man did not "pass by on the other side," but stopped and tended to the wounded man, and he did not stop there, he continued to care for him through his own ministrations and the money he left with the innkeeper. He went out of his way to help someone else, someone he did not know, someone who was not (in a literal sense) his "neighbor" at all. There are many other principles implied in this story. This parable illustrates the power of the analogical style to communicate a great deal in a few words.

The analogical style is favored in cultures that concern themselves with appropriateness and preservation of ideas and principles. Native-American myths and stories teach members of their cultures significant truths about the harmony between persons and nature, the cycles of nature and life, and the enduring truths of their religions. In Muslim cultures, stories from the history of Islam are often used to communicate religious principles. And, as we have mentioned, the use of story and narrative is also important in many Asian cultures. Indeed, it is probably the case that narrative is more pervasively used as a form of "argument," than the rational approach included in this text and in many Western courses in reasoning and argument!

All cultures develop value systems that indicate acceptable modes of conduct and thus premises of which arguers can make use to argue for their claims. When you are talking with a person from a culture different from your own, you should consider whether that person shares your values. If not, you would be well advised to consider what that person *does* consider to be important before you begin making your arguments. Furthermore, not every culture shares Western culture's preference for logical argument and empirical evidence. If you want to influence people from a culture different from your own, you might want to consider using stories or metaphor to communicate your ideas. While this book will focus on Western modes of argument, we do want to make the point that they are not the only way of effectively presenting your ideas to others.

ARGUMENTATION AND ETHICS

Just as arguments can be used to help people make better decisions, arguments can also undermine and harm people. As with any tool, arguments have the capacity to improve our lives or to damage them. The difference rests in how the arguer elects to use arguments and how recipients evaluate them.

When arguers use arguments to oppress others, mislead their audiences, evade the truth, and deceive the public, the repercussions can be felt for generations. Millions of people in Europe died because the Nazis believed Adolf Hitler's argument that their misfortunes were caused by the Jewish people. Many lives and careers were ruined in the early 1950s when the public believed Joseph McCarthy's false claims and accusations about Communist infiltration. President Richard Nixon and his advisors sought to conceal illegal activities through half-truths and evasions during the Watergate cover-up. During President Reagan's administration, Oliver North, an aide to the National Security Council, admitted that he had lied and misrepresented the facts regarding the Iran/contra arms dealings in earlier testimony.

Because arguments have the potential to do great harm, people involved in arguments have a responsibility to be vigilant about the quality and integrity of arguments they present and receive. In other words, all people involved in arguments share an ethical responsibility. *Ethics is the study of what is morally right or just.* When we abide by the prescriptions of our ethics (for example, we do not lie, attempt to cause injury to others, or deceive) our arguments are considered ethical. However, when we use the power inherent in arguments to persuade people based on deception or argumentative trickery, then our arguments are considered unethical.

As citizens of a democratic society and as private individuals, we must be critical of the arguments addressed to us and scrupulous in presenting arguments to others. Evasion, deception, and misrepresentation cause public distrust, poor decision making, and occasionally outright harm and injury to individuals. We must, therefore, be aware of the quality of our arguments and knowledgeable about standards that will enable us to distinguish arguments that are ethically or morally right from those that are wrong. The remainder of this chapter, therefore, will consider the question, "What is an ethical argument?"

We are constantly influenced by ethical codes for conduct, whether they are formally stated or informally understood. Because ethics are often not formally stated, however, we are challenged with making the "right" decision based on what we believe is the correct action. For example, what would you do if you found a $100 bill on a sidewalk outside of a store? If there is no identification on the money, do you keep it? Do you give it to the clerk in the store? Do you take it to a police station? This can be a difficult choice and your decision will depend on what you believe to be the correct or just choice. Another ethical issue is raised by the *Mason Country Journal,* a newspaper in Shelton, Washington, that routinely publishes the names of rape suspects and victims alike (including juvenile rape victims). The paper's argument is that its job is to publicize the full record of Shelton and rapes are a part of that record. However, releasing the names has disrupted the lives of many women and young girls. Is that ethical? The answers are not always clear.

Ethicists have long considered the nature of ethical conduct and how different ethical requirements and rules emerge from a variety of contexts. While understanding how ethics function in any given context can be difficult, ethics in argumentation generally operate at two levels: a *content* level and a *relationship* level.

First, some ethical principles govern the content of arguments. Such ethics evaluate whether the claim, evidence, reasoning, and attempt to influence are moral, good, or just. Such a position was taken by Wayne Minnick when he wrote that an ethical communicator should

> reject all frauds, deceptions, concealments, specious arguments; cultivate the capacity for careful investigation and judicial and reflective deliberation of controversies and problems; endorse only those positions whose truth-claim merits his advocacy; must use intrinsically sound methods; use ethically neutral methods in ways that are consistent and can be defended by reliable evidence and sound reasoning.[14]

Minnick's position seems reasonable enough. If we speak the truth and use care in selecting appropriate arguments, then we are behaving ethically.

Richard L. Johannesen wrote in *Ethics in Human Communication* that what is ethical or unethical can be evaluated from many different perspectives including religion, politics, and law.[15] From the religious perspective, arguments are evaluated by a series of "thou-shalt-nots" that distinguishes right from wrong. For example, lying, slander, and deception are all considered unethical as described in a religious document such as the Bible. The political perspective derives its ethics from a set of values and criteria unique to the political system. Johannesen noted:

> Naturally each different political system could embody differing values leading to differing ethical judgments. Within the context of American representative democracy, for instance, various analysts pinpoint values and procedures they view as fundamental to optimum functioning of our political system. . . .[16]

These values include respect for the dignity and worth of the individual, fairness and equality, freedom, and the ability to understand and participate in democracy. Anything that enhances these values is viewed as ethical, and acts that undermine them are viewed as unethical. Yet, making such a clearly defined distinction is not always so easy. While the standards for determining what is ethical might seem simple and clear, often they are not—especially when different people hold widely different values and views of what is ethical or not.[17]

For example, consider the issues surrounding physician-assisted suicide. Is it appropriate for a physician to assist patients in killing themselves? Should there be any restrictions on such help? What types of rules are appropriate? These are questions that have been asked more and more as technologies have been able to keep terminally ill patients alive longer.

Euthanasia presents the medical profession with an important dilemma. From the time of Hippocrates, physicians have been instructed never to take life. The view has been that life should be preserved and lengthened but never shortened. Asking a doctor to kill a patient is difficult and strikes at the heart of most medical codes of ethics. Should the United States allow doctors to practice euthanasia?

The Netherlands has allowed physician-assisted suicide for several years. In fact, The Netherlands is the only country in the Western world that allows the practice, and currently 2000 to 3000 patients commit suicide each year with the aid of a physician. The U.S. equivalent (adjusting for the difference in population) would be between 40,000 and 60,000.[18] The concern is that the high numbers reflect abuse. The Dutch government was forced to change its euthanasia laws when it discovered that many of the cases of suicide not only involved people who were not competent to make the decision but many who were euthanized involuntarily.

In the United States, more and more doctors are beginning to prescribe lethal doses of medication to patients who are mentally competent but in the last phases of a terminal illness. The state of Oregon is the only state to legalize physician-assisted suicide. Perhaps no one is better known for euthanasia than Dr. Jack Kevorkian, dubbed by the media as Dr. Death. He has presided over dozens of suicides and has helped people take their own lives through his "suicide machine," the use of carbon monoxide poisoning, and other methods. Each of his patients presumably wanted to die and had asked for his help. From a legal point of view what he did was not wrong, and although Michigan passed several injunctions barring Kevorkian from assisting in further suicides, he has won every court case brought against him. So, if one considers the standards for what is deemed ethical, the questions become Did Kevorkian show respect for the dignity and worth of the individual? Was he fair and equal? and Did the people have the right to make their own choice? These are important issues and ones that cannot be easily decided.

It should be clear from the preceding discussion that ethical judgments are difficult to stipulate because, in part, they vary widely from culture to culture. As we discussed earlier, ethics highlights what is an appropriate moral stance. Therefore, ethics are dependent on values that are generated culturally. What remains constant among cultures, however, is that each culture imposes restrictions on the content of argument and defines appropriate action. Almost every culture and every subculture has ethical codes that prescribe what can and cannot be argued and what is and is not ethical.

The relational level, the second level at which ethics in argumentation operates, focuses on whether an arguer has enhanced or diminished the relationship among the arguer, recipient, and field. If an arguer seeks to harm the intellectual integrity of the recipient or covertly seeks to damage or undermine the relationship with the recipient, the arguer has acted unethically.

Whenever a person engages in arguments with another, a relationship is created and that relationship is an important part of the process of argumentation. Wayne Brockriede put the relational level in perspective when he wrote an article called "Arguers as Lovers."[19] Brockriede noted that beyond the content of argument transactions, "the relationship among the people who argue may afford one useful way of classifying argumentative transactions."[20]

Brockriede, as the title of his article suggests, takes the position that arguers, in their attempt to influence and relate to their recipients, should act as lovers toward their audiences and need to respect and understand the needs of their recipients. The goal or ethically correct choice for the arguer is to approach the audience as a partner rather than coercing them.

Brockriede wrote that the relationship between arguers and their audiences can be classified as three different types: rapist, seducer, and lover. When arguers rape, they view their relationship with the audience as a unilateral one. The arguer will tend to objectify the audience and will seek to manipulate the recipients. As Brockriede claimed, "The rapist wants to gain or to maintain a position of superiority—on the intellectual front of making his case prevail or on the interpersonal front of putting the other person down."[21]

Whether or not we like to admit it, argument rape is a common practice and many people engage in it without even thinking. But we live in an adversarial society in which one person's success often means another's failure and where success at whatever cost is prized over failure. It can be easy for arguers—who may not even be aware of their actions—to "rape" their recipients. Even our language describing arguments suggests this. We often say:

> I beat their arguments.
>
> I destroyed their position.
>
> I demolished the competition.

Yet, each of these examples points to our tendency to objectify and treat people who oppose us as less than human.

A second type of relationship between arguer and recipient is seducer who seeks to win covertly through charm or deceit. As Brockriede noted:

> The seducer's attitude toward co-arguers is similar to that of the rapist. He, too, sees the relationship as unilateral. Although he may not be contemptuous of his prey, he is indifferent to the identity and integrity of the other person. Whereas the intent of the rapist is to force assent, the seducer tries to charm or trick his victim into assent.[22]

There are many ways for arguers to trick their recipients. Different types of fallacies make faulty arguments appear reasonable and believable. When employed by a crafty arguer, fallacies may cause audiences to believe in faulty arguments. Similarly, withholding information, telling half-truths, taking evidence out of context, fabricating evidence, among other deceptions, all provide arguers with the means of fooling audiences.

The third type of relationship between arguer and recipient is that of lover. The arguer as lover seeks to empower the recipient through argument and to expand and enlighten the recipient. The lover, according to Brockriede, wants "power parity" in which arguer and recipient share equally in the exchange of arguments. Brockriede noted: "whereas the rapist and seducer argue against an adversary or an opponent, the lover argues with his peer and is willing to risk his very self in his attempt to establish a bilateral relationship."[23]

The arguer-as-lover relationship views the process of giving reasons in argument as a person-centered enterprise. Its central tenet was summarized by Thomas Nilsen when he concluded that: "Whatever develops, enlarges, enhances human personalities is good; whatever restricts, degrades, or injures human personalities is bad."[24] For Nilsen, this meant that arguers should always give their recipients a "significant choice," which means that arguers should provide their audiences with enough information to draw their own conclusions.

The arguer-as-lover relationship can enhance personal development and improve the quality of life. The relationship is based on the arguer's candidness and efforts to preserve free and well-informed choices by all parties to an argument.

SUMMARY

Culture is important to the understanding of argument practices, because a person's values arise from his or her cultural background. Values can be used as premises for argument and are also vital to argument ethics, or standards for good argument. This chapter considers how culture affects argument practices and how values influence a view of ethical argument practices.

Cultures are systems of shared meanings that are expressed through different symbolic forms such as rituals, stories, symbols, and myths that hold a culture together. Cultures are not necessarily tied to race or citizenship but rather are enacted by people who share common values and life experiences. Cultures include subcultures, each of which has its own traditions, rituals, and norms. Arguers should consider the values held by the cultures and subcultures to which their audience members belong when they construct arguments, because different cultures assign different levels of importance to different values.

Various cultures also favor particular styles of argument. Western culture favors the quasi-logical style, which is rooted in science and formal logic. The quasi-logical style relates claims to each other deductively and makes use of logical connectives such as "thus" and "therefore" when advancing claims. Asian-American, Latino, African-American and Native-American cultures generally favor the presentational and analogical styles of argument. The presentational style takes its model from poetry and uses a rhythmic flow of words and sounds, parallel clauses, and visual metaphors to move the audience through aesthetic appeal. The analogical style makes claims by calling to mind stories or fables known in the culture that imply principles and ideas favored by the arguer. While this book focuses on the quasi-logical style of argument, people who seek to influence recipients from non-Western cultures might effectively use one of the other two styles in their arguments.

Misleading or deceptive uses of argument can cause great harm to society and to individuals and, for this reason, argument practices should be governed by sound ethical principles. Ethics is defined as the study of what is morally right or just, but sometimes this is not easy to determine. This is because the question of what ethical standards should be applied to an argument may depend on the culture or situation in which the argument occurs.

Ethical argument practices are related both to the content of the argument and the relationship between the arguer and his or her audience. Ethicists who have written on argument content believe that content that is ethically sound is content that furthers open inquiry, quotes evidence in context, and makes use of sound reasoning. On the relational level, arguers can attempt to manipulate and objectify their audiences, or charm and trick them, or empower and enlighten them. Only the third of these three further opens inquiry and choice among recipients.

Regardless of the cultural or ethical perspective one chooses for argument, one should keep in mind that in any argument situation, there are many diverse values at work, many argument styles and strategies available, and many ways to further sound decision-making and ethical practice.

EXERCISES

Exercise 1 Below are some passages by various authors. Each one is speaking predominantly in the quasi-logical, presentational, or analogical style. (*Please note that passages in either of the last two styles may not appear to be arguments according to the strict criteria we proposed in Chapter 1.*) For each passage, which of the three styles do you believe the speaker or writer to be using? Provide a justification for your choice. Then, decide which values seem to be favored in the passage and how the speaker or writer is prioritizing them. What alternative values could be weighed against the ones the speaker or writer seems to favor?

1. While every society has its rich and poor, inequality is mainly a matter of degree. In 1974, when the gap between the incomes of the richest and poorest Americans was at a historic low, the top 10 percent of U.S. households had incomes 31 times those of the poorest 10 percent and four times those of median-income households. By 1994, those numbers were 55 times the poorest and six times the median. Not only is inequality growing; its growth is accelerating. Inequality surged between 1991 and 1993 as the most recent recession lowered incomes for all but the richest Americans. Executives killed jobs in ways that would be illegal in Germany and France—for example, shutting down plants in some regions and relocating them in jurisdictions with right-to-work laws. Wall Street rewarded the executives with a mid-recession rally that boosted the value of their stock options.

   Michael Hout and Samuel R. Lucas, "Narrowing the Income Gap between Rich and Poor," *Chronicle of Higher Education,* August 16, 1996, B1.

✸ 2. The meaning of "the virtual" is obscure. What is its relation to "the real"? Is it somehow a mimicking? an approximation? a double? the antithesis of the real? Does it inhabit, so to speak, its own space, its own plane? (For a long time it has been a technical term in physics and in art history in discussions of perspectivism.) In the same semantic field are a number of related notions—actual, counterfactual, specular, replicated, simulated, artificial—whose connections, with respect to the human sensorium and cultural reception, await their analyst.

   Iain A. Boal, "A Flow of Monsters: Luddism and Virtual Technologies," in *Resisting the Virtual Life: The Culture and Politics of Information,* James Brook and Iain A. Boal, eds. (San Francisco: City Lights, 1995), 7.

3. The continuing "debate" over the National Information Infrastructure, the so-called information superhighway, has so far been a staged event. Mass-circulation magazines like *Newsweek* and *Time* have run cover stories about the coming "revolution" that are little more than regurgitations of industry PR. Lifestyle magazines like *Wired* and *Mondo 2000* stimulate consumer demand for new gadgets and informed acquiescence to governmental and corporate policies—in the name of a spurious "liberation" and "empowerment." Buzzwords like "interactive" and "choice" are frequently employed. "Choice," however, means no more than a consumer choosing a product offered by the seller of services or commodities, perhaps video-on-demand or database services.

"Interactive" means the ability to punch in your credit card number and order products via screen commands from home. The very language of interactivity and the new data communications is being subverted by this emphasis on one-way flow and sales.

Jesse Drew, "Media Activism and Radical Democracy," in *Resisting the Virtual Life,* p. 75

4. No [Black] Muslim smokes—that was another of our rules. Some prospective Muslims found it more difficult to quit tobacco than others found quitting the dope habit. But black men and women quit more easily when we got them to consider seriously how the white man's government cared less about the public's health than about continuing the tobacco industry's *billions* in tax revenue. "What does a serviceman pay for a carton of cigarettes?" a prospective Muslim convert would be asked. It helped him to see that every regularly priced carton he bought meant that the white man's government took around two dollars of a black man's hard-earned money for taxes, not for tobacco.

Malcolm X [assisted by Alex Haley], *The Autobiography of Malcolm X* (New York: Ballantine Books, 1965), 259.

✻ 5. When necessary, I've acted without Congress. Our administration has approved 67 separate welfare reform experiments in 40 states to move people from welfare to work. Fully three-quarters of all welfare recipients are living under new rules right now.

The *New York Times* has called it a quiet revolution in welfare. Today, 1.3 million fewer people are on welfare than the day I took office, and child support collections are up 40 percent.

For three and a half years, I've worked with Congress to craft legislation that replaces welfare with work.

Bill Clinton, "Text of Clinton's Weekly Radio Address," *Allpolitics:* online, Internet. 13 July 1996. http://allpolitics.com/news/9607/13/clinton.radio/transcript.shtml

6. I have a message for our youth. I challenge them to put hope in their brains, and not dope in their veins. I told them like Jesus, I, too, was born in a slum, but just because you're born in a slum, does not mean that the slum is born in you, and you can rise above it if your mind is made up. I told them in every slum, there are two sides. When I see a broken window, that's the slummy side. Train that youth to be a glazier, that's the sunny side. When I see a missing brick, that's the slummy side. Let that child in the union, and become a brickmason, and build, that's the sunny side. When I see a missing door, that's the slummy side. Train some youth to become a carpenter, that's the sunny side. When I see the vulgar words and hieroglyphics of destitution on the walls, that's slummy side. Train some youth to be a painter, or an artist—that's the sunny side. We need this place looking for the sunny side because there's a brighter side somewhere. I am more convinced than ever that we can win, because there's a brighter side somewhere. . . . I just want young America to do me one favor. Just one favor. . . . Exercise that right to dream.

Jesse Jackson, "The Rainbow Coalition," in *Contemporary American Speeches,* 7th ed., Richard L. Johannesen, R. R. Allen, Wil A. Linkugel, eds. (Dubuque, Iowa: Kendall/Hunt, 1992), 391.

7. Let us build a Middle East of hope where today's food is produced and tomorrow's prosperity is guaranteed, a region with a common market, a Near East with a long-range agenda. We owe it to our own soldiers, to the memories of the victims of the Holocaust. Our hearts today grieve for the lost lives of young and innocent people yesterday in our own country. Let their memory be our foundation we are establishing today, a memory of peace on fresh and old tombs.

    Shimon Peres, "Statements by Leaders at the Signing of the Middle East Pact," *New York Times,* September 14, 1993, A6.

8. [When I studied history and political theory in Paris], all foreigners had to take a French composition class. Over the year, the format of this class never varied. A subject was set, everyone had one week to turn in an outline and two or more to write the composition. Then the three-week cycle would begin again with the assignment of a new topic. The format of the composition never varied. Each one had to be written in three parts, with each of these parts further divided into three parts. Although I knew many of my classmates took to this style easily, for me this was a completely alien way of writing. My way had been to read, think, and make notes on little pieces of paper. I would spread these notes out in my room, across my bed, desk, and floor. Then I would immerse myself in their contents, move them around into bits of text, and frequently rewrite sections. Now, under pressure from the new rules, I developed a technique for getting by. I did my reading and thinking, wrote my notes and bits of text, spread them out in my room, and let my composition emerge—but I did all this in the first week periodically adjusting the emerging composition so that it would grow with the right number of divisions and subdivisions. After a week of hectic activity, I extracted an outline in three parts. I turned in that outline and put the completed composition in my desk drawer, where it waited two weeks for its turn to be handed in to the instructor.

    [I wrote in a "soft" style]—a flexible nonhierarchical style, one that allows a close connection with one's objects of study. . . . Our culture tends to equate the word "soft" with inscientific and undisciplined as well as with the feminine and a lack of power. . . . "Soft" is a good word for a flexible, nonhierarchical style, one that allows a close connection with one's objects of study.

    Sherry Turkle, *Life on the Screen: Identity in the Age of the Internet* (New York: Simon & Schuster, 1995), 50, 56.

✱ 9. Under scrutiny, a revealing pattern emerges in much of the recent literature that denies the comparability of the Holocaust and other examples of genocide: The advocates of Holocaust uniqueness resort to many of the same assertions used by those who deny that the Holocaust ever occurred. Over and over again, dubious massaging of the data leads one author after another to minimize drastically the death toll in other genocides; to claim that the deaths that did occur during those other "tragedies" were routine wartime casualties or the result of "natural causes" such as disease; to deny evidence of official intent to commit genocide.

    David E. Stannard, "The Dangers of Calling the Holocaust Unique," *Chronicle of Higher Education,* August 2, 1996, B2.

10. My father was extremely ambitious; he had gone to college and later opened his own business. Because he was having stomach problems, he went to stay with his mother back in Philadelphia; he died of stomach cancer ten days later. I was only six years old when he died, so I didn't know him very well, but he spent a lot of time trying to teach me how to read. My brother, who was one and a half years older than me, would read to me. At one point my parents told him to stop reading to me or else I would never learn to read myself. I cried and cried and thought, "I'll show her," and I learned to read. I've gone through life with that sense of "I'll show them."

Dr. Lorraine Hale, in *On Women Turning 50* (San Francisco: Harper, 1993), 199.

Exercise 2 Almost daily we are faced with decisions that have a moral or ethical character. Consider the following example and decide what the most ethical course of action is.

What should we do when bad money supports good causes? If, for instance, organized crime offered the Scouts a million dollars, should the Scouts take the money? Should they publicize it or should they keep it secret? While this may seem far fetched, it really isn't. While tobacco companies are not the same as organized crime, their products contribute to more than 440,000 deaths a year to say nothing of the suffering inflicted on surviving family members. Yet, tobacco companies support good causes. Consider:

- Many sporting events are sponsored by tobacco companies and some would argue that women's tennis would never have become a high-profile, high-paying sport if it were not from the support of companies such as Virginia Slims.
- Tobacco companies support political candidates and give Democrats and Republicans alike large amounts of money for their campaigns.
- The Partnership for a Drug-Free America receives large financial support from the tobacco industry, enabling it to get its message and programs across.
- Tobacco money also supports the American Civil Liberties Union, the NAACP, the Urban League, the National Women's Political Caucus, and the Poetry Society of America. Beyond that, tobacco money supports many different children's charities, environmental groups, and even some health organizations.

There are many more examples. The problem is that money is tight and budgets are being cut and when the tobacco industry offers to help, then good programs survive and flourish. But is there a larger issue at stake? For instance, the Coalition for the Homeless no longer takes money from the tobacco industry because of its source. Amnesty International USA no longer takes money from the industry. Yet, the ACLU has no difficulty taking money from the industry because it allows the organization to survive and do good work to help people.

And the tobacco industry is only one example. There are many other instances of foreign industries and organizations supporting specific candidates for office in the United States. Is there a problem when bad money allows good organizations to be effective?

Consider the following issues:

1. What are the ethical considerations inherent in bad money supporting good causes?
2. Formulate an argument on both sides of the issue. Why is it all right to take the money and why should we reject the money?

3. Considering all the information you have been presented, should "good causes" take the money?
4. Do cultural considerations play a role in the decision to take the money or not?
5. In general, are there some basic ethical guidelines that might help us decide when to accept money and when not to? What might these criteria be?

NOTES

1. Joseph Wenzel, "On Fields of Argument as Propositional Systems," *Journal of the American Forensic Association* 18 (1982): 204.
2. This example was taken from Barbara Johnstone, "Linguistic Strategies and Cultural Styles for Persuasive Discourse" in *Language, Communication, and Culture: Current Directions,* Stella Ting-Toomey and Felipe Korzenny, eds. (Newbury Park, Calif.: Sage, 1980), 144.
3. Charles Conrad, *Strategic Organizational Communication,* 2nd ed. (Fort Worth: Holt, Rinehart, & Winston, 1989), 4.
4. Tad Tuleja, *Fabulous Fallacies* (New York: Harmony Books, 1982), 1.
5. Stokely Carmichael, "Black Power," in *Black Protest: History, Documents and Analysis,* Joanne Grant, ed. (New York: Fawcett Premier, 1968), 459.
6. Barbara Jordan, "Democratic Convention Keynote Address," *Contemporary American Speeches,* 7th ed., Richard L. Johannesen, R. R. Allen, and Wil A. Linkugel, eds. (Dubuque, Iowa: Kendall/Hunt, 1992), 371 and 373.
7. John E. Young, "30 Families and All Their Worldly Possessions," rev. of *Material World: A Global Family Portrait,* by Peter Menzel, *World Watch,* March/April 1996: 36.
8. Johnstone, 150–51.
9. Johnstone, 148.
10. Martin Luther King, Jr., "I Have a Dream," in *Contemporary American Speeches,* 368.
11. Johnstone, 151.
12. Johnstone, 149.
13. Luke 10: 29–37.
14. Wayne L. Minnick, "The Ethics of Persuasion" in *Ethics and Persuasion: Selected Readings,* R. Johannesen, ed., (New York: Random House, 1967), 38.
15. Richard L. Johannesen, *Ethics in Human Communication* (Prospect Heights, Ill.: Waveland Press, 1981).
16. Johannesen, 20–1.
17. An interesting discussion of how ethics change and develop over time can be found in Johannesen, 17.
18. *Time* 15 April 1996: 83.
19. Wayne Brockriede, "Arguers as Lovers," *Philosophy and Rhetoric* 5 (1972): 1–11.
20. Brockriede, 2.
21. Brockriede, 3.
22. Brockriede, 4.
23. Brockriede, 5.
24. Thomas R. Nilsen, *Ethics of Speech Communication,* 2d ed. (Indianapolis: Bobbs-Merrill, 1974).

CHAPTER 3

Argument Occasions

CHAPTER OUTLINE
- Nature of Occasions
  - Argument Spheres
  - Argument Fields
- Argument Situations
- Summary
- Exercises

KEY CONCEPTS

argument occasions
argument fields
field-dependent standards

field-invariant standards
rhetorical situation
exigence

The following story has become something of an urban myth—the story of the woman who spilled hot coffee in her lap and sued McDonalds because she was burned. Her judgment was for $2.9 million dollars. Many people have heard of the case, most think the verdict is an indication of the decline of justice in this country and how lawyers are beginning to make it impossible for a business to manufacture anything without being sued. "Of course coffee is hot. If you spill it on yourself, you will get burned," they will say. Most people, however, are not familiar with the case and a description of it follows:

> February 27, 1992, was a date on which Stella Liebeck's life changed dramatically. She was an active and energetic 79 year old woman. She had just retired from a long career as a department store cashier.
>
> On that morning, she did not have time for breakfast at her daughter's house. Her son, Jim, was catching an early flight out of Albuquerque, New Mexico, and to get him to the airport on time, she had to leave at dawn. After dropping off Jim at the airport, Stella and her grandson, Chris Tiano, pulled into a McDonalds restaurant drive through to buy breakfast. Stella ordered and then went into the restaurant to add some cream and sugar to her coffee. She returned to the car and attempted to get the top off her coffee. "I took the cup and tried to get the top off," she later testified. She looked for a place to put it down, but the dashboard was slanted and there was no cup-holder in her Ford Probe. She described what happened next: "Both hands were busy. I couldn't hold it so I put it between my knees and tried to get the top off that way." With a strong tug the top came off and scalding coffee poured all over her lap. She screamed and tried desperately to get the pants from her sweat suit off as the 170-degree coffee burned. By the time she and Chris reached the emergency room, Stella had suffered second and third-degree burns across her buttocks, her thighs and her labia. All that she remembers is the pain.
>
> While the jury initially awarded her $2.9 million for pain, suffering, and injuries, a judge later cut the amount to $640,000. Yet her case became one of the leading cases for tort reform in Congress—an attempt to diminish runaway damage claims in lawsuits. Was her case unjust? Was her case another example of lawyers trying to get all they can out of the system? The answer may not be as easy as it seems on its face.
>
> Liebeck spent seven days in the hospital and then three more weeks recuperating at home. During that time her movement was limited and she was in constant pain from the burns. She was again hospitalized for skin grafts over the affected areas of her body and during this time, while practically immobilized, her weight dropped 20 pounds to 83 pounds while suffering the pain from the grafts.
>
> Initially she was not interested in suing. In a letter she wrote to McDonalds, she asked that they turn the temperature of the coffee down and asked for $2,000—the amount of her out-of-pocket expenses. McDonalds offered her $800. Upon further investigation, Liebeck discovered that McDonalds had been sued in the past for keeping its coffee too hot and that McDonalds had received more than 700 burn complaints over 10 years. Yet, the coffee continued to be sold at the same, burning temperature.[1]

When most people hear of this case, they conclude that Liebeck represents another person who was able to "beat the system." Coffee is hot—that is not the fault of McDonalds. If people are burned, that is their own fault. We live in a litigious society where examples such as this illustrate the need to change the legal system. Sherman Joyce, president of the American Tort Reform Association, argued that Liebeck's case pointed out "a lot of the problems with the system. . . . It demonstrates that the system needs reform."[2] At the same time, Robert H. Scott, the trial judge in the case, wanted to send McDonalds a stern warning. He said that it "was appropriate to punish and deter" McDonalds given its history of burns.[3] And members of Congress moved quickly to pass legislation to reduce the amount of damages a plaintiff could collect.

This case illustrates how a common set of facts—what happened to Stella Liebeck—can be examined, reviewed, and debated among different groups of people who arrive at very different conclusions. Members of the legal community thought that punitive damages would deter McDonalds from unsafe and unnecessary practices. Political lobbyists used the case to illustrate the need for reform and argued that the punitive award was an abuse. Politicians looked for ways to act on the perceived abuses and wrote legislation to minimize any future abuses.

People from different associations and groups see different things in the world around them. They talk of different subjects and have their own rules of discourse. Lawyers, for instance, have very strict rules for what can serve as evidence for an argument. In science, certain types of reasoning are considered superior. Scientists tend to look for cause and effect and tend not to reason from analogy. Arguments should be proven objectively. This chapter will focus on argument occasions. It will look at why members from different fields and situations interpret arguments differently and how arguers can use knowledge of occasions to better craft arguments.

NATURE OF OCCASIONS

Just as the context elements of culture and ethics provide the background and context for understanding and interpreting arguments, occasions are the impetus for argument. *Argument occasions consist of the specific fields and situations in which arguments arise.* Occasions include a variety of elements such as timing and place—when and where to present arguments.

Liebeck's case provides some important clues as to how argument occasions function. Liebeck's case became a fence around which arguments for and against tort reform have been debated. Although tort reform had been an issue for several years, her case provided an opportunity to bring the debate into the open. Further, it showed a clash between two powerful communities of people: lawyers and politicians. Many members of the legal professional saw this as an example of how well the justice system works in America. A single, elderly woman can beat a giant corporation when the corporation does something wrong. The political community, however, saw this case as another abuse of legal power.

Argument Spheres

Perhaps the clearest way to explain argument occasions is through the model in Figure 3–1. This is a model of argument spheres that are bound by time and place and constrain the way arguments are produced and interpreted. Thomas B. Farrell and G. Thomas Goodnight in their discussion of argument spheres suggested that the members of any given culture channel their concerns, ambitions, goals, and plans among many other possible issues through vast superstructures that help them to focus or coordinate their arguments.[4] We discussed cultures in Chapter 2 as collections of people who share meanings,

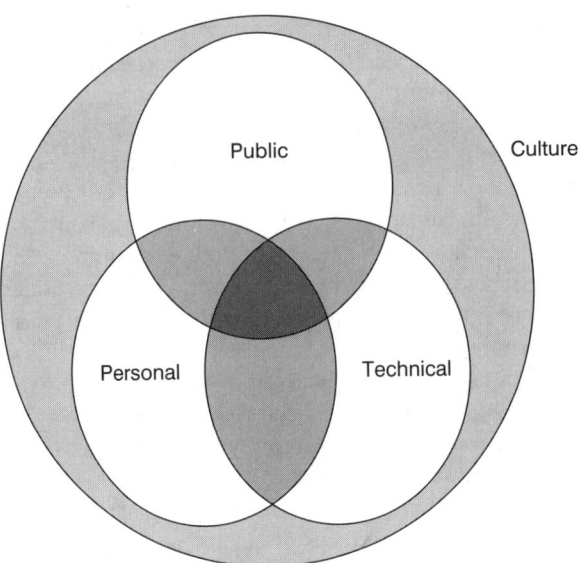

FIGURE 3–1 Argument Spheres

traditions, institutions, and the like. When the members of a given culture seek to argue within the culture, they look for culturally appropriate methods, or what Farrell and Goodnight refer to as superstructures, to help them communicate. These superstructures, which they referred to as spheres, vary from culture to culture but can be represented by three dominant spheres: personal, technical, and public. These three spheres exist within the culture and they overlap. Cultural and ethical rules affect the arguments produced in each sphere and some arguments can coexist in each sphere.

The personal sphere contains the relatively informal arguments among people in typically casual settings. As we discussed in Chapter 1, personal arguments are those among friends or family and are not typically characterized by careful attention to evidence and reasoning but are governed by the interpersonal rules for arguments generated in the particular relationship. The rules and procedures for personal arguments are determined by the relationship and not by some external force such as the government. The technical sphere contains arguments that adhere to rules that are more formalized and rigorous and tend to be generated by particular groups of people such as doctors or lawyers. Arguments in this sphere might include the arguments made in academic papers and essays, legal arguments, scientific arguments, and religious arguments. If one can identify explicit rules for evidence, appropriateness, reasoning, or audience then the argument is probably in a technical sphere. Unlike personal arguments, these arguments are evaluated by an external community of people that applies the standards of the community. The public sphere contains arguments that are intended for public or general audiences. These arguments are evaluated by publicly understood and accepted standards for criticism and analysis. Public arguments include the kinds of arguments politicians might make or that a public relations officer for a corporation might present.

Editorials in newspapers typically are written for the public sphere. Whereas the public sphere has relatively formalized rules for appropriateness (for example, one cannot make slanderous comments about another), the rules are understood and used by a broader public than the technical sphere, which focuses on a particular community of people.

Each sphere is bound by two dominant characteristics that determine both its content and size. First, the content appropriate to each sphere is governed by the rules or conditions within the sphere. As we discussed earlier, the legal profession has rules and conditions for argument that are very different from those of the scientific or political communities. Arguments are appropriate and acceptable when channeled to the appropriate sphere for that argument. For instance, it might seem odd to have a member of an argumentation class begin to discuss problems and concerns in a private relationship. Even if the arguments are strong and valid, the rules of what appropriately is placed in the technical sphere (the classroom) are different from what appropriately is placed in the personal sphere (the relationship).

Second, arguments need to be adapted to the appropriate sphere for which they are intended. Consider, for example, how arguments change as Liebeck's case is placed into different spheres. Initially she had no intention of suing McDonalds. She wrote them a letter asking for the cost of her out-of-pocket medical expenses (about $2,000) and a request to reduce the temperature of their coffee. This was a personal argument. It was governed by the rules created by the relationship between McDonalds and Liebeck. McDonalds offered $800 dollars, which was not an acceptable amount. At that point, Liebeck turned to a professional who might help her persuade McDonalds to pay for her treatment. The professional was a member of the legal community who worked to focus the arguments at a technical level toward a judge and jury and argued that the coffee was a defective product and that it was unsafe according to the law. The jury awarded Liebeck $2.9 million on the strength of technical arguments. The verdict and the award were based on the rules established in the legal profession. These were highly formalized rules developed and understood by a highly specialized community. The media then carried the story to the public, which heard that a person was awarded almost $3 million for burning herself with hot coffee. The standards for judging the argument at a public level were very different and the award was seen as unreasonable because commonly held public standards and beliefs are that coffee is hot. This is why pro–tort reform protesters later carried signs saying "She spilled it on herself." Publicly, the trial and award did not make sense.

Arguments are shaped and judged differently depending on the sphere in which they operate. In Figure 3–1, each sphere overlaps each other sphere. This is because some arguments that are personal may also meet the requirements of the public or technical spheres. Similarly, technical arguments may fit one or more of the other spheres, or arguments may be adapted such that they can fit multiple spheres.

Certain arguments have an appeal beyond the sphere in which they were produced. In such cases arguments may be criticized and evaluated by multiple sets of standards as different communities attempt to understand and evaluate them. An interesting example of an argument that was adapted to both the technical and public spheres is the one presented in Rachel Carson's book, *Silent Spring*.[5] This book was written initially for a technical audience about the dangers of a pesticide, DDT, in the environment. Carson warned that DDT was destroying the integrity of robins' eggs and posed a serious long-term threat to the ecosystem. Her argument was heard beyond the technical community to which it was addressed, and the book soon found its way to bookstore shelves, and her arguments became the basis for public legislation to ban the pesticide in this country. Similarly, technical works such as dissertations or academic papers may occasionally appeal to the general reader when they put forth ideas that appeal to different communities.

Arguments do not reside in any given sphere forever. For any given argument, the sphere may be larger or smaller as time progresses and this is the subject of argument occasions. Carson's book today would receive less attention than in 1970 because the public sphere for that argument is very small; DDT has already been banned and the time for the argument has passed. Similarly, the arguments in the book would exist in a relatively small technical sphere because the claims in the book have already been accepted. Other arguments, however, may find that their opportunities within any given sphere are large as interest increases. The following section focuses the two concepts that restrain the size and shape of argument spheres: argument fields and argument occasion.

Argument Fields

Argument fields are similar, in many ways, to cultures. They provide arguers with a context for making and interpreting argument, and they provide arguers with a common ground or framework for conducting disputes. Consequently, distinguishing between what constitutes field and a culture is not always clear. Fields share many characteristics with cultures, and occasionally the distinction between the two can become blurred. Perhaps argumentation theorist Joseph Wenzel put it best when he said that although field can be very difficult to define, they do refer to "*some* sort of universe of discourse."[6] However, whereas cultures provide a backdrop for argument practices and understanding, fields provide the rules for arguing. They provide the specific procedures by which arguments are developed and evaluated.

The very fact that an argument takes place in a law court, a corporate board room, a medical care setting, or an art class may influence the procedures that are used and the standards that are applied to make arguments and judgments about arguments. Argument fields define the rules for engagement and resolution. In other words, they determine what kind of evidence and support will be considered appropriate support for a claim. All general cultures have specific argument fields. Some fields are highly defined with very rigid rules and other fields are loosely defined with norms for arguing.

In *The Uses of Argument* and subsequent works, philosopher Stephen Toulmin emphasized the importance of argument fields in understanding and interpreting argument.[7] Although his original definition was ambiguous, later scholars have come to agree that he viewed *argument fields as sociological contexts for arguments marked by patterns of communication that participants in argumentative disputes can recognize.*

The arenas in which arguments are developed influence the forms of argument, the bases on which inferences are made, and the means for deciding disputes. They are both social and communicative phenomena. In other words, fields for argument are made by people through interaction; they act as the source for the conventions and criteria used in conducting arguments and they are an important feature of arguments.[8] Of the three spheres, the technical sphere is the one most rigidly defined by fields.

Argument fields include such examples as law, ethics, medicine, science, and aesthetics. Furthermore, each of these fields has subfields (e.g., tort law, family law, criminal law) that themselves function as fields of argument. Describing what fields exist at any given moment can be difficult because we are constantly surrounded by and involved in many different fields. Nevertheless, the field in which arguments are produced affects the nature of the argument; as the field changes so does the way the argument is constructed. Robert Rowland made the point that it "seems obvious that arguments vary by field."[9]

Although fields can be complex and difficult to isolate, generally, fields share five common characteristics. First, they are a human creation.[10] This means that fields develop over a period of time through social interaction. Second, fields are developed by people with shared goals.[11] People sustain interaction and develop fields when they share objectives and purposes. In science, for example, the purpose is to identify the laws of nature; in ethics, the purpose is to distinguish what is good and morally right from what is not; and in medicine, the purpose is to promote health by preventing and curing illness. Third, fields develop specialized language and rules.[12] When people converse to achieve their objectives, there are certain rules of conduct as well as language that facilitate their objectives. We may call such specialized language *jargon* but for the members of a field, the language carries unique meanings. Fourth, people may belong to many fields.[13] Humans share many different objectives and adhere to many different sets of rules. Therefore, we can be members of as many fields as serve our interests or objectives. Fifth, a field will survive only as long as the field serves the common purpose of its members and as long as it can adapt to changing objectives.[14] When a field no longer serves its members and cannot adapt to meet their needs, it will disappear.

Any field can be described by these five dimensions. For example, if we look at the field of law, we would say first that law is a human creation. Lawyers were not needed until human beings began developing rules and laws for governance and developed a need to have a group of people interpret and apply the rules. Second, the legal field consists of people with shared goals. Lawyers and judges work to apply the law in civil and criminal matters to punish wrongdoers and seek justice. Third, members of the legal field develop their own specialized language to describe activities and directions in their field. They talk about *writs* (which are any legal document that is used for a court action), *habeas corpus* (which is a type of document used to release someone from unlawful imprisonment because of lack of due process), *praecipe* (which are *writs* that command a defendant to do the thing required or show just reason why he or she cannot), and *estoppel* (which prevents someone from acting in contradictory ways to the detriment of another party), among many other terms. Fields develop a unique language that unites and binds their members and gives them a language within a language (in this case a legal language within English) that identifies them as members of a community or field. Fourth, members of the legal fields may also belong to many other fields. For instance, many politicians are either practicing or former attorneys and judges. Some lawyers move into education and teach at law schools. Finally, lawyers need to be able to adapt to changing conditions and times for the field to survive. As new laws are passed, members of the legal community need to remain current so that the correct rules and precedents are applied to their cases. As laws become more complex, attorneys often find themselves in very specialized areas within the field. They may, for instance, specialize in laws pertaining to intellectual property or real estate, among many other areas. Failure to adapt to changing rules and laws can lead to individual members of the field being disbarred or to the dissolution of the field.

Toulmin, among others, has concluded that arguments are judged according to the standards of the field for which they are produced.[15] Different standards are applied in the field of law, for example, than in the field of politics. And standards used in either of these fields are different from those in medicine or education. For example, consider the debate that has surrounded President Kennedy's assassination for decades. The FBI and prosecutor's office (legal field) in 1963 believed there was sufficient evidence to indict Lee Harvey Oswald for the murder. Witnesses saw him rush by with a panicked expression. He fit the general description of a man who left the school book depository building, and when he was arrested Oswald yelled "Well, it is all over now" and tried to shoot one of the arresting officers.[16] The legal field has rules for evidence and is swayed particularly by physical evidence (the rifle, Oswald's fingerprints) and eyewitness testimony (what he said before the shooting, his behavior after the shooting). In the legal field, this was enough for an indictment.

Yet, the scientific community did not think Oswald could have acted alone in the assassination. An 8-mm home movie of the assassination recorded by Abraham Zapruder showed precisely when the shots were fired and showed which bullets hit the President. Rifle experts timed the lapse between the shots and then tested the rifle allegedly used to assassinate Kennedy. The rifle, they concluded, required a minimum of 2.3 seconds between shots to operate the bolt and re-aim. Because Oswald shot three times—and assuming the first bullet was in the chamber—the total time required by Oswald if he acted alone was a minimum of 4.5 seconds; yet Zapruder's film shows that 4.8 seconds were necessary, which made it possible but not very likely that Oswald could have reloaded, aimed, and fired in the time allowed. Furthermore, the second bullet fired has been dubbed by conspiracy theorists as the "magic bullet." What made this bullet appear magical is that it appeared to strike Kennedy and then change direction and hit Governor Connally. Because bullets travel in straight lines, and because few thought that one bullet could do as much damage as this appeared to have done, the scientific community was unconvinced of the single assassin theory.[17]

In 1964, the Warren Commission (political field) was convened and again in 1978 the House Select Committee on Assassination was created. Their conclusions were that one man had the time to aim and fire and that even the "magic bullet" could have passed through both President Kennedy and Governor Connally. There was no second gunman, the two panels found, and there was no one other than Oswald who could have committed the crime.[18]

A few years ago, a British television company attempted to re-create the trial of Lee Harvey Oswald that never actually took place. The program's producers flew all the participants to London, where the trial took place. Defending Oswald was Gerry Spence who was a very successful defense attorney and known for defending clients such as Karen Silkwood and Imelda Marcos. Vincent Bugliosi, the prosecutor in the Charles Manson case, prosecuted Oswald. The jury was drawn from a pool of Dallas voters and the judge was also drawn from Texas. The witnesses in the case were either eyewitnesses at the time, the recorded testimony of eyewitnesses, or experts who had testified in either the Warren or House Select Committee hearings. At the conclusion of the trial, the jury concluded that Oswald was the assassin and returned a unanimous verdict of "guilty."[19]

It is interesting that for several decades, more than 200 books, a dozen documentary films, and a Hollywood feature film have been dedicated to this one event in history. While there are many explanations for the continued interest in Kennedy's assassination, one reason is that members of different fields continue to offer conflicting opinions and support them with different forms of evidence and reasoning. In the field of medicine, pathologists have suggested that the bullet's path is inconsistent with the lone assassin theory. Yet, legal and political fields seem to have enough evidence to conclude Oswald's guilt. And members of the scientific community argue that one person did not have time to fire all of the shots. Conflicts among fields are brought about by different rules of what constitutes acceptable reasoning or evidence and can lead to confusion among different audiences.

Argument fields are important for arguers and critics alike because they provide us with a means of judging arguments. When we evaluate arguments to determine whether they are true or false, good or bad, valid or invalid, we apply two sets of tests: field-dependent standards and field-invariant standards.[20] *Field-dependent standards are the rules, norms, and prescriptions guiding the production of arguments in a particular field.* These are the standards that the particular field identifies as appropriate for evaluating arguments. Therefore, legal standards pertaining to hearsay evidence applied to legal arguments would constitute field-dependent standards.

Field-invariant standards apply generally, regardless of the field of argument. All arguments must have the required parts of an argument: claim, evidence, reasoning, and attempt to influence. This requirement is invariant, in other words, regardless of the field, an argument should have these parts. Similarly, if evidence and reasoning are used inappropriately (perhaps the evidence is fabricated) or the audience's emotions are played upon by the arguer to avoid criticism or thoughtful judgment, then the argument would be considered fallacious regardless of the field.

Arguers should be aware of the requirements of the fields in which they argue. The selection of a field for argument implies the grounds to be used in making a decision. The legal field uses precedent (decisions rendered in earlier, similar cases) and various types of charges (extortion, property damage, manslaughter, and so forth) to judge issues supporting the claim. Argument fields also imply certain peculiar burdens or requirements that must be addressed. A jury, for instance, must believe a defendant guilty beyond a reasonable doubt. Furthermore, the legal field implies specific rigorous rules of evidence (hearsay is inadmissible, affidavits must be notarized, testimony must come from witnesses or disciplinary experts, and so forth). Yet, in other fields these rules may not apply at all.

The notion of an argument field is valuable because understanding fields helps arguers understand many of the rules and conventions for judging between competing claims in a controversy. Depending on which standards from which fields are applied to arguments, the results can be very different. This is why it is important for advocates to be aware of the fields from which they argue and to learn as much about the field for argument as about the subject they are arguing.

ARGUMENT SITUATIONS

The contents of argument spheres change over time. Arguments that may have been appropriate at one point in time in the personal sphere may develop and move to a technical or public sphere. Some arguments drop out of all three spheres over time as arguments are accepted, rejected, or become irrelevant. For instance, there was a time when arguments developed over whether the Earth was round like a ball or flat like a plate. Arguments that began as personal discussions became the subject of technical discussions in the scientific community and finally became large public discussions that culminated in events such as Columbus's sailing across the Atlantic. Arguments about the shape of the world moved back and forth among the spheres but over time moved out of the spheres as the discussion was no longer controversial and the idea was universally accepted.

As with so many other human events, in argumentation timing is everything. Arguments (or any form of communication) may be interpreted very differently at different times. All communication is generally bound by its particular occasion. For example, the first edition of this book was published in 1989 and used many examples of arguments about the Soviet Union and the Cold War. If these same arguments were made today, they would be considered outdated and inapplicable given current events and the dissolution of the U.S.S.R. *Argument occasion refers to the rhetorical situation of the argument.* Perhaps the person most noted for his development of the "rhetorical situation" is a theorist named Lloyd F. Bitzer.[21]

The rhetorical situation is a natural context of persons, events, objects, relations, and an exigence that strongly invites arguments. Therefore, every argument exists in a particular and unique occasion. The occasion is made up of the audience, the arguer, the experiences of the audience and arguer, and what Bitzer refers to as exigence. *Exigence can be defined as "an imperfection marked by urgency; it is a defect, an obstacle, something waiting to be done, a thing which is other than it should be."*[22] In other words, arguments are not developed randomly but are instead called into existence by some exigence—there is some cause or reason for us to argue. When Martin Luther King, Jr., presented his "I Have a Dream" speech, he presented it to a particular audience at a particular time. He was responding to decades of discrimination and he was urging action on a pending comprehensive civil rights bill. His audience was comprised of more than 250,000 people who had come to Washington, D.C., to protest for civil rights. It was the largest demonstration ever held in the United States to that time and the situation required a cornerstone address. King's address met the exigence of the situation.

Not all exigencies, however, require such important arguments. Presenting an argument in class to fulfill the requirements of an assignment may address the exigence of the assignment, but it also addresses an exigence in a larger sense. *An exigence is also a contemporary problem or issue that needs to be addressed.* This is why classroom assignments address significant or important issues as opposed to the trivial. The exigence is like a question waiting for an answer. The point is simply that particular occasions call

> ## HOW SITUATIONS CHANGE WITH TIME
>
> Timing makes a great deal of difference in when and where arguments are made. Consider the following claims:
>
> > "Computers in the future may weigh no more than 1.5 tons."—*Popular Mechanics,* 1949
> >
> > "I think there is a world market for maybe five computers."—Thomas Watson, chair of IBM, 1949
> >
> > "There is no reason anyone would want a computer in their home."—Ken Olson, president of Digital Equipment Corporation, 1977
> >
> > "Who the hell wants to hear actors talk?"—H. M. Warner, Warner Brothers, 1927
> >
> > "Stocks have reached what looks like a permanently high plateau."—Irving Fisher, Professor of Economics, Yale University, 1929
> >
> > "Everything that can be invented has been invented."—Charles H. Duell, Commissioner, U.S. Office of Patents, 1899
> >
> > "640K ought to be enough for anybody."—Bill Gates, 1981

for particular arguments, and speakers who are able to identify and understand the requirements of the rhetorical situation may be able to develop arguments that "fit" the needs of the argument context.

Generally, argument occasions have four characteristics. First, the occasion invites arguments. Our arguments are in response to some problem, proposition, or other issue that we are attempting to address. Without a problem there is little reason for argument. King's "I Have a Dream" speech was designed in response to a problem of racial inequality. If the United States was truly integrated—if King's "Dream" had already been fulfilled—there would have been no need for the speech and it is unlikely King would have presented it.

Second, the argument must be fitting to the occasion. Even though arguers may be able to identify a problem, not just any argument will fit the situation. If King, for instance, had written a speech about the need for more space exploration or better pay for migrant farm workers, the speech would not have fit the situation because the audience and occasion would not have been appropriate for the subject. Similarly, if an advocate makes an argument that is not relevant or does not address the important issues of a dispute, then the argument does not fit.

Third, situations prescribe the criteria for a fitting response. If we agree that a response must fit the situation, the requirements for the fit should be clear. This means that if King's speech fit the situation, then the criteria for judging the fit must be identifiable such that King could have understood them and adapted the speech to them. King knew that he was expected to offer a message of hope to those engaged in the struggle for civil rights, acknowledge the sacrifices many had made, call for redress of discrimination against persons of color, and emphasize the importance of nonviolent protest. He did all of this so admirably and his speech so fit the occasion that it has always been regarded as a masterful speech.

Fourth, argumentative situations are impermanent. This means that just as situations arise and invite argument, they also dissolve or become unimportant. Just as some questions go unanswered, so do situations. Situations, then, are temporary and if unanswered will dissipate and lose their significance. Had King chosen not to speak during the demonstration, his opportunity for argument would have been lost and "I Have a Dream" might have been nothing more than a manuscript somewhere. Even if he had spoken a day later, the situation would have dissipated as the demonstration broke up and people went home.

SUMMARY

Arguments are produced for particular occasions and are judged by their time and place. This chapter examined how argument occasions influence the way arguments are created, understood, and evaluated. Occasions are an important part of an argument's development because they shape the way arguers attempt to influence recipients. Generally we talked about argument occasions as the intersection of two concepts: argument spheres and argument fields. These two concepts help us understand how to produce and evaluate arguments.

Argument spheres are the contexts in which people argue. Recipients understand arguments and coordinate them through their own frames of reference through the use of argument sphere. Generally, argument spheres are of three types: personal, technical, and public. When people argue in personal spheres, the arguments are relatively informal and casual. Arguments in the technical sphere are governed by more rigorous and specialized rules, which serve to specify the types of acceptable evidence and reasoning. Public-sphere arguments are arguments that are produced and evaluated in a public arena. They are intended for public audiences and are criticized using public standards. Depending on the sphere the arguer operates in, arguments are adapted and criticized using the rules or conditions of the given sphere.

Argument fields are similar to culture in many ways. Like culture, they also help provide a context for making and interpreting arguments. However, fields are more than cultural contexts, they are specialized contexts that determine the rules for acceptable evidence, the types of issues to be considered, the rules or procedures for conducting argument, the requirements for proving a case, and even the specialized language in which arguments are expressed. Examples of such fields are law, medicine, and science. Fields are important in judging between competing claims because they provide the basic principles in which many forms of reasoning are based. Some standards for judging arguments are field dependent and arise from the particular context in which the argument is made. Other standards are field invariant and apply to all arguments regardless of their contexts.

Argument situations change over time. Arguments that would have been appropriate for a given audience at a given time may not be appropriate years or even days later. Arguments change as people, issues, and knowledge about the world change. Argument situations refer to the rhetorical situation of the argument. Bitzer contended that a rhetorical situation arises from the context of person, events, objects, relations, and exigence, which together call for an argument to be produced. Argument occasions have four characteristics. First, the occasion asks for an argument to be offered. Just as a question invites an answer, an argument occasion invites an argument. Second, the argument must be a fitting answer to the occasion. The answer offered should be relevant to the question asked. Third, the standards for judging a fitting response should be embodied in the situation. The arguer should know how to adapt the arguments to the occasion. And fourth, argument occasions are temporary. Situations arise, they exist, and if left unanswered, they disappear.

CHAPTER THREE   Argument Occasions

EXERCISES

* *Exercise 1* We have discussed the role of argument fields in

    - providing grounds for decisions
    - implying requirements for what audiences expect from argument
    - implying rules arguers will follow in conducting arguments

    One example of a field in which argument occurs is medicine. Based on what you know about fields, how would you answer the following questions?

    - What kinds of grounds do medical doctors use in their research papers, public presentations, or in the diagnosis of a disease?
    - What constitutes acceptable evidence for medical arguments?
    - In what spheres do medical doctors operate?
    - What are the audience expectations of this field?
    - What are some conventions or rules followed by doctors?

Exercise 2 What fields are you associated with? Using the description of fields presented in the text, how would you characterize these fields?

Exercise 3 In this chapter we discussed how argument occasions can be used to understand the environments in which arguments exist. Part of our discussion focused on argument spheres, argument fields, and argument situations. Read the case study and consider the following questions:

1. What field(s) operate in the case study? Can you identify the field-invariant and field-dependent standards that were used in the argument to restrict the media?
2. What role does argument situation play in understanding the argument?
3. In the chapter we presented four characteristics of an argument occasion. These were:

    - the occasion invites arguments
    - the argument must be fitting
    - situations prescribe the criteria for a fitting response
    - argumentative situations are impermanent

4. How well do you think the argument below and its surrounding situation meet these criteria?

    "Make Professional Baseball Subject to the Antitrust Laws"

Mr. Speaker, the game of baseball has provided Americans of all ages with a source of entertainment since the first professional game was played in 1869. It truly is the American past-time. But in recent years ugly labor disputes have tarnished the game and hurt baseball fans. One of the reasons why the players have felt compelled to go on strike—including the present strike action—is that the baseball owners are exempt from U.S. antitrust laws.

As a former athlete from the University of Pittsburgh, and a staunch supporter of all working people, I believe that this is a detriment to the great game of baseball. The antitrust exemption has denied the players the same bargaining tools and leverage currently enjoyed by other professional athletes. While I won't even attempt to characterize athletes whose average salary is well over $500,000 a year as victims, they should be afforded the same rights and bargaining opportunities as other professional athletes.

Clearly, the American people aren't concerned with the details of the dispute. They don't care about salary caps, free agency or arbitration. All they want is for the bickering and posturing to end, and for the umpires to yell "Play Ball!" Since the players went on strike last August, all efforts to mediate the dispute have failed. Clearly, the owners have indicated that they no longer have the best interests of baseball in mind and they have lost the trust Congress placed in them back in 1922 when they moved to exempt Major League Baseball from U.S. antitrust laws. Removing this exemption may be the only way to end the strike and save the 1995 season.

That's why today I am introducing the Professional Baseball Antitrust Reform Act of 1995. This bill provides that professional baseball teams and leagues composed of such teams shall be subject to all antitrust laws. The bill also states that the Congress finds the business of organized professional baseball is in, or affects interstate commerce, and therefore the existing antitrust laws should be amended to reverse the result of the decisions of the Supreme Court of the United States, which exempted baseball from coverage under those laws.

In introducing this legislation, I am not professing to take sides in the dispute. I believe both parties share some of the blame for the sorry state of the game of baseball. My desire is to force the union and the owners to sit down, negotiate in good faith, and come to an agreement that both sides can live with. Professional football and basketball are both subject to U.S. antitrust laws. Interestingly enough, both sports are doing extremely well financially, both sports have salary caps—and player income has never been higher. Professional baseball players and owners should stop posturing and take a look at basketball and football (it's not hard to do—with the National Hockey league owners locking the players out there's not much else for them to watch).

Owners take heed: enactment of my legislation won't bankrupt the game nor would it prevent you from imposing a salary cap. Players: don't think that this bill will be a panacea for all your problems. Bargain in good faith and remember that most Americans would give their right arm to be a bench warmer for a Major League team and earn $150,000 for 6 months work. Think about it.

Mr. Speaker, I urge all of my colleagues to co-sponsor the Professional Baseball Antitrust Reform Act of 1995.

Hon. James A. Traficant, Jr., House of Representatives, *Congressional Record,* Wednesday, January 4, 1995, E51–2.

NOTES

1. This description of Stella Liebeck's case was adapted from Aric Press, Jenny Carroll, and Steven Waldman, "Are Lawyers Burning America?" *Newsweek* (March 20, 1995): 32–5.
2. Press et. al., 35.
3. Press et. al., 35.
4. Thomas B. Farrell and G. Thomas Goodnight, "Accidental Rhetoric: The Root Metaphors of Three Mile Island," *Communication Monographs* 48 (1981): 271–300.
5. Rachel Carson, *Silent Spring* (Boston: Houghton Mifflin, 1994).
6. Joseph Wenzel, "On Fields of Argument as Prepositional Systems," *Journal of the American Forensic Association,* 18 (1982): 204.

7. Stephen Toulmin, *The Uses of Argument,* (Cambridge: Cambridge University Press, 1958), 13–5. Further information can be found in Charles A. Willard, "Argument Fields and Theories of Logical Types," *Journal of the American Forensic Association,* 17 (1981): 129–45.
8. Charles Kneupper, "Argument Fields: Some Social Constructivist Observations," in *Dimensions of Argument: Proceedings of the Second Summer Conference on Argumentation,* George Ziegelmueller and Jack Rhodes, eds. (Annandale, VA: Speech Communication Association/American Forensic Association, 1981), 80–7.
9. Robert Rowland, "The Influence of Purpose on Fields of Argument," *Journal of the American Forensic Association,* 28 (1982): 228.
10. Charles A. Willard, "Argument Fields" in *Dimensions of Argument,* 21–42.
11. Willard, 41.
12. R. Rowland, "Argument Fields" in *Dimensions of Argument,* 56–79; and "The Influence of Purpose on Fields of Argument," 228–45.
13. Rowland, 64.
14. Kneupper, 82.
15. Toulmin, 33.
16. Gerald Posner, "It Was Him All Along," *Night & Day* (October 17, 1993): 8.
17. Posner, 12–13.
18. Posner, 12–13.
19. Vincent Bugliosi, *And the Sea Will Tell* (New York: Ivy, 1991), 632–4.
20. Toulmin, 33.
21. Lloyd F. Bitzer, "The Rhetorical Situation," *Philosophy and Rhetoric,* 1 (1968): 1–15.
22. Bitzer, 4.

SECTION **TWO**

Communicating Arguments

CHAPTER 4

Arguers, Recipients, and Argumentation

CHAPTER OUTLINE

- The Audience and Argumentation
  - Selecting the Starting Points
  - Supporting Reasoning
  - Using Evidence
  - Organizing Arguments
  - Additional Concerns about Audience
  - Analyzing the Audience
- The Arguer and Argumentation
  - Message Sources and Their Influence
  - Enhancing Credibility through Argument
- Fallacies Related to Audience
  - *Ad Hominem*
  - *Ad Populum*
  - Appeal to Tradition
  - Straw Arguments
- Summary
- Exercises

KEY CONCEPTS

strategies
source credibility
initial credibility
derived credibility

compliance
identification
internalization
expertise
trustworthiness
reluctant testimony

fallacy
ad hominem
ad populum
appeal to tradition
straw arguments

A student recently planned a speech to give to his argumentation class on piracy of computer software. Because the assignment required him to advocate a policy, he decided to try to convince his listeners that certain forms of software copying should be made legal. He gathered extensive information from the computer science and business libraries and publications of software manufacturers. In a technical but succinct analysis, he described how legalizing software duplication would provide economic and educational benefits for society. When he completed his presentation, he was certain that he had impressed and convinced his listeners with his complete information, thorough research, and carefully constructed reasoning. Can you imagine his surprise and disappointment when he discovered that his argumentation had failed?

The audience members said that they were bored and confused by his technical jargon, that he had not made the reasons for his position clear to them, and that they would need to know more before making a decision as to whether they favored his position. The few people in the class who did have some knowledge of the topic claimed he had cited only biased sources who stood to gain from indiscriminate software copying and had neglected the importance of copyright laws and protection. As you might imagine, this is an actual example rather than a hypothetical one. This student had somehow gone astray in planning and executing his speech. What had gone wrong?

Clearly, the student had done many things correctly. He had selected a topic on which he was well informed and in which he was interested. He had carefully researched the topic and had collected evidence to support his points. He had organized his speech logically and used sound reasoning. Unfortunately, he failed to consider some fundamental questions about his audience and their attitudes that were vital in getting his message accepted. These included: How much does the audience already know about the topic? What are the audience's present values and beliefs about software licensing? What sources are they likely to accept as credible? How should the speech be organized so that the arguments will have the greatest impact? How many arguments can be developed in the time available? What are the audience's attitudes toward the arguer and what can the arguer do to appear more believable to recipients?

This speaker had a good, well-substantiated, carefully reasoned argument, but he had forgotten his audience—its capacities, interests, and perceptions of him as a speaker. You may recall that in Chapter 1 we described three perspectives on argument—logical, dialectical, and rhetorical. The first perspective is concerned with the soundness of an arguer's premises and reasoning, the second with argument as a process of inquiry to uncover significant issues, and the third with argument in a social and political context and with the characteristics of audiences to whom arguments are directed. In other chapters of this book, we will consider the logical perspective on argument, including reasoning structures, case construction, and tests for argument. In this chapter, we will consider the rhetorical perspective—how arguments are adapted to audiences and how the audience's view of the speaker affects the argument's success.

When arguments occur, the people for whom they are intended do not function as blank slates or logic machines responding only to the validity of an arguer's reasoning or evidence. Audiences are also invariably influenced by the rhetorical aspects of the message situation. These include the audience's own past experience, knowledge, and values; their inclination to believe what the arguer says; the language the arguer uses; and the way the argument is presented. This chapter will emphasize the ways in which such factors influence the persuasiveness of arguments. It will explain how audience members' knowledge, values, and attitudes affect the use of premises, selection of evidence, and support for inferences. It will also consider how arguments can be organized to have the greatest impact on audiences and how arguers can enhance their own credibility so as to make their claims more persuasive.

Therefore, this chapter will focus on persuasive strategies. *Strategies are means used to adapt arguments and make them appealing to audiences.* The use of strategies does not require you to abandon your position or fundamentally alter your analysis. Rather, communicating strategically sometimes requires you to change the way a message is structured and presented. After all, arguments have a function and that function is to win acceptance for claims by getting audiences to attend to, understand, think about, and respond to a message.

THE AUDIENCE AND ARGUMENTATION

At the beginning of this chapter, we described a student who prepared and presented an unsuccessful speech on software licensing. His speech failed to persuade his audience because he forgot a basic fact about persuasive arguments. Arguments are not prepared for the benefit of their author, nor are they meant to be written and filed away somewhere. Instead, they are intended for a particular set of audience members and must be adapted to be persuasive to that specific group.

These people—potential readers of or listeners to an argumentative message—should influence the planning and preparation of an argument in at least four areas: selecting starting points for premises and evidence, finding backing or support for the arguer's reasoning, applying evidence in support of claims, and deciding what order to use in advancing various claims. One purpose of this section is to explain why and how audiences' values, knowledge, needs, and interests are relevant to these aspects of argument preparation. A second purpose of this section is to suggest some methods arguers can use to find out information about their audiences before they construct their arguments. Sometimes arguments are prepared before they are presented; at other times arguments must be adjusted and adapted as arguers proceed. In either case, audience analysis can make arguments more persuasive, and the last part of this section will suggest how this can be done.

Selecting the Starting Points

In Chapter 1, we observed that, in order to function as evidence in an argument, a statement must fall below the level of dispute—that is, audience members must agree with it. If a statement is uncontroversial and accepted by the people to whom the argument is made, then the arguers can get started "on the right track" and proceed to build an argument chain. Otherwise, the arguer will run into trouble and may be derailed. Consider the following two examples from sales interviews:

Car Salesperson: This late model is a wonderful deal. The gas mileage is exceptional and the car only has 30,000 miles on it. For $15,000 you can't beat it!

Car Buyer: Oh, yes I can! I saw the same make, model, and year at Alternative Motors for $14,500, and it only had 20,000 miles on it!

ACME Representative: As you know, the most important things to look for in copiers are versatility and the number of features they offer. Our new model reduces, enlarges, and sorts up to twenty copies and has seven print selections.

Client: All these features are relatively unimportant to me. After my experience with your last copier, my concern is reliability. How many times will I have to call for repairs when it doesn't work?

In both cases, the arguers made incorrect assumptions about their arguees' values and priorities. The car salesperson assumed that the buyer would agree that no better deal was available and the copier representative assumed that the customer would value versatility over reliability, convenience, and other factors that might influence the client's purchasing decision. False starts such as these undermine arguers' credibility and make successful presentation of their claims especially difficult.

It is important, therefore, to have some knowledge of the audience's values and attitudes so as to be assured that premises will be accepted and not challenged or rejected. What are the recipients' needs and interests? What are their priorities? In the topic area in which the argument is made, what do they value? Finding out the answers to such questions will ensure that the process of making the argument goes smoothly.

Furthermore, arguers should be aware of their audience's level of understanding and knowledge of the topic. Premises and evidence that are not comprehended will not go far in getting recipients to accept arguments. Consider the following example:

Computer Salesperson: The P6 computer has 16 MB of memory, a 1-MB cache, and 12X CD.

Client: Why is 16 MB of memory important? What's a cache? What's a 12X CD?

In order to get her client interested in the product, this salesperson will have to explain how the computer will meet the client's needs in terms that are meaningful at her client's level of understanding.

As you select the starting points for your arguments, you should be certain that they are points that fall below the level of dispute for the audience you have in mind. The facts you present should be viewed as facts rather than being open to question; the values to which you appeal should be values to which your audience and its culture subscribe. The assumptions you make should be assumptions that even audience members skeptical about your position would also make. No matter how good the quality of your argument's organization, reasoning, and presentation, if you do not begin with points accepted by your audience, they will reject what you say. Of course, many audiences are very heterogeneous, and it is sometimes hard to discover the values, assumptions, and facts on which all audience members would agree. Methods for analyzing specific audiences to discover such information will be described later in this chapter.

Supporting Reasoning

In Chapter 1, we noted that an argument's reasoning constructs a link between its evidence, or starting point, and the claim that the arguer wants the audience to accept. Selecting *reasoning recognizable to the audience* is just as important as selecting a *starting point acceptable to them*. We will discuss particular *forms* of reasoning, such as cause and analogy, in Chapter 8. For now, the point we want to emphasize is that the reasoning you use should itself be accepted by your audience. If you use an analogy to make a comparison, for example, the two things you compare should be viewed as similar by your audience. If you make a causal connection (e.g., between legalizing software duplication and economic benefit), then the audience should understand what you are doing, and you should make your causal connection clear to them. Consider the following argument made by a defense attorney attempting to persuade a jury not to convict a defendant based on circumstantial evidence:

Defense Attorney: Just because the defendant was seen leaving the victim's home the evening of the murder, owned a 22-caliber gun of the type used in the crime, and had recently quarreled with the victim, we cannot conclude he is guilty. His guilt must be proven beyond a reasonable doubt.

The attorney's *claim* is "you should not vote for a conviction." His *evidence* is that the defendant was *only* seen leaving the home, owned a 22-caliber gun, and had quarreled with the victim. His *reasoning* is unstated but is probably that the signs shown in the evidence are insufficient to support a conviction. Why? Because in our judicial system an accused person is assumed to be innocent until proven guilty beyond a reasonable doubt. If challenged, the defense attorney would further support his reasoning by stating this principle, which he knows is recognized and accepted by the members of the jury.

As a second example, consider a student making a classroom speech opposing capital punishment. Here she attempts to refute an argument often put forward by supporters of capital punishment:

Some people have argued that capital punishment saves taxpayers money because it costs society $35,000 per year to keep an inmate in prison. Over a lifetime that amounts to hundreds of thousands of dollars. I would argue that that does not mean we should put a person to death. How can we put a monetary value on human life, particularly when there is the chance that the accused may be proven innocent?

Here the arguer's *evidence* consists of her opponent's cost argument; her *claim* is that cost is an insufficient reason for putting a person to death; and her *reasoning* comes from the prioritization of human life in our culture. Her reasoning, then, is based culturally in the sanctity of human life—a value not all cultures share. Her argument is likely to succeed in a Western culture that orders values in the same way that she does because she has adapted her reasoning to the reasoning habits of her audience.

Knowledge about the audience, therefore, can provide materials useful for supporting reasoning. Principles, conventions, rules, laws, value hierarchies, and other cultural artifacts act as resources arguers can call upon in constructing their arguments. Arguers preparing their arguments should ask questions about their audiences such as: What principles and laws are recognized by my audience? How do audience members order their values and priorities? What rules or conventions do they accept and follow? By determining the answers to such questions, an arguer can locate a foundation for the reasoning and inferences drawn in the argument as a whole.

Using Evidence

An arguer who knows how audiences are likely to respond to the use of evidence will generally be more effective than one who does not. A good deal of experimental research has been done on the use and effectiveness of evidence in speeches and arguments. The results of this research have at least three implications for the planning and presentation of arguments.

First, your argument will be more effective if you use authoritative evidence than if you do not use it. Researchers who study the persuasive effects of messages have found that arguers who use evidence are more influential with their audiences.[1] This means that unless you yourself are a widely recognized expert on a topic, you should use evidence from authorities accepted by your audience. No matter how thoroughly you have prepared or how much you know about your topic, your audience is unlikely to take your word alone as sufficient support for your claims.

Second, you should be aware of authorities that the audience is likely to perceive as credible and unbiased on a given topic. Calling upon the statements and observations of individuals perceived as credible enhances your credibility. For example, the Rev. Jesse Jackson is generally considered to have had experience in the area of civil rights. Likewise, most people view Lee Iacocca as a leader in American business and as a role model of the values and ideals in his field; for this reason, he is considered credible when the condition of the American automobile industry is discussed.

You should also be aware of the audience's perceptions of bias in authoritative statements. In Chapter 7 we will see that a biased source is one who has personal, political, or economic reasons for supporting a particular point of view. A biased source has a "hidden agenda"—a vested interest in the outcome of the matter being discussed. Audiences are suspicious of biased sources and are likely to reject arguments based on their opinions.[2] Before an arguer cites the American Tobacco Institute's claims that there is no causal link between smoking and cancer or the National Rifle Association's arguments against gun control, the arguer should consider the effect of these authorities on the audience. Even if the facts or opinions of such authorities are well founded, what they say may be rejected by an audience because of its suspicion of their motives.

Third, you should introduce facts and information that are "news" to the audience rather than relying on information already well known to them. When people initially encounter evidence that shocks or disturbs them, they make an effort to reconcile or cope with it. Once the evidence has entered their cognitive systems and they have dealt with it, they are much less impressed or disturbed by it when they encounter it again. For this reason, research on the effects of evidence shows that people are more influenced by novel information than by information they have heard before.[3] The implication of this is that you should have some idea of your audience's prior exposure to information on your topic before you prepare your argument. Facts already known to your audience will not be as effective as new information gleaned from current in-depth research such as that which we will describe in Chapter 7. New information that dramatizes the nature and extent of a problem or value discrepancy will be more likely to change or influence the attitudes and values of your audience.

In summary, persuasion research on the use of evidence shows that you should use and cite external evidence, draw from authorities that your audience views as credible, and use novel information and statistics. Your use of evidence is one of the most important factors in your argument. If you have done your research and have a sense of the information that your audience will understand and accept, you will be more likely to produce an effective argument.

Organizing Arguments

Students of argument frequently ponder the order in which to organize the arguments they have constructed. They often ask themselves such questions as: "Should I openly state my conclusion or thesis or leave it implicit?" "Where should I place my strongest arguments so they will have the greatest possible impact on the audience?" "Should I organize my argument around possible objections to my position?" "Should I use all my arguments, even the weaker ones?" and "Should I present both sides or one side of the question?" Arguers who ask such questions want to organize their arguments so that audiences will respond to them favorably. Although their decisions will probably be affected by the requirements of the topic being discussed and the nature of the situation, some information based on research about audience reaction to various patterns of organization may be helpful.

Should one openly state one's conclusion when making a controversial argument? Researchers have compared the use of explicit conclusions with conclusions that were implied or left unstated and have found that explicitly stated conclusions were generally more effective.[4] One researcher speculated that when claims are not explicitly stated, audiences fill in the gaps with claims and arguments of their own—ones that frequently go against what the arguer had intended.[5] The arguers in such cases can lose control of the argument. If the audience is intelligent and the argument very clearly organized, the audience may be favorably influenced even if the conclusion is not stated. Otherwise, arguers who fail to state their claim clearly may lose the concurrence of their audience.

Should one present both sides of an issue or only one side when making an extended argument? In answering this question, one should consider at least three factors besides the nature of the audience. The first is the nature of the topic itself. When two courses of action are obviously available and are recognized as such, for example, it is desirable to consider them both. A second concern is the time or space available for the argument. If time allows, a thorough analysis of all aspects of a topic is usually the best course of action. If time is limited, however, one must often develop thoroughly only the side one favors so that sufficient evidence and reasoning can be used to support one's claims. A third concern relates to the ethics of argumentation as we discussed it in Chapter 2. Arguers have an obligation, so far as is possible, to fully inform their recipients about available alternatives so that they can make informed decisions about the best choice or course of action. For this reason, slighting or misrepresenting opposing points of view is undesirable.

Research into the characteristics of audiences has revealed a fourth concern affecting whether one- or two-sided messages are better. Certain audiences do respond more favorably to one-sided presentations.[6] These include audiences already favorably predisposed to the arguer's thesis and those who are poorly informed about the topic. Both types of audiences are evidently confused or disoriented by complex or discrepant information.

When the audience is well informed or disagrees with the arguer's position, a two-sided analysis is more effective. People who know both sides of the argument or who oppose the arguer's position will rehearse counterarguments as they listen or read, and they will not concentrate on the argument while it is being presented. Furthermore, they will view a two-sided argument as more credible because it appears fair and well informed. Finally, hearing both sides of the issue causes audience members to be more resistant to opponents' later efforts to argue against the arguer's position.

A two-sided analysis should not be confused with the sort of organizational format that uses objections to the advocate's position as starting points around which the message is organized. A message organized in this way would begin with a preview like: "I will present three major objections to drug testing and show why they are untrue." This type of approach to a controversial issue is usually ineffective for two reasons. First, by merely *listing* objections to a proposal (without explaining the reasons behind them) and then extensively responding to them, one "stacks the deck" against the position one opposes and arouses audience suspicions about one's fairness and objectivity. Second, to begin with the objections to one's point of view gives the impression that one is on the defensive. Audiences are reminded of the opposing viewpoint and may focus on that rather than on the thesis the arguer is trying to uphold. Therefore, if a two-sided message is used, the arguer should give approximately equal time to both sides of the question.

Sometimes advocates wonder about how selective they should be about the arguments they use. Usually, they have a large number of potential arguments available. Should they use them all? Or should they be selective, using only the best and most cogent in support of their thesis? Generally, selective application of only the strongest arguments is the better course of action. Ruth Anne Clark, a persuasion theorist, explains why:

> There is a major danger in this policy [of using weak arguments]. Members of the audience who are predisposed to disagree with the advocate will look for some justification for discounting the validity of the entire message. Although it seems reasonable that such individuals would simply ignore arguments they do not agree with, often this is not the case. If an argument seems invalid or insignificant, they will concentrate on it, frequently ignoring all other arguments. A week later, if someone asks them what the message was about, they may recall only the argument they found invalid.[7]

Clark's observation reminds us of why we should not use weak arguments indiscriminately. Not only do they undermine our credibility, but they also give those who are opposed to our proposal a reason not to accept it.

The recognition that the arguments available for construction of a message have various degrees of strength implies another question about the relation between the audience and the organization of the message: Where should the stronger arguments be placed? People interested in this question have studied the cognitive processes and recall patterns people use when they respond to arguments. They have found that audiences are most likely to remember what comes at the beginning and end of messages.[8] This is called the primacy-recency effect. Whether placement of a strong argument at the beginning or at the end of a message is more effective depends on situational and other factors, but arguers are generally well advised to place their strongest arguments at either of the two positions.

Additional Concerns about Audience

The implications of an audience-centered orientation to argument construction that we have explored do not exhaust the ways in which a concern for audience affects argument success. Consistent awareness of the audience enhances the effectiveness of most arguments. Too often, arguers seem almost exclusively concerned with why they hold a view rather than with why their audiences ought to subscribe to it.[9] Considering the audience's orientations should affect the arguer's choices throughout composition of the message.

First, you should consider whether the audience is as concerned about or interested in the topic as you are. Often the first challenge you must overcome is audience apathy or indifference. The more remote the topic from the daily lives or concerns of the audience, the harder you will have to work to make it immediate and significant. Vivid examples of the nature and impact of the problem or situation, description of its effect on the daily lives of audience members, and carefully selected information regarding its scope and importance can help to overcome audience indifference. All this should come relatively early in the message.

Second, you should match the focus of your argument case to the concerns of your audience. As you will see in later chapters of this book, you as an arguer have a wide range of choices for designing and organizing your analysis. In deciding which format to use, you should ask yourself, "What is my audience most concerned about?" If their concern is the moral and ethical dimensions of a topic, then a value analysis such as that described in Chapter 10 would probably be your best choice. (Topics such as abortion, euthanasia, and capital punishment are prone to value-based analysis.) If the audience is most concerned about the existence and causes of a problem, then a problem solution or comparative advantages format such as that discussed in Chapter 11 might be your best choice. (Such topics as juvenile crime or drug and substance abuse are candidates for this sort of analysis.) Since your time to discuss your topic will be limited, it is advisable to select organizational formats that allow you to focus on the issues that are of greatest concern to your audience.

Third, you should be aware of beliefs or reservations that might interfere with the audience's willingness to accept your thesis. What problems or facts likely to be known by the audience might undermine your analysis? For example, suppose someone wanted to argue that the drinking age should be lowered to 18 nationwide. Anyone defending such a proposal would have to address the problem of a rise in DWI arrests and alcohol-related auto accidents among young people. Or suppose an advocate argued that defense spending should be dramatically curtailed and the funds used for other purposes. The audience would need to be reassured that such a measure would not reduce our military preparedness and expose the nation to war or to military aggression. Although it is inadvisable to devote one's entire message to refuting possible objections, advocates should consider and deal with obvious objections that would readily occur to many or most audience members.

Analyzing the Audience

Hopefully, our description of the many ways audience values and attitudes affect your argumentative success has convinced you that knowing your audience is vital to the success of your argument. Your next question might be: How is information about my audience to be obtained? It is important for you to decide what you need to know about your audience, to construct questions that enable you to gather this information, and to devise a means of collecting it. In this section, we will briefly describe some strategies for collecting such information.

The characteristics of an audience that we have thus far described in this chapter apply to audiences in general and are based on research on a broad range of audiences in our society. As we have pointed out, in general audiences tend to hear or read evidence in support of your claims, remember best the arguments that come at the beginning and end of your message, discount authorities they consider biased, and react negatively (and disproportionately) to weak or bogus arguments. You should keep these general tendencies in mind when making most arguments.

In addition, any recipients of any argument in a particular situation will have special needs, interests, values, and attitudes unique to that group. How do you find these out? While most of the strategies for discovering them are common-sensical, they are often overlooked. For example, how often has a salesperson approached you in person or on the telephone and made a sales pitch without bothering to ask you any questions about your possible needs or interests concerning the product? If you are in a situation in which you can ask questions of an arguee or members of an audience so as to obtain information relevant to your topic, do so. Often arguments in an interview, conversation, or discussion can be made much more successfully if arguees are simply asked about their interests, concerns, needs, and values. Such questions as the following are helpful:

> Could you please describe what you know about _____?
>
> What are the sources of your information on _____?
>
> What individuals or publications do you regard as authoritative on this topic?
>
> What aspects or features of _____ concern you most?
>
> What changes, if any, would you like to see in areas related to _____?

Of course, the answers to such questions will be helpful only if they are put to use to help you decide on what premises to base your argument, what information will be novel and interesting to the arguees, what authorities to use for evidence, what values to emphasize, and what alternatives to advocate.

Furthermore, if you will be speaking or writing for a larger group, it is important to obtain information about the group as a whole. If you know in advance that you will be making an argument to a specific group, you can talk with group members, read the group's publications, or attend meetings of the group. Obtaining information about the group will yield knowledge of the members' ages, political and religious affiliations, educational levels, economic status, ethnicity, and occupations. Since these factors often influence audience members' values and interests and indicate their level of intelligence and knowledge about the topic, obtaining such information will help you to make decisions about how to organize, explain, and present your claims. At best, the process of adjusting your argument to your audience will be a result of generalization and educated guessing, but information you obtain about your audience will nevertheless give you something to go on as you make choices in preparing and communicating your argument.

THE ARGUER AND ARGUMENTATION

In the 1968 presidential campaign, opponents of Richard Nixon mass-produced a campaign button portraying a picture of a shifty-eyed Nixon and below it the question "Would you buy a used car from this man?" The button's producers were attempting to impugn Nixon's source credibility. *Source credibility refers to an arguer's ability to be believed and trusted by recipients.* The buttons functioned as an argument with an implied claim: "If you wouldn't trust this man enough to buy a used car from him, you should not elect him president." The buttonmakers counted on the public's recollection of charges that Nixon had illegally used campaign funds in 1952, that he had used questionable campaign tactics in the past, and that he had been an ill-humored bad sport after losing a campaign for governor of California in 1962. The button was intended to remind the public of all this and to cause them to question once again Nixon's trustworthiness and sense of integrity. Factors such as expertise, trustworthiness, and integrity cause people to accept claims because they have confidence in the character of the person making them. Such factors also contribute to an arguer's source credibility.

The importance of credibility as a factor in persuasion has been recognized at least since the time of Aristotle's *Rhetoric,* written over 2000 years ago. Aristotle identified the personal character of the speaker as one of the three modes of persuasion and called it *ethos.* (The other two modes are *pathos,* the way the audience's emotions put them in a certain frame of mind, and *logos,* the rational proof offered within the message.) Of *ethos,* Aristotle said:

> Persuasion is achieved by the speaker's personal character where the speech is so spoken as to make us think him credible. We believe good men more fully and more readily than others: this is true generally whatever the question is, and absolutely true where exact certainty is impossible and opinions are divided. This kind of persuasion, like the others, should be achieved by what the speaker says, not by what people think of his character before he begins to speak.[10]

Aristotle's statements about credibility bring out four points that should be kept in mind when we consider its relationship to argumentation. First, credibility is not a characteristic that the arguer possesses but one that is *attributed* to the arguer by the recipients. When Aristotle said that the "speech is spoken so as to make us think [the speaker] credible," he emphasized the fact that how the speaker appears and what he or she does lead recipients to form certain impressions and beliefs, both about the speaker and about the claims that are made. These impressions and beliefs then influence the recipients so as to cause them to accept or reject the speaker's message.

A second and related point is that credibility is a field- and context-dependent phenomenon. If credibility results from what recipients perceive about the arguer rather than from intrinsic characteristics of the arguer, then it will vary from one time and situation to another, depending on what an arguer does or says. For example, once elected, Nixon found his credibility rising after foreign policy successes such as his trips to China and Russia and the settlement of the Vietnam war, and dropping sharply once the revelations about Watergate became known to the public.[11] Even within a speech or during reception of a message, the credibility of an arguer may increase or decrease depending on how recipients perceive and react to the points made by the arguer.[12]

The third point Aristotle made is that we value credibility most "where certainty is impossible and opinions are divided." If we ourselves cannot check out facts to find out whether a claim is true or if the claim is value-based rather than fact-based, we will rely upon credibility heavily as a source of our belief. Four decades of research in social psychology and communication have confirmed the importance of credibility.[13] Having reviewed this research, R. Glen Hass concluded, "Few areas of research . . . have produced results as consistent as the findings that sources high in expertise and/or trustworthiness are more persuasive than those low in these qualities."[14] The implications of this for argument, of course, are that you should design your arguments so as to enhance your audience's perceptions of your expertise and trustworthiness. The last section of this chapter will suggest means of enhancing credibility so as to make your arguments more persuasive.

The fourth point Aristotle made is to distinguish between credibility "achieved by what the speaker says" and that attributed to the speaker based on prior reputation. This latter form is called initial credibility. *Initial credibility is based on an arguer's credentials, status, and reputation as known to recipients before they hear or read the message.* Although initial credibility is an important factor in persuasion, its role is based largely on the extent to which a speaker's audience finds the speaker to be attractive or influential. *Derived credibility results from what is said in the message—the quality of the claims and evidence used and the ways arguers employ their own expertise to get their claims accepted.* Compared with initial credibility, derived credibility depends much more on what the audience thinks about the arguer's claims, the extent to which they produce counterarguments, and their assessment of the quality of an arguer's evidence.

Because this is a book on argumentation and because we focus upon the rational dimensions of a message, we will emphasize derived credibility. Specifically, the remainder of this section will consider how credibility works generally to enhance the persuasiveness of arguments. After a brief explanation of the noncognitive factors in the persuasiveness of a message source, we will focus on cognitive factors—how the expertise and trustworthiness of an argument source influence acceptance of its claims. Having explained this process, we will offer specific recommendations for structuring arguments so as to enhance the recipients' impressions of an arguer's expertise and trustworthiness.

Message Sources and Their Influence

Social psychologists who have studied persuasion and compliance gaining have identified three major ways that people get others to comply or agree with their requests or claims. They are compliance, identification, and internalization.[15] The first two depend heavily on nonlogical responses to messages and are independent of many of the reasoning processes described in this book. The third, however, is closely related to the quality of argument in a message and will be carefully considered later in this section.

Compliance is the use of rewards and punishments by a powerful source to get recipients to believe or act in a certain manner. A very familiar example is shown in the way students undertake an academic assignment. They recognize that the teacher possesses the means to reward for the work in the form of a favorable grade, so they carefully structure their work to conform to the teacher's expectations. In order for a person to get acceptance of a position through rewards and punishments, other people must believe that person has the resources to reward or punish them and cares whether or not they comply.[16] Argumentation, however, is not a necessary condition for compliance. A teacher *may* attempt to justify an assignment; a supervisor *may* explain a work order. But such actions are not required in order for the outcome they desire to be produced. The power they possess by itself causes others to do as they say. This form of influence is therefore relatively unimportant for our own purposes.

Identification is influence that occurs because people find a source attractive and wish to enhance their own self-concepts by establishing a relationship with the source. People identify with other people whom they like and admire. People often want to be like someone else who possesses traits similar or complementary to their own. This identification plays a prominent role in advertising. Because we want to be attractive and sexy like the models in their ads, we buy Jordache jeans. Because we admire the athletic prowess of Dennis Rodman or Ken Griffey, Jr., we are persuaded to buy the athletic shoes and products that they endorse. Ray Charles's musical ads for Pepsi appeal to a wide range of the American public, whereas Ed McMahon's endorsement of Publisher's Clearinghouse gives that operation credibility for some audiences.

Hass has observed that attitudes changed through identification "are not incorporated into the individual's system of beliefs and values; nor are they maintained independent of the message source."[17] In other words, people's acceptance of an argument because of identification is not related to message content but instead to the identity of its source. If the source loses his or her attractiveness or changes the claim in the message, then the recipients will change their own positions as well. This was demonstrated in a rather amusing experiment that showed the influence of attractiveness. Experimenters designed a questionnaire, and a female confederate volunteered to assist by contributing to the group discussions the experimenters would lead. She would make the same responses in both discussions, and the same people would participate in both groups. For one discussion, she was made up to look very attractive with a stylish hairdo, chic clothing, and becoming makeup. In the other condition, she appeared repulsive with ugly clothing, messy hair, and the trace of a moustache on her upper lip.

The results showed that in the attractive form she was much more effective in influencing the group.[18] The group's reactions were based solely on her attractiveness and not on cognitive processes. They had not thought about her message or about its quality.

Unlike compliance and identification, internalization is based on the thought recipients give to the content of a message. *Internalization is a process in which people accept an argument by thinking about it and by integrating it into their cognitive systems.* While attitudes and beliefs acquired because of compliance or identification often fade or disappear when the message source loses power or attractiveness, attitudes and beliefs that are internalized often persist and are maintained.

Before continuing our discussion of internalization and the form of source credibility connected with it, we should pause to stress here that, like all category schemes, this three-part division of source influence by means of compliance, identification, and internalization is somewhat oversimplified. Power, attractiveness, and content-related credibility often are closely related in any given argumentative situation. If a confident, attractive, highly respected supervisor explains a new marketing plan to subordinates and details a strategy for implementing the plan, that supervisor has clearly influenced the subordinates in all three ways simultaneously. Furthermore, one study of attractiveness revealed that attractive persuaders also tended to be perceived as better communicators, more highly educated, and better informed.[19] In many situations, then, it would be very difficult, if not impossible, to separate any one of these three forms from the other two.

Nevertheless, researchers have linked internalization most closely to what is actually said in the message. People who believe an argument because of its content are most affected by two aspects of the arguer's credibility—expertise and trustworthiness. *Expertise is the possession of a background of knowledge and information relevant to the argument being made.* It depends on whether people believe an arguer knows the correct position on a topic. *Trustworthiness depends on whether people believe the arguer is motivated to tell them the truth.*[20] Although expertise and trustworthiness are often established partly by initial credibility (the arguer's reputation for being knowledgeable, sincere, and honest), what the arguer actually says and does while presenting the argument is even more vital.

There are five situational factors that determine the importance of expertise and trustworthiness in judging an arguer's credibility. First, expertise and trustworthiness are especially influential when the question being discussed appears to have a "right" and "wrong" answer. For example, if the question is whether violence on television causes violent behavior in children, we are more likely to accept the claims of a media scholar who has studied the relationship than we are the claims of the "average" parent. However, if the question relates to values and preferences, such as what television programs are most enjoyable and entertaining, we may be heavily influenced by persons we find attractive.[21]

Second, the less involved people are in a message and the less knowledge they have of the topic, the more influenced they will be by the credibility of the source. Presumably, people with low levels of knowledge and interest are not prepared or inclined to think about the content of arguments or to weigh the merit of claims and evidence advanced in their support. Arguers with low credibility who must address uninformed and disinterested recipients must therefore cope with a greater challenge than arguers with high credibility.

Third, people who hear and read arguments from arguers with varying degrees of credibility will tend to forget who made the argument and remember only its content. So people who are initially influenced by an arguer's credibility will later forget the source and remember only the arguments made. Researchers call this the "sleeper effect." While research experiments showing this phenomenon have been somewhat inconsistent, they do indicate that often people forget the identity of a message source and remember only what was said.[22]

Fourth, expertise seems particularly important when recipients disagree strongly with the position an arguer favors. In a situation in which the position advanced is very controversial and in basic disagreement with the recipients' position, a highly credible source will be more persuasive than one who has less credibility. In one experiment reported by Richard E. Petty and John T. Cacioppo, the argument concerned how many hours of sleep per night were necessary. It was attributed either to a Nobel Prize–winning physiologist or to a YMCA director. The highly credible source influenced recipients even when he advocated extreme positions (such as two or three hours of sleep per night). When the less-expert source advocated the same extreme position, however, recipients were much less likely to believe it.[23] The researchers in this study concluded that the more extreme the discrepancy between an arguer and his or her audience, the more pronounced will be the influence of credibility in producing attitude change.

Fifth, as we emphasize in the last section of this chapter, it is vital that recipients perceive a source as being free of bias and vested interest and concerned primarily with their welfare. Researchers have found that subjects were more influenced by a message when they thought arguers were unaware they were being overheard and thus did not intend to persuade them.[24] Research has also shown that when arguers are expected to have a personal interest in one side of an issue and actually favor the other side, they have high credibility. This indicates, for example, that a union officer who opposes a strike will be more likely to be believed than one who advocates a strike simply because he would be expected to do the latter. These results and others indicate that recipients' perception of arguers' objectivity, fairness, sincerity, and disinterestedness all contribute to their trustworthiness and thus to their credibility.

Enhancing Credibility through Argument

An arguer with low credibility, such as a student or entry-level worker, faces a challenge every time he or she produces a persuasive message. That challenge is to enhance credibility through and by means of the message itself. This sort of derived credibility comes from features of the message and depends on the arguer's ability to cause listeners to believe that the arguer has their best interests at heart. When the arguer's prior reputation and qualifications are not a major factor in audience perception, the arguer has to implement strategies for enhancing credibility discussed in this section.

As an arguer, you will usually have three goals in regard to your credibility: (1) to get the attention of the audience focused on the content of your message; (2) to make an initial favorable impression on the audience; and (3) to cause the audience to form a favorable impression of your expertise and trustworthiness. The first two are preliminary but necessary conditions for the development of the third. Initial impressions are based on your attractiveness and self-presentation. Although those impressions are superficial, they are important. Arguers who cause negative perceptions because of careless appearance or an offhand or grating manner create a deficit against which they must work in order to get their message fairly considered. If the argument is orally presented, such matters as appearance, delivery, and vocal mannerisms will be significant. If it is in written form, poor style, misspellings, and other visual cues will affect the reader.

Once you have made a favorable personal impression, your next task is to win a favorable consideration of your claims and evidence by holding your audience's attention and keeping them engaged in your argument. This is essential to the process of internalization by which audiences integrate new beliefs and attitudes into their cognitive systems through actively considering your claims. Useful strategies for maintaining attention include use of examples close to the recipients' experiences, concrete information, good style, personal narrative, novel and unknown facts, and other materials contributing to the immediacy of the message. As we noted in the last section, people who have low involvement in the arguer's topic and little prior knowledge of it will attend more to the credibility of the source than to the content of the message. The low- to moderate-credibility arguer, therefore, should expend effort in getting recipients to actively attend to and consider the message.

The next item an arguer should have on the agenda is to enhance recipients' perceptions of his or her expertise and trustworthiness. Expertise is enhanced by showing that the position advocated is well supported and thus "correct." Trustworthiness is developed when arguers show that they have no biases or vested interests that they are trying to hide from their recipients. Seven specific strategies for accomplishing these ends will be described here. The first four relate to expertise and the last three to trustworthiness.

1. *Show that you or the sources you use have experience with the topic.* Before they will seriously consider your position on a topic, audiences must be reassured that you have studied the matter. Obvious as this might sound, the frequent use of unqualified and inexperienced sources to support claims shows that it's a practice often neglected. When the executive director of the Attorney General's Commission on Pornography was interviewed for a magazine article, he wasted no time in attempting to establish the credibility of its chair.

   > Mr. Hudson is the new U.S. Attorney for the Eastern District of Virginia. He previously served for a number of years as the commonwealth attorney for Arlington County, Virginia. *The Washington Post* and other critics of Mr. Hudson have repeatedly noted that Arlington County is completely free of illegal obscene material.[25]

   Clearly, this author expected to establish the commission's credibility by showing the extent to which its chair had direct experience cleaning up pornographic materials in an area where he served as U.S. Attorney.

2. *Use as many qualified sources as possible.* Qualified and respected sources have a "halo effect." They endow those who cite them with their own credibility. If a well-intentioned and earnest but inexperienced and unqualified arguer assures us of something, we may be equally likely to believe as not to believe her. But if the same speaker cites a number of respected authorities in support of her claim, the claim gains cogency. The impact of many authorities in support of a

position seems to be well recognized by the author of a letter to a newsweekly who opposes using chimpanzees instead of humans in AIDS research.

> Even Dr. Anthony Fauci, head of the National Institute of Allergy and Infectious Diseases, says that the initial phase of a genetically engineered vaccine could be tested in human volunteers before chimpanzee experiments are finished. Other strong proponents of early human tests are Dr. Robert Pollack of Columbia University and Dr. Donald Francis, a virologist at the Centers for Disease Control who recently changed his mind regarding the necessity of testing first on chimpanzees.[26]

This author's use of authorities illustrates the effectiveness of using sources with a variety of backgrounds who have independently reached the same conclusion.

3. *Use sources the recipients are likely to respect.* Sources that one audience might perceive as highly respectable may not be respected by another audience. For example, a labor union officer might be highly credible with union members but have very low credibility with management on the subject of working conditions and employee benefits. In arguing against federal aid to higher education in a popular conservative magazine, William F. Buckley, Jr., readily selected individuals whom his reading audience would accept as authorities on higher education.

> About 35 years ago, the presidents of Harvard, Johns Hopkins, Stanford, Brown, and other colleges issued a manifesto warning against federal aid to education. Their point was that such aid inevitably meant federal control, and of course they were correct.[27]

4. *Use sound reasoning and avoid fallacies.* Recipients who are involved in an arguer's message and who are being persuaded through the process of internalization will often detect weaknesses in the inferences an advocate makes and will think of counterarguments. Well-educated or intelligent recipients often have native reasoning skills and can criticize the arguments of others. As we observed earlier in this chapter, a weak and easily rejected argument will often do more harm to one's case than no argument at all because it will raise doubts in recipients' minds about the arguer's credibility on all the other issues in the message.

5. *Demonstrate fairness.* As we observed earlier in this chapter, audiences often become suspicious when they believe an arguer is presenting a one-sided or biased treatment of an issue. Directing *ad hominem* attacks at opponents, ignoring or superficially citing their points of view, twisting or misconstruing their position, or engaging in other similar practices are not only unethical but also have a "boomerang effect" because they cause audiences to suspect an arguer of unfairness and to distrust his or her overall trustworthiness. Notice how the arguer in the following example, who is attempting to persuade her friend that mandatory seat belt laws are unconstitutional, makes an overt attempt to establish her fairness:

Colleen: Do you wear a seat belt?

Patty: Yes.

Colleen: I just want to say that I wear a seat belt for my own reasons. I think it's safer to wear a seat belt. I just think the question here is: Is this law constitutional or not?

By showing that she was not opposed to seat belts *per se* but concerned only about the constitutionality of laws requiring them, Colleen showed that she was reasonable and wanted to be fair about the argument she was making.

6. *Use reluctant testimony. Reluctant testimony is testimony made by sources who speak against their own vested interest.* Anyone who furnishes evidence against his or her own interests or prejudices is likely to be highly credible to most audiences. After reviewing research on this effect, Petty and Cacioppo concluded that "the source who violates our expectations by being trustworthy when we expected untrustworthiness is especially effective."[28] The student who argues that tuition should be increased to maintain quality in education, the teacher who maintains that competency tests for teachers are necessary, and the lawyer who supports no-fault divorce laws are all likely to be believed. That is because they are all advocating positions opposite to the ones they would be expected to advocate.

7. *Avoid inconsistency.* People who take a strong position on an issue and then reverse it lose considerable credibility in the eyes of the public. Sudden reversals in position give people the impression that one does not think through one's position very well and lacks a sense of principle. In the 1992 presidential election, for example, Bill Clinton pledged to support legislation that would allow gays and lesbians to serve in the military. After he was elected, however, he gave in to military leaders and backed away from his earlier promises. Instead of allowing gays and lesbians to serve openly, his administration allowed service only on the condition that soldiers not reveal their sexual orientation. Many observers viewed Clinton's eventual support of the "don't ask, don't tell" policy as being very inconsistent with his earlier unconditional support for these groups.

FALLACIES RELATED TO AUDIENCE

A fallacy is an argument that is flawed by irrelevant or inadequate evidence, erroneous reasoning, or improper expression. In other words, a fallacy is an incorrect argument. Appendix D examines various types of fallacies When language is used inappropriately—either intentionally or unintentionally—and obscures and confuses the meaning of an argument, a fallacy has occurred. Fallacies are persuasive because they are false arguments that may seem reasonable and acceptable but are based on erroneous assumptions or invalid reasoning. Too often they are unrecognized by recipients and receive little attention either by critics or audiences.

The ability to think and act critically is dependent in many ways on our ability to understand how arguments work and to identify flaws that may appear. Identifying fallacies is an important skill to develop because it will help you to understand when an argument should or should not be persuasive and to examine the roots of your decisions. The following section will concentrate on the types of fallacies that derive from the relationship between arguers and recipients.

When arguers present arguments to direct a recipient's attention away from the central argument and to some other irrelevant argument, then the advocate has committed a fallacy to misdirect the audience's attention. Most often, fallacies of this type are called *ad* fallacies. *Ad* is Latin for "to," and fallacies of misdirection are often called *ad* fallacies because they appeal to the audience and not to the arguments. When an arguer shifts attention away from the argument and to the audience or something else, then the arguer has committed this fallacy.[29]

Such arguers may appeal to our stereotypes or prejudices about people, our tendency to go along with the crowd, our admiration for celebrities and famous people, or our respect for past practices. By appealing to such prejudices, which are often irrelevant to the claim made, arguments *ad* circumvent the substantive issues that should be considered in reaching a decision. Various forms of this category of fallacies include personal attacks on the arguer, appealing to audience emotions, and taking advantage of the audience's ignorance and gullibility to get a claim accepted.[30] In this section we will discuss four of the most common fallacies in this category—*argumentum ad hominem, argumentum ad populum,* appeal to tradition, and straw arguments.

Ad Hominem

The issue an arguer raises and the meritoriousness of the arguer's claim are usually separate from the personal character, behavior, or characteristics of the arguer, yet the *ad hominem* fallacy diverts attention from the issue at hand and focuses instead on the personal character of the argument source. Translated literally as "to the person," *the* ad hominem *fallacy launches an irrelevant attack on the person or source originating an argument instead of responding to substantial issues raised in the argument.* For such an argument to qualify as a fallacy, the accusation must be irrelevant to the claim at issue and an effort to divert attention from it.

To illustrate this fallacy, let us consider two examples of it:

Parent: I am really concerned about your grades this past semester. You were always such a good student in high school and now you have slipped to straight Cs. I think you need to study more and forget about seeing so much of your friends.

Student: Why are you always on my back for not studying? *Your* grades in college were nothing to write home about!

In raising the issue of the student's grades, the parent makes three points—that the student had done well in the past, that his grades had slipped, and that he needed to cut back on his social life and study more. The student does not acknowledge or respond to any of these points but instead accuses the parent of being a slovenly student so as to put the parent on the defensive.

Mary: I think that 18-year-olds should serve a mandatory two years in the military. The United States should serve as a leader in the free world, and that requires a strong military to keep the peace. Often, however, our best people choose not to serve and avoid combat whenever they can. A mandatory service requirement would not be unreasonable.

George: The only reason you favor this is because you're a woman and women are not allowed to serve in combat zones. So, if your idea were instituted tomorrow, I would probably find myself fighting and in danger of losing my life while you would probably have some safe, cushy job here in the States.

In this case, Mary makes the argument that the United States might have a stronger leadership role and international presence by requiring all 18-year-olds to serve two-year terms. George, on the other hand, avoids the argument by attacking Mary's motivations and character instead of responding to the argument.

One way to detect *ad hominem* responses such as these is to be alert to instances in which an indictment of an argument seems intended to divert the discussion away from the central issues it raises so as not to respond to them. There are, however, many occasions in which the arguer's character is and should be a central issue. Assessment of the integrity of political candidates in election years may be an important part of determining whether they are fit to hold office. Questioning the qualifications of a source is also legitimate when one is responding to argument from authority in which the evidence offered is the statement of a source other than the arguer. An argument is *ad hominem* and fallacious only when it is used to circumvent and avoid a legitimate issue by arbitrarily attacking the person who raised it.

Ad Populum

Literally, *ad populum* means "to the people." *An* ad populum *fallacy occurs when the substance of an argument is avoided and the advocate appeals instead to popular opinion as a justification for the claim.* Consequently, the argument's claim is predicated on popular beliefs and opinions rather than on reason and evidence. Consider the following three examples:

> The President's approval rating has dropped to less than 35 percent. This is the first time during his term that his rating has dropped this low and proves, I think, that he is doing a very poor job.

> Most new parents buy Dr. Spock's *Baby and Child Care* book to learn about the care and feeding of newborn infants. So, it seems obvious that Dr. Spock has the best book available.

> Eighty-five percent of those polled believe fluoride in water causes cancer. Therefore, we should ban fluoride from our water supplies because of its consequences.

Each example presumes that if enough people believe something, it must be true. In fact, popular belief may even run counter to objective reality. Fluoridation does not cause cancer; at least there is no statistical validation for the popular conclusion. Appealing to popular beliefs, however, hides the reality of the argument and substitutes an extraneous issue.

As you can see in these three examples, just because many people agree about something does not necessarily mean it is true. The president's popular approval rating, taken alone, is not an absolutely reliable indicator of the quality of his work. Dr. Spock's book may contain no useful advice and still be a best-seller. And fluoride may actually prevent cancer, yet popular opinion might say otherwise. The point is that public opinion cannot control the factual nature of the world; public opinion only reflects the opinions and attitudes of a large group of people. If the claim of the argument does not involve the attitudes and opinions of people, arguments appealing to opinions commit *ad populum* fallacies.

We can think of many more examples to illustrate this point, and some have important social and economic consequences. Consider what happens when people stage a "run" on a bank or other financial institution. When this happens, depositors fear that the bank's financial situation is uncertain and a panic spreads throughout the depositors. When people begin withdrawing their money, others interpret this action as a sign of the bank's insolvency and begin to withdraw their money. The result is that the bank becomes insolvent because of popular opinion.

We are not suggesting here that arguments based on popular opinions are fallacious *per se*. Sometimes the argument seeks to focus on opinion. For instance,

> The latest Gallup Poll showed that the Superbowl is the most popular television event in history.
>
> Overwhelming popular support elected the president to office.
>
> The *Cosby Show* was the most popular sitcom of all time.

In these cases, appeals to popular opinion are warranted because the crux of the argument is what the public thinks. The *ad populum* fallacy occurs only when the issues involved are not related to public opinion. Skillful argument critics should be able to discern the difference between arguments that depend on popular opinion and those that use popular opinion to avoid discussion of issues. Argument recipients who detect *ad populum* fallacies should attempt to redirect the arguments back to the issues at hand.

Appeal to Tradition

Presumption is the assumption in favor of existing beliefs and states of affairs when proposals for change are made. Presumption exists as a convention of argument that reflects people's tendency to favor what is presently in practice until a good reason for changing it is offered.

Appeal to tradition attempts to convert that convention or practice into a right or a rationale for not making a change even when a good reason for doing so is offered. *The fallacy of appeal to tradition occurs when someone claims that we should continue to do things the way we have always done them simply because we have always done them that way.* Appeal to tradition takes advantage of people's reverence for past practice and attempts to avoid dealing with meritorious reasons for changing it.

Appeals to tradition are based on the often mistaken assumptions that what has worked in the past will work well in the future, that conditions have not changed, and that there is no better way of doing things. Consider the following true example (from a college curriculum committee meeting).

Professor Smith: We should change the college grading scale to include plus and minus grading distinctions. A recent study by this committee indicates that there is a big difference between a B+ (94 out of 100 on most exam scales) and a B– (82 out of 100). Further defining the range of grades gives more precise information about a student's performance in the course.

Professor Jones: Why should we change? We've had simple letter grades without plus or minus distinctions in this college for over ten years and it's worked fine.

Professor Smith presented a good reason for changing the grading system—that the change will provide more precise information about student performance. Instead of responding to Smith's substantive argument, Jones merely appealed to tradition, saying that the way things have been done in the past should continue. When a cogent and meritorious argument for making a change occurs, then, the fallacy of appeal to tradition ignores the rationale given for change and assumes that traditional practice is the "best" way of doing things.

Straw Arguments

Straw arguments are often called "strawperson" or "strawman" arguments. They occur often in debates, discussions, and other situations where there is interactive argument. *The straw argument fallacy attacks a weakened form of an opponent's argument or an argument the opponent did not advance.* In committing this fallacy, arguers use as evidence an argument not advanced by their opponents but nonetheless an argument that bolsters their own position. It is very well described by Edward Damer in his book on fallacies:

> There are several different ways in which one may misrepresent an opponent's argument or position. First, one may state it in a perverted form by utilizing only a part of it, by paraphrasing it in carefully chosen misleading words, or by subtly including one's own evaluation or commentary in it. Second, one may oversimplify it. An opponent's complex argument can be made to look absurd when it is stated in a simplified form that leaves out important qualifications or subtle distinctions. Third, one may extend the argument beyond its original bounds by drawing inferences from it that are clearly unwarranted or unintended.[31]

As we will emphasize in Chapter 12 when we discuss the analysis and criticism of arguments, arguers should begin by grounding their arguments and criticisms on fair and reasonable representations of an opponent's argument. To do anything less is unethical. Consider the following examples of the straw argument fallacy:

Mary: I think it's time that this university begins to computerize its departments. Just think, if all the secretaries and all the professors were linked together by computer, access to student records would be more efficient, and students would save time and get better-quality advising.

Derrick: Yeah, but if we computerized everything it would take forever to teach the secretaries and professors to use the system, which would end up wasting more time than it saves.

Derrick took one aspect of Mary's proposal—the investment of time needed to get a computer network functioning—and discussed obvious problems with it. He did not, however, respond to the central issue she raised—the long-term gain in efficiency and quality of student service. By ignoring the major thrust of her argument, he created a straw argument. Here is another example:

George: With AIDS being the problem it is, I think this country is going to have to get tough. I think that within the next decade we're going to have to enforce some kind of mandatory AIDS testing for everyone.

Harry: What a bad idea. This country would never have the ability to pay for testing. If we can't afford it, we shouldn't do it.

Here Harry selected an issue irrelevant to the thrust of George's argument and tried to divert the argument onto an entirely different track. If a large portion of the population is being infected and people are dying, then the major issue of public safety raised by George must be addressed. But Harry ignores it and instead attacks a strawperson—the cost of testing.

SUMMARY

This chapter emphasizes a *rhetorical* perspective on argument—a concern with adapting arguments to specific audiences and with building up the arguer's credibility through arguments as they are made. How are arguments designed and constructed so as to be suited to the particular audiences for whom they are intended? How do arguers ensure that they will receive a favorable hearing or reading because they are perceived as well informed and trustworthy? This chapter is directed at answering these two questions and at providing recommendations for audience analysis and for developing one's own credibility.

Arguments have a particular purpose—to influence another person, a group, or a gathering of individuals. The interests of recipients should be taken into account in many dimensions of argument construction. First, the premises used should be statements audience members can safely be expected to agree with. If recipients reject an arguer's starting point, the arguer will not get far. For this reason, the arguer must have some knowledge of preexisting audience beliefs and predispositions.

Second, the principles and values held by recipients can be called upon to support the inferences made by an arguer. Most reasoning is based upon assumptions, principles, and value hierarchies that can be called into play if the reasoning is questioned. Arguers seeking acceptance of their claims, then, should use reasoning forms that the audience recognizes and should make links between their evidence and their claims that audiences will understand.

Third, understanding audience orientations should influence the process of selecting evidence. Research on the use of evidence has shown that recipients are more likely to accept arguments supported by evidence than those that are not, that they are highly suspicious of authorities whom they regard as biased, and that they are much more influenced by information that is novel than that which is "old hat." Again, only an awareness of audience knowledge and beliefs can ensure that an advocate will select his or her evidence with these factors in mind.

Fourth, audience influence also affects the way messages should be organized. Research on various audiences has shown many behaviors that are generally true of most audiences and of which arguers should be aware: (1) Explicitly stated conclusions are more effective than unstated conclusions. (2) Whether one should present one or both sides of a question depends on whether audiences are well or ill informed on a topic and whether they agree with the arguer's position. (3) Weak arguments should not be used because they are often the only ones recipients remember. (4) The arguer's strongest arguments should be placed at either the beginning or end of the message because such placement will make a greater impression and will be more easily remembered.

A concern for audience orientation should also affect other aspects of the argument. How difficult will it be to get and hold the audience's attention? What issues are foremost in the audience's mind and what form of analysis might best deal with them?

What reservations and objections does the audience have and how might they best be dealt with? Sensitivity to such questions will cause the arguer to construct an argument effectively and appropriately tailored to the audience for which it was intended.

Incorporating audience beliefs, values, and attitudes into the planning of argument requires one to know something about the recipients. Such information can be gathered in a number of ways. First, one can inform oneself about the general tendencies of most people when they attend to persuasive messages. Second, one can strategically question arguers to find out about their interests, concerns, needs, and values before making one's argument. And third, if one is speaking or writing for a large group, one can read its publications, talk with its members, and attend its meetings. Doing so will provide information about members' knowledge, education, occupations, ages, and economic status that may be useful in adapting the argument to the audience.

Another audience-related factor in the persuasiveness of arguments is the recipients' perception of the arguer's source credibility. Source credibility refers to an arguer's ability to be believed and trusted by recipients. Credibility is not an inherent characteristic of the arguer but varies according to the situation and what the arguer says and does. There are two kinds of credibility—initial credibility, which arises from the arguer's preexisting credentials, status, and reputation; and derived credibility, which results from what is said in the message. Argumentation is more closely related to derived than to initial credibility.

Social psychologists have identified three major ways that people get others to comply with their requests. The first is *compliance*, or the use of rewards and punishments to compel action. The second is *identification*, or influence that occurs because recipients find a source attractive and want to emulate him or her. And the third is *internalization*, in which recipients adopt a new attitude or belief by integrating new information into their cognitive systems. Only internalization, which results from the thought audiences give to the content of an argument—the quality of its claims and evidence—is directly related to the processes we have described in this book.

Internalization occurs when a source is perceived to possess expertise and trustworthiness. Expertise depends on whether an arguer is viewed as knowing the correct position on a topic. Trustworthiness is the extent to which recipients believe the arguer is willing to communicate that position for their benefit. Expertise and trustworthiness are most important when the topic is fact-based and susceptible to a correct answer, when the positions of arguer and recipient are widely discrepant, and when the source appears to be free of bias and vested interest. Other research findings indicate that over time people tend to remember the content of a message more than the source from which it came. Also, people who are disinterested and uninformed about a topic will rely more on whether its source appears credible than on what they think of the message content.

Arguers should be aware that, in order to win favorable consideration of their messages, they must make a good initial impression on recipients and gain and hold their attention. Credibility plays a role in this entire process. Arguers who have moderate or low credibility with audiences initially must develop their derived credibility through construction and presentation of the message. Seven strategies for doing this are described in this chapter.

Arguers should demonstrate their own and their sources' experience with the topic. They should use a large number of diverse, qualified sources and depend upon sources their recipients are likely to respect. They should avoid weak or easily rejected arguments that might cause doubt in recipients' minds about their overall credibility on other issues in the message. They should demonstrate their fairness by providing a balanced treatment of the topic, avoiding inconsistency, and citing sources likely to be perceived as trustworthy by the audience. The effectiveness of an argument is often highly dependent on the recipients' perceptions of the arguer's credibility; awareness of this influence will assist arguers in getting their claims believed and accepted.

Finally, arguers should seek ways to avoid making fallacies that mislead audiences. Fallacies are mistakes in arguments that undermine the recipients' ability to critically understand and evaluate arguments. This chapter discussed four such fallacies: *ad hominem, ad populum,* appeal to tradition, and straw arguments.

CHAPTER FOUR Arguers, Recipients, and Argumentation

EXERCISES

Exercise 1 Select a situation in which you have recently made or will soon make an argument to a particular recipient or group of recipients.

   A. Think of at least three strategies you could use to find out information about your audience's values and attitudes.

   B. How could you incorporate the information you would gather into the planning of your message? Specifically, what changes or adjustments could you make in your argument to design it for this particular audience?

   C. What strategies could you use to appear credible to this audience? How could you enhance the credibility of your arguments so they would be accepted?

Exercise 2 This chapter provided a number of strategies arguers could use to relate their arguments to the orientations of their audiences and to enhance their own credibility. These included:

   A. Use premises the audience accepts.
   B. Use audience values and principles for backing.
   C. Cite authorities the audience is likely to respect.
   D. Use novel evidence.
   E. Keep the audience interested and involved in the argument.
   F. Focus on issues about which the audience is likely to be concerned.
   G. Be aware of possible audience objections and reservations.
   H. Appear attractive and emphasize similarities you share with the audience.
   I. Emphasize your own and your source's experience with the topic.
   J. Use unbiased and reluctant testimony.
   K. Avoid inconsistency.

Examine each of the arguments below in which the speaker or writer adheres to or violates one or more of these strategies. Decide whether the audience would respond more or less favorably to the argument because of what is said. Also, decide which of the strategies the arguer uses or violates. Some information about the audience is provided.

* 1. From Martha D. Lamkin, manager of the Indianapolis Office for the U.S. Department of Housing and Urban Development, "Power: How to Get It, Keep It, and Use it Wisely," a speech delivered to Women in Communications, Inc., Indianapolis, Ind., October 24, 1986. Reprinted in *Vital Speeches of the Day* 53 (1986): 153.

   > I mentioned at the outset that Machiavelli's essay, "The Prince," gave power a bad name. Perhaps it's up to a woman, Rosabeth Moss Kanter, to reverse this perception. Her book, entitled *The Changemasters*, makes the point that organizational genius is 10 percent inspiration and 90 percent acquisition—acquisition of power (that is information, resources, and support) to move

beyond the formal job charter to influence others to accomplish organizational objectives.

2. From Zane G. Todd, chairman of the board, Indianapolis Power and Light Company, "Electric Power: A Look Back, a Look Ahead," a speech delivered at Franklin College, Franklin, Ind., October 21, 1986. Reprinted in *Vital Speeches of the Day* 53 (1986): 149.

> We are all for a clean environment. None of us wants dirty air or polluted water. But the environmental standards set by our Federal Government were set far above the danger levels. In a word, they were "harsh." While we in our industry complained that these restrictions would inflict punitive costs on our customers, the Government was adamant. They reasoned that these high costs were justified because, in addition to protecting the environment, they would impose energy conservation. As a result, about 20 percent to 25 percent of your electric bill goes to pay for environmental improvements.

3. From "Marginalia," a column in *The Chronicle of Higher Education* (June 3, 1987): 2.

> A reader found this ad on a bulletin board at the University of Delaware and sent a copy to us:
> ONE DAY RESUME PRINTING SERVICE
> A resume which produce exceptional results is one that is *clean* and *distinctive in appearance*. Your resume must be *attention getter*, more *readable*, and *attractive* with a *visual impact* then competitive resumes. . . .
> We'll do our own, thanks.

4. From Anton J. Campanella, president of New Jersey Bell, "Public Education is Turning the Corner," a speech delivered to the New Jersey Council of Education, Bridgewater, N.J., October 3, 1986. Reprinted in *Vital Speeches of the Day* 53 (1986): 81.

> But the quality of our state's public education system is of vital concern to me. I'm concerned as a parent, as a citizen, and as a business leader.
> My wife was a teacher.
> Our three sons attended public schools.
> I've served on my local school board and two college boards of trustees.
> But my status as president of one of New Jersey's largest private employers ensures that education is far more than a passing interest to me. My company, like many others, looks to our public education system for the human resources—the people—we need.

* 5. From Glenna M. Crooks, director of the policy division of the American Pharmaceutical Association, "How to Make a Difference: Shaping Public Policy," a speech delivered to the First Annual National Conference on Women's Health, Washington, D.C., June 18, 1986. Reprinted in *Vital Speeches of the Day* 52 (1986): 756.

> When I first began to work on this topic I was a government official assigned to attend an international meeting of policymakers, theologians, philosophers and scientists to discuss the ways in which the religious values and cultural ethics of a nation affected the ways in which health policy was made. . . .

CHAPTER FOUR   Arguers, Recipients, and Argumentation   **91**

> They assigned me a title, "Policymaking in America," and I set out to explore how I made my living in the public policy arena. My social science perspective shifted into high gear. I read the Declaration of Independence and the Constitution and observed the actions of my contemporaries in government, associations and as individuals in a new light. My observations impressed and awed me. I saw a process that I have come to passionately believe in and promote; one that in my opinion truly capitalizes on the great strengths of the nation.
>
> Some of my friends and colleagues here today know that I have just returned from the Soviet Union where I led a group of health professionals in an international professional exchange. As a result of that experience and my observations of such an oppressive society, my views about the strengths and value of our consensus-building passions as Americans are even stronger. It is one of our greatest national treasures.

6. R. L. Crandall, chair and president, American Airlines, Inc., "The Volatile Airline Industry," a speech before the Economic Club of Detroit, February 23, 1987. Reprinted in *Vital Speeches of the Day* 53 (1987): 468.

> It's a pleasure to address such a distinguished audience as the Economic Club of Detroit, for two reasons: First, because I suspect many of you are frequent flyers on American, and I always like to be among our best customers. Second, because, for a long time, the name Detroit has been synonymous with transportation—admittedly, of the four-wheeled, rather than the airborne kind, but transportation nonetheless.

7. From Margarita Papandreou, president, Women's Union of Greece, "Women in Politics: Human Rights a Dominant Force," a speech delivered at the National Organization for Women in Denver, Colo., June 13 15, 1986. Reprinted in *Vital Speeches of the Day* 52 (1986): 744.

> Perhaps [during the early stages of the contemporary women's movement], we didn't pay enough attention during our struggle for equal rights to that heavy sack, that sandbag, we carried on our backs . . . the responsibility for the house, the children, the oldsters. So, when the doors were finally opened to us . . . for education, for entry into so-called male jobs and professions, for political participation, etc., there we were, standing at the door, a man next to us, we—our bag—a staggering weight as we moved forward to take advantage of our new opportunities.

8. Ronald Reagan, president of the United States, "President's Response to the Tower Commission Report: Iranian Affair," a speech delivered to the American people in Washington, D.C., March 4, 1987. Reprinted in *Vital Speeches of the Day* 53 (1987): 323.

> Let's start with the part that is most controversial. A few months ago I told the American people I did not trade arms for hostages. My heart and my best intentions still tell me that is true, but the facts and evidence tell me it is not.
>
> As the Tower board reported, what began as a strategic opening to Iran deteriorated in its implementation into trading arms for hostages. This runs counter to my own beliefs, to Administration policy, and to the original strategy we had in mind. There are reasons why it happened but no excuses. It was a mistake.

NOTES

1. These studies are summarized in James C. McCroskey, "A Summary of Experimental Research on the Effects of Evidence in Persuasive Communication," *Quarterly Journal of Speech* 55 (1969): 169–70.
2. McCroskey, 172.
3. McCroskey, 174–5.
4. Stewart L. Tubbs, "Explicit versus Implicit Conclusions and Audience Commitment," *Speech Monographs* 35 (1968): 14–95.
5. Tubbs, 18.
6. This research is effectively summarized in Bert E. Bradley, *Fundamentals of Speech Communication*, 4th ed. (Dubuque, Iowa: William C. Brown, 1984), 346–8.
7. Ruth Anne Clark, *Persuasive Messages* (New York: Harper & Row, 1984), 28.
8. This research is summarized by Robert N. Bostrom in his *Persuasion* (Englewood Cliffs, N.J.: Prentice-Hall, 1983), 178.
9. Clark, 17.
10. Aristotle, *Rhetoric*, 1356a.
11. Bradley, 66.
12. R. Brooks and T. Scheidel, "Speech as Process: A Case Study," *Speech Monographs* 35 (1968): 1–7.
13. See, for example, R. Glen Hass, "Effects of Source Characteristics on Cognitive Responses and Persuasion," in *Cognitive Responses in Persuasion*, Richard E. Petty, Thomas M. Ostrom, and Timothy C. Brock, eds. (Hillsdale, N.J.: Lawrence Erlbaum Associates, 1981), 141–72; Bostrom, 63–87; Gary Cronkhite and Jo Liska, "A Critique of Factor Analytic Approaches to the Study of Credibility," *Communication Monographs* 43 (1976): 91–107; Jesse G. Delia, "A Constructivist Analysis of the Concept of Credibility," *Quarterly Journal of Speech* 62 (1976): 361–75; and James C. McCroskey and Thomas J. Young, "Ethos and Credibility: The Construct and Its Measurement after Three Decades," *Central States Speech Journal* 32 (1981): 24–34.
14. Hass, 154.
15. Hass, 142–51. Hass's account is based on H. Kelman, "Compliance, Identification, and Internalization: Three Processes of Attitude Change," *Journal of Conflict Resolution* 2 (1958): 51–60.
16. Hass, 149.
17. Hass, 144.
18. J. Mills and E. Aronson, "Opinion Change as a Function of the Communicator's Attractiveness and Desire to Influence," *Journal of Personality and Social Psychology* 1 (1965): 173–7.
19. S. Chaiken, "Communicator Physical Attractiveness and Persuasion," *Journal of Personality and Social Psychology* 37 (1979): 1387–97.
20. Hass, 143.
21. Hass, 153.
22. Richard E. Petty and John T. Cacioppo, *Attitudes and Persuasion: Classic and Contemporary Approaches* (Dubuque, Iowa: William C. Brown, 1981), 89–94.
23. Petty and Cacioppo, 64, report a study by S. Bochner and C. A. Insko, "Communicator Discrepancy, Source Credibility, and Opinion Change," *Journal of Personality and Social Psychology* 4 (1966): 614–21.
24. Hass, 159.
25. Connaught Marshner, "Inside Look at Pornography and the Commission," *Conservative Digest* (August 1986): 29. This is an interview with Alan Sears.
26. From a letter to the editor by Murray J. Cohen, M.D., in *The Chronicle of Higher Education* (April 1, 1987): 44.
27. William F. Buckley, Jr., "On the Right," *National Review* (August 1, 1986): 46.
28. Petty and Cacioppo, 64.
29. Fallacies of this type were identified as a group by C. C. Hamblin, *Fallacies* (London: Methuen, 1970): 135–76. He traced the origin of this group of arguments to Francis Bacon's *Advancement of Learning* in the early 1600s. Bacon identified four types of "idols," or prejudicial habits of thought, that affect reasoning. Hamblin (p. 146) noted that after Bacon the study of fallacies included the study of the influence of psychological factors on human reasoning.
30. Hamblin (p. 41) lists the Latin names for the first type of these as *Ad Hominem* and *Ad Passiones*. Hamblin noted that there are many varieties of "argument ad" and concluded that "We feel like adding: Ad *Nauseam*—but even that has been suggested before."
31. T. Edward Damer, *Attacking Faulty Reasoning*, 2d ed. (Belmont, Calif.: Wadsworth, 1987): 128–9.

CHAPTER 5

Language and Argument

CHAPTER OUTLINE

- The Nature of Language
  - Language and Meaning
  - Language and Abstraction
  - Connotations and Denotations
- Language in Argument
  - Language, Thought, and Perception
  - Functions of Language
  - Using Language in Argument
- Fallacies of Language Use
  - Equivocation
  - Amphiboly
  - Emotive Language
- Summary
- Exercises

KEY CONCEPTS

language
abstraction
denotative meaning
connotative meaning
euphemism
terministic screen
emotive function
phatic function

cognitive function
rhetorical function
metalingual function
poetic function
presence
fallacy
equivocation
amphiboly

President Abraham Lincoln delivered the Gettysburg Address on November 19, 1863. It began:

> Four score and seven years ago our fathers brought forth on this continent a new nation, conceived in liberty, and dedicated to the proposition that all men are created equal.[1]

Is there any significance to the words used by Lincoln? The speech itself certainly carried with it an importance and elegance suitable not only for 1863 but for the twentieth century as well. But do the actual words used to convey the message carry with them any particular significance? Lincoln's opening could just as easily have begun:

> Eighty-seven years ago those who came before us established in this country a new system of government created in freedom and based on the idea that all people are created equal.

Is there a difference? The content has remained the same, but the words used to express the message are now simpler and perhaps more contemporary. But the change in language seems to change more than just the words; some of the force and spirit of the original version is gone.

The language Lincoln used to express his message was not chosen randomly—nor is the language used to express everyday arguments. Even if we are not aware of our language choices, we adhere to the rules of grammar and vocabulary inherent in our language. The stronger our command of language, the better able we are to select which words to use—but all of us make choices about how to phrase and develop the language of arguments. As you will see later in this chapter, the eloquent language Lincoln used contributed not only to the beauty of his address, but also to its persuasiveness. Harold Zyskind in his study of Lincoln's address noted that, although the occasion was ceremonial (dedication of the cemetery at Gettysburg), the address itself was argumentative and was designed by Lincoln to persuade members of his audience to rededicate themselves to the reunification and continuance of the federal government after the Civil War.[2] Gilbert Highet, writing of Lincoln's address, observed:

> No one thinks that when he was drafting the Gettysburg Address, Lincoln deliberately looked up these quotations and consciously chose these particular patterns of thought. No, he chose the theme. From its development and from the emotional tone of the entire occasion, all the rest followed, or grew—by the marvelous process of choice and rejection which is essential to artistic creation.[3]

In the course of devising and framing arguments, we select the words by which our claims and their support are expressed. These words have a profound impact on the use and interpretation of arguments because their significance lies not in the words themselves, but in what they come to mean for the people who use them. The effects of language depend upon the degree of concreteness and emotive significance of the words themselves.

George Orwell once lamented about the decline of the English language. He argued that when people use language inaccurately or sloppily, they cloud the ability of others to think clearly. They make the language unclear such that their thinking becomes unclear. He said

A man may take to drink because he feels himself to be a failure, and then fail all the more completely because he drinks. It is rather the same thing that is happening to the English language. It becomes ugly and inaccurate because our thoughts are foolish, but the slovenliness of our language makes it easier for us to have foolish thoughts. The point is that the process is reversible.[4]

As we discussed in Chapter 1, the ability to think critically about arguments is important for both arguers and analysts. When language is used inaccurately and sloppily, it becomes a barrier to our ability to think critically and argue intelligently about problems. The importance of understanding how language is used and misused was highlighted by Howard Kahane when he commented: "it is quite useful for students to gain insight into how language, the medium through which they obtain information from others, can be and often is used to obfuscate and otherwise deceive the unwary."[5]

Too often arguers obscure their true meanings by using words that are ambiguous. Just as often, arguers decide to use words that may sound complex and intelligent but have the effect of unintentionally obscuring their meaning. For example, consider the language of computers. Jargon words such as RAM, ROM, byte, BPS, 32-bit slot, and the like may be clear to others who are involved with computers but may be confusing to those without common frames of reference or a common understanding of the language.

Orwell's argument is important. If we communicate our ideas clearly, we are able to engage our audiences' minds in more complex and accurate ways. If we are not clear, then our ideas may become lost in our audiences' confusion. We need to be careful with our language choices and we need to avoid patterns of confusing language choices. Orwell said: "If one gets rid of these habits one can think more clearly, and to think clearly is a necessary first step towards political regeneration. . . ."[6]

This chapter will examine the nature and functions of language in general and then make specific recommendations regarding its use in argument. By the end of this chapter, you should be able to explain how language works to influence arguers and recipients of argument. You should also be able to control how your arguments are received and understood by controlling your use of language when you make arguments.

THE NATURE OF LANGUAGE

There are over 3000 languages in the world. Each one of them, including English, has a grammar and a vocabulary that control its use and structure. Throughout your primary and secondary education, you learned about the grammar and vocabulary of the English language. You learned grammar as a set of rules—for example, that each English sentence requires both a subject and a verb.

Language is the systematic coordination of grammar and vocabulary used to convey meaning. Grammar and vocabulary are the two components of language and the tools used to communicate meanings among people. Language is a very powerful tool—one of the most powerful available to human beings. Michael Calvin McGee wrote that language functions as an important unifying tool.[7] Recall the discussion from Chapter 2. In that chapter we talked about how cultures develop around systems of shared meanings. People who share a language share a set of cultural assumptions and a way of

> **SYMBOLS ON THE INTERNET**
>
> Language is made up of a collection of symbols and a grammar for their use. Over time, language adapts and new symbols are added. Following are a collection of some of the symbols that have made their way into the language of the internet.
>
> | :-} | Smiley face | :-$ | Orthodontics smiley |
> |---|---|---|---|
> | 8:} | Bow in hair smiley | =:-() | Scared smiley |
> | :-}8 | Bow tie smiley | :-@ | Screaming smiley |
> | 0:-} | Innocent smiley | :-8 | Smiley eating a pickle |

thinking. Language is a powerful means by which cultures are developed and continued from generation to generation.

Within every language certain words convey very complex and important meanings to the members of those cultures. Within the United States, for example, words such as "democracy," "honesty," or even "apple pie" carry meanings that are important to the members of the cultures. McGee made this point when he argued that these special words "are the basic structural elements, the building blocks of ideology. Thus they may be thought of as 'ideographs,' for, like Chinese symbols, they signify and 'contain' a unique ideological commitment; further, they presumptuously suggest that each member of a community will see as a gestalt every complex nuance in them."[8] The members of a given culture, then, resonate with the many and complex meanings of the ideographs within their language. These words serve as an organizing and unifying principle for culture that provide members with a common frame of reference for understanding the world around them.

When we argue, the words we choose to use are powerful and important. They function on many levels and have the capacity to change recipients' minds in different ways. Understanding our choices and developing ways of using language is central to being an effective and ethical communicator. The focus of this chapter, then, is to examine how language communicates meaning among people. How is language used to convey meaning? Specifically, what are the implications for argument of the ways language works in communication and argument?

Language and Meaning

Language is such a powerful tool that sometimes when we think we have mastered it, we find that it has the ability to master us. A few years ago, a segment on a TV program called "Candid Camera" illustrated this point well. The program's producers placed signs over two adjacent public telephones. One sign read "Men" and the other sign read "Women." Interestingly, even when one or the other phone was not being used, lines developed in front of the "Men" phone or the "Women" phone. The act of labeling a telephone as men's or women's changed the way people used them.

The "Candid Camera" example is a humorous illustration of the power words have over our actions and thoughts. Some words are considered taboo and we don't typically

CHAPTER FIVE Language and Argument

allow their use in public. Instead, we refer to the "four-letter words" or the "seven dirty words" that cannot be used on radio or television.

Nevertheless, words by themselves have no intrinsic meaning. They acquire meaning only insofar as people use them to describe their world. This is the point made by C. K. Ogden and I. A. Richards in their book *The Meaning of Meaning*.[9] Their argument was that humans are symbol users who develop symbols to stand for thoughts and ideas in their minds. The mental image, also known as a representation, is the result of direct experience or imagination. For example, if John Smith sees a green pine tree, he develops a representation of the tree through direct experience. John is also able to imagine a green pine tree that he has never seen—based on his past experience with pine trees.

Communication involves the process of transforming such representations into symbols. Therefore, the user's mental image of a tree is translated into the word "tree," and the language provides the tool for sharing representations, or meanings, with other language users. Ogden and Richards' model is illustrated in Figure 5–1.

The referent is the actual material object referred to in language. The symbol is the word used to refer to the referent. The reference is the association the language user makes between the symbol "pine tree" and the material object that the user has experienced.

The major point this model makes is that the symbol is connected with the referent *only by way of* an association made by the language user. In other words, the meaning of the word rests in the people using the word. Therefore, the connection is *indirect* and represented by a broken line in Figure 5–1. What is the implication of this for communication? Because there is no direct relation between symbol and referent, there is room for misunderstanding. Two language users could make the connection differently and therefore have two diverse understandings of what is meant by "pine tree." Language user 1 may think of a giant evergreen tree, while language user 2 may think of a dwarf pine. It is not difficult to imagine the misunderstandings in language use that arise when symbols are ambiguous or when language users have widely discrepant experiences with some set of referents. Because of this, the level of abstraction and concreteness of words and symbols in the language system affects the precision and accuracy of communication.

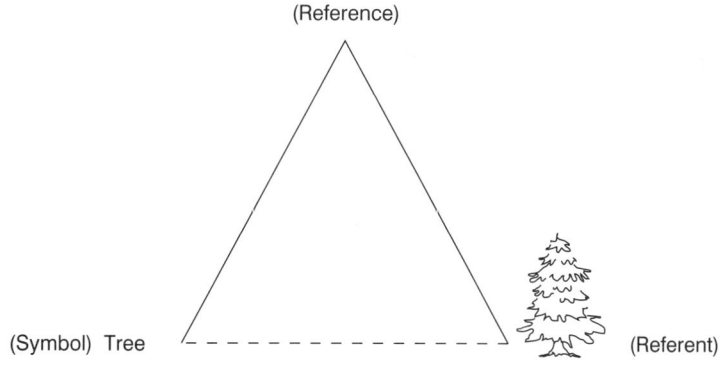

FIGURE 5–1 Symbol, Reference, and Referent

Language and Abstraction

Because the relationship between the symbol and the referent is subject to variation, communication is not 100 percent efficient. Variations occur for many reasons. Members of different cultures may have different meanings for symbols. Members within the same culture may not always share the same frame of reference. In either case, complex meanings can become lost or changed because communication is not completely efficient.

For communication to be entirely efficient, the representation in the recipient's mind should be identical with the representation in the speaker's mind. In other words, if Sue says, "There is a tree outside my window," a hearer would have to be able to know exactly to which tree Sue is referring. This is not possible, because the symbol used is not the referent. It is only indirectly related to the referent through the user's mind.

Language serves as a vehicle for conveying meaning between a source and receiver. When we speak, we not only select words and gestures we think will effectively communicate our thoughts and intentions, but we also select those we think will have some meaning for the recipient. For example, this book could have been written for high school students. Although the language used would convey meaning for everyone reading the book, a college student would probably find it simple and boring. Similarly, the book could have been targeted toward a graduate-level course. It would convey meaning, but high school students would find it very difficult to understand.

The difference in each case is the knowledge and experience the recipient is able to use in understanding the language. If the recipient has a great deal of knowledge about argumentation, the book would not need to dwell on aspects of definition or concrete examples. Instead, it could develop more abstract and theoretical discussions and the language used could be more complex. The complexity of the connection between the referent and the symbol is measured by the relative abstractness of the symbol. *Abstraction refers to the degree to which relevant characteristics are omitted in language.* As a recipient's knowledge of a subject increases, the language used to convey the subject can be more abstract. Consider the following:

Kari: Would you go to my car and get my book?

Mark: Sure, but what book in what car?

Kari: My car is the white Nissan Altima license plate KARI-1. I need my argumentation textbook.

Mark: Sure, no problem.

In the first part of the conversation, Kari assumed that Mark knew which car was hers and what book she wanted. Her language choices were relatively vague and abstract because she assumed he had a level of knowledge that would supply the missing details. After it became apparent that Mark was unsure about which car and book, Kari added more information to help make the request clearer and less ambiguous.

When we argue, we use language we assume the recipients can understand. We develop examples and speak with a level of abstraction and ambiguity that is appropriate for the given audience. It is important, however, to recognize that not all recipients have the necessary background and experience to understand abstract language. Based on the advocate's understanding of the particular recipients being addressed, relatively more or less ambiguous language and examples may be used to convey the argument.

CHAPTER FIVE   Language and Argument

S. I. Hayakawa was noted for his work in the area of language abstractness and the development of the abstraction ladder.[10] He argued that when we use language we choose to make it more or less abstract as the situation warrants. His abstraction ladder looks much like that in Figure 5–2.

The bottom of the ladder represents the most concrete—and least abstract—form of language. It uses symbols that represent the referent as specifically as possible. The top of the ladder, however, is the least specific. A manufactured item can be almost any human-made product. A listener hearing more specific language would be better able to develop a mental representation of the referent than a listener hearing the more abstract language.

Abstract language is, by its nature, ambiguous. Arguers selecting ambiguous language run the risk of being misunderstood. Why, then, would a speaker choose to use abstract language? The answer can be found in the nature of the audience. For instance, most people have never seen John's car. If he refers to it and wants to persuade his listeners to buy it, they would be unable to create an accurate mental image if the language

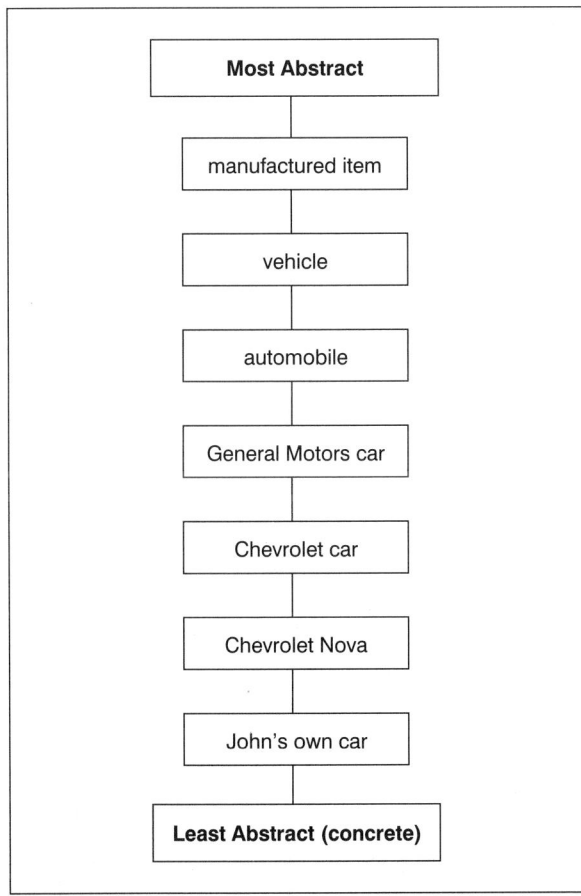

FIGURE 5–2 Hayakawa's Language Abstraction Ladder

he uses is too specific for them to understand. Therefore, as a speaker he needs to orient the recipients with language they can understand by using more abstract, commonly understood language. He might say:

> Come buy my car. It is a Chevrolet Nova built in one of the General Motors plants in California.

By blending the concrete with the abstract, arguers are able to orient their recipients to the reference and then move to more concrete symbols. We do this often because it is important that recipients understand the context or orientation of the argument. Even the process of giving directions involves a careful blend of the concrete with the abstract. If a speaker invites someone to her home and says "I live at 4111 North 37th Street," she assumes that the recipient understands what city and how to get there. The address alone is very concrete. But if the recipient was from another city or country, the speaker would need to be more abstract until the recipient was oriented. For instance she might have to say:

> I live in the United States
>
> I live in Seattle, Washington.
>
> If you take Interstate 5, get off on Exit 165.

In this case, the speaker begins providing directions with a common frame of reference, which may be relatively abstract, and then provides greater focus and concreteness as the discussion moves forward. The significance of appropriately placing words on the ladder of abstraction when making arguments will be explored further in the last section of this chapter.

Connotations and Denotations

The triangle of meaning and abstraction has several important implications for arguers. If one recognizes that people may interpret words differently depending on the degree of abstraction, then an arguer should be able to consciously select words that affect people in the way the arguer intends.

The process to be used in selecting words can best be understood by considering the two poles of meaning in language use. Each word when used has a denotative meaning and also a connotative meaning. *The denotative meaning is the objective meaning held by language users in general.* A word's denotative meaning is usually found in dictionaries. Dictionaries record the meanings of words generally agreed upon and established in the culture as a whole. Denotative meanings are relatively stable, and are agreed upon by most language users at any given point in time. *Connotative meanings, however, are the subjective meanings a given individual holds of symbols used in a particular situation.* Connotative meanings have emotive significance and are unique for the individual. Words used by language users, therefore, have both denotative and connotative significance.

For example, consider the word "fag." *Webster's New Collegiate Dictionary* defines "fag" as "toil or drudgery."[11] Yet, if you were to call someone a "fag" referring to the nature of that person's work, odds are that person would respond impolitely. This is because the meaning of the word "fag" is found not in the word itself, but in the person

> **LOST SYMBOLS**
>
> Symbols are important to our thinking and communicating processes. Without them, the communication becomes nearly impossible and the ability to share complex thoughts is remote at best. Language symbolizes the importance of things by naming them or giving them a symbol. People, for example, are important because we have names. Some symbols, however, are almost lost in the huge collection of English symbols. For example:
>
> Aglet—the covering on the end of a shoelace.
> Duff—the decaying organic matter found on a forest floor.
> Harp—the small metal hoop that supports a lampshade.
> Phosphenes—the lights you see when you close your eyes hard.
> Piggin—a small wooden pail with one long stave used as a handle.
> Quarrel—a small, diamond-shaped pane of glass, like that used in lattice glass.
> Solidus—the oblique stroke (/) used between words or in fractions such as 7/8.
> Zarf—a holder for a handleless coffee cup.

to whom the word is addressed. Similarly, in the 17th century, the word "Good-bye" was seen as blasphemous because it contracted the Lord's name. The correct phrase to use when parting was "God be with you," and the shortened form was seen as inappropriate and disrespectful. Over time, the meaning of words change and adapt as the culture changes and as words become used and acquire new or different meanings.

To illustrate this point, examine the following list of words and write down the first word or phrase that comes to mind:

feminist

Miss America

Texan

construction worker

student

Take a look at your list. You will find that the words you most closely associate with each of these words are your own personal definitions—or connotations—for each of these symbols. The denotative definitions that are found in *Webster's* are the objective, generally agreed-upon definitions for the list of words:

feminist: someone who believes the theory of the political, economic, and social equality of the sexes.

Miss America: young unmarried female who is representative of America

Texan: someone from Texas

construction worker: a person employed to build

student: one who attends school

The odds are that your personal meanings are different than the denotative meanings for the same set of symbols. This holds some important ramifications for speakers of a given language. Whenever you construct a message or argument designed to persuade a listener, you must deal with not only the meaning of the language as you know it, but also with the meaning of the language the way the listener understands it.

Our language is full of words that have been replaced by other words carrying less negative or more positive connotations. This is the function of euphemisms. *Euphemism is a linguistic device for replacing words and phrases that carry a negative connotation with words and phrases that carry a positive connotation.* (Of course a speaker intending to convey a negative feeling might also substitute negative words for positive words.) For example,

Positive Term	**Negative Term**
daytime drama	soap opera
indiscretion	moral wrong
inappropriate	illegal
air support	bombing
terminated	fired
destabilize	overthrow
intelligence gathering	spying
sanitation engineer	garbage collector
correctional facility	prison
low-income	poor
freedom fighters	revolutionary guerrillas
passed away	died

There are many other possible examples, but in each case words with the same denotative meaning may be substituted for one another with the objective of changing the connotative meanings.

This section has illustrated three characteristics of language. First, the meaning of language depends on language users because symbols by themselves have no intrinsic meaning. Second, language can be abstract or concrete, and arguers must decide what degree of abstraction is appropriate for a given situation and audience. And third, because language allows room for variable interpretations of the meanings of symbols by both the speaker and the listener, meanings of symbols may vary. While denotative meanings are the objective meanings of words agreed upon by the language users, connotative meanings are the subjective interpretations of words that depend on the individual symbol user. Arguers should be sensitive to the fact that the words they use have both denotative and connotative meanings when they are interpreted.

LANGUAGE IN ARGUMENT

We have discussed the variability in the meanings of words from one context to another and from one language user to another. Not only does language affect the accuracy of understanding and interpretation of arguments, but it also influences our perception of our experience. This section will show how language shapes the way recipients think and therefore demonstrate its power in influencing human thought.

Language, Thought, and Perception

What is the relationship between language and thought? Simply stated, language molds and shapes our thoughts. It influences both our perception of the world and what we think about it. For example, imagine the implications of your instructor telling you that you will be comprehensively examined on the exact wording of each definition in this book—and nothing else. Immediately, the instructor's wording would begin to affect how you would think about studying the course material:

> comprehensively examined
>
> exact wording
>
> each definition
>
> nothing else

The use of this wording, then, would shape your perception of how to study the book and cause you to concentrate on argumentation terminology, perhaps much more than on argument analysis, construction of messages, and many other topics covered in this book.

Of all the means an advocate has for arguing, language is perhaps the most important. Through the skillful use of language, the arguer is able to help shape and change a recipient's perception of an issue and push the recipient toward a new action or way of thought. Although it is an integral facet of arguing, language is often overlooked in favor of understanding argument parts and tests of evidence and the like. But it serves a central and important function.

The words we use to communicate shape and focus the attention and thoughts of recipients. To demonstrate this, turn to the next page and circle every "the." When you have finished, the odds are that you can say how many instances of "the" appeared and even describe their physical placement. But you would probably not be able to recall the use or frequency of any other word on the page, the subjects discussed on the page, or any misspellings such as "teh." The reason is that the linguistic instruction focused your perception to isolate a particular symbol and this in turn focused your thoughts so that unrelated stimuli were systematically excluded.

In the mid-1950s, Edward Sapir, an anthropologist, and his student, Benjamin Whorf, advanced the hypothesis that people experience their world through language.[12] While they did not say that our thoughts are bound by language, they did argue that language and vocabulary influence our thought patterns.[13] Another noted intellectual, Kenneth Burke, introduced the notion of "terministic screens" to illustrate the role language plays in human perception.[14]

A terministic screen is a linguistic filter through which human beings perceive their world. In other words, our definitions of the world, our environment, our relationships with others, and ourselves are created through the exchange of symbols. We know who and what we are because of the exchanges and interactions we have had with other people and our environment. Therefore, language—the tool we use to interact—serves to define our world. Language, according to Burke, allows us to see and understand our world and in essence affects how we experience it.

By way of illustration, Burke uses the example of a photograph. If you took three pictures of a house, each with a different color filter, each picture would be different—even though the subject remained the same. The filters give significance, substance, and contrast to different items in the picture. Likewise, language acts like a filter. The words we use to express ourselves lend different meanings to our world. Our linguistic filter shapes what we see. This is one reason an exact translation of English into French or Greek or any other language is impossible, because the nature of the filters is different.

A dramatic example of the influence of language on thought and perception is provided in George Orwell's *1984*. The novel takes place in a totalitarian society. The novel's hero, Winston Smith, has long resisted the strong and pervasive force of the government to control thoughts, emotions, and actions. Part of the government's attempt to control thought is contained in the new language of the government called Newspeak. In the following passage, Syme, Smith's colleague, discusses the *Newspeak Dictionary* with him.

> "The Eleventh Edition is the definitive edition," he said. "We're getting the language into its final shape—the shape it's going to have when nobody speaks anything else. . . . You think, I dare say, that our chief job is inventing new words. But not a bit of it! We're destroying words—scores of them, hundreds of them, every day. We're cutting the language down to the bone. . . .
>
> "It's a beautiful thing, the destruction of words.
>
> "You haven't a real appreciation of Newspeak, Winston," he said almost sadly. "Even when you write it you're still thinking in Oldspeak. I've read some of those pieces that you write in the *Times* occasionally. They're good enough, but they're translations. In your heart you'd prefer to stick to Oldspeak, with all its vagueness and its useless shades of meaning. You don't grasp the beauty of the destruction of words. Do you know that Newspeak is the only language in the world whose vocabulary gets smaller every year?
>
> "Don't you see that the whole aim of Newspeak is to narrow the range of thought? In the end we shall make thoughtcrime literally impossible, because there will be no words in which to express it. Every concept that can ever be needed will be expressed in exactly *one* word, with its meaning rigidly defined and all its subsidiary meanings rubbed out and forgotten. . . . The Revolution will be complete when the language is perfect. . . ."[15]

This passage holds an important message for any language user. Although the English language contains more than 450,000 words, the average American speaking vocabulary is only about 3000 words. Our tendency is to use highly abstract words so that by being vague we are able to discuss broad and complex subjects with very few symbols. We have begun to use words placed more highly in the abstraction ladder and let one word do the work of several. The shades of meaning are lost as the vocabulary contracts,

CHAPTER FIVE   Language and Argument   **105**

and the arguer's intention is convoluted when the arguments are expressed in general or simple terms as opposed to the appropriately concrete and specific terms.

An arguer has the ability to change thought and perception through the use of language. But it is important that an advocate be aware of the influence words have on a recipient. Words restrict as well as enhance thought, and argument should develop opportunities for thought. The point here is that arguers should be conscientious users of language. Language should be used to its fullest extent to convey the arguer's intentions, and should be as clear as possible to the recipients to avoid unwanted and unnecessary ambiguity.

Functions of Language

When we argue, we use and adapt our language choices to fit the argument and situation. The way in which language is used in argument to influence is affected not only by the available vocabulary and the terms used but also by the ways in which language functions. In conveying our messages to others, we express our thoughts in ways that enable us to reach our objectives in the particular situation. For instance, sometimes we want our messages to inspire an audience. Other times we want our messages to humor an audience. We use language that enables us to achieve the particular outcomes we seek.

One observer has classified the functions of language into six categories: emotive, phatic, cognitive, rhetorical, metalingual, and poetic. Often we use combinations of these functions to give our messages and arguments dimension and depth. In any case, our decisions about how we want to affect our audiences should guide the choices we make with regard to language.

The emotive language function is used to express and convey the feelings, attitudes, and emotions of the speaker. When we use our words to convey and arouse emotions within the listener, we are using language emotively. Language used emotively in argument is highly dependent on connotative meanings and the responses they evoke in the recipient. Consider the following statements about the Playboy Foundation:

> Although it calls itself a "foundation," it is actually an arm of Playboy Enterprises, a profit-making corporation that pollutes the moral environment and stands accused of victimizing women and children by portraying them as sex objects.[16]

The author here is attempting to make the argument that the Playboy Foundation contributes to the moral degradation of society. His language is heavily connotative and seeks to develop anger within the readers. Words such as "profit-making," "pollutes," and "victimizing" fulfill an emotive function in that the author both expresses his feelings and seeks to arouse the same feelings in the recipients.

Advertising is a common source of argument that is grounded in the emotive functions of language. In her book *The Beauty Myth,* Naomi Wolf argues that the media and advertisers create a "fear of fat" and link women's self-esteem to particular stereotypes of beauty.[17] Jerry Nix, a salesperson, described his job as: "Everything in sales is a battle. First, it's the battle with other salesmen to get the best customers, then it's a battle to overcome the customer's reluctance to make a decision, then it's the battle to find approved credit, then you've got to battle to get delivery arranged. You're getting pressure all the way around, and you just have to be able to deal with it."[18] Again the symbols convey the arguer's emotional intensity in the hope of creating a similar intensity among recipients.

The phatic function of language is used socially to reinforce the relationship among parties to a communicative exchange. Language used phatically includes greetings, farewells, and "passing the time of day." The emphasis is not on the context of what is said but on the exchange of pleasantries as an expression of mutual good will. Consider the following example:

Amy:	Hi, John, how are you doing?
John:	Fine, how are things with you?
Amy:	Same old stuff. Work until the weekend, you know how it is.
John:	Sure do. Seems the work keeps on piling up.

In this passage, there is very little information or content exchanged. The focus of the conversation was simply to recognize one another, exchange a greeting, and talk briefly about a relatively noncontroversial topic—work. Phatic communication may be a bridge to a more in-depth conversation that might follow this exchange or it might simply end at this point. Since the phatic function is relevant to the relationship among arguers rather than to the topic in question, it may affect the rhetorical dimension of argument while having little influence on its logical content.

The cognitive function of language is used to inform. Unlike the emotive function, which relies primarily on the recipients' connotative meanings for its impact, language used cognitively is primarily denotative and neutral. It is intended to inform recipients of something they do not know. It can also have the effect of alarming recipients or getting them concerned about a situation or problem of which they were unaware. However, while the effect may be alarm or some other emotion, the cognitive function is concerned primarily with providing information. Consider the following example:

The Warning Signs of Suicide

Teenage suicide is increasing dramatically. It is the third leading cause of death for people aged 15 to 24 years and the sixth for people aged 5–14. Since 1950, the teen-age suicide rate has tripled. In an effort to curb this increase, professionals warn that family members, friends and teachers should be aware of the following symptoms that might indicate a teen in trouble:

- Change in eating and sleeping habits.
- Withdrawal from friends, and family and regular activities.
- Violent actions, rebellious behavior or running away.
- Drug and alcohol use.
- Unusual neglect of personal appearance.
- Marked personality change and unusual moodiness.
- Persistent boredom, difficulty concentrating, or a decline in the quality of schoolwork. General apathy toward school and family.
- Frequent complaints about physical symptoms, often related to emotions, such as stomachaches, headaches, and fatigue.
- Loss of interest in pleasurable activities and outside activities.

- Feelings of depression and despair.
- Reckless driving.
- Not tolerating praise or rewards.[19]

The primary function of this passage is to inform readers of a little-known fact—that suicide is the third leading cause of teen death—and of measures to be taken about it. To the extent that the piece alarms readers and gets them to take precautions, however, it is relevant to argument.

The rhetorical function of language aims to direct or influence thoughts and behaviors. It is persuasive. This is generally the type of language use primarily associated with argumentation. The process of motivating hearers to accept a claim is rhetorical because it seeks to effect some substantive change in the listener's attitudes, values, or beliefs. The following excerpt, again about teen suicide, exemplifies language used rhetorically:

> If you are feeling suicidal right now, please tell someone. Before making an irrevocable choice, you owe it to yourself to talk about it with someone else. To locate a suicide prevention service in your community, just call your telephone operator and ask for the number.
>
> If a child or adolescent says, "I want to kill myself," or "I'm going to commit suicide," always take the statement seriously and seek evaluation from a child and adolescent psychiatrist or other physician. People often feel uncomfortable talking about death. However, asking the child or adolescent whether he or she is depressed or thinking about suicide can be helpful.[20]

Unlike the earlier passage about suicide, this makes an explicit attempt to influence the reader. It calls upon readers to take action and uses imperatives to address them directly. It also uses a greater number of connotative terms—"irrevocable choice," "owe it to yourself," and "helpful"—than the informative piece. The rhetorical function of language can be effective in engaging and influencing recipients and thus persuading them.

Metalingual language comments upon language use itself rather than upon objects or ideas in the world. Its focus is on how language is used and why. Language is used metalingually in argument when arguers make claims about someone else's use of language for purposes of criticism or refutation. For example, if you were to attack an opponent's argument by showing that he or she had used one of the language fallacies identified in Appendix D, you would be using a metalingual function of language to make an argument. Or, consider as an example Highet's appraisal of language use in the Gettysburg Address:

> It does not spoil such a work of art to analyze it as closely as we have done; it is altogether fitting and proper that we should do this: for it helps us to penetrate more deeply into the rich meaning of the Gettysburg Address, and it allows us the very rare privilege of watching the workings of a great man's mind.[21]

Highet here is commenting upon his own comments upon the language and composition of the Gettysburg Address. His own metalingual use of language is essential to his ability as a critic to assess and interpret the speech in a certain way. He thereby supports his own interpretation by making an argument.

The poetic function of language emphasizes the structure and artistry of expression in a message. Language used poetically is designed to be aesthetically appealing and distinctive. In it we look for creativity, uniqueness, figures of speech, rhythm, and melody. While the poetic function of language is not intended to persuade readers or listeners to action, it can affect arguments. Arguments that are finely and artistically expressed hold their listeners' or readers' attention, contribute to their enjoyment of discourse, and thereby increase the likelihood that recipients will accept the claims stated or implied by the discourse. Recall the original and "plain" versions of the opening words of the Gettysburg Address cited at the beginning of this chapter. Which version influenced you more? Most rhetorical critics would concur that it should be the first one, largely because of the artistry of its language.

As we have intimated, none of these six functions occur in a pure form in common speech. Depending on the arguer, the situation, or the recipients, any two or more of these six functions may combine in any instance of language use. The claim of an argument often functions rhetorically. The language used to make a claim is intended to effect some change in the listener. But the claim is based on evidence that emphasizes the cognitive function to make information or ideas available. The reasoning connecting the evidence to the claim may be rhetorical if it helps persuade the listener, or it may be cognitive if it provides backing for the claim, or it may even be metalingual if it highlights how the language was used in the evidence. Furthermore, the entire argument using the rhetorical, cognitive, and metalingual functions of language may be poetic if it is structured in an aesthetically pleasing manner.

Lincoln's address provides several examples of how the different uses of language can be blended into a single argument. The situation, in particular, helped provide the immediate impetus for Lincoln's selection of language. The address was intended to commemorate war dead as well as to serve as a turning point in the Civil War. Lincoln said:

> It is rather for us to be here dedicated to the great task remaining before us—that from these honored dead we take increased devotion to that cause for which they gave the last full measure of devotion—that we here highly resolve that these dead shall not have died in vain—that this nation, under God, shall have a new birth of freedom—and that government of the people, by the people, for the people, shall not perish from the earth.[22]

The closing of Lincoln's address illustrates several functions. First, it is cognitive. It asks us to think about and informs us of the war dead. Second, it is rhetorical because it asks us to rededicate ourselves—at least in attitude—to picking up where the dead concluded. And the structure is aesthetically appealing. For example, Lincoln uses parallel repetition to emphasize and provide richness to his argument:

> government of the people
> by the people
> for the people

Such poetic use of language provides a richness, a rhythm, and a harmony to the speech.

Therefore, we can conclude that in any given argument, language can function in more than one way simultaneously. The functions of language in arguments should indicate to you the importance of language in determining an argument's persuasiveness and the likelihood that an audience will accept it. Having examined the role of language function, let us turn now to some specific guidelines for using language in the construction of arguments.

Using Language in Argument

Understanding the functions of argument can help you better construct effective arguments. That language is used referentially, artistically, and persuasively in arguments means that it must be understood, adhered to, and remembered to be effective. Certain strategies for the choice of language and phrasing in your arguments will make them clearer, more vivid, and more persuasive. In his essay "Politics and the English Language," George Orwell warned that if we allow our language to become imprecise and ambiguous, each one of us contributes to the decline of our society. To avoid such decline, he offered the following six guidelines that all communicators should use in the presentation of ideas:

1. Never use a metaphor, simile or other figure of speech which you are used to seeing in print.
2. Never use a long word where a short one will do.
3. If it is possible to cut a word out, always cut it out.
4. Never use the passive where you can use the active.
5. Never use a foreign phrase, a scientific word or a jargon word if you can think of an everyday English equivalent.
6. Break any of these rules sooner than say anything outright barbarous.[23]

Orwell's point was simply that we need to be vigilant when it comes to our communication skills and language use. Our ideas and argument should be clear. We should work to minimize confusion and maximize common understandings and shared meanings. What follows are general guidelines and principles for language use, not hard-and-fast rules. As you recall from previous sections, the use of language in argument depends as much on the situation and the listeners as it does on the argument itself; however, these guidelines will help to ensure that you make the best possible use of the resources language has to offer.

1. *Use clear language.* Clarity is comprised of two factors: selecting language at the appropriate level of abstraction for the recipient, and avoiding convoluted or ambiguous language. Matching the concreteness of the word choice to the experience of the arguee and expressing oneself simply and directly ensures that the argument will be understood as the arguer intended that it should be.

As we noted earlier in the chapter, the appropriate use of abstraction/concreteness depends on the relationship between the arguer and arguee. If the arguee does not know of or understand very concrete references made by the arguer, the language is too concrete. Likewise, if the arguer and arguee understand each other's personal references or the background to the argument, then more concrete terms can be used.

For example, consider someone trying to persuade a friend to take up a training program for running:

John: It isn't as difficult as you think to build speed and endurance.

James: Really?

John: Last summer I alternated sprints with long easy runs. On weekends I ran 10Ks—the St. Patrick's Day Dash, the Beat the Bridge, and the Symphony. By fall, I was able to run a seven-minute mile in a 10K run.

James: You're right! That sounds do-able!

John uses very specific concrete references—"sprints," "10Ks," and names of particular races—because he assumes that his friend James is familiar with the running scene. Because he has designed his argument to appeal appropriately to James's interests and knowledge, John's language choice is effective. If James were naive about running, then John would have to use terms at a higher level of abstraction—using "runs at alternating paces" for "sprints," "runs along a preset 6.2 mile course" for "10Ks," and the complete names and dates of the various races. Only by using more generalized references could John be sure that an inexperienced runner would understand and relate to his argument.

The second requirement of clarity is simplicity. Often when people have a choice, they will tend to use convoluted and ambiguous language to convey their argument when simpler language might be just as effective. But such practices as circumlocution (using an unnecessarily large number of words to express an idea) and obfuscation (using words confusingly) do not have to be intentional. Their unintentional use often muddles up arguments and interferes with their effectiveness.

Because the objective of the arguer is to get the audience to understand the argument, the language used should be as simple and concise as possible:

> In my well-considered interpretation of the events preceding this encounter and considering what others have said to me as well as my own background, I think we should increase the expenditures for the bus fare by 10 cents.

A simpler way of conveying the same message is:

> I think we should raise the bus fare by 10 cents.

Generally, when an arguer has a choice, the words used should be as direct and simple as possible to get the message across. If the argument is not understood or if there is confusion about what the arguer actually is claiming, the argument will not be effective.

2. *Define terms when necessary.* If an arguer's argument hinges on a particular term and if there's a chance that an arguee might not understand the term in the way the arguer intended, then the term should be defined. By providing clear definitions, the arguer can help reduce unwanted connotations or ambiguities that might otherwise develop. For example:

> I think that regardless of the politics in any given country, we should provide the people with support—by support I don't mean military aid, I do mean economic and food assistance.

By defining "support," the arguer avoided possible pitfalls from a misinterpretation of what "support" is used to mean. Definition helps shed the connotation of military assistance and makes the claim more concrete.

3. *Express arguments vividly.* An important dimension of an argument's persuasiveness is the vividness with which it is expressed. We can select words and modes of expression that depersonalize what we say and make it seem distant and remote from the audience. Using the passive voice, the antecedentless "it," and complex formal language makes what we say less vivid. Compare the following two arguments (which say essentially the same thing):

> Sometimes the debate over abortion asks the wrong question. What is truly at issue is not a balancing of the rights of one person against the rights of another. Rights are not zero sum, and they do not shrink when they are extended to someone else.[24]

> Sometimes the abortion controversy is directed at incorrect issues. It is believed that one person's prerogatives are counterbalanced against another's. Individuals' rights are not differentially assigned so that rights accorded to some individuals are removed from others.

The second passage uses the passive voice and such formal words as:

> prerogatives
>
> counterbalanced
>
> differentially assigned
>
> accorded

The original version uses active voice and everyday language. In addition, it employs colorful terms and metaphor to engage readers and enliven their interest, such as:

> asks the wrong question
>
> truly at issue
>
> balancing . . . against
>
> zero sum
>
> shrink

When we make a problem or a description come alive for the arguee, we endow it with what one theorist calls "presence."[25] *Presence is a quality of argument that moves things near to us in space and time so they act directly on our sensibility.* This quality is best demonstrated by the following story:

> A king sees an ox on its way to sacrifice. He is moved to pity for it and orders that a sheep be used in its place. He confesses that he did so because he could see the ox, but not the sheep.[26]

We care much more about what is immediate to us than about that which is distant. Vivid language increases the immediacy of the arguer's subject and point of view.[27] By engaging his or her audience's care and concern, the arguer can use vividness to make arguments more effective.

4. *Avoid sexist and racist language.* Our discussion of the Sapir-Whorf principle, terministic screens, and the examples from *1984* earlier in this chapter made the point that language can limit and shape the way its users think and act. Women, minorities and

other economically and culturally oppressed groups have become increasingly sensitive to language use that labels and disparages or devalues them. Many language users are unaware of how their conscious forms of expression reflect unconscious assumptions about groups that may be a part of their audience. When those assumptions are negative and are negatively reflected in the claims an arguer makes, the argument's effectiveness is undermined.

Sexist use of language occurs in many of our habits. When we are referring to a group of mixed gender, we often use the masculine pronoun. The structure of our language typically gives men first priority.

> The men and women in this room . . .
>
> The men and women of this university . . .
>
> Mr. and Mrs. Smith

And women traditionally abandon part of their identity or definition upon marriage by giving up their "maiden" names.

Furthermore, women are often portrayed as children. The expression "women and children first" testifies to the linguistic equality women share with children. There are many terms used to define women as children or subhuman people. For instance, a woman may be called a "babe," "chick," "doll," or "fox."[28] Likewise, women are referred to as girls—even when they are 20, 30, 40, 50, and even 60 years of age ("The office girls got this for you").

In framing arguments, arguers often allow sexism to creep into their expression in very subtle ways. Can you detect it in the following paragraph?

> The standards of achievement in this profession are set by the men who have been most productive. The exceptional manager should recognize that his productivity depends upon his sales team and the women in his office staff.

A number of sexist uses of language are embedded in this passage. In the first sentence, "men" is used to refer generically to all practitioners of the profession (and they are *productive*). Again, in the second sentence, "the manager" is referred to by the masculine possessive pronoun "his." Furthermore, supervisors are characterized as male, while clericals ("the office staff") are assumed to be female. Slips such as these should be avoided.[29] Although nonsexist language rarely, if ever, alienates recipients, sexist language is almost certain to do so.

Unconscious racism in language use is also highly problematic. In the century following the Civil War, America became increasingly committed to equality among races and ethnic origins. In such Supreme Court cases as *Brown v. Board of Education* in 1954, in the Civil Rights Act of 1964, and in Affirmative Action measures, efforts have been systematically made to eliminate discrimination against minority groups.

These measures were important, but failed to provide for equality because, at least in part, they did nothing to override the attitudes of the people opposed to racial and ethnic equality. The laws changed, the language did not, and because language helps to shape a culture's reality, the attitudes were fostered by the language.

Civil rights leader Stokely Carmichael recognized the power of language as a barrier to racial equality when he spoke in 1967:

> The need of a free people is to be able to define their own terms and have those terms recognized by their oppressors . . . for white people to be allowed to define us by calling us Negroes, which means apathetic, lazy, stupid, and all those other things, is for us to accept those definitions. We must define what we are and move from our definitions and tell them to recognize what we are.[30]

Blacks and other minorities have objected to labels and terms of reference having negative connotations. The key terms to keep in mind when discussing minorities and minority issues are "respect" and "equality." Minorities should not be set apart unless there is good reason to do so, and if they are, they should be referred to in nonoppressive ways. At one school, a discussion was held concerning salary differentials related to people's ethnic origin. Caucasians discussing the issue continually referred to themselves as "majority faculty." This self-reference reasserted their status within the system. When reminded that a term such as "nonminority faculty" might be more neutral, one officer responded that he was not about to make that concession. Evidently, he was well aware of the role language plays in reasserting power relations between Caucasians and minority groups in this country.

In framing arguments in language, arguers should make every possible effort to engage, befriend, and appeal to the recipient through the medium of their expression. Conversely, they should systematically avoid sexist and racist language along with obscenity or other inappropriate word choices. Nothing is to be gained by insulting or alienating recipients. It is in the arguer's best interest to word arguments with care, taste, and sensitivity for those to whom the argument is directed.

FALLACIES OF LANGUAGE

A fallacy is an argument that is flawed by irrelevant or inadequate evidence, erroneous reasoning, or improper expression. In other words, a fallacy is an incorrect argument. Appendix D examines various types of fallacies, however, when language is used inappropriately—either intentionally or unintentionally—and obscures and confuses the meaning of an argument, a fallacy has occurred. Fallacies are persuasive because they are false arguments that may seem reasonable and acceptable while being based on erroneous assumptions or invalid reasoning. Too often they are unrecognized by recipients and receive little attention either by critics or audiences.

The ability to think and act critically is dependent in many ways on our ability to understand how arguments work and to identify flaws that my appear. Identifying fallacies is an important skill to develop because it will help you to understand when an argument should or should not be persuasive and to examine the roots of your decisions. The following section will concentrate on the types of fallacies that derive from poorly used language.

Language plays an important role in the way arguments are perceived and interpreted. Most fallacies of language use are intentional and occur when arguers equivocate, use amphiboly, or use emotive language to get their claims accepted by deliberately trying to evade issues and avoid presenting solid evidence and reasoning in favor of what they advocate. How they succeed in these efforts will become clear as we examine the various strategies employed in arguers' fallacious use of language.

Equivocation

Many words have more than one meaning, and occasionally arguers may exploit the ambiguity in language to make a fallacious claim. One way to do this is through equivocation. *The fallacy of equivocation exploits the fact that a word has more than one meaning so as to lead to a false conclusion.* For example, someone might say, "You shouldn't take that course in reasoning that is supposed to improve your ability to argue; you argue too much with your friends now!" Here the meaning of the term "argue" has shifted from "reasoning and correctly supporting claims" to "engaging in interpersonal squabbles." The arguer has made a false causal connection between the two based on the ambiguity of the meaning of the term "argue."

Equivocation is often used in deceptive advertising. For example, an advertisement that appeared in several national publications proclaimed that "Parents can receive a FREE college education" for their children. On its face, the bold letters across the top of the ad made a fairly spectacular promise that the average person might have a difficult time ignoring. For most people, the word "free" means without charge, cost, or obligation. But the word "free" means something very different to the producers of the ad. To them, "free" meant that parents needed to invest a substantial sum of money in their "tax-free open-end mutual funds and unit trusts" and pay for a variety of administrative "charges and expenses." The point was that if enough money was invested, then the interest produced should be sufficient to send a child to college. But placing money into a long-term investment is not "free" because there is an opportunity cost to having the money committed and there are administrative and other charges that are not "free." Words mean different things to different people and when word choice misdirects the audience's understanding of the argument, then an equivocation has taken place.

The question the recipient needs to ask is whether the argument contains any language that might be misconstrued by the arguer. If the answer is yes, then the recipient should ascertain what the words are intended to mean so that both recipient and arguer share a common understanding of the argument.

Amphiboly

Equivocation exploits ambiguities in word meanings, but *amphiboly exploits ambiguity in grammatical structure to lead to a false or questionable conclusion.* Just as there are many types of grammatical structure, there are many forms of amphiboly. For example, an advertisement might claim:

> New, improved product X is unquestionably more effective.
>
> Our product is new and improved.

More effective than what? New and improved compared to what? Here we have comparative adjectives used but no object provided for comparison. Perhaps product X is being compared with the "original" product, or perhaps with other brands of the product. We don't know.

Here is another example. An arguer claims that "When we compare the danger of spreading AIDS with the incursion of privacy involved in widespread AIDS testing, we must conclude that it is a risk we have to take." Is the antecedent of "it" the spread of AIDS or the incursion of privacy? Until we know what the arguer is referring to, the meaning of the claim is unclear.

An excellent example of the exploitation of amphiboly appeared in an article on the writing of recommendation letters. The article was in response to a number of defamation suits that had been filed against people who wrote unfavorable letters of recommendation. Faced with the problem of writing an honest letter without subjecting themselves to lawsuits, many letter-writers are puzzled about what to do. Robert J. Thornton, in his Lexicon of Inconspicuously Ambiguous Recommendations (LIAR, for short) recommends the circumspect use of amphiboly. Here are two examples:

> To describe a candidate who is woefully inept: "I most enthusiastically recommend this candidate with no qualifications whatsoever."

> To describe a candidate who is so unproductive that the position would be better left unfilled: "I can assure you that no person would be better for this job."[31]

Because of the ambiguity in the way the sentences are constructed, the reader of the first sentence assumes that the recommendation is unqualified (when it is actually the *candidate* who is unqualified). The reader of the second sentence may interpret it to mean that the candidate is the best alternative (when hiring *no one* would be the best alternative). Such examples remind us to be on the lookout for intentional and manipulative ambiguity. If we are confused about what the arguer meant by the wording of a claim, there may be a good reason for our confusion!

Emotive Language

The language used to express thoughts and ideas often is a potent force in influencing our opinions and actions. As one philosopher of argument observed, "An emotional appeal to us for some specific action may be so powerful as to inhibit our capacity to exercise critical judgment on the reasons offered in favor of the action urged."[32] *The fallacy of emotive language manipulates the connotative meaning of words to establish a claim without proof.* It attempts to persuade an audience by getting them to respond emotionally to images and associations evoked by the language used rather than by judging the quality of the arguer's evidence and reasoning.

Emotive language is often used by politicians, advertisers, and propagandists to get acceptance for ideas that cannot be effectively supported through reasoning and evidence. The idea behind the fallacy of emotive language is to set up associations in the audience's mind with either pleasant or favorable values and attitudes (in order to win acceptance for an idea) or with unpleasant experiences or disfavored values (to get an idea rejected). Language is therefore used suggestively and can have an unconscious influence.

President Harry Truman can serve as an interesting example. In 1962, a historian, Herbert Feis, contacted Truman with several questions about Truman's decision to use the atomic bomb on Hiroshima and Nagasaki during World War II. Truman had been the subject of much criticism on his decision and he responded with an emotionally laden letter that he never sent:

> My dear Mr. Feis:
>
> You write just like the usual egghead. The facts are before you but you'd like to garble them. The instruction of July 25th, 1945 was final. It was made by the Commander in Chief after Japan refused to surrender.
>
> Churchill, Stimson, Patterson, Eisenhower and all the rest agreed that it had to be done. It was. It ended the . . . War. That was the objective. Now if you can think of any other "if, as, and when" egghead contemplations, bring them out. . . .

> It is a great thing that you or any other contemplator "after the fact" didn't have to make the decision.
>
> Our boys would all be dead.[33]

While Truman's response may be understandable, it does not address the criticisms posed by others, nor did it address Feis's request for information about the decision on whether to use the bomb to end the war. Instead, Truman used several emotionally charged words to place the researcher on the defensive. Terms such as "egghead," "contemplator 'after the fact,'" and "dead" all help charge the letter.

Advertisements for many "self-improvement" cosmetics and health products often use emotive language to appeal to the prospective buyer's desire for a sudden and dramatic improvement in personal appearance. An advertisement for tan accelerator claims that

> Once in a generation there's a breakthrough so revolutionary it can change forever the way people tan.

Terms such as "breakthrough" and "revolutionary" are intended to convince consumers that the product's effects must be singular and a striking advance over other tanning methods. Or, consider this claim from a weight-loss ad:

> After years of research and testing, a scientist from Princeton University has finally developed a *miracle* weight loss formula which has clearly proven to be the *strongest fat-burning compound in the entire world!* [This product] is so *radically powerful* that it can actually make the *slim and shapely* figure of your *dreams a reality*. [Emphasis added]

Readers who are seeking a "radically powerful" "miracle" formula to make them "slim and shapely" may be persuaded by the emotive language of this advertisement. But the "Princeton scientist" is not identified, nor is the method used in the supposed study explained. Educated recipients of arguments should be skeptical of product claims that promise "revolutionary breakthroughs" and "miraculous results." Language such as this is often substituted for hard evidence and valid reasoning in order to make arguments and claims persuasive.

SUMMARY

Language should not be used unconsciously or without concern; rather speakers should deliberately adapt language to their audience. Arguers, in particular, can enhance or inhibit their effectiveness through the uses they make of language. The purpose of this chapter was to enable arguers to understand, use, and criticize language as used in argument.

Language is the systematic coordination of grammar and vocabulary used to convey meaning. Although it is often thought of as a tool we use, language is also a tool that influences us and others. Words have meanings through the use and interpretations people make of them, but people's perceptions and experiences are also profoundly influenced by language itself. Since words and what they refer to are connected only by way of the thoughts of language users, there is room for misunderstanding in communication. By controlling the way they use language, arguers can prevent misunderstanding and enhance their own effectiveness in communication.

Words used to refer to objects or experiences have certain characteristics that influence their use in language. They are abstract (having general reference to broad classes of objects) or concrete (referring to specific or particular objects or experiences). They are also used denotatively as symbols with objective, generally agreed-upon meanings, or connotatively as symbols with subjective or emotive meaning for each individual. People manipulate words by replacing negative connotations with positive ones. These result in euphemisms such as "daytime drama" for soap operas, "projects" for slums, and "correctional facility" for prison.

In the 1950s anthropologists Edward Sapir and Benjamin Whorf proposed the theory that our system of language contributes greatly to how we think about and experience our social world and our physical reality. This can be demonstrated by such examples as George Orwell's *1984* in which a totalitarian government exercises thought control over its people by systematically altering the language they speak.

The way language is used in argument is influenced by the six functions of language when it is used. Language is used emotively to express the feelings, attitudes, and emotions of people. Sometimes this results in fallacious argument when arguers intend to mislead recipients, or when recipients are unduly influenced by connotative language and the arguer's conviction rather than the facts of the matter under discussion. The phatic function of language, which is used socially to reinforce relationships between parties, seldom plays a role in argumentation. Used cognitively, language informs people about matters on which they are uninformed. It plays an argumentative role if providing the information alarms people and changes their attitude toward a problem or condition. Language used rhetorically is expressly intended to direct or influence thoughts and behaviors and plays a major role in argument. Language used metalingually comments on the role of language itself and has an argumentative function when language is used to get a claim accepted or rejected. The poetic function of language emphasizes the structure or artistry of a message rather than its content, and plays a role in argument when the form of expression is used to hold recipients' attention and influence them to accept a claim. In any given argument, language may function in multiple ways simultaneously to enhance communication of the argument to the audience.

Understanding how language functions can assist arguers in getting their arguments understood, remembered, and adhered to by recipients. Four guidelines for using language can assist in this process. First, arguers should be clear. They should employ language that is sufficiently concrete to keep their messages interesting. They should also speak or write simply, avoiding convoluted or ambiguous language. Second, arguers should define any terms that their recipients might misunderstand. This is particularly true when the terms have an important role in the argument and the arguers' usage of the terms departs from ordinary usage. Third, arguers should express their arguments vividly. Using active rather than passive voice, personalized constructions, and nonformal language along with colorful terms and metaphor will engage recipients and cause them to be more likely to accept an arguer's claim. Fourth, arguers should avoid sexist or racist language. Although few arguers intentionally try to offend recipients, many do so inadvertently by expressing their ideas in ways that set women and minorities apart as having less status in society than men and Caucasians. Concerted efforts to eliminate discriminatory forms of reference and ways of speaking will ensure that no recipients are inadvertently alienated by the way an argument is expressed.

Fallacies occur when mistakes are made in the construction of an argument. Arguers may commit fallacies intentionally or inadvertently. In either case, it is important to recognize where and when fallacies occur because they can be very persuasive and yet not reasonable or rational. Too often recipients respond to the claims being made and not to the underlying support.

This chapter identified three types of fallacies related to the use of language: equivocation, amphiboly, and emotive language. Equivocation occurs whenever an arguer obscures the meaning of an argument by exploiting the fact that a word has more than one meaning. In such cases the arguer may be saying one thing while the audience—reacting to a different meaning—may be persuaded to do something else. Amphibolies are fallacies similar to equivocation. With amphibolies, arguers exploit ambiguities in a language's grammar to lead recipients to an erroneous conclusion. Finally, emotive language is the use of highly emotionally charged words that arguers use to cause a reaction in a recipient such that the recipient avoids any critical analysis of the argument. Fallacies of language have the potential to obscure the true meanings and implications of an argument and both argument producers and consumers should understand how they work.

EXERCISES

✱ *Exercise 1* In this chapter, we discussed Lincoln's Gettysburg Address. Following is a complete version of the speech. Read the speech and locate every use of language made by Lincoln. Next to each example, place

EM	for emotive function of language
PH	for phatic function of language
CO	for cognitive function of language
RH	for rhetorical function of language
ME	for metalingual language
PO	for poetic function of language

You may want to color-code each type of language using a felt marker for ease of identification. Once you have completed this task, tally each type of language used by Lincoln in the following space:

Language	Number of Times Used
Emotive	
Phatic	
Cognitive	
Rhetorical	
Metalingual	
Poetic	

What types of language were used most frequently? Least frequently? Why do you think Lincoln chose to use these types of language? Do they help or hurt the speech? How?

The Gettysburg Address

Four score and seven years ago our fathers brought forth on this continent a new nation, conceived in liberty, and dedicated to the proposition that all men are created equal.

Now we are engaged in a great civil war, testing whether that nation, or any nation so conceived and so dedicated, can long endure. We are met on a great battlefield of that war. We have come to dedicate a portion of that field, as a final resting place for those who here gave their lives, that that nation might live. It is altogether fitting and proper that we should do this.

But, in a larger sense, we cannot dedicate—we cannot consecrate—we cannot hallow—this ground. The brave men, living and dead, who struggled here have consecrated it, far above our poor power to add or detract. The world will little note, nor long remember what we say here, but it can never forget what they did here. It is for us the living, rather, to be dedicated here to the unfinished work which they who fought here have thus far so nobly advanced. It is rather for us to be here dedicated to the great task remaining before us—that from these honored dead we take increased devotion to that cause for which they gave the last full measure of devotion—that we here highly resolve that these dead shall not have died in vain—that this nation, under God, shall have a new birth of freedom—and that government of the people, by the people, for the people, shall not perish from the earth.

CHAPTER FIVE   Language and Argument   **119**

Exercise 2   Originally, S. I. Hayakawa proposed an abstraction ladder with Bessie the Cow as the most concrete symbol on the ladder. In the following space, draw an abstraction ladder that has you as the most concrete symbol.

Most Abstract
10.
 9.
 8.
 7.
 6.
 5.
 4.
 3.
 2.
 1.

Most Concrete

If you were introducing yourself to someone you had never met before, at what level would you begin?

Exercise 3   Each of the following words has a denotative and connotative meaning. Next to each word write the first definition that comes to mind and then look the word up. Is there a large difference? Why? Do you think your peers' answers would be closer to the connotative definitions you generated or the denotative definitions you looked up? Test it on five friends. What did your test show?

	Connotative	Denotative
school teacher		
Buick		
boss		
turkey		
sex		
trip		
work		
career		
education		
car		
emotional		

Exercise 4 The question of whether English should be the "official" language of the United States has been the subject of much debate. Read the following case study and consider the following questions:

- What functions of language are apparent in this argument?
- Based on what you know about how language affects our thoughts and perceptions, what would be the effects of making English our "official" language?
- Do you think that Bill Emerson used language effectively in his argument?
- Should the United States have an "official" language?

"English is Our Common Thread"

Mr. Speaker, many times before I have taken to the floor to speak about the importance of the English language. For decades, English has been the de facto language of the United States. In recent years, 19 States have designated English as their official language. Support for these efforts has been overwhelming. I strongly believe that English should be the official language of the United States Government. I have been a persistent sponsor of such legislation, and I will again today introduce the Language of Government Act.

At the same time, however, I want to recognize the important contributions of other languages through a sense-of-the-Congress resolution. In an increasingly global world, foreign languages are key to international communication. I strongly encourage those who already speak English to learn foreign languages.

As a nation of immigrants, America is comprised of people of all races, nationalities, and languages. These differences make our Nation the wonderful place it is. While being different, all of these people can find a common means of communication in the English language. English is the common thread that connects every citizen in our great Nation.

Hon. Bill Emerson, House of Representatives, *Congressional Record* (January 4, 1995): E13.

"English Language Tax Credit"

Mr. Speaker, I rise today to introduce an important piece of legislation that I believe to be an integral part of the official English movement. As you may know, I am the author of H.R. 123, the Language of Government Act which seeks to make English the official language of the United States Government. This legislation is the perfect complement to the Language of Government Act. It recognizes the need for a highly skilled labor force and provides a tax credit to employers for the cost of providing English language instruction to their limited-English-proficient employees.

Many Americans lack the language skills and literacy necessary to take full advantage of roles as responsible citizens and productive workers. While many employers acknowledge the need to educate their workers and have demonstrated an interest in establishing on-site training programs for their employees, the high cost of doing so often prevents them from taking any concrete action. This legislation will provide them with an incentive to offer this crucial instruction to their employees and make the workplace a friendlier, and less daunting environment for non-English-proficient employees.

Hon. Bill Emerson, House of Representatives, *Congressional Record* (January 4, 1995): E24.

"The Language of Government"

Mr. Speaker, today I am pleased to introduce once again the "Language of Government Act." America is a nation of immigrants. As President Franklin Delano Roosevelt once said, "All of our people all over this country—except the pure-blooded Indians—are immigrants or descendants of immigrants, including those who came over here on the Mayflower."

Indeed, we are a diverse lot. We are a country of many peoples, each with an individual cultural heritage and tradition. It is not often that people of so many varying cultures and backgrounds can live together in harmony, for human nature often leads us to resist and fear those who are different from us. Yet despite our differences, we do have a common bond. We have a common tongue, the English language, that connects us to one another and creates our national identity. It is this unity in diversity that defines us as uniquely American.

The time is right for passage of this important, unifying legislation. H.R. 123 offers a balanced, sensible approach to the common language issue. This legislation states that the government has an affirmative obligation to promote the English language, elevating that goal to official capacity. At the same time, the bill seeks to set some common sense parameters on the number and type of government services that will be offered in a language other than English. We do not need nor should we want a full scale multilingual government. But, if we do not address this issue in a forward-thinking, proactive manner, that is just what we would allow to develop.

I want to stress that the "Language Of Government Act" is not "English only." It simply states that English is the language in which all official United States Government business will be conducted. We have an obligation to ensure that non-English speaking citizens get the chance to learn English so they can prosper—and fully partake of all the economic, social, and political opportunities that exist in this great country of ours.

The late Senator Hayakawa, founder of this movement, was a prolific writer and I offer you one of my favorite quotes of his:

> America is an open society—more open than any other in the world. People of every race, of every color, of every culture are welcomed here to create a new life for themselves and their families. And what do these people who enter into the American mainstream have in common? English, our shared, common language,

As Americans, we should not remain strangers to each other, but must use our common language to develop a fundamental and open means of communication and to break down artificial language barriers. By preserving the bond of a unifying language in government, this nation of immigrants can become a stronger and more unified country.

Hon. Bill Emerson, House of Representatives, *Congressional Record* (January 4, 1995): E35.

NOTES

1. Abraham Lincoln, "Gettysburg Address," as cited in Philip B. Kunhardt, Jr., *A New Birth of Freedom* (Boston: Little, Brown and Co., 1983), 240.
2. Harold Zyskind, "A Rhetorical Analysis of the Gettysburg Address," *Journal of General Education* 4 (1950): 202–12. For other analyses of the rhetorical effects of this speech, see Ronald F. Reid, "Newspaper Response to the Gettysburg Address," *Quarterly Journal of Speech* 53 (1967): 50–60; and Barbara Warnick, "A Ricoeurian Approach to Rhetorical Criticism," *Western Journal of Speech Communication* 51 (1987): 227–44.
3. Gilbert Highet, "The Gettysburg Address," in *Readings in Speech*, 2d ed., Haig A. Bosmajian, ed. (New York: Harper, 1971), 227.
4. George Orwell, "Politics and the English Language," in *Collected Essays* (London: Mercury Books, 1961), 357.
5. Howard Kahane, *Logic and Contemporary Rhetoric: The Use of Reason in Everyday Life,* 4th ed. (Belmont, Calif.: Wadsworth, 1984), 158.
6. Orwell, 357.
7. Michael Calvin McGee, "The 'Ideograph': A Link between Rhetoric and Ideology," *Quarterly Journal of Speech* 66 (1980): 1–16.

8. McGee, 7.
9. C. K. Ogden and I. A. Richards, *The Meaning of Meaning* (London: Kegan, Paul Trench, Trubner, 1923).
10. S. I. Hayakawa, *Language in Thought and Action* (New York: Harcourt, Brace, 1964), 180.
11. *Webster's New Collegiate Dictionary,* s.v. "fag."
12. Benjamin L. Whorf, *Language, Thought, and Reality* (New York: John Wiley & Sons, 1956).
13. Whorf, 134.
14. Kenneth Burke, "Terministic Screens," in *Language as Symbolic Action* (Berkeley: University of California Press, 1966), 44–57.
15. George Orwell, *1984* (New York: Signet, 1977), 45–7.
16. Cliff Kincaid, "Playboy Hugh Hefner's Politics of Hedonism," *Conservative Digest* (August 1986): 16.
17. Naomi Wolf, *The Beauty Myth: How Images of Beauty Are Used Against Women* (New York: Doubleday, 1991).
18. Mike Maharry, "Selling," *The News Tribune* (October 1, 1995): E4.
19. Adapted from American Academy of Child and Adolescent Psychiatry, "Teen Suicide." *www.cmhcsys.com/factsfam/suicide.htm* (Mental Health Net & CMHC Systems, 1997); Sharon Caron, "Suicide Prevention," www.commnet.edu/qvctc/classes/conflict/suicd.html, 1997; "Warning Signs of Suicide, *USA Today,* September 19, 1986: 10A.)
20. Growth House, Inc., *www.growthhouse.org/suicide.html,* 1997.
21. Highet, 227.
22. Kunhardt, 241.
23. Orwell, "Politics," 366–7.
24. Jack Kemp, "Why Abortion Is a Human Rights Issue," *Conservative Digest* (August 1986): 40.
25. Chaim Perelman and Lucie Olbrechts-Tyteca, *The New Rhetoric: A Treatise on Argumentation,* trans. John Wilkinson and Purcell Weaver (Notre Dame, Ind.: University of Notre Dame Press, 1969), 116.
26. Vilfredo Pareto, *The Mind and Society* (New York: Harcourt, Brace, 1935), II, 1135, as cited in Perelman and Olbrechts-Tyteca, 116.
27. A wonderful little guide to making one's style more vivid is W. Strunk and E. B. White, *The Elements of Style,* 3d ed. (New York: Macmillan, 1979).
28. Haig A. Bosmajian, *The Language of Oppression* (Lanham, MD: University Press of America, 1983), 118.
29. An excellent guide to how to avoid sexist and racist language is the *Publication Manual of the American Psychological Association,* 4th ed. (Washington, D.C.: American Psychological Association, 1994), 50–60.
30. Stokely Carmichael, Address to students at Morgan State College, January 16, 1967, cited in Bosmajian, 45.
31. Robert J. Thornton, "Lexicon of Inconspicuously Ambiguous Recommendations," *Chronicle of Higher Education* (February 25, 1987): 42. Copyright 1987: *Chronicle of Higher Education.* Reprinted with permission of author.
32. Irving Copi, *Informal Logic* (New York: Macmillan, 1986), 114.
33. Monte M. Poen, ed., *Strictly Personal and Confidential: The Letters Harry Truman Never Mailed* (Boston: Little, Brown, and Company, 1982): 34.

SECTION THREE

Parsing Arguments

CHAPTER 6

Argument Claims and Propositions

CHAPTER OUTLINE
- The Nature of Claims and Propositions
- Formulating a Proposition
    - Controversiality
    - Clarity
    - Balance
    - Challenge
- Types of Claims
    - Factual Claims
    - Value Claims
    - Policy Claims
- Continuum of Claims
- Summary
- Exercises

KEY CONCEPTS

propositions
issues
controversiality
clarity
double-barreled
balance
challenge
burden of proof

presumption
factual claims
relational claim
predictive claim
claim of historical fact
value claims
values
policy claims

In all situations in which disputes arise and arguers argue, claims are made. As we said in Chapter 1, a claim is the end point of an argument: "an expressed opinion or conclusion that the arguer wants accepted." Usually, before an argument is made, the arguer has made a decision and is committed to a position that the arguer is prepared to support and defend. Being able to identify an arguer's claim and to distinguish it from the evidence and reasoning used to support it will enable you to analyze and criticize competently the arguments of others.

Knowing the characteristics of well-stated claims will enhance your ability to construct arguments yourself. This chapter will discuss the nature and characteristics of claims and propositions, suggest criteria that distinguish good claims and propositions from bad ones, and identify the various types of claims and propositions.

THE NATURE OF CLAIMS AND PROPOSITIONS

Whenever we argue, we use claims and propositions. Both serve an important function in argument because they help define and focus the direction of arguments. At this point, it is useful to make a clear distinction between claims and propositions. Argument claims, as they were defined in Chapter 1, are the end points of an argument. They are supported by reasoning and evidence and focus on a single issue or idea. When we argue, we may develop many different subarguments and each of those subarguments has a claim. Claims are relevant to the evidence and reasoning that serve to support them.

Beyond the claims of individual arguments, however, lie propositions. *Propositions are overarching or main claims that serve as the principal claim of an extended argument.* This means first that propositions are a type of claim. They are the primary point made by an arguer. Second, propositions focus the field of discussion. They define and limit the issues that are available to arguers in a dispute. For instance, if two advocates argue over the proposition that "The United States federal government should provide more financial aid for college students," the proposition includes some issues and excludes others. *Issues are the points of potential disagreement related to a proposition.* Propositions set the boundary of acceptable and reasonable issues about which we might argue. In other words, they create a propositional area that defines what issues are appropriate for the discussion. In the case of financial aid, several issues are apparent:

Is there enough financial aid currently?

Can the government afford more education money?

Are there sources of unused financial aid that could meet the need?

Should this be addressed by private sources of funding instead of government?

Do students forgo their education because they cannot afford it?

Should government support public and private education?

Just as these issues might be included in a conversation about financial aid, this proposition also excludes other issues. For example, issues about space flight, the right to die, and health care have nothing to do with the area created by the proposition. Advocates, therefore, could not appropriately develop arguments that focus on issues beyond the scope of the proposition because such arguments would not be relevant.

Because propositions represent collections of issues, they indicate relevant arguments that both support and deny the proposition. If, for example, an advocate argued that American college students do not receive sufficient financial aid, an opponent could appropriately argue that there are millions of dollars of unclaimed scholarships each year and that additional aid is unnecessary.

Propositions are supported by collections of individual arguments that are developed from the issues within the propositional area. These individual arguments are all related in some way to the proposition and may either support or deny it. Propositions thus provide the framework for individual arguments in a question. See Figure 6–1. In this figure, all the potential and relevant issues for discussion are contained within the field. These include A, B, C, D, E, F, G, and H. In the financial aid example, such issues might include who can afford school, how much aid is available, how much more is needed, what an appropriate amount of aid is for a given student, and what criteria we should use to determine who receives aid and who does not.

Irrelevant issues are excluded by the proposition's boundary. In the figure, these issues are represented as I, J, K, L, and M. Examples of irrelevant issues might be whether students should work instead of attending college, whether universal military service would be beneficial, or whether conservation is a means of saving our resources. These issues do not address the central question advanced in the proposition. It is important for advocates to be clear as to what issues fall within the propositional area and are therefore relevant and what issues fall outside the proposition and are therefore irrelevant.

However, just because the proposition contains issues does not mean that an advocate constructing an extended argument has to address them all. Arguers select from the available issues and construct extended argument cases supporting or denying the proposition. Some issues may never be addressed. The choice rests with the advocate who decides what is appropriate for a given audience and situation.

Often, claims and propositions are stated explicitly; but not always. Occasionally, someone will ask the arguer, "What point are you getting at?" because the claims are

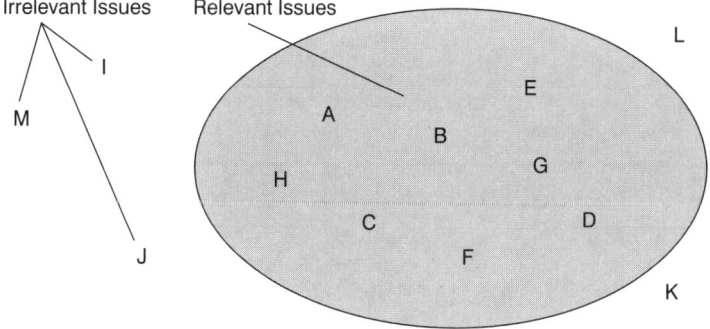

FIGURE 6–1 The propositional area includes relevant issues and excludes irrelevant ones.

implicit or unclear. Arguers who want to be understood should respond by clearly and explicitly stating their claim or proposition. Consider the following example:

Lisa: You know the Webers are coming over tonight?

Nigel: Of course I know! Why do you think I got out the grill and cleaned it?

Lisa: It's too bad Perry's gone this week.

Nigel: Why? I'm enjoying the peace and quiet.

Lisa: Yes, but I miss having him around to do certain chores.

Nigel: Like what, for instance?

Lisa: Like mowing the lawn, for instance.

Nigel: Oh, you want me to mow the lawn, is that it?

Lisa wanted Nigel to mow the lawn for two reasons: They had guests coming over for a cookout, and the regular lawn mower was out of town. But her statements made no sense to Nigel until he discovered that her claim was "I think you should mow the lawn."[1]

In essays, speeches, and other forms of one-way communication, claims are usually stated at the beginning or at the end of the argument. This placement occurs because arguers like to either state their position and then support it or to present evidence or reasoning followed by a conclusion. Where are the claims in the following paragraphs?

Dogs can teach us a lot about gift-giving and generosity. They can also teach us about our most basic experiences of grace and mutual responsibility. Gilda Radner once observed that "I think that dogs are the most amazing creatures; they give unconditional love. For me they are the role model for being alive." In fact, dogs are a part of an "anti-economy." They give without requiring payment. The care without stipulation or reservation. These characteristics of dogs led Agnes Repplier to comment: "Our dogs will love and admire the meanest of us, and feed our colossal vanity with their uncritical homage." If all people modeled their behavior after dogs, we would live in a much happier world.[2]

The labels we use affect how others perceive us and how we see ourselves; they shape how we see others and how we want to be seen by them; they are used by those in power to define the rest even as they struggle to define themselves. They shape who we are.[3]

The beginning sentence in the first paragraph put forward the claim that the remainder of the paragraph supported, and the final sentence in the second paragraph did the same. Someone wanting to identify the central claim in a paragraph can also watch for terms like "therefore," "then," and "so" that show the conclusion is coming.[4]

On the other hand, informally developed arguments—such as arguments developed among friends in a conversation—may not have clearly placed claims. This is because claims often emerge and develop as we argue. We tend not to begin discussions with a claim and proceed in a rationally considered development of the claim.

Propositions often emerge and are formulated over time. Initially, they are tentatively stated and then honed and refined as participants become knowledgeable about vital issues in a dispute. For example, prosecutors study the particulars of a case before bringing charges; legislators study and revise bills before they are introduced; doctors study a patient's symptoms before issuing a diagnosis; and most of us think and read about social and political problems before we venture to express opinions about them.

Long essays, speeches, extended discussions, and lengthy conversations in which efforts to argue and influence are taking place, frequently contain a network of related claims that are combined to support a proposition. Figure 6–2 is an illustration of this.

Figure 6–2 displays a network of claims supporting the proposition "lack of a clear policy for treating patients in irreversible comas is a problem in our society."[5] The proposition is supported by a hierarchy of subsidiary claims—principle subclaims, secondary subclaims, and sub-subclaims. The principal subclaims state four major problem areas—lack of a definition of "death," rapid technological advancement, physical liability, and inconsistent procedures for decision-making. Each of these four principle subclaims is in turn supported by clusters of secondary subclaims and sub-subclaims. Taken together, the subclaims form an argument chain that reaches from the level of dispute to the proposition. The further the proposition is away from the level of dispute, the more layers of subclaims are necessary to prove the proposition.

Some propositions are relatively close to the level of dispute and can be proven with very short and simple lines of argument. A claim such as "Leif Ericson was the first to discover the New World" would probably not require as many levels of claims because of its factual nature. The more complex and controversial a proposition, the longer the chain of arguments required to support the proposition.

In extended arguments such as the one illustrated in Figure 6–2, argument claims begin with assumptions or factual statements (in columns 1 and 2) that function as evidence because they are accepted by all parties to the discussion. They therefore fall below the level of dispute and act as starting points linked together through reasoning and evidence to support further claims. The network of claims as a whole in turn supports a main claim or proposition that possesses certain characteristics arising from its role as a central thesis. Because the proposition functions as it does within the context of an extended argument, it can be identified only within that context.

Depending on the field in which they occur, extended arguments supporting a main claim or proposition appear in many forms. In journalistic circles, they may appear as editorials; in criminal law, as cases constructed by the prosecution or defense; in business, as recommendations to management; in religious settings, as sermons and theological discussions; and in academic research as articles in scholarly journals.

The field of argument determines the form of proposition for an extended argument. In a parliamentary setting, propositions may appear as motions ("I move that we abolish the university's core curriculum in general education."). In argumentative discussions, they may be expressed as an opinion ("MTV is a menace to the morality of today's youth."). In legal cases, they appear as indictments ("The state charges John Smith with reckless driving."). In medicine, they take the form of diagnosis and recommended treatment ("The patient appears to have a uterine fibroid tumor; surgery to remove it is recommended.").

Failure to identify a proposition can cause an extended argument to become confused and unprofitable. Russel R. Windes and Arthur Hastings provided an excellent

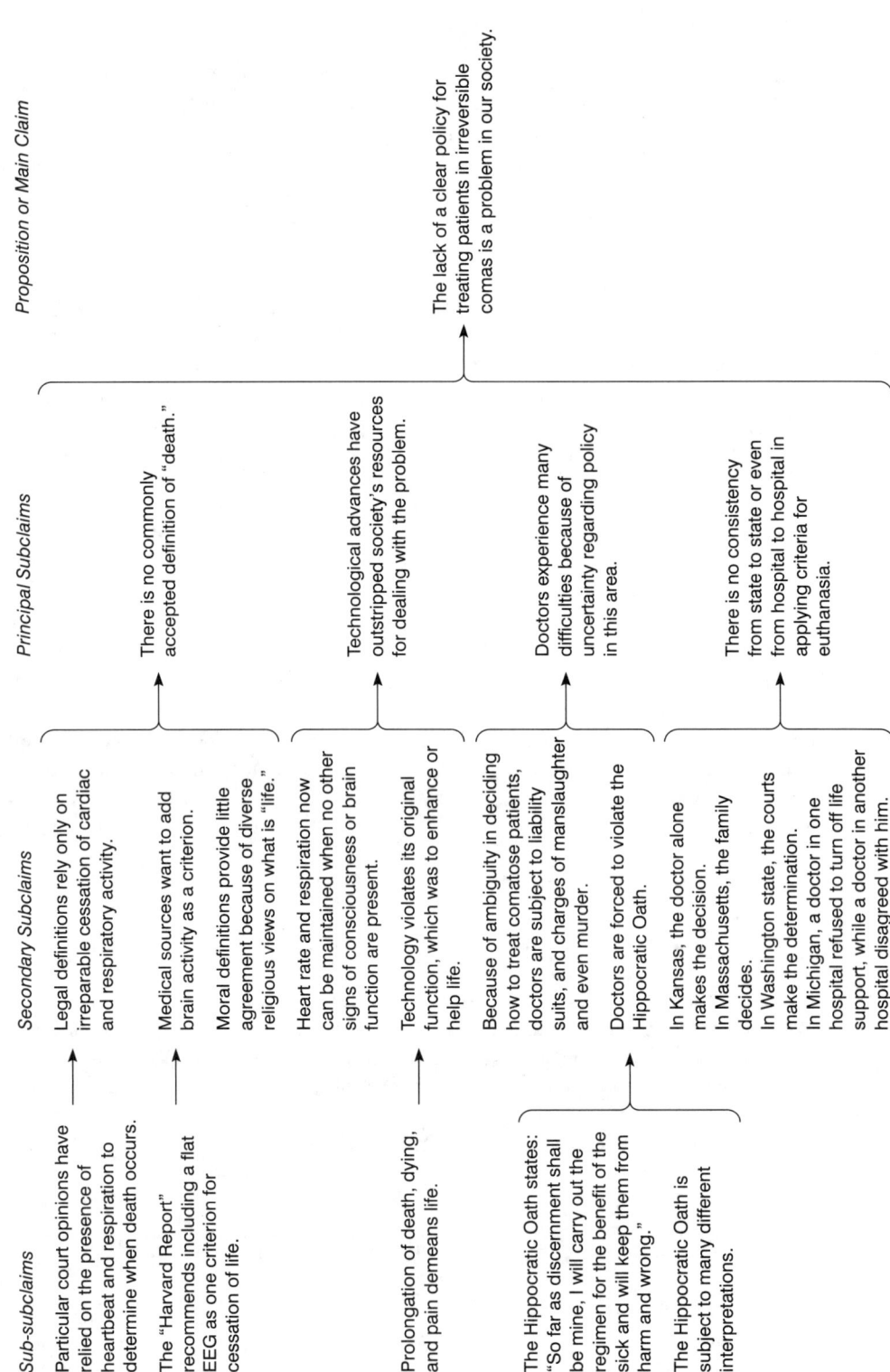

FIGURE 6–2 In a network of related claims, sub-subclaims support secondary subclaims, which support principal subclaims, which support the proposition or main claim.

historical example of a public argument that became muddled because no central thesis was identified. Referring to criticisms of public education that were made in the 1950s and 1960s, Windes and Hastings wrote:

> Rightist groups have launched what amounts to a concealed and nationwide attack on public education. Their general proposition is difficult for the observer to state and seemingly impossible for them to state themselves. But it is probably similar to the following: Contemporary public education is failing to preserve the "American way of life." . . . Unfortunately . . . rather than debating the real issues in education—financing, teacher training, and curriculum—these advocates have concerned themselves with pseudo-propositions. . . . In public meetings, rightist advocates deliberate over the censorship of textbooks, the indoctrination of students, what is to be done about teachers and administrators who are "soft on subversives," and how to make schools more patriotic.[6]

Because the advocates in this example had not formulated a coherent statement of what they proposed and because the public and school administrators were unsure of exactly what it was they wanted, they had difficulty accomplishing anything concrete.

In this case, then, there was controversy but no specifically stated proposition. Since a proposition provides the focal point for issues in a dispute, the absence of a clearly formulated statement of the main claim to be argued is problematic. In some situations in which you will argue, the proposition will be formulated by another party to the dispute or by some agent authorized to state it in advance. At other times, however, you yourself will be able to state the proposition to be supported. Such an opportunity might arise in interpersonal argument when no one has clearly formulated the central question to be discussed. You may also need to formulate a proposition for an essay or speech you plan to make. The next section, therefore, discusses the criteria for clear, precise propositions.

FORMULATING A PROPOSITION

People who engage in argument expect certain things to happen. Their expectations grow out of the conventions or implicit "rules" for conducting arguments that influence argumentative discussions in our society.[7] Because people expect that arguments are made for specific purposes and are directed toward specific goals, arguers need to formulate their propositions and statements of opinion to meet others' expectations. This section will consider the basic requirements for expressing well-developed propositions and claims. Claims and propositions need to be both controversial and clear. In addition, propositions need to be balanced and challenging.

Controversiality

All claims and propositions should be controversial. *If a claim or proposition is controversial, it states a position that is not currently accepted or adhered to by the audience.* As we noted in Chapter 1, argumentative theses are concerned with matters that are controversial. After all, if the parties to an argument already agree to the claim, what need is there to argue? In fact, claims that are not controversial probably serve the function of evidence. People do not argue about things such as whether the earth is round or whether murder is wrong. Instead, we use our understanding of these accepted claims as evidence to ground other claims. In deciding upon a topic or a thesis to defend, the advocate should select something that will be important and controversial to an audience. For example, if you addressed students in the United States and decided to defend the proposition, "Education is beneficial to society," or to argue that "Freedom is important in a democracy," you might be met with ambivalence or disinterest from your readers or listeners. They might wonder why you felt such a thesis needed to be defended since everyone already agreed with it.

Sometimes the controversy is not apparent to argument recipients. They may be unaware of the controversy, or the issues may be so complex or incomprehensible as to make it difficult for the audience to understand the controversy. Often this is the case with scientific discoveries. Articles published in scientific journals may be controversial and interesting but if the recipients do not have the expertise, education, or background to interpret the argument, they may not perceive or understand the nature of the controversy.

When issues require the recipients to have specialized knowledge or background, the arguer has two responsibilities. First, the arguer should provide the recipients with sufficient information about issues to make them aware of the controversy. And second, the arguer should provide sufficient depth to the issues to develop the recipients' capabilities to make reasoned judgments about the arguers. For example, if the arguer were going to discuss means for resolving conflicts in the Middle East, the arguer would have to provide the recipients with sufficient history and cultural knowledge to be able to make a reasonable interpretation of the arguments.

The arguer must explain the necessary background and assumptions to the recipients for the audience to understand the basis of the argument and its controversiality. The recipients should be aware and understand the focus of the argument. The responsibility of the arguer is to provide the recipients with sufficient background and information to make them aware of the controversy and have sufficient depth of information to make reasoned judgments about the argument.

In deciding on a proposition for discussion or debate, it is wise to canvass newspapers and other current periodicals. What is controversial and the subject of public attention at one time may be of little interest later on because the matter has been settled or because other issues seem more pressing. The questions of what was to be done about the polio epidemic or of whether we should have a national draft were very controversial at one time. But a vaccine was found for polio and the all-volunteer army seems to be working well at present. The controversiality of a proposition may depend on what issues are timely and of significant public interest.

Clarity

When people engage in argument, they expect to know what the goal of the argument is and how they will know when the dispute is resolved. As we observed in the last section of this chapter, ambiguous, unclear, muddled claims and propositions generally lead to muddled argumentation. *Clarity refers to how well a claim focuses arguments on a particular set of issues.* People need to know where they are starting in order to decide when they have finished. If, through ambiguous wording, the claim allows multiple interpretations or fosters misunderstanding, then it is not clear. Consider Figure 6–3. If a

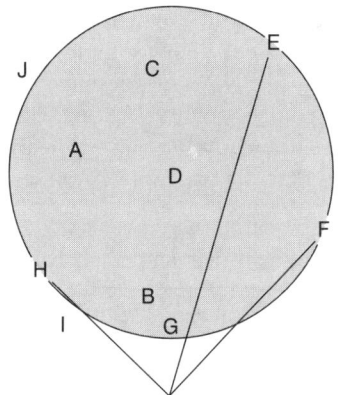

Issues that are not clearly included or excluded

FIGURE 6–3 Ambiguously Worded Claims

proposition is stated clearly, the relevant issues included in the propositional area are focused; it is clear which issues are relevant to the proposition and which are not. But if a proposition is ambiguous, the relevant issues are less apparent and arguers may find themselves discussing extraneous matters or tangential issues.

One major source of confusion in stating propositions is the use of ambiguous terms that are interpreted one way by one party to the dispute and another way by the other. Since each party is interpreting the proposition differently, each arguer has a different starting point and is probably going in a direction unanticipated by the other. For example, consider a dispute between two professors discussing the merits of nongraded credit options for students. Both are unaware that there are actually *two* such options at their university. One option (Credit/No credit) is offered on a classwide basis. (All students take the class on a Credit/No credit basis.) The second option is Satisfactory/Nonsatisfactory, which can be elected by individual students in courses where other students take the course for a grade. Professor Jones, who teaches a Credit/No credit course, is talking with Professor Smith.

Prof. S.: I think the pass/fail grading system is just a way of letting students goof off.

Prof. J.: That's not true! The students in my class work just as hard as they would for a grade!

Prof. S.: Oh, come on! They just use pass/fail grading to make life easier for themselves. It's the easy route to accumulating credits.

Prof. J.: That would only be true if students worked only for grades. Some are motivated more by the subject matter and the pleasure of learning.

Prof. S.: You surely are an idealist. Everyone knows that it's the concrete payoffs that allow students to get ahead that really motivate them.

Prof. J.: All I can speak from is my own experience.

This discussion is not going in a profitable direction, primarily because of the ambiguity of the phrase "pass/fail grading system." For example, if Professor Jones made it clear that he was speaking of the Credit/No credit designation that is mainly used for activity-based and performance courses (internships, readers' theatre, orchestra, etc.), his statements about motivation and the pleasure of learning might be more readily accepted by Professor Smith. Here are two more examples of ambiguous terms in propositions:

Euthanasia should be allowed when the patient and family consent to it.

Does "euthanasia" in this claim refer to removal of life support systems (passive euthanasia) or to administering drugs or other means to induce death (active euthanasia or "mercy killing")?

Grades are not an efficient means of determining a student's intelligence.

Does "determine" here mean "to obtain knowledge of" or "to bring about as a result"? Both are accepted dictionary definitions, yet they lend very different interpretations to the claim! Examples such as these show the desirability of using precise and exact terms when one states claims.

A second source of confusion and lack of clarity in stating claims is the "double-barreled" statement. *Double-barreled claims advance two or more claims simultaneously and, as with ambiguous terms, often lead arguers in separate directions because the relevant issues for each part of the claim are different.* Because double-barreled claims and propositions include issues from two or more propositional areas, arguers often find it difficult to focus on and define the area under dispute. If a proposition or claim has two different objectives, it is best divided by the arguer. Figure 6–4 illustrates the problems of double-barreled claims. In this diagram, the double-barreled claim encompasses issues that support one of the claims and not the other. The result is that an arguer is faced with confusion regarding which issues are relevant and which issues are not.

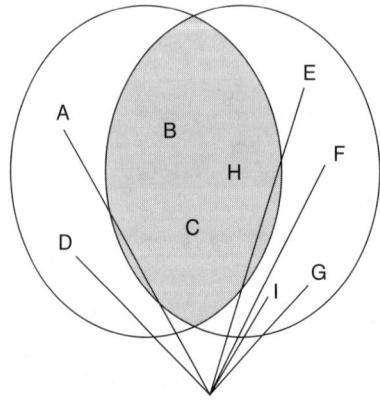

Issues that do not fit clearly within the proposition

FIGURE 6–4 Double-Barreled Claims

Confusion because of double-barreled claims has occurred in the example of the discussion between Professors Smith and Jones. Smith's claim really is that "opportunistic students exploit the pass/fail grading system." Consequently, Smith and Jones are actually discussing two issues simultaneously—whether nongraded options have an effect on student learning and performance and whether students are likely to take the "easy way out." If Smith had more clearly stated his claim and if Jones and Smith had agreed on what the main claim was to be, their discussion might have been less diffuse and more profitable. Here are two additional examples of double-barreled claims broken into two separate claims:

Double-barreled claim:	The U.S. federal government should cut the income tax rate to stimulate the economy.
Claim 1:	The U.S. federal government should cut the income tax rate.
Claim 2:	Cutting the income tax rate will stimulate the economy.
Double-barreled claim:	If corporations test employees for drugs, they should also test for alcohol, which is the biggest drug of all.
Claim 1:	Alcohol is the "biggest" (most frequently used) drug of all.
Claim 2:	Drug testing should be combined with alcohol testing by corporations that test for substance abuse.

The desirability of breaking double-barreled claims into separate claims is illustrated by the rules of parliamentary procedure. *Robert's Rules of Order* state that only one proposal or claim can be considered at a time. If someone proposes a motion with a dual idea, the motion should be divided into separate motions that can be debated separately.[8] Dividing related but separate ideas allows participants in a discussion to recognize their starting point and to know when they have reached their goal. Stating individual ideas separately enables arguers to recognize the points on which they agree and the points on which they disagree, thereby conforming to the conventions of argument and promoting productive, orderly discussions.

Balance

A productive, fair discussion of the issues in a dispute can result only when the topic of discussion is stated in a form with which both parties feel comfortable. Recipients can only be drawn into a discussion and persuaded by the evidence an arguer offers when they are convinced that the arguer has a balanced perspective on the topic. *Balance is the requirement that the issues for and against a proposition be included equally in the propositional field.* When the topic is specifically and clearly stated in neutral language, the field is left open for both its proponents and its opponents to discuss it freely. In fact, a neutral, dispassionate statement of the proposition is a convention in many forums of argument. In law, the charges brought against a defendant are stated neutrally and are agreed upon before the trial can begin (Ms. Jones committed libel against Ms. Davis; Mr. Smith is charged with driving while intoxicated.). In business management, decision makers usually discuss a specific policy or course of action that has been recommended (Should we acquire the Widget Company as a subsidiary of our operation?

Does the preliminary information we have on this product line indicate that it should be heavily promoted?).

When a proposition for discussion is stated in connotative or prejudicial language, however, the "deck is stacked" against the viewpoint that opposes the proposition because the issues available to the opposing arguers have been limited or tainted by the emotionally loaded language. Furthermore, speakers and writers who state their theses in ways that reveal personal biases cause their audiences to become suspicious. Consider, for example, the following propositions:

> The space race is the world's biggest money waster.
>
> Unprincipled recidivists should be put away for life.

Propositions such as these overstate one's case and close off rather than promote open discussion because extraneous language serves to limit the issues available to the arguers. Propositions that avoid connotative language, superlatives, and stereotypes encourage all parties to the dispute to consider all available options and decision proposals. The propositions given above could be rephrased so as to be more neutral. As a general rule of thumb, the wording of the proposition should be agreeable to all parties of a dispute.

> Funds invested in space exploration should be significantly reduced.
>
> Repeat offenders should receive life imprisonment.

Challenge

One of the characteristics of an argument that we discussed in Chapter 1 is that it is an attempt to influence someone else. *Challenge means that an arguer's claim confronts recipients' existing values, beliefs, or behaviors.* Generally, the arguer who initiates the dispute by stating the initial claim expresses dissatisfaction with a prevailing belief or state of affairs. The arguer tries to change the other's attitudes or behavior to something different from what the attitudes or behavior would be if no argumentation took place.

A proposition for argument or debate should, therefore, challenge what people already believe or do. This is more than the requirement of being controversial. Whereas controversy refers to how ready a recipient is to agree to or believe in a proposition or claim, challenge focuses on changing the recipient in some way. This convention is based on the principle that there is no reason to defend an already accepted practice or belief unless it is questioned or criticized. Richard Whately, a 19th-century educator and clergyman, described this convention and its implications for argument.[9] He observed that in most argumentation there was a *presumption* and a *burden of proof*. The presumption favors the position that, because it is already accepted, "preoccupies the ground" in a controversy until some challenge is made against it. The person initiating the dispute therefore has the burden of proof entailed in making such a challenge.

The metaphor of preoccupying ground that Whately uses is carried through in the associations we make when we hear the word "claim." A land claim is a claim to a parcel of land owned or possessed by someone else. The agency or the institution against which the claim is made enjoys no other advantage than the prerogative to retain the land if the claim is not upheld and accepted.

Therefore, the implication of Whately's concepts is that arguers who advance claims should challenge existing beliefs, policies, and states of affairs. Those who put forward proposals or advocate new ideas assume the *burden of proof, which obligates arguers to provide good and sufficient reasons for changing what is already accepted.* Those who defend existing beliefs and practices enjoy the *presumption that is the predisposition to favor an existing practice or belief until some good reason for changing it is offered.* The following claims do not challenge existing beliefs and practices and thus do not fulfill the burden of proof requirement:

> School desegregation is desirable.
>
> Washington State should continue to rely on sales and property taxes for revenue.
>
> The legal drinking age should be 21.

Propositions such as these do not advocate change, and if arguments supporting them were not made, the policies and conditions they advocate would continue anyway. The following propositions, on the other hand, assume a burden of proof for the person who defends them because they challenge beliefs and policies that are presently accepted.

> A nationwide system of magnet schools is desirable.
>
> Washington State should implement an income tax.
>
> The legal drinking age should be set at 15 nationwide.

Because they raise the possibility of innovations and new policies, such propositions challenge the present system and fulfill our expectation that attempts at influence be necessary and justified.

TYPES OF CLAIMS

Both claims and propositions occur in various forms and types. Knowing which type of claim is in question helps the arguer decide what issues or questions to address. Some claims refer to sources or conditions that can be readily checked for verification. Other claims, such as those involving social values or policies, require more complex forms of support. For example, in Figure 6–2, the claim restating the Hippocratic Oath can be verified merely by referring to the text of the oath itself. If the group discussing euthanasia were to question whether "prolongation of death, dying, and pain demeans life," however, it would have to spend some time defining the terms of the claim and generating criteria to decide whether certain practices "demean life."

Many category schemes for classifying claims have been proposed.[10] The simplest and most frequently used scheme divides claims into the categories of fact, value, and policy. We will use this scheme here because it includes the major types of claims used as subjects of argument and because the sets of issues each type generates can be distinguished from the sets of issues generated by the other two.[11]

Factual Claims

Factual claims make inferences about past, present, or future conditions or relationships. In making such inferences, we reason from something that is known or assumed to be true to something that is unknown or disputable. These inferences occur in numerous forms and in Chapter 8 we will discuss these and explain how one makes the link from what is known to what is claimed. If a statement is about a condition or relationship that is already known and readily apparent to participants in the argumentation, it functions as *evidence*, or, in a network of claims, as a sub-subclaim used as a starting point for argument. (Remember from Chapter 1 that previously established claims can be used as evidence in new arguments that build on them.)

Some statements of fact are straightforward and easily established, therefore not disputable. For example,

> Mary weighs more than John.
>
> The flight cannot leave because of heavy fog.
>
> Central Airlines has the worst record for losing baggage in the United States.

Such statements are unlikely to serve as propositions for extended arguments because they are relatively easy to verify or prove. On the other hand, propositions of fact as discussed in Chapter 9 are much more difficult to prove because the information we need to establish them is not available or because such information is subject to varying interpretations. Such claims could function as propositions and be supported and attacked in extensive argument.

One type of factual claim that states a controversial position is the relational claim. *A relational claim attempts to establish a causal relation between one condition or event and another.*

> Capital punishment deters crime.
>
> Smoking marijuana harms your health.
>
> Violence on television affects children's behavior.

Researchers have completed many studies on each of these topics, and their results do not agree. Sifting through and comparing information on such topics is worthwhile because the inferences made in the claims are so controversial. In Chapter 8 we will discuss procedures for analyzing and supporting such claims.

A second type of factual claim that makes an argumentative statement about what will happen is the predictive claim. *A predictive claim is based on the assumption that past relationships and conditions will be repeated in the future.* Because information that might prove such claims is often not available, predictive claims often serve as the subject of argumentation. For example,

> A staffed space mission will reach Mars by 2015.
>
> Our economy is headed for a massive depression.
>
> A severe shortage of teachers will occur by the year 2005.

Such claims are usually supported by descriptions of long-term trends and statistically based projections; they also involve studying causal relationships that may be affected by unanticipated developments and events.

A third type of controversial factual claim is the *claim of historical fact, which rests on the strength of probable evidence to which we have access.* Because historical records and artifacts are damaged, destroyed, or lost as time passes, evidence supporting historical claims may be as unavailable as that supporting predictive claims. Extensive controversy has surrounded the following claims:

> The Shroud of Turin was worn by Jesus in the tomb.
>
> The author of *On the Sublime* was not Longinus.
>
> Lee Harvey Oswald was the sole assassin of John F. Kennedy.

Supporters of such claims collect and describe as much circumstantial evidence as possible to convince skeptics that their claims are true. Historical claims cannot be positively proven because direct evidence to support them is unavailable.

Three types of factual claims that can serve as the subject of argument, then, are relational claims, predictive claims, and historical claims. Relational claims connect two conditions and infer that one of them has brought about or will bring about another. Predictive claims are grounded in the assumption that past events will be repeated in the future and make a claim about some future occurrence. Historical claims are descriptive and informational and are usually based on a preponderance of evidence that a particular account or interpretation of past events is the correct one. All three deal with matters that are disputable because the information we would need to establish them conclusively is insufficient or unavailable. They describe how or why something has come about or will come about in ways that are controversial and subject to argument.

Value Claims

Value claims assess the worth or merit of an idea, object, or practice according to standards or criteria supplied by the arguer. The focus of argumentation about values is the values held by participants in a dispute. *Values are fundamental positive or negative attitudes toward certain end states of existence or broad modes of conduct.*[12] Such fundamental attitudes influence our conceptions of what is desirable or undesirable in a given situation. Joseph W. Wenzel has noted that "values exist in an intersubjective realm of agreements that are the fabric of a community; they exist in the actions and discourse of persons constructing, sustaining, testing, and revising the rules by which we will live and act together."[13] Examples of values expressing fundamental conceptions of desirable end states are equality, salvation, self-fulfillment, and freedom; those regarding models of conduct are courage, honesty, and loyalty.

Values govern our choice-making and indicate to us what we ought to believe and do. When we make value claims by assigning a value to an object, practice, or idea, we are actually making recommendations to others. Following are examples of value claims:

> Capital punishment is beneficial to society.
>
> Private schools provide better elementary and secondary education than public schools.
>
> Degas's paintings are ethereally beautiful.

In each of these claims, a value judgment is made. The first deals with social benefit, the second with quality, and the third with aesthetic merit. The claims also involve an object of evaluation that may be an idea, a practice, a person, or a thing. Analysis of value claims must be located within some field or framework that implies the standards or criteria for the value judgment. For example, judging capital punishment according to its social benefits might involve a utilitarian standard whereby we try to determine whether capital punishment provides the greatest good for the greatest number of citizens. Criteria suggested by a utilitarian standard might include the following:

- Does capital punishment actually prevent capital crimes?
- Does implementing capital punishment save more lives than it takes?
- Does capital punishment discriminate against minorities?

More will be said about the analysis of issues in value claims in Chapter 10.

Policy Claims

Policy claims call for a specific course of action and focus on whether a change in policy or behavior should take place. Policy claims frequently deal with complex social, political, or economic problems, but they may also deal with actions on a much smaller scale. In the conversation between Nigel and Lisa near the beginning of this chapter, Lisa's implication that Nigel should mow the lawn must be considered a policy claim. Other examples of policy claims are:

> The King County government should legalize prostitution.
>
> Sales of handguns to private citizens in the United States should be banned.
>
> You should not smoke cigarettes in public places.

When making policy claims, arguers express either a dissatisfaction with present practices or a belief that a change in practices or behavior would be an improvement. The types of issues generated in policy claims and methods for analyzing them will be explained in Chapter 11.

CONTINUUM OF CLAIMS

Although the previous section detailed the difference among the three types of claims—fact, value, and policy—our point was not that they exist independently from one another. They are not discrete and separate. Rather, they exist along a continuum of claims such as that illustrated in Figure 6–5.

Fact-based claims are found at the far left of the continuum. These claims serve as the foundation for both value and policy claims. We are not inclined to make value or policy claims in the absence of fact claims. For example, to argue the value claim that

| Fact-Based Claims | Value-Based Claims | Policy-Based Claims |

FIGURE 6–5 Continuum of Claims

"Restricting access to the internet for children is desirable" we must also understand and accept certain fact-based arguments. These might include:

> There are pornographic sites on the internet that might harm children.
>
> There is language on the Web that is not suitable for children.
>
> There are topics on the internet that children are not developmentally ready to understand.

Fact claims are the basis for making most of our value and policy claims. They provide arguers with a foundation for the claims that follow.

Similarly, value claims assume the existence of certain facts and serve as the basis for making policy claims. We might make the claim, for instance, that "Censoring pornographic material is desirable." This value claim assumes the existence of certain facts (the existence of pornographic material) and at the same time provides a justification for a policy action (pornography should be banned). All three types of claims, therefore, are linked together by networks of subsidiary or foundational claims: fact claims supporting value claims, value claims supporting policy claims, and policy claims assuming facts and values.

Such a network can be seen if we were to discuss the policy claim: "Sales of handguns to private citizens in the United States should be banned." In this case, we might consider one or all of the following claims:

> The number of handgun deaths and injuries in our country is appalling. (value claim)
>
> The licensing and regulation of handgun sales is inconsistent from state to state. (fact claim)
>
> Eliminating handguns will decrease the number of unpremeditated and accidental gun injuries. (predictive fact claim)
>
> The "right to bear arms" is not as important as the public's right to safety and freedom from harm. (value claim)

An examination of the network of claims supporting policy propositions will always reveal subsidiary claims of fact and value. Furthermore, a value proposition such as "compulsory national service for all U.S. citizens is desirable" will involve decisions about policy (What is to be done to provide the needed service? Does "compulsory national service" mean a universal draft, required public service, or some other practice?).

Arguers need to keep in mind that because different types of claims are interdependent, they are not always easily distinguished from one anther. For example, if an arguer claimed that "Driving above the speed limit is harmful," the claim seems to come to rest somewhere on the continuum between fact and value. The term "harmful" implies a value. What is meant by harm? How do we evaluate harm? At the same time, we can assume that excessive speed results in a fact of harm. Similarly, if we argue the claim that "It would be good for the United States to criminalize cigarettes" we find that the claim contains both a valuing term (good) and a policy directive (to criminalize cigarettes).

Between each classification (fact, value, policy) there is a "gray zone" in which claims may hold both fact and value elements or value and policy elements. Furthermore, no claim exists independently. Because certain facts are true, we tend to value things. Because certain values are important, we tend to make policies. Similarly, our policies reflect our values, which in turn reflect our understanding of how the world works (facts). Claims of various types often occur in conjunction with each other and are interdependent. If arguers can identify and distinguish them, however, they will be able to focus on the issues and vital questions that the claims imply.

SUMMARY

Claims and propositions serve important argument functions. They focus arguers' attention on the purpose of the argument and imply the issues that need to be decided before a dispute can be resolved. Extended arguments, whether they are in the form of conversations, discussions, speeches, or essays, include a network of claims that combine to support a proposition, or main claim. Skillful arguers should be able to identify the main claims and principal subclaims in the arguments of others. They should also be able to phrase their own claims so that they conform to others' expectations. By phrasing their claims appropriately, arguers will be more successful in constructing extended arguments.

People who participate in arguments expect the subject to be controversial or open to dispute. Anyone who advances a claim should be able to explain why it needs to be justified and supported. Arguers should therefore advance claims about which there is likely to be disagreement. People participating in arguments also expect them to be clear; that is, they want to know what the issues are and what is required to resolve them. Arguers stating claims should therefore avoid ambiguous terms, statements with multiple meanings, and statements that introduce multiple issues simultaneously. Furthermore, stating claims in a biased or prejudiced way forestalls open discussion of the options to be considered. Claims should therefore be stated objectively, and stereotypes and connotative terms should be avoided. Finally, people expect arguers to take issue with prevailing attitudes and practices. If an arguer attempts to influence someone, he or she must make a claim that would change what would continue to be done or believed had the argument not taken place. In presenting an argument for change, the arguer assumes the burden of proving there is good reason for the change to be made.

There are three major types of claims that are made in arguments. Each type of claim calls for a different type of analysis to identify the issues that the claim implies. Claims of fact make inferences about the past, present, or future conditions or relationships. Sometimes factual claims are readily verifiable and agreed upon by all parties to the dispute, or come to be agreed upon as the argument progresses. At other times, factual claims cannot be conclusively established because the needed information is unavailable, in conflict, or subject to conflicting interpretations. Value claims assess the worth or merit of something according to standards supplied by the arguer. The focus of disputes on value claims is on the fundamental attitudes (values) of participants in the argumentation. Value disputes may involve ethical, aesthetic, or moral judgments. Policy claims call for a course of action or change in the beliefs of others. They usually express dissatisfaction with present practices or a belief that a change in policy or behavior will bring improvement.

Finally, it is important to remember that claims are not separate and discrete. Rather, they are interrelated along a continuum of claims in which each type of claim is interdependent with the other two.

EXERCISES

Exercise 1 In this chapter, four criteria were described that enable you to decide whether a proposition is well formulated. They are:

CHAPTER SIX   Argument Claims and Propositions   **143**

- *Controversiality.* The proposition should state a thesis that is potentially disputable rather than one about which most people would agree.
- *Clarity.* The proposition should be clearly and precisely stated; ambiguous terms and double-barreled claims should be avoided.
- *Balance.* The claim should be stated in objective, neutral language rather than in a way that reveals the personal biases or prejudices of the person making the claim.
- *Challenge.* The proposition should confront an audience's prevailing beliefs, values, or state of affairs.

Using these criteria, criticize the following propositions. Are they well formulated? If not, why not? How could they be reformulated so as to function more effectively?

* 1. Exercise is good for one's health.
  2. Plea bargaining is a good and essential means of case disposal.
  3. The United States should withdraw from the United Nations.
  4. The United States should reduce its deficit by cutting wasteful social programs.
* 5. Euthanasia is a desirable and necessary medical practice.
  6. People who are HIV-positive should not be allowed to teach in public schools.
  7. All schools should adopt school uniforms for their dress code.
  8. The United States should eliminate its military forces.
  9. Schools should become more rigorous.
  10. Degenerate and perverted pornographic material should be pulled from every bookstore and magazine stand in America.
  11. Good sales people are effective.
  12. The increasing legalization of casino gambling has only made the rich richer and the poor poorer.
  13. Washington State should stabilize its revenues by imposing an income tax.
* 14. Women should have access to abortion on demand.
  15. Education is good.
  16. Automobile emissions should be reduced.
  17. America's industries need to invest in manufacturing if the United States is to be internationally competitive in the 21st century.
  18. People who own large cars with big engines are wasteful, stupid, and trying to destroy our environment.
  19. Parties are a way of life in college.
  20. An egg has as much protein as a hot dog.

Exercise 2 This chapter discussed a continuum of claims within which three types of claims could be identified: fact, value, and policy. Fact claims make inferences about past, present, or future conditions or relationships; they can be explanatory, predictive, or historical. Value claims judge an idea, object, person, or practice by some value standard or set of criteria. Policy claims advocate a course of action that is not currently followed. Where would you place each of the following criteria on the continuum of claims?

* 1. Extraterrestrial beings visited Earth during prehistoric times.
  2. Every state should require all teachers to pass a proficiency examination.
  3. All nations should destroy their biological weapons.
  4. Illegal immigrants generally take jobs U.S. citizens do not want.
  5. Discrimination is never justified.
  6. Marijuana should be legalized in all 50 states.
  7. Mandatory seat belt laws violate our constitutional rights.
  8. Polygraph evidence is better than eyewitness testimony in criminal trials.
  9. Pornography causes sex crimes.
  10. Required automotive emissions tests are an inefficient means of ensuring clean air.
  11. The U.S. welfare system has abandoned the poor.
  12. The United States should not interfere in the social, political, and economic affairs of other nations.
  13. Movies made in America have more graphic violence and gratuitous sex than they did ten years ago.
  14. Higher education in America is the best in the world.
  15. Colleges and the Universities should stress technical and applied subjects over the liberal arts.

Exercise 3 Select three topics on which you would like to develop an argumentative case. A list of suggested topics is given, but you may choose some other topic area. What is important is that you already know enough about the topic to construct claims related to it. Within each topic area, construct a proposition of fact, a proposition of value, and a proposition of policy. Be sure that the propositions you supply adhere to all the guidelines for working propositions supplied in this chapter and listed in Exercise 1. Here is an example:

Topic area:	Alcohol Abuse
Proposition of Fact:	Alcohol-related accidents cause more deaths than any other cause in the United States.
Proposition of Value:	Alcohol is a more dangerous substance than marijuana.
Proposition of Policy:	The allowable BAC (blood alcohol content) in drivers should be significantly reduced across the nation.

Suggested topics (or select three of your own):

AIDS	inner cities
poverty	censorship
environment	abortion

CHAPTER SIX   Argument Claims and Propositions

religion
foreign policy
illegal drugs
political campaigns
gun control
trade barriers
financial aid

consumer protection
legalized gambling
crime
endangered species
restricting drivers
capital punishment
animal rights

NOTES

1. Lisa's original "claim" was actually a veiled request to mow the lawn. When requests are supported by reasons, they function as arguments. Study of such argument forms occurs in Sally Jackson and Scott Jacobs, "Structure of Conversational Argument: Pragmatic Bases for the Enthymeme," *Quarterly Journal of Speech* 66 (1980): 251–65; and Jacobs and Jackson's "Conversational Argument: A Discourse Analytic Approach," in *Advances in Argumentation Theory and Research,* J. Robert Cox and Charles Arthur Willard, eds. (Carbondale, Ill.: Southern Illinois University Press, 1982).
2. Adapted from Stephen H. Webb, "It's a Dog's Love," *UTNE Reader* (January/February, 1996): 61.
3. Kevin P. Phillips, "Is the Party Over?" *Seattle Times* (July 20, 1986): A16.
4. More techniques for identifying claims and conclusions on the bases of contextual cues will be discussed in Chapter 12.
5. These claims are drawn from a group discussion of the topic "What policy should be enacted in regard to patients in potentially irreversible medical situations?" The discussion occurred at the University of Washington on May 8, 1983. Student participants were Steven McCornack, Ann Hurd, Leigh Chang, Anne Bigelow, Carrie O'Connor, Liza Thomas, and Margo Welshons. This discussion predated a significant Supreme Court decision that ruled that patients have the right to refuse medical treatment and to write living wills precluding extraordinary measures to prevent death.
6. Russel R. Windes and Arthur Hastings, *Argumentation and Advocacy* (New York: Random House, 1965), 51–2.
7. A good deal of work has been done in elaborating the conventions or "rules" of argument. By a rule, we mean "a regularity (formalized ... written, understood, or tacitly observed) that defines an activity." See Gary Cronkhite, "Conventional Postulates of Interpersonal Argument," in *Argument in Transition,* David Zarefsky, Malcolm O. Sillars, and Jack Rhodes, eds. (Annandale, Va.: Speech Communication Association/American Forensic Association, 1983), 697. See also Frans van Eemeren and Rob Grootendorst, *Speech Acts in Argumentative Discussions* (Dordrecht, The Netherlands: Foris Publications, 1984).
8. *Robert's Rules of Order* (New York: Jove Publications, 1977): 30, 131.
9. Richard Whately, *Elements of Rhetoric,* Douglas Ehninger, ed. (Carbondale, Ill.: Southern Illinois University Press, 1963), 112–3.
10. For example, some authors break proposition types down into fact/value (including descriptive, predictive, or evaluative statements that assert the existence or worth of something) and policy, which advocates a course of action. See George Ziegelmueller, Jack Kay, and Charles Dause, *Argumentation: Inquiry and Advocacy,* 2d ed. (Englewood Cliffs, N.J.: Prentice-Hall, 1990), 14–5. Church and Wilbanks describe another unique category scheme that divides propositions into those of inference, value, and policy, with the category of inference subdivided into trait, relational, historical, and predictive inferences. See Russell T. Church and Charles Wilbanks, *Values and Policies in Controversy* (Scottsdale, Ariz.: Gorsuch Scarisbrick, 1986), 35–42.
11. A fourth type of claim is the claim of definition or classification. Examples would be "This is

an act of burglary" and "By 'euthanasia,' I mean the removal of life support from terminally ill patients." To support claims such as these, the arguer justifies the definition or classification by referring to a source that others find acceptable. The arguer may also have to show that the chosen definition is applicable. Only rarely do definitive claims serve as central theses in argumentation; they more frequently function as subsidiary claims when participants disagree about how to define a term in the main claim or proposition.

12. Daryl J. Bem, *Beliefs, Attitudes and Human Affairs* (Belmont, Calif.: Brooks/Cole, 1970), 16.
13. Joseph W. Wenzel, "Toward a Rationale for Value-Centered Argument," *Journal of the American Forensic Association* 13 (1977): 153.

CHAPTER 7

Evidence: The Foundation for Arguments

CHAPTER OUTLINE
- The Nature of Evidence
- Types of Evidence
- Evaluating Fact and Opinion Evidence
    - Reliability
    - Expertise
    - Objectivity
    - Consistency
    - Recency
    - Relevance
    - Access
    - Accuracy of Citation
- Evaluating Statistical Evidence
- Fallacies of Evidence
    - Begging the Question
    - *Non Sequitur*
- Research Strategies for Locating Evidence
    - Site Types
    - Source Types
- Summary
- Exercises

KEY CONCEPTS

statistics
artifacts
reliability
expertise
objectivity
bias
external consistency
internal consistency

accessibility
primary source
secondary source
sample
representative sample
begging the question
non sequitur

As critics and consumers of argument, we should be aware of the vital role evidence plays in argumentation and decision-making. Russel R. Windes and Arthur Hastings have suggested that the acceptance of conclusions and decisions in the absence of evidence "has resulted in decisions and actions which have led to indescribable human suffering and misery—to wars and material destruction, to political inequities and the suppression of human rights, to economic catastrophes, to unjust persecutions, to mob violence, and to superstition and prejudice."[1] If you believe that accepting unsupported or poorly supported claims is harmless, consider Nazi Germany.

The Nazi propaganda machine sought to isolate and ostracize the Jewish people. To do this, Nazi publications claimed that Jews had caused the country's economic ills, had committed atrocities against German women and children, and were devious and untrustworthy. In support of their claims, the Nazis presented either no evidence (only innuendo) or phony evidence. But if a claim is made often enough, people begin to believe it,[2] and the German people did. One result was the Holocaust in which millions of Jewish people were put to death.

Not only do we need to be aware of the absence or misuse of evidence in arguments we hear and read, but we also should be mindful of the need to use evidence in arguments we make. Particularly in situations in which an arguer is unknown to an audience or does not have an established reputation with them, evidence is vital in establishing the credibility of claims and arguments the arguer makes. Researchers who have studied the effect of evidence on the persuasiveness of arguments have found that speakers unknown to or only moderately respected by an audience will be more successful if they use evidence to support their claims.[3] As recipients, critics, and producers of arguments, then, it is important for us to be aware of the vital role played by evidence.

In Chapter 1, we defined evidence as "facts or conditions objectively observable, beliefs or premises generally accepted as true by the audience, or conclusions previously established." Evidence is what we produce whenever we are asked to prove something or when someone asks us "How do you know?" or "What have you got to go on?" This chapter will discuss the nature and types of evidence, procedures for locating evidence in libraries and resource material, and guidelines for the use of evidence to support arguments. After you have read this chapter, you should be able to recognize evidence, conduct research to find support for your arguments, and evaluate the quality of evidence used in your own and other's arguments.

CHAPTER SEVEN   Evidence: The Foundation for Arguments   **149**

THE NATURE OF EVIDENCE

Our definition of evidence from Chapter 1 indicates that evidence is not simply concrete facts or observable behavior. Rather, the defining characteristic of evidence is that it is accepted by the audience and can be used to support statements (claims) that are not accepted. The three ways in which evidential statements can function will be discussed in this section so as to reveal the nature of various forms of evidence.

First, evidence can stem from objectively observable conditions in the world. For most people, this is what evidence is. Evidence is simply what we can see and hear, feel, touch, and smell. For instance, your desk can serve as evidence that is objectively observable; so can the color of the sky or the number of people in your argumentation class. These are things that can be seen or discovered by anyone looking for them.

Second, beliefs or premises generally accepted as true by the audience can function as evidence (as long as they do not clearly disagree with directly observable evidence). This view of evidence can be problematic for some people because it means that evidence is not always concrete. However, the concept of level of dispute introduced in Chapter 1 can provide a useful means for understanding this view of evidence. Evidence can be used as support because it lies below the level of dispute. If evidence fell above the line, then it would become a focal point for argument instead of support for a claim. For instance:

> According to Paul Talbot, president of the Fremantle Corporation, which sells the international rights to the television series *Baywatch,* the program is now seen in 144 countries, which makes it the most-watched television program ever.[4]

> If one were to analyze how a typical, hour-long *Baywatch* episode distributes its time, one would find the following:
>
>   cavorting on the beach, 2 minutes 32 seconds
>   references to female lifeguard locker room, 2
>   shots of lifeguards running on beach, 5
>   shots of lifeguard bodies, 3
>   approximate time devoted to dialogue, 9 minutes, 21 seconds[5]

In the first case, the evidence says that *Baywatch* was the most-watched program in the world. That might be controversial to some, yet the source is an expert and most people in an audience would probably concede that Mr. Talbot is in a position to know how widely the program is distributed. Therefore, an audience is likely to accept the statement as evidence because of its source. The second example of evidence, however, does not come from an expert source. Yet it would still function as evidence because any audience member might reasonably expect to verify the figures by watching an episode of *Baywatch* and because the statistics do not seem unreasonable and are probably acceptable to most members of an audience. As long as audience members find the statements acceptable and reasonable, they can function as evidence. If, however, the audience believed that *Dallas* was the most-watched television program ever, then Talbot's statements would need further support and would function as a claim. The arguments' initial starting points would no longer serve as evidence because they fell above the level of dispute.

Third, conclusions that have been previously established can function as evidence. In the argument above, if you accept that Talbot is an expert in the distribution patterns of the program and you trust what he is saying, then he could use that statement as evidence to support an additional claim. For example, he might argue that *Baywatch* is the best program that has ever been aired because it is the most popular. If the audience accepts that claim as being true, the level of dispute rises until the proven claim falls below the level. The proven claim can now be used as evidence for the next claim and so on. The process of using proven claims as evidence to support further claims is called *argument chaining*.

A prospective car buyer can provide a useful example of how people might commonly use evidence. There are many publications to help car buyers choose from hundreds of makes and models. One of the most prominent of these is *Consumer Reports*, which tests dozens of automobiles each year. These tests and surveys can provide the prospective buyer with a wealth of evidence: the price of the car and options, predicted reliability, comfort and convenience, ease of service, drivability, and performance. With the information from *Consumer Reports*, John, a prospective car buyer, goes looking for a new car. He drives many makes and models and notes the features in each of the cars he tests. With all of this information, he selects the car he wants and sits down to bargain with the dealer.

The *Consumer Reports* evidence is useful to John in making an argument with the dealer for a better price. He can tell the dealer that he likes the car but the $15,000 price is too high because the consumer magazines claimed that the dealer paid only $8,000 for the car in the first place. He can also claim that the car was not quite as comfortable, reliable, or gas-efficient as he had hoped, and perhaps he should look elsewhere for another car. In each case, John appeals to evidence to support his claims about the car.

Suppose, however, that the dealer rejected John's $8,000 figure and asserted that the particular car with its options cost him a good deal more. John's original evidence would then become a claim because it would be disputed and the subject of argument.

This illustration points to the nature of evidence. Evidence is not always concrete nor is it always certain. In fact, evidence can be placed on a continuum from concrete, objectively observable, certain evidence to evidence that is probably true. For instance, John knew the car existed. He could make an argument for the car's existence and have little difficulty getting people to agree with him. John could use any of the car's physical features as evidence without much fear of contradiction. On the other hand, suppose John argued that *Consumer Reports* conducted a reliability study on the car. Evidence from such a study is not directly experienced by the participants in an argument, and because neither party had a concrete experience with the evidence there is room for dispute. It could be that no such study was conducted or that John's interpretation of the study is wrong or that the study was biased. The results of the study and John's interpretation of them are probable but not certain. Sometimes evidence functions as fact; at other times it functions as opinions or premises accepted by the audience.

TYPES OF EVIDENCE

Evidence can be divided into two broad classifications—fact and opinion as to fact.[6] Facts may be thought of as things people believe to be the case either because they have experienced them firsthand or because they regard them as the truthfully reported experiences of others.[7]

Generally, there are two ways in which people come to believe something is a fact. First, they may verify it through their own observations or experiments. In other words, they can see, hear, feel, touch, or taste it. Most phenomena perceived by our senses are easily accessible, but some are not. Scientists seeking to prove the existence of atoms have conducted experiments allowing them to see the physical effects of atoms. They have used cloud chambers that help them trace atomic trails or computer simulations. If someone did not believe in the existence of atomic particles, their existence could be demonstrated by these or other methods.

A second way people come to believe in something as a fact is through common experience. We can talk about the history of the United States and the Civil War. While none of us have directly experienced the Civil War, it is part of our common heritage. We do not question it because we accept it as a fact, a historical occurrence well substantiated in many sources. Factual evidence can be further divided into types. Each type, in turn, can be verified by observations, experiments, or common experience.

1. *Reports and descriptions are nonnumerical or narrative accounts of some object or occurrence.* They often occur in arguments as examples and illustrations and may make a passing reference to something or describe it at some length. Here are two examples of this type of evidence:

    Tombstone, Arizona, a Wild-West town known for mock gunfights, plank sidewalks, hitching posts, and Western atmosphere, passed a measure requiring horses to wear diapers or dung bags to help keep the streets clean. People thought it looked pretty silly, but it is having an effect on keeping the streets clean.[8]

    Last year, a few days before the holiday that some people equate with fireworks. . . . [J. R. "Don"] Schmidt lost portions of his thumb and two fingers on his right hand.
    The logger and some friends had gone to Hood Canal to discharge fireworks purchased from a stand on an Indian reservation.
    "My buddy lit a cherry bomb with a cigarette lighter, then handed it to me to toss. It had a short fuse. It went off too soon," Schmidt explained.[9]

    Reports and factual descriptions such as these lend immediacy and vividness to many arguments. They help recipients identify with the characters and relate to the situations described. And they bring home or dramatize situations or conditions that might otherwise seem remote and unimportant.

2. *Statistics are facts and figures that have been systematically collected and ordered so as to convey information.* Generally, statistics provide a quantitative summary of the characteristics of a population or sample (selectively chosen instances) of a population. Statistics may take the form of averages, numerical comparisons, percentages, totals, or estimates, for example. Sometimes arguers use statistics alone or in combination with reports and descriptions to help build a multidimensional foundation for arguments. Following are some examples of statistics:

    According to Temple Law's career office, their students fare quite well [in the job market]. Temple reports that nine months after graduation, 93% of the class of 1994 was employed, pulling down a median salary of $39,000.[10]

> More than 800 anti-smoking lawsuits have been filed since 1954. . . . There are 46 million smokers in this country and 400,000 smoking-related deaths each year.[11]

Statistics lend credence to arguments by showing that problems and conditions are not limited to isolated instances but instead affect many people in many different types of situations. The first set of statistics above shows that Temple Law School has had a high success rate in placing graduates into the legal field, the second set that there are many smokers and smoking-related deaths in this county. Statistics are useful in showing the breadth of a problem, and reports and descriptions are used often to show its depth or human consequence.

3. *Artifacts are physical evidence that helps to prove an argument. An artifact is simply a physical object that a speaker might use to prove a point.* For example, exhibits in a trial are artifacts. X-ray films showing the damage caused by smoking are also artifacts, as would be letters of job offers for the graduates of law schools. Artifacts may also take the form of demonstrations. Often a trial lawyer will demonstrate how a piece of evidence works in order to make a point. Teachers will have students do an exercise or science experiment to illustrate a concept. These are artifacts that help support claims. Since we are influenced more strongly by what we see and experience than by what we hear or read, artifacts can be a very effective form of factual evidence because they involve the recipients of argument in multidimensional ways.

When advocates make arguments that are based on their own firsthand knowledge and understanding of the facts, then they are making arguments grounded in fact-based evidence. However, sometimes the facts surrounding an issue are excessively complex or large such that an advocate cannot reasonably review all the factual material. In such cases, arguers turn to others who have examined the factual evidence and distilled it into meaningful compilations or opinions.

The second broad type of evidence, then, is opinion as to fact. Opinion evidence is someone's interpretation of the meaning of factual evidence. Whereas facts are based on direct or indirect experience, opinions are judgments about how an event or state of affairs is to be understood, evaluated, or dealt with. In using opinion evidence, the advocate uses the statements of others' judgments and estimations to support his or her own claims. Consider the following opinion statement and the claim it might support:

> Recently, psychologists presented at the annual American Psychological Association convention in Toronto an in-depth examination of the American Presidents. Opinions from more than 100 experts were sought and the raters designed and completed a battery of standardized tests designed to evaluate each of the Presidents. Several of these tests included more than 100 questions. Their goal was to develop a personality profile of each of the past US Presidents and develop a rating system to help guide voters in future elections. The psychologists looked at many dimensions including their: level of neuroses, openness to the experience of others, intelligence, extroversion, agreeableness, among others. Their conclusions included the following.
>
> Ronald Reagan was the least neurotic of all the Presidents. Richard Nixon was the most. Thomas Jefferson was the most intelligent and Theodore Roosevelt was second. Warren G. Harding was the least open to the experience of others and he was the least conscientious. Bill Clinton was the second least conscientious. George Washington was

rated as the most conscientious. James Madison and Abraham Lincoln were rated among the most agreeable. Theodore and Franklin Roosevelt were among the most extroverted, Bill Clinton was third.[12]

The factual data compiled by the pyschologists is extensive and overwhelming. It would take a single arguer weeks to read through it all and, assuming the advocate had the appropriate education, she or he might be in a position to use it as factual evidence in support of a claim. However, for most people, the quantity of factual evidence and the expertise required to understand it means that arguers often rely on the opinions of others in developing their own arguments. Using this study as opinion evidence an arguer might be able to make the following argument:

Claim: George Washington was the best President we have had.

Evidence: Psychologists presented a paper at the American Psychology Association Convention in Toronto that concluded he was the most conscientious of all our presidents, in the upper third in intelligence, open to the opinions of others, and an agreeable President.

Reasoning: These elements, taken together, make Washington the most balanced of all our Presidents because he exhibited far above average abilities in each of the areas studied by the psychologists.

Just as arguers can draw on factual evidence in the form of reports, statistics, and artifacts, arguers can also draw on the opinions of others about what reports, statistics, and artifacts mean. In other words, just as there are three types of factual evidence, there are three parallel types of opinion evidence. These include opinion as to reports and descriptions, opinion as to statistics, and opinion as to artifacts.

EVALUATING FACT AND OPINION EVIDENCE

Just as a house or any structure is only as strong as the foundation on which it is built, so is an argument only as strong as the evidence used to support it. As arguers and as recipients of argument, we need to be aware of the quality of evidence so that we can judge others' arguments and select strong evidence to support our own arguments.

The remainder of this section will list and describe criteria to be applied to various types of evidence. Applying criteria such as reliability, expertise, objectivity, consistency, recency, and relevance to our own and others' evidence supplies us with a system for judging the quality of support provided for claims. The result can only be to make us better critics and users of argument.

Reliability

One question many audiences ask about a source is whether or not the source is reliable. *A reliable source is one that has proven to be correct many times in the past.* An excellent example of a reliable source is cited by Robert P. Newman and Dale R. Newman in their book on evidence:

[Senator J. William] Fulbright's overall record of prophecy is pretty good. He warned President Truman that unless atomic energy were put under international control, there would be a monstrous arms race and proliferation. . . . He told Secretary [of State John Foster] Dulles that arms shipments to India and Pakistan would lead to war between the two. He . . . warned President Kennedy the Bay of Pigs would be a fiasco.[13]

Given Senator Fulbright's accuracy record for predictions, political leaders would have done well to attend to his opinions. People naturally trust sources and other people who have been proven right in the past. Thus we are likely to put our confidence in a Wall Street newsletter that accurately predicts stock market fluctuations or in *Consumer Reports*, whose product assessments have repeatedly proven to be correct.

Expertise

Studies on factors affecting whether or not a source is believed have indicated that the most important factor is the recipients' perception of the source's competence.[14] *Expertise is the possession of a background of knowledge and information relevant to the subject matter under discussion.* Generally, we determine whether or not someone is an expert in a subject area by examining or considering the nature and extent of his or her experience with the topic. Education and formal training in a subject are one index as to whether a person is qualified. Experience may be gained in other ways, however. Any given senator would not necessarily be considered an expert on the conduct of Pentagon business, whereas a senator who had chaired the Senate Armed Services Committee for a number of terms would probably be considered an expert on the status of American armed forces. Any person who has published favorably reviewed books or articles on a subject is generally accepted as an expert on that subject. Furthermore, people who hold elective offices in professional organizations are highly regarded because it is assumed that they are respected by their peers.

Because of the importance of expertise in establishing the acceptability of evidence with most audiences, it is vital for arguers to fully cite their source's qualifications and experience with the topic. Instead of saying "Jon Smith concluded that NutraSweet should have been more thoroughly tested before it was approved by the Food and Drug Administration," an advocate should say "Dr. Jon Smith, a nutritionist at the University of Florida, recently reported in the *New England Journal of Medicine* after twelve years of investigation that. . . ." Unless the source's qualifications and experience with the topic are fully reported to recipients, they will have no way of making any judgment about the source's expertise. Emphasizing the source's credentials can enhance the argument's persuasiveness by showing that evidence is taken from someone whose knowledge and experience can be trusted.

Objectivity

Recipients feel confident in trusting sources they believe are objective about the topic of the argument. *Objectivity refers to a source's tendency to hold a fair and undistorted view on a question or an issue.* An objective source does not have views strongly colored by a personal emotional investment in one ideological viewpoint on the topic. We can hardly expect a member of the John Birch Society to provide a well-balanced discussion of the influence of the political left on contemporary American society. Nor can we expect a union leader to provide a complete account of corruption within his organization. We should not expect all sources to be completely impartial in their analyses of issues. After all, if they did not have a viewpoint to argue, they would not be making a claim or supporting a point of view. We should expect sources to be unbiased, however. *A bias is an unreasoned distortion of judgment or a prejudice on a topic.* A biased source often has a personal stake in the outcome of an argument and thus is unlikely to provide a fair account of differing points of view. A representative of the American Tobacco Institute (which is funded by tobacco companies) is unlikely to openly acknowledge the health hazards of smoking cigarettes. Nor is the National Rifle Association objective on the subject of gun control. Arguers using such sources are likely to discover that their recipients are aware of the biases of such groups and suspicious about any information taken from them.

Consistency

Recipients of an argument expect evidence used to be consistent with other information and with itself. Consistency with other information is called external consistency. *External consistency is the agreement of evidence with sources of information other than the source being used.* Concerning this form of consistency, Douglas Ehninger once remarked:

> Because nature is not uniform and because people's actions are often unexpected or unpredictable, the fact that a given piece of evidence differs in form or content from other evidence bearing on the same point does not necessarily mean that it is false or inaccurate. Such deviation from the norm is, however, a justifiable cause for suspicion.[15]

A piece of evidence that runs counter to what is already believed or known about a topic is therefore not necessarily wrong, but the arguer using it has the burden of proving that the evidence is correct and can be reconciled with other seemingly incompatible facts the audience already believes or accepts. After all, the mainstream of opinion, or even of what is thought to be "knowledge" is not always correct. For example, Galileo argued that the earth revolved around the sun at a time when most people believed the sun revolved around the earth. Columbus believed that one could reach the East by sailing west at a time when most people thought someone attempting that would fall off the edge of the earth. However, when evidence fails to agree with other credible facts and sources, it can be detrimental to acceptance of an argument.

Advocates can increase the acceptability and believability of their arguments by using a sufficient amount of evidence from different sources to show that their support is externally consistent. Recipients of arguments can assure themselves that evidence is externally consistent by comparing it with facts they already know or information to which they have access.

Evidence should also be internally consistent. *Internal consistency is the absence of self-contradiction within information provided by a source.* When political leaders and other public figures contradict themselves, the media and the public take great delight in pointing this out. One recent political advertisement made the claim that Medicare was five years from bankruptcy. Fortunately, one Congressional leader had a plan to save it. The plan was to raise benefits to those on Medicare. The advertisement was on its face inconsistent. If Medicare is going bankrupt, increasing the distributions will not be the solution. The inconsistency in the ad suggested there was more to the story than appeared in the argument.

Similarly, the tobacco industry has been under tremendous pressure to reduce its advertising and in particular to eliminate the "Joe Camel" ads that many critics charged were aimed at children. The response by the tobacco industry was that the advertisements did not affect purchases, rather, smokers were loyal to their brands. Therefore, campaigns such as "Joe Camel" were not targeted at getting young people to smoke but rather at reinforcing brand loyalty. Again, this argument is inconsistent. If people are loyal to particular brands and if advertising does not promote smoking, then the advertisements would have no effect and are a waste of money. Yet, they continue.

Few things are more damaging to an arguer's credibility than the appearance of inconsistency or self-contradictions in statements that are made. While it is cliché to charge politicians with this offense, consistent internal contractions or broken promises make people wary of politicians. When arguers contradict themselves, they diminish the level of trust and credibility they have with their audiences.

Recency

As a general rule, arguers should be aware of whether their evidence is or is not sufficiently current on the topic of their argument. The extent to which evidence must be recent varies with the topic under discussion. Advocates examining foreign policy, AIDS research, or international terrorism should rely on the most recent evidence available because our knowledge about such topics and the events that bring them to our attention change almost daily. Evidence about the world, objects, people, or anything else that changes needs to be current.

Other topics may be less affected by the comparative recency of evidence. Evidence relating to human rights or capital punishment, for example, may be of more enduring usefulness because conditions and values relating to these topics are less subject to change. Consequently, speakers appealing to values such as "life, liberty, and the pursuit of happiness" are arguing from safe ground because such values are an enduring part of American political life regardless of when the appeal was made.

Relevance

It is not uncommon for an arguer to present something that *sounds like* evidence and to connect it with a given claim when, in fact, the evidence is unrelated to the claim as made. Consider the following example of an ad for pain relief medication.

Evidence: Nine out of ten doctors recommend aspirin for headaches.

Claim: Aspirin is a powerful all-purpose medication.

A close examination of these two statements quickly reveals that the claim goes well beyond what is warranted by the evidence. First, the doctor stipulated a specific purpose for aspirin use and did not say it was "all-purpose." Second, the doctors made no statement about the aspirin's potency. So the evidence as stated does not relate to the claim as made.

One might think that irrelevant or unrelated evidence would be obvious, but often it isn't. The evidence is frequently somewhat related but does not directly support the claim because of the way it is worded or qualified. To detect this problem, we should be aware of the way the language and focus of the claim relate to the language and focus of the evidence. The following excerpt from a student's paper will illustrate how irrelevant evidence might *appear* to support a claim when, in fact, it does not.

A 1982 Safe Schools study showed that 36% of all secondary schools paddle children in a typical month. For junior high schools the figure jumps to 61%. Children all across the United States are being legally beaten under our laws.

The arguer uses a very connotative term—"beaten"—in her claim. Is this term, normally associated with child abuse which is illegal, to be equated with paddling? Furthermore, do the arguer's statistics show that this is happening "all across the country"? The answer to both of these questions is "probably not." The study makes no mention of geographical location, and punishment deemed legal by the courts should not be equated with abuse. Therefore, the claim departs from and exaggerates the evidence given to support it.

Access

When an arguer cites opinion as to fact about a situation or event, recipients should expect the source of that opinion to have been in a position to observe directly the matter in question. *Accessibility depends on whether or not someone offering an opinion is or has been in a position to observe firsthand the matter being disputed.* A person who has not directly experienced something must rely on reports or summaries provided by others or on impressions based on limited information. But any time we hear or read something secondhand, certain features and aspects are filtered out by the perspective and viewpoint of the person who reports it to us. The features identified and reported may not at all be the ones we would notice if we had an opportunity to observe the situation ourselves firsthand. The further we move from the original situation as directly observed by eyewitnesses, the greater the possibility for misinterpretation or error.

Newman and Newman emphasize the importance of accessibility to a reporter's ability to collect accurate and credible evidence.[16] They argue that we can be much less sure of reports coming from geographically remote foreign-language–speaking countries than we can of information from English-speaking countries. Their reason is that many reporters and observers in the foreign countries can observe only what local governments want them to see and can hear only about what the local governments want them to be told (particularly if the reporters or observers do not speak the host country's language). Furthermore, a senatorial junket or a two-week assignment in a country does not provide a congressperson or a reporter with sufficient exposure to situations to make accurate judgments. An important question to ask when we judge opinion evidence, then, is "Has the source had an opportunity to observe directly the matter in question, as well as the knowledge and experience to interpret competently what he or she has observed?"

Accuracy of Citation

When we make a decision on the basis of someone else's argument, we generally have certain expectations about the evidence presented to us. We hope it has been fully reported, is of the best possible quality, and is not misrepresented or intentionally distorted. Information that is second-rate or distorted does not provide reliable grounds for decision-making. Arguers and recipients of argument should be aware of the ethical obligation to cite accurately the sources used to support arguments. There are many ways to interpret and communicate evidence so as to mislead recipients about its nature or quality, and not all involve deliberate falsification. Everyone would agree that adding to or altering a source's words is unethical, but often selectively omitting words or sentences is also ethically questionable. The overarching question is "Does the manner in which an arguer cites a source give recipients an accurate and faithful picture of the nature and intent of the evidence?" To clarify the implications of this question, we will consider *some* of the practices to be avoided.

1. *Omitting words to make the evidence more favorable to the arguer's claim.* Quotations from sources should be faithful to the context from which they are taken. If the citer of the source omits qualifying words or phrases or otherwise alters the meaning of the original, the practice is unethical. It is not difficult to completely reverse the meaning of a quotation by leaving part of it out. For example, an arguer once claimed that

> For a man who is supposed to be a champion of democracy, it is odd that Lincoln said: "You can fool all of the people some of the time." This doesn't show much faith in the judgment of the people.

While this claim uses Lincoln's words, its interpretation was flawed because it does not address the remainder of Lincoln's statement, which was

> You can fool some of the people all the time and all the people some of the time, but you can't fool all the people all the time.

A practice of misrepresentation through omission with which we are all familiar is the movie advertisement that quotes movie critics' statements. For example, the *Boston Tribune* reviewed *Attack of the Killer Ants,* a horror film aimed at the teenage audience. The reviewer reported that "The only way this movie could be best picture of the year is if children under the age of sixteen are the only people allowed to vote for best picture this year." Yet, within three days the movie marquee announced "According to *Boston Tribune*— . . . Best Picture of the Year. . . ." Omitting statements from quotations to make them support one's point is easy to do but is wrong because it misleads and deceives the audience.

2. *Failing to distinguish between primary and secondary sources. A primary source is the original source of the evidence.* The primary source is the source in which the evidence first appeared. Eyewitness accounts; original documents (letters, diaries, personal notebooks); and transcripts of speeches as originally delivered are examples of primary sources. Primary sources provide the most immediate possible account of what was said by the source at the moment it was uttered.

Secondary sources are sources that compile, analyze, or summarize primary sources. Secondary sources often provide an interpretation or a restatement of what was originally said. For example, Thomas Jefferson's own correspondence about events leading to the Declaration of Independence is a primary source; an account of the Revolutionary War period in a history book is a secondary source. An original editorial is a primary source; a reprinting or summary of that editorial is a secondary source.

Arguers should use primary sources whenever possible because they are authentic and there is less possibility for error when they are used. When original or primary evidence is unavailable, arguers may use secondary sources, but they should always report that the information was cited in a secondary source and give the secondary source credit. Information in a secondary source may have been shortened, changed, or edited. For example, the *Reader's Digest* often changes and alters the articles it republishes. It is therefore important for recipients to know that the arguer is not citing the original source.

3. *Failing to give all relevant information about the source from which the evidence was taken.* When sources are cited, complete information about where the evidence was found and the qualifications of the sources should be given. This includes the name of the author (if one is available), his or her qualifications, the date the statement was made, and the place of publication.

> Dr. James I. Brilhart, professor of anthropology at the University of California at Berkeley, argued in the January 12, 1980, issue of *Time* that "There is no such thing as a primitive language."

The arguer should provide enough information about the source that the recipients could track down the information and read it themselves if they wanted to. Fully disclosing the sources of one's information makes the argument appear credible and the arguer trustworthy.

Alluding to one's sources vaguely ("according to several articles that have appeared recently") is unacceptable. Not openly dating the information is deceptive. What if an arguer decided to leave out the date in the statement about primitive language cited above? A good deal of research has been done on language behavior recently and, if the recipients thought the comment was current, they would be deceived.

Ethical requirements for using evidence, then, include citing the words of the author so the citation conforms to his or her intentions and to the context, distinguishing between primary and secondary sources, and providing recipients with complete information about the source's qualifications and where the evidence was found. Omission or addition of words or information to make the evidence appear more favorable to one's claim is unacceptable.

EVALUATING STATISTICAL EVIDENCE

One should keep in mind the adage "Figures lie and liars figure." All of the standards we have just proposed for fact and opinion evidence apply equally well to statistics. Statistics are the end result of a process subject to human bias and human error. Questions on a survey can be loaded; the people surveyed can be subjectively chosen; comparisons may be made of noncomparable units; and reports of findings can be slanted. Actually, statistics are often no more reliable than other forms of evidence, yet people often think statistics are true. As Newman and Newman laconically observed,

> If you would not believe a man who testifies that he has seen a flying saucer, do not believe him when he claims to have seen fourteen flying saucers each measuring twenty-two feet in diameter and weighing eleven tons.[17]

Gathering, using, and assessing statistics nevertheless present problems and challenges different than in other forms of evidence. This section will alert you to difficulties that frequently arise when arguers use statistics to support their claims. As an advocate, you should take care to avoid these pitfalls in conducting your own research. As a recipient of argument, you should scrutinize the statistics you hear and read and be alert to some of these practices.

1. *Using pseudo-statistics.* Sometimes we hear statistics applied to phenomena and situations in which it is difficult if not impossible to imagine how the statistics could have been compiled using good statistical methods. Here are three examples:

> According to *Esquire* magazine, February, 1964, Judy Garland sang "Over the Rainbow" 1476 times.
>
> Seven out of every ten Americans cheat on their income taxes.
>
> *Mega Foods* has developed a revolutionary line of *Food* Vitamins and *Food* Minerals that are up to sixteen times more effective than the so-called "natural" vitamins and we can prove that with scientific research.

While the first case appears innocent enough, a closer look invites criticism. Specifically, how does anyone know precisely how many times Garland sang "Over the Rainbow"? Did someone count every time the song was sung in rehearsal, on stage, and in the shower? It is unreasonable to assume that this statistic could be accurate because there is almost no way it could have been collected. Similarly, the second piece of evidence would be difficult to arrive at reasonably. In order to collect the figure seven out of ten, what would a researcher have to do? Ask a group of people which one of them cheats? How would each of the respondents interpret what is meant by "cheat"? Given people's concern about tax audits, how many would honestly say they cheat? And how would "scientific research" determine that a certain brand of vitamins and food supplements is precisely sixteen times more effective than the natural alternative? Would respondents have to feel sixteen times better? Would they need to be sixteen times more resistant to disease? Was the study based on the self-reports of people taking the vitamins and supplements or on some other measure? We don't know.

2. *Comparing noncomparable units.* In essence, this practice, which emerges most frequently when longitudinal trends are reported, involves comparing dissimilar items while assuming they are the same. For example, due to inflation, the value of the dollar has declined. The 1993 dollar does not have the same value that the 1963 dollar did. This is why salary comparisons and commodity prices are always "corrected for inflation" when across-time comparisons are made. A similar problem arises when advocates use the federal government's crime statistics. The definition of what constitutes a felony or a misdemeanor varies from one time or location to another. When new types of crimes are included in the class of felonies, the felony rates appear to increase simply because the method of classification has changed.

3. *Using an unrepresentative sample. A sample is a population or group of people or objects that researchers survey when a study is conducted.* Most researchers do not have the time, money, or ability to survey or study every individual in a given state or the country. Consequently, researchers must draw upon a group or sample of people small enough to work with. Conclusions about their sample are then generalized to a broader group. One example is the studies of college students that conclude that seventy percent

will graduate after four years and find employment in their chosen field. This statistic was arrived at by surveying a group of students and then generalizing the conclusions to all other students. Certain questions need to be answered before such evidence should be used or accepted. Was the sample representative? Was the sample too small? Was the sample randomly selected?

A representative sample is one that possesses all the characteristics of the larger group from which it is drawn. For example, if the general population of college students on which a study is done is 35 percent college freshmen, 20 percent college sophomores, 10 percent juniors, and 35 percent seniors, then a representative sample is one made up of approximately the same proportion of individuals. In this sense, a representative sample is a group drawn from a larger group that shares most of the larger group's characteristics.

One of the best-known examples of use of an unrepresentative sample is the *Literary Digest*'s 1936 poll of voters that showed that Republican Alfred Landon would defeat Franklin D. Roosevelt by winning 57 percent of the vote. When Roosevelt won and Landon's share was only 37.5 percent, the *Digest* was so discredited that it had to cease publication. The problem with the *Digest* poll was it was based on an unrepresentative sample. The *Digest* mailed postcard ballots to people listed as owning automobiles and having telephone service. But the poorer classes who supported Roosevelt did not have such luxuries and thus were not included. This is why the poll results were so skewed in favor of Landon and so misleading.[18] The *Digest* should have sampled registered voters to get its results.

4. *Using poor statistical methods.* Sound methods for gathering statistical information should guard against redundancy and bias when responses are counted. For example, surveys that count some of the respondents twice or those that count only people who are highly motivated to respond are using poor statistical methods.

One example is the compiling of casualty statistics during the Vietnam war. Officers in the various services frequently sought totals of the number of enemy dead after battles. Various platoons were dispersed to conduct body counts, but there was no way to ensure that one platoon would not duplicate another's count. Furthermore, it was difficult to distinguish civilians from soldiers because many Vietnamese soldiers did not wear uniforms. Combat conditions also made counts very difficult to conduct. Nevertheless, casualty totals, however inaccurate, were reported.[19]

Another example is the media polls that ask viewers to call a toll-free number to express support for or opposition to an idea. One Seattle television station recently asked viewers to phone one of three numbers to express support for one of three potential state songs the legislature was considering. "Roll On Columbia" received the largest number of votes. The station projected a winning song based on the assumption that those who were motivated enough to call in were representative of the state population—a shaky assumption at best.

FALLACIES OF EVIDENCE

Fallacies that relate to evidence occur when arguments are grounded poorly. This happens when arguers use evidence that is of poor quality or, in some cases, nonexistent. Poorly grounded arguments tend to confuse reasoning or claims with evidence. When arguers commit this fallacy, they are asking recipients to draw conclusions from premises that are either missing or inappropriate to the claim. As you may recall from our earlier discussion of evidence, there are many tests of evidence that help critics determine whether evidence is relevant, reliable, and valid. When arguers ground their arguments in evidence that fails the tests of evidence, then a fallacy of evidence occurs. While many such fallacies are possible, following are significant and prevalent forms of problems with evidence or lack of evidence.

Begging the Question

The fallacy of begging the question assumes as a premise or as evidence for an argument the very claim or point that is in question. Often, when arguers beg the question they are accused of circular reasoning because they use the argument's premises as their claims and reason that one supports the other when, in fact, there is little or no difference. Arguers who beg the question fail to seek external support for their claims so that they assume the point they are expected to prove. Consequently, the evidence for such claims is not externally valid and, in fact, cannot be validated through external sources.

You may recall that when we discussed the level of dispute in Chapter 1, we pointed out that in an argument one begins with evidence (statements that the audience accepts) and moves to prove a conclusion that is not yet accepted. Begging the question fallacies, however, are circular because they depend upon premises whose truth is assumed rather than established.

There are many ways to beg the question. Two of them are illustrated in the following examples.

> The soul is immortal because it lives forever.

In this example, the arguer has simply stated the claim in two different ways. "Living forever" may be a definition of "immortal," but stipulating a definition does not constitute proof of immortality's existence. Put simply, the evidence in the argument cannot possibly be verified.

> We must accept the traditions of men of old time who affirm themselves to be the offspring of the gods—that is what they say—and they must surely have known their own ancestors. How can we doubt the word of the children of the gods?[20]

The issue here is whether the ancestors' word can be trusted. To address the issue, the author commits an *ad verecundiam* (appeal to authority) fallacy to claim that we should trust their authority because their word on the matter is authoritative! This is a very clear example of the kind of circular reasoning often found in fallacies that beg the question.

When we suspect that a question-begging fallacy has been committed, we should determine whether premises independent of the claim have been offered to support it and, if they have, whether these premises are any more certain or acceptable than the claim itself. If the arguer has not offered accepted or proven evidence to support the claim, then he or she has begged the question.

Non Sequitur

This Latin phrase, literally translated, means "it does not follow." *The non sequitur fallacy contains a claim that is irrelevant to or unsupported by the evidence or premises purportedly supporting it.* In other words, the arguer grounds the argument in evidence that fails to support the claim advanced.

This fallacy, also known as "irrelevant reason," occurs very frequently. We are likely to be misled by it because the reasons or premises offered to support a conclusion somehow resemble the type of evidence that would be necessary to support it. People often present standards that *look* like evidence and connect them with claims in the same topic area, but actually the statements have no logical relation to each other. Consider the following two examples of *non sequitur* arguments:

> Plea bargaining affects many people. In the second quarter of 1993 in King County, there were 2,115 burglaries, 62 robberies, 109 rapes, and 2 murders.

In this argument, the first sentence is intended to be the claim and the second the evidence for it. But they are unrelated. The evidence does not tell us how many perpetrators of the listed crimes were arrested or charged, nor does it contain any information as to whether the charges were plea bargained. The only claim the evidence proves is there was crime in King County in 1993. The argument is clearly a *non sequitur.* The next one is more subtle.

> The United States is the only industrialized country in the world where teenage pregnancy is increasing. The Guttmachur study found that the U.S. pregnancy rate is twice that of Canada, England, or France, and seven times that of the Netherlands.

The first sentence is intended to be the claim and the second serves as evidence. Someone attending to this argument who is not aware of *non sequiturs* might easily be fooled. But notice that the evidence does not say that the pregnancy rate is *increasing,* only that it is higher than in other countries. To prove there's an increase, we would need comparable rates for different time periods showing that rates have increased in the recent past.

Non sequiturs are often subtle and yet seem obvious when they are pointed out. To detect them, we need constantly to ask, "What kind of evidence would be needed to support this claim?" and "Does this evidence qualify?"

RESEARCH STRATEGIES FOR LOCATING EVIDENCE

Computer programmers used to have the saying "garbage in, garbage out," which meant that the functioning of any program was only as good as the data input. The same is true of any argumentative speech or essay you might devise; your argument will be only as good as the quality of thought and the information that go into it. It is for this reason that research is vital to the success and effectiveness of your speech or essay. We have discussed the standards by which the facts, statistics, and opinions you use can be judged. The quality of your evidence will depend on the quality of the sources from which you take evidence, and that in turn will depend on your ability to do research and to find the high-quality sources that meet your needs.

Unfortunately, undertaking research these days is not an easy task. The variety and proliferation of places to do research, as well as the number of different kinds of sources available, present a daunting challenge to the novice researcher. What we aim to do here is to provide some basic guidelines and tips for locating materials to use in your argument. Our task, too, is complicated. First, nearly anything we say here about the use of electronic resources in doing research is liable to become dated in the near future. Second, we know that some of you who read this may be experienced researchers, or at least experienced at some forms of research, while others will have had very little experience with large libraries and electronic resources.

Before we begin discussing strategies for research, we want to remind you again of the importance of narrowing your topic and deciding on a specific question or proposition for discussion. (For in-depth discussion of this process, see Chapter 6.) As you begin your research, you will need to have decided whether you will be arguing a proposition of fact, value, or policy. You will also need to *narrow* broad categories so that they can be satisfactorily treated in the time you have available. For example, one probably cannot adequately discuss the entire topic of Affirmative Action in a short speech or essay, but one could specifically consider Affirmative Action in educational admissions or in certain hiring practices in that amount of time. Likewise, "gun control" would be too broad. What kinds of guns and what kinds of control would you specifically treat? Beginning by narrowing your topic will save you research time, because you will have a clear idea of what specific subjects you are searching *for* (assault weapons, handguns, restrictions on gun dealers, waiting periods, etc.), and this will focus your research and lead you to sources that will be directly relevant to the claims you want to make.

Our aim here is to save you some work by presenting an overview of the kinds of resources available and the best places to begin your research. We will deal with two categories of sources—types of *sites* for research, and types of *sources* where information can be found. Site types include online (electronic) sources, hard-copy (printed) sources, and CD-ROMs. Source types include books, periodicals, newspapers, government documents, general reference works, and other sources.

Site Types

One of the first choices you will have to make as you begin your research is *where* to begin. If you are connected to an online service or to the internet via a modem from home, you may choose to do your research from the comfort of your own study or dorm room. This choice would only be possible because of online resources available through remote access. At present, many of the processes executed through online connections can often be done more quickly and easily in a library or a "wired" computer laboratory in your school or college. (A "wired" environment is one that is connected to electronic services through a high speed cable rather than through a telephone line.) Since the environments and means for transmitting information online will change rapidly over the next few years, the best advice we can give you is to compare the efficiency and ease of working in the environments available to you and select the one that best meets your needs.

Also at present, there are some drawbacks to staying away from the library. First, some of the best full-text services such as Lexis/Nexis are only available at reasonable cost to students and library users in the library. Second, other services such as ERIC (the Education Resources Information Center) and Web browsers (indexes that search contents of the internet) run more quickly in a "wired" environment. Third, many sites may provide only an abstract and source information and not the full text of a document. For those, you must go to the "hard-copy" original source. And that, of course, is located in the library. At the end of this chapter, we will provide some exercises that enable you to do research in various environments, and you can judge the ease and effectiveness of working in these venues for yourself.

Online Sources

Online sources include the various databases and the World Wide Web. *Database* services are available through your college library and provide you with the ability to search various kinds of sources for the information you need. In 1996, such databases included the *Expanded Academic Index* (indexing scholarly and general interest periodicals), the *National Newspaper Index* (indexing five major newspapers), ERIC (indexing journals and documents in the field of education), the *Legal Resource Index* (including law reviews, bar association journals, and legal newspapers), and the *Business Index* (including business, management, and trade journals). A very effective way to begin research is to locate the names and functions of the various databases in your own library and search those. To *search* a database, follow these steps:

1. Identify the database you want to search.
2. Read the instructions for searching that database (usually in a help file, or ask your librarian).
3. Identify the *field* you want to search (author, title, subject, keyword, etc.)
4. Select any "limit options" to limit your search by type of source, date, etc.
5. Retrieve the list of sources in which you are interested.
6. Print or make a record of the sources you want to consult.

When you record your sources, be sure to include *all the source information you will need to document the source for your assignment* and *all the information (call number, etc.) you will need to locate the source in the library.* Careful record-keeping from the beginning of your research effort will save you a good deal of time at the end when you are preparing the assignment for submission to your instructor.

Other online research may include browsing the resources on the internet. The internet is a vast international network of computer networks connecting computers ranging from individual personal computers to supercomputers.[21] The World Wide Web, which is carried on the internet, is a hypertext gateway to the internet where resources (home pages, gopher sites, etc.) are interconnected via hypertext links.[22] Hypertext is any block of text that can be linked to other blocks of texts. At this time, there are two points we want to make about the World Wide Web and the internet:

1. To access information on the Web, you will need to have access to a Web search engine (such as Webcrawler or Alta Vista) or a Web subject directory (such as Yahoo). (Search engines search the contents of the internet using terms or words you provide; subject directories group or cluster web sites by type or subject category.) To research successfully on the Web, you will need to learn *how* to use the search mechanism by reading its help files and experimenting with it.
2. Since (as we have noted) the Web includes all sorts of Web sites or home pages, you will have to distinguish sources that are *not* credible (Joe Blow's home page)

from sources that *are* credible. In judging the credibility of a site, apply the criteria for evidence we presented earlier in this chapter, for example:

- Is the site author a credible authority or agency?
- Is the site current?
- Can the information it provides be corroborated with other sources?
- Is the information posted on the site objective, or is it posted by a special-interest or a biased party?

To help you begin your research on the Web, we have included some Web sites that can be regarded as highly credible and reliable (Figure 7–1). While these sites may not still be online at the time you read this book, the agencies who have posted them will probably still have a site that you can locate.

One of the drawbacks of the Web is its fugitive nature. Sites disappear. The servers (computers) that provide them malfunction; the people who maintain the sites move on to other activities; the agencies and organizations that maintain the sites reorganize or close down. When you make use of a site, you should be sure to document that source as you would any hard-copy source you might consult by reporting the name of author (if given), title of the text (underlined), publication medium (online), name of the archive or service, name of the computer network, and the date you consulted the source. Also, it is essential that you report the online address (displayed in the bar above the text you consult) so that someone could check your citation by consulting the address him/herself. It might also be a good idea to print the page from which you are drawing your information so you can verify it later.

Hard-Copy Sources

Your local or school library is a very fruitful source of all sorts of print-based information. When combined with high speed online data bases, these hard-copy sources can quickly and easily yield valuable information for your argumentative speech or essay. To be an effective researcher, you will need to accurately assess the quality of print materials and to be able to find the most useful sources on the library shelves. Our discussion of the various kinds of hard-copy sources at the end of this section should help you make optimal use of print materials.

The criterion of *quality* should always be considered as you do your research. As you locate, read, and record information, remember to regard your sources with a critical eye. Your first inclination may be to limit your research to accessible, popular periodicals and newspapers, such as *USA Today*, *Reader's Digest*, trade magazines, and news magazines such as *Time*, *U.S. News & World Report*, and *Newsweek*. These publications are NOT designed to provide analytical, in-depth coverage of major national and local issues, and we urge you not to rely on them as your sole source of information. While your search for evidence could begin with popular publications written for a mass audience, it should not stop there. Having gained basic information on your topic, you should move on to professional journals, government documents, scholarly books, and other, more advanced materials. These are generally written by experts and/or reviewed by authorities.

"COOL" WEB SITES (credible, objective, current, useful):

1. http://coombs.anu.edu.au/ResFacilities/DemographyPage.html
   Demography and population studies: Census information, Social Science Data Center, U.S. Census Bureau, Population Reference Bureau. Many links to census and demographic data in the United States and abroad.
2. http://www.stat-usa.gov/
   U.S. Department of Commerce: Budget of the U.S. government for upcoming year, export and international trade, personal income, consumer price index, retail sales, employment statistics, etc.
3. http://www.law.indiana.edu/law/v-lib/lawindex.html
   Indiana Law School, links in three categories: (1) Legal information by organization type (law schools, law firms, U.S. government servers, etc.); (2) Legal information by topic (Constitutional law, environmental law, torts, etc.); (3) Search tools (various law search engines and indices).
4. http://thomas.loc.gov/
   Federal government site on current legislation: Up-to-date summary by topic of bills introduced in current Congressional session, complete text of Constitution and all amendments, Index to activities of various congresspersons, new legislation in Congress in current week, searchable daily proceedings on floors of House and Senate, index to *Congressional Record*, etc.
5. http://marvel.loc.gov/homepage/lchp.html
   Part of Library of Congress services: links to decisions of the U.S. Supreme Court, decisions of federal circuit courts, home pages for various federal departments.
6. http://ericir.syr.edu
   A federally funded national information system that provides a variety of products and services on a broad range of education-related issues: Includes http addresses and links for American universities, the CIA, the *Chronicle of Higher Education*, the Library of Congress, the National Institutes of Health, the White House (labeled "concise guide to internet resources").
7. http://chronicle.merit.edu/
   Maintained by the *Chronicle of Higher Education:* The most useful information available only to subscribers, but does include valuable statistics on higher education, including characteristics of institutions, faculty, and students.
8. http://www.ed.gov/index.html
   Department of Education: Guide to initiatives for education—learning objectives for the 21st century, technology in education, etc.
9. http://lcweb.loc.gov/global/executive/white_house.html
   Executive branch of federal government: includes executives' press briefings, memoranda, executive orders, proclamations, speeches, town halls, appointments, nominations, and awards; inaugural addresses of all U.S. Presidents; link to White House WWW site (www.whitehouse.gov).

FIGURE 7–1 "Cool" Web Sites

You can also ensure that you have a thorough understanding of your topic and its complexities when you have read a *variety* of sources. Each type of source offers a different type of information and a different slant on the topic. Newspapers and news magazines report the "facts" from a supposedly "objective" point of view (although each publication has a political slant of some kind). Journals and many magazines offer *analyses* of events, often presenting many divergent perspectives and views. Books offer in-depth consideration of the topic from the point of view of a single individual or set of authors. By examining sources of different kinds, you will get a broad range of viewpoints and information of many varieties. The student who consults two journals, two books, and an encyclopedia on a topic will probably have more information of better quality than the student who reads three news magazines and two brief newspaper articles. In the last part of this section, we will discuss the specific virtues of various types of print sources. The sort of sources you use will relate to the nature and currency of your topic and the approach you plan to use in your argument.

CD-ROM Sources

A CD-ROM (compact disk—read only memory) is physically the same as an audio CD, but instead of storing music it stores computer data.[23] If your home computer has a CD drive and the capacity to "read" CD stored data, some of the CDs on the market may be useful to you in your research. Your reference librarian will probably have a source such as *CD-ROMs in Print* for the current year that indicates what is available in this format. The 1996 version of this source listed such products as *Grolier Encyclopedia Americana* (containing all thirty volumes of the 1995 edition of the *Encyclopedia Americana*), *Fast Reference Facts* (containing some 5000 facts taken from the ready-reference files of libraries), the *National Health Care Debate* (containing the full text of virtually all proposed health care legislation), and a *U.S. Government Periodicals Index* (but see the library reference sources to government periodicals in the next section).[24]

CD-ROMs have advantages and disadvantages. For those with the appropriate computer setup, CD-ROMs can provide a multimedia experience including sound and moving pictures of pretty high quality. CD-ROMs are storage devices, however, and this means that the individual user cannot change the contents of the disk. Because of the static nature of the information stored on CD-ROM, some databases that used to be on CD-ROM have gone online. Also, while much of the information online can be had for free from your local library, the material on CD-ROM is available only to those who purchase the CD-ROM or who can use one in a library. Because of their high storage capacity and comparatively low cost, CD-ROMs will continue to find a market. As to how effective they are as general research tools for your purposes, only future technological development and your own needs will determine that.

Source Types

Each type of source—book, periodical, newspaper, government document, or general reference work—presents a unique set of advantages and disadvantages to the researcher seeking information. The purpose of this section is to identify what each source type has to offer and to mention a few of the most valuable sources in each category.

Books

Books on a topic are usually easy to find and obtain. The researcher searches through a computerized catalog or a card catalog, locates the book, and identifies relevant information. While many books (particularly those by expert authors who ground their observations in information) may be very useful, there are certain disadvantages to consider. First, books are often dated by the time they appear. Producing a book often takes two years or more from the time it is written. So, if your topic requires you to have very recent information, then books may not be the best place to begin your research. Second, books take time to read. Therefore, if you draw heavily from a book and depend on its information for your argument, you should be sure that it is a credible source. You should obtain information regarding a book's authoritativeness, particularly if you plan to cite the book frequently. You can discover the author's qualifications by checking the back of the book or the book jacket or by consulting biographical resources that provide information about the author's credentials (Such as *Who's Who;* see Figure 7–2). You can also read reviews of the book. The *Book Review Index,* for example, contains an author listing with abbreviated citations to reviews in over 450 publications in the fields of general fiction and nonfiction, humanities, and social sciences. If you have trouble getting information about the author's credentials or reviews of the book, ask your librarian for help.

Periodicals

Periodicals are sources published periodically—weekly, monthly, quarterly, semiannually, or annually. They include popular magazines as well as professional journals. Periodicals are useful sources of information for topics of current interest because they are often up to date. Periodicals offer contemporary opinion on current events and issues as well as chronologies and relevant facts.

As with other sources, you should be careful to ascertain the credibility of the periodical as well as of the author of the particular article you are consulting. Certain periodicals provide lengthy, credible articles by experts in various fields. Examples would be *Commentary, Harper's, Fortune, The Atlantic, The Progressive, Congressional Digest, Congressional Quarterly,* and *Current History.* Some magazines have a definite editorial slant. *The Progressive* and *New Republic,* for example, are considered to be on the liberal end of the spectrum, while *National Review* is considered conservative.

To locate information on your topic in magazines, determine the relevant database for the type of periodicals you want to consult. Databases are usually organized by *field.* The following fields presently have databases indexing periodicals in that area—architecture, literature, business, law, public affairs, medicine, psychology, physical sciences, engineering, computing, and anthropology. And, as we have pointed out, there is a general periodical index—the *Expanded Academic Index.* Therefore, you should determine which fields are most likely to contain periodicals relevant to your topic and ask your librarian to direct you to the databases that index those periodicals. Once you have located articles and abstracts that seem to contain relevant information, consult your library catalog to find out the periodical's call number, and then locate the journal or magazine on the shelves in your library. Be sure to record all the information about the periodical while you are in the database—volume number, date, and page number,

> **VALUABLE HARD COPY SOURCES** (quick, easy, widely available, useful)
>
> 1. *Encyclopaedia Britannica*
> The most scholarly English language encyclopedia available, this reference work is divided into a micropaedia, a macropaedia, and an index. The revised 15th edition (1991) was the most recent available at this writing. The micropaedia is an independent ready-reference source with short articles on a wide range of topics. The macropaedia contains monograph-length articles written by an expert on the subject. The index to this work is the way to use it to best advantage.
>
> 2. *Encyclopedia Americana*
> This is a good, comprehensive encyclopedia particularly strong in information about Americans, American towns and cities, and other subjects particular to the United States. The articles are generally short and on specific subjects, but many lengthy articles on broad topics are also included.
>
> 3. *Facts on File*
> This world news digest is very current and emphasizes news events in the United States. It gathers material from 70 major newspapers and magazines condensed into short, factual reports, and it is arranged geographically by region.
>
> 4. *World Almanac*
> This useful and comprehensive American almanac contains statistics on social, industrial, political, financial, religious, educational, and other subjects.
>
> 5. *Who's Who in America*
> The best-known and generally most useful of works of this type, this source focuses on notable living men and women who are selected because of their accomplishments or positions. The entries contain biographical information, addresses, and lists of works by the individual.
>
> 6. *Dictionary of American Biography*
> This source provides biographical information about noteworthy persons who are not living. Each entry includes signed articles and bibliographies.
>
> 7. *Statistical Abstract of the United States*
> This invaluable compendium of statistics is compiled by the Bureau of the Census. It has topically organized chapters on population, banking, finance, insurance, social welfare, environment, energy, agriculture, manufacturing, etc. It has a comprehensive and easy-to-use index. If you need to find a statistic, it's probably there!

FIGURE 7-2 Valuable Hard-Copy Sources

for example. Then, finding the article once you have found the periodical on the shelves should be a simple matter.

Newspapers

Newspapers are indispensable sources providing the most current information on major events, issues, and persons. Aside from their editorial pages, they provide mainly factual information, although certain newspapers, like certain magazines, may have an editorial slant that influences their news coverage. Since metropolitan newspapers appear daily, they provide the most up-to-date coverage of current events. Most major newspapers are indexed so that articles can be quickly and easily located.

Most newspapers are on microfilm. Actual copies of the newspapers are kept for only a short time by libraries, then they are photographed and put on microfilm reels for compact storage. To consult them, you must locate a reel, load it on to a microfilm reader, and roll through the reel until you find the newspaper article you are seeking. This is time-consuming but only minimally problematic. You can use newspaper indices to find out how long an article is, what its contents are, and how useful it will be to you. Then you can make an informed decision on whether microfilm consultation is worth your time. Consulting microfilm takes only a little more time than consulting the hard copy of the newspaper itself.

The *National Newspaper Index* catalogues material in *The New York Times, Washington Post, Wall Street Journal, Christian Science Monitor,* and *Los Angeles Times.* Other prominent newspapers, such as the *London Times, Chicago Tribune,* and *San Francisco Chronicle,* are also individually indexed. Some newspapers have been placed on CD-ROM. Consult your librarian to find out the best and most efficient way to access the newspaper texts you want to read.

Government Documents

Government documents provide a rich source for your research, both online and in hard copy. Government web sites (such as those listed in Figure 7–1) provide a great deal of information that is well indexed, credible, and *free,* because the government's role as information provider is financed through the federal government rather than through proprietary, for-profit sources. Many students are intimidated by the volume and complexity of resources in government documents, yet they need not be. Librarians working with government documents collections generally recognize the public's need for guidance in using government collections and are very helpful. Also, the policies for recording and cataloging government proceedings and resources are rapidly changing, so the help of a librarian knowledgeable about government documents is most valuable.

As indicated in our description of web sites in Figure 7–1, the U.S. government compiles sizable amounts of useful data on such matters as the demographics of the U.S. population, current bills in Congress, recent decisions of the U.S. Supreme Court and federal circuit courts, proposed initiatives and changes in the law, U.S. foreign policy around the world, and many other topics that may be relevant to your argument research. The *Congressional Quarterly Weekly Report* offers an informative weekly summary of congressional action and developments, including sections such as "Inside Congress," "Economics and Finance," "Defense and Foreign Policy," and "Government and Commerce." Catalogs of government publications (as compiled by various commercial services) are available in most libraries. The Marcive Catalog, for example, is a CD-ROM that begins in 1976 and includes a catalog of congressional bills, hearings, reports, issue papers, and statements by experts indexed by title or series, author or agency, subject, and document number. The *Index to U.S. Government Periodicals* provides author and subject access to over 170 government periodicals on a variety of subjects. The *Congressional Record* prints the debates and proceedings of Congress on a daily basis. It includes speeches, voting records, and other material, including anything Congress members want inserted in it. Because Congress members can edit any of their speeches or remarks before they are printed in the *Record,* this is not an entirely accurate record of what they actually said.

General Reference Works and Other Sources

General reference works—such as encyclopedias, dictionaries, biographical dictionaries, fact books, and compendiums—are often the quickest and easiest way to locate particular facts and information. Your local public or college library probably contains a good collection of reference works in all of the above categories. Figure 7–2 lists and describes some of the most prominent and frequently used reference works.[25] We have identified encyclopedias most appropriate for adult and college audiences (as opposed to those written for school-aged audiences). As we noted when discussing books and articles, biographical dictionaries are useful for discovering the credentials of the authors you cite in your argument. Fact books and compendiums are particularly useful if you want to discover the background or development over time of an issue or event. We encourage you to consult these readily available and easy-to-use sources as you gather evidence to support the claims in your argument.

One additional resource you might want to consider is information gained through interviews of local experts or persons knowledgeable on your topic. Since the information you cite in your formal argument must be independently available to your listeners or opponents, statements made to you in interviews are not a viable source of opinion evidence. Interviews are useful, however, in helping you to discover sources on your topic that you might not have discovered in your research, and interviewees can also help you to determine if you are "on the right track" in your thinking and your argument.

If you do decide to interview a source, there are five guidelines to keep in mind.[26] First, allow time to set up an appointment in advance; busy interviewees are often unavailable on short notice. Second, prepare for the interview by doing research on the topic so that you will appear well informed and credible in asking your questions. Try to limit your questions to matters you yourself have been unable to locate elsewhere. Third, before the interview, plan a schedule of questions that are open-ended and cover all the major topics about which you are concerned. Fourth, record the interview carefully, either in writing or by means of a tape recorder (with the interviewee's permission). In case the recorder did not work or your notes are hard to make out, be sure to transcribe the information immediately after the interview while it is still fresh in your mind. Fifth, be sure to express your appreciation in writing to the interviewee as soon as possible after the interview.

Various researchers develop various methods and strategies for finding the information they need to support their argument. Some prefer online resources and supplement them with printed material when necessary, while others prefer browsing the library shelves and using reference materials. Others prefer to begin with pro/con analyses of issues relevant to their topic so as to get an overview of the various arguments and perspectives that experts have identified. Still others prefer to begin by reading a credible book on the topic to get a sense of its development and history. Each person develops a style and a preferred method for doing research. In this section, however, we have identified some *principles* to keep in mind: use credible, adult-level materials rather than those written for a mass audience; corroborate your information by referring to a variety of sources on the topic; record source information as you locate it so as to have it ready to place in your bibliography; use only information that could be verified by a third party. If you follow these principles and test your information according to the guidelines for evidence discussed earlier in this chapter, then you will have a compelling and well-grounded argument that will be respected by your listeners—both those who agree with you, and those who do not!

SUMMARY

It is vital to be aware of the absence or misuse of evidence in arguments we hear and read and of its importance in the arguments we make. As defined in Chapter 1, evidence includes objectively observable facts and conditions, generally accepted beliefs or premises, and previously established conclusions. The purposes of this chapter are to discuss the nature and types of evidence, to provide guidelines for using evidence, and to explain how to locate and organize evidence when doing research.

Evidence functions as such because it is accepted by recipients and can be used to support other statements. If participants in an argument dispute a statement, it cannot function as evidence because it is not agreed upon. Generally, evidence falls into two broad classifications—fact and opinion as to fact.

Factual evidence comes from our observations and experience. It includes reports and descriptions of events or phenomena, statistics, and artifacts that are actual objects used to support an argument. Factual evidence is expected to mirror physical reality.

Opinion evidence is someone's interpretation of the meaning of factual evidence. When an arguer uses opinion evidence, he or she uses the statement of someone else to support a claim. Opinion evidence from experts is useful when an arguer does not have a great deal of personal experience with the subject of the argument.

We should be aware of the quality of evidence so that we can judge the quality of support for our own and others' arguments. Evidence should come from reliable sources who have proven correct many times in the past. Sources for evidence should have expertise in the subject matter of the argument, and it is important that audiences be informed of sources' qualifications when evidence is given. Sources should be objective, offering an undistorted and fair view of the question or issue. Evidence should be consistent, both with itself and with evidence from other sources. It should also be of recent vintage, particularly on topics in which conditions change over time. Evidence offered to support a claim should be directly relevant to the claim as stated rather than tangential or irrelevant. People who testify about a situation should have had access to it and an opportunity to observe it firsthand. Otherwise, the evidence is hearsay and less reliable. Finally, arguers who cite the statements of others should be accurate. They should not violate the context or intended meaning behind a quotation by omitting crucial words, making secondary sources seem to be primary, or omitting information about the source's qualifications or where the information was found.

Like other forms of evidence, statistics are often subject to bias and human error as well as errors by the people who use them. There are certain problems unique to the discovery and use of evidence, however. First, we should be aware of pseudo-statistics, those that are applied to phenomena and situations in which it is difficult to imagine how they could have been compiled using good statistical methods. Second, we should be cautious about comparing noncomparable units that seem to be of the same class but that are actually different. Third, we should use a representative sample, one that includes all the important characteristics of the group from which it was drawn.

Fallacies of evidence occur when arguers use poor evidence or no evidence at all. When arguers ask recipients to draw conclusions from premises that are either missing or inappropriate to the claim, their arguments fail the tests of evidence. One fallacy of evidence, begging the question, results when an arguer equates evidence with the conclusion it is intended to support. A second fallacy of evidence, *non sequitur,* occurs when the evidence offered is irrelevant to the claim made.

Because arguments are only as good as the quality of evidence from which they are drawn, research is vital to mounting a credible argument. Therefore, relying exclusively on popular magazines and trade books is not sufficient to obtaining good information and statistics. Professional journals, government documents, and scholarly books will provide extensive, credible information on topics for argument.

Developments in computer-mediated communication and CD-ROM resources have broadened the choices researchers have for finding evidence. Online sources include various databases and the World Wide Web. Strategies for accessing, evaluating, and recording information from these sources are included in this chapter.

Other sources come in hard-copy (print) form. Library databases may lead the researcher to books, but the researcher should check the author's credentials carefully and should realize that information from books on some topics is often dated.

Periodicals and newspapers provide very current information on most topics. Periodicals range in bias from the extreme left to the radical right. They also range from popular and trade magazines to scholarly journals. Researchers can avoid relying on slanted or inexpert information by being aware of the nature and editorial biases of the periodicals they use and by consulting a wide range of periodicals. Newspapers are very current and useful when you need a chronology of facts and events related to a certain topic. Most major metropolitan newspapers are indexed. *The New York Times* is the national newspaper of record, and *The Washington Post* and the *Los Angeles Times* are also highly regarded.

Other sources of information include encyclopedias, biographical dictionaries, pamphlets and brochures, interviews, and media broadcasts. The chapter suggests guidelines and lists specific indexes and catalogs for each of these forms of evidence. The type of information source selected depends on the arguer's purpose and the topic being treated. Since the support offered for arguments is an important factor in whether they are accepted, arguers should locate and use a large quantity of high-quality evidence.

EXERCISES

Exercise 1 The following passages help illustrate correct and incorrect uses of evidence. For each passage try to identify the primary weaknesses by applying the following criteria as discussed in this chapter.

Tests of Evidence. Apply each of the following tests to the passages:

Reliability	Evidence should be drawn from sources that have proven to be correct many times in the past.
Expertise	Evidence should be drawn from sources having a background of knowledge in relevant information.
Objectivity	Evidence should be taken from sources who hold a fair and undistorted view on a question or issue.
Consistency	Evidence should agree with other sources and should be consistent with itself.
Recency	Evidence should be based on the most current information available.
Relevance	The facts and evidence presented should be relevant to the claim that is made.

CHAPTER SEVEN   Evidence: The Foundation for Arguments **175**

Access | Evidence should be drawn from sources who have observed firsthand the matter being disputed.

Accuracy | Citations should be complete and the sources of evidence fully identified.

Fallacies of Evidence. Look for any mistakes in evidence use. As you may recall from the chapter, the two fallacies we discussed were:

Begging the Question | This assumes as evidence for an argument the claim that is being made.

Nonsequitur | This occurs when an arguer makes a claim that is unsupported by the evidence.

Now, here is the evidence to be evaluated.

* 1. Mr. Herbert Kause convincingly argued last month that pregnant women should restrict their intake of caffeine. According to studies he conducted over the past six years, he has found strong evidence that supports the conclusion that caffeine is dangerous to unborn children.

  2. Recently, at the University of Wisconsin, a study was conducted on listening and study patterns of freshmen students in a Speech 101 course. This study found that students in this course exhibited a lack of concentration in their studies and note-taking. Therefore, we can conclude that college students have poor study skills.

  3. In a special advertisement on Zenith Data Systems, Enrico Pesatori, Zenith Data Systems president and chief executive officer, said, "We have taken many major steps over the past 18 months to respond to our customers' needs for innovative, aggressively priced products, and to adapt to the upheaval in the PC industry. The product lines we have developed will clearly distinguish Zenith Data Systems in the marketplace."

  4. But, in actuality, almost 25,000 people are involved in fatal alcohol-related accidents per year. Of these 25,000 people, over 25% are under the age of 21. This means we are losing over 6000 young people per year because of alcohol. There are several reasons a nationwide drinking age should be enforced. Statistics show that raising the age would save over 750 young lives per year nationwide.

* 5. We should reinstitute the military draft in this country. After all, we should recall John F. Kennedy's famous words "Ask not what your country can do for you, ask what you can do for your country." Our country is currently in a military force crisis and a military draft is something we can do for our country.

  6. As the National Rifle Association has argued, if handguns were made illegal, then only those people who abide by the law would be barred from obtaining handguns. The criminals and the smugglers and racketeers would still have them.

  7. A nationwide survey of college freshmen by Alexander W. Astin in 1991 revealed that 85.5% of those polled agreed that the government is not doing

enough to control pollution. Water and air pollution controls should definitely be increased.

8. According to the Environmental Policy Institute and the Health and Energy Institute, "The Food and Drug Administration allowed irradiation of canned bacon in 1963 based on Army research. Five years later the FDA rescinded the approval, saying that the tests had been improperly structured and sloppily conducted."

9. A cosmetic company conducted a study of prospective customers for a new skin lotion. They sent 10,000 questionnaires to these customers asking them to compare the new product with a variety of other products. Ninety percent of those responding favored the new skin lotion; therefore the cosmetic company should proceed with production of the new lotion.

* 10. Dr. Harvey Brenner concluded a study of unemployment in 1975. He argued that for each 1% increase in the unemployment rate, the death rate increases by 36,667 lives. Therefore, the federal government should take immediate action to decrease the levels of unemployment in this country.

11. Disco music has some important side effects. The United Press reports that "Disco music causes homosexuality in mice and may make no exception where men are concerned" according to a study at the Aegean University. The study also found that disco music caused deafness among pigs.

12. Cheating in school has reached epidemic proportions. In a study conducted at a large eastern university, researchers discovered that 88.3 percent of the students cheated at some point in their academic career.

13. Cats are more popular than dogs as pets because people like them better.

14. American families are on a collision course with their own culture. We watch a great deal of television and media violence. Children are not doing as much homework as they used to.

15. The *Cecil Textbook of Medicine* reported in its 5th edition on page 1031 that "in a series of patients studied post-mortem more than 90 percent complained of shortness of breath."—From the *Journal of Irreproducible Results,* 40(2), (1995): 15.

Exercise 2 Find an editorial in a local newspaper or magazine and analyze the evidence in it. When you are done you should be able to do the following:

1. What types of evidence did you discover?
2. What were the strengths and weaknesses of the evidence?
3. Did you discover any fallacies?

Exercise 3 Below are a number of pieces of information that could be relevant as evidence for certain claims in argumentative speeches or essays. To complete this exercise, divide the class into groups of three or four. Within each group, each individual should decide on the certain *types* of resources (e.g., the internet, CD-ROMs, books, periodicals, newspapers, etc.) in which to look for the answers to these questions and inform the other group members where s/he plans to look. When everyone has had an oppor-

CHAPTER SEVEN   Evidence: The Foundation for Arguments   **177**

tunity to locate the information in question, reconvene your group. Then, consider the following questions:

1. Did everyone find the same answer to the question? What was it?
2. If different sources differed in the answer, how can the discrepancy be resolved?
3. How long did it take to find the answers to the questions in the various sources available? (That is, which sources were the easiest to use and the most efficient?)
4. How credible and in-depth is the information provided in the various sources?
5. Based on your experience, develop a "position statement" to share with the class about your group's views on the best strategies and venues for conducting research to locate evidence.

Now here are the questions to answer:

1. What are the demographics (age, income, profession, etc.) of internet users?
2. What is happening to the hole in the ozone layer?
3. What have been major instances of terrorism against U.S. citizens (at home or abroad) during the past 12 months?
4. What is the most effective form of birth control currently available?
5. What bills related to gun control are currently being considered by the U.S. Congress?
6. What are said to be the major causes of domestic violence (spousal and child abuse) in the United States?
7. What are the most promising treatments presently available for AIDS?
8. What are the gun control laws in four nations not including the United States?
9. How promising is solar power as a major energy resource?
10. What is the current status of the deforestation of rain forests? Who benefits from clearing the forests?

Exercise 4 In 1954 the Supreme Court decided the case of *Brown v. Board of Education of Topeka*. This decision overturned the 1896 ruling of *Plessy v. Fergson*. In *Plessy*, the court had argued that separate facilities (in this case train cars) but equal treatment guaranteed equal protection to people of different races and ethnicity under the law. The *Brown* decision argued the proposition that separate is inherently unequal (proposition of fact). Read the decision by Chief Justice Warren (below) and consider the following:

1. Underline each example of evidence you can find.
2. Do you think separate can be equal? What arguments presented in this case convince you or fail to convince you?
3. How would you describe the use of evidence in this argument? Does the decision seem to rest on one type of evidence more than others?
4. How would you evaluate the use of evidence? Was it used appropriately?
5. If you were going to deliver a similar argument in front of a community group, would you use the same evidence? If not, what other types of evidence might you use to support your argument?

These cases come to us from the States of Kansas, South Carolina, Virginia, and Delaware. They are premised on different facts and different local conditions, but a common legal question justifies their consideration together in this consolidated opinion.

In each of the cases, minors of the Negro race, through their legal representatives, seek the aid of the courts in obtaining admission to the public schools of their community on a nonsegregated basis. In each instance, they had been denied admission to schools attended by white children under laws requiring or permitting segregation according to race. This segregation was alleged to deprive the plaintiffs of the equal protection of the laws under the Fourteenth Amendment. In each of the cases other than the Delaware case, a three-judge federal district court denied relief to the plaintiffs on the so-called "separate but equal" doctrine announced by this Court in *Plessy v. Ferguson*, 163 U.S. 537. Under that doctrine, equality of treatment is accorded when the races are provided substantially equal facilities, even though these facilities be separate. In the Delaware case, the Supreme Court of Delaware adhered to that doctrine, but ordered that the plaintiffs be admitted to the white schools because of their superiority to the Negro schools.

The plaintiffs contend that segregated public schools are not "equal" and cannot be made "equal," and that hence they are deprived of the equal protection of the laws. Because of the obvious importance of the question presented, the Court took jurisdiction. Argument was heard in the 1952 Term, and reargument was heard this Term on certain questions propounded by the Court.

Reargument was largely devoted to the circumstances surrounding the adoption of the Fourteenth Amendment in 1868. It covered exhaustively consideration of the Amendment in Congress, ratification by the states, then-existing practices in racial segregation, and the views of proponents and opponents of the Amendment. This discussion and our own investigation convince us that, although these sources cast some light, it is not enough to resolve the problem with which we are faced. At best, they are inconclusive. The most avid proponents of the post-War Amendments undoubtedly intended them to remove all legal distinctions among "all persons born or naturalized in the United States." Their opponents, just as certainly, were antagonistic to both the letter and the spirit of the Amendments and wished them to have the most limited effect. What others in Congress and the state legislatures had in mind cannot be determined with any degree of certainty.

An additional reason for the inconclusive nature of the Amendment's history with respect to segregated schools is the status of public education at that time. In the South, the movement toward free common schools, supported by general taxation, had not yet taken hold. Education of white children was largely in the hands of private groups. Education of Negroes was almost nonexistent, and practically all of the race were illiterate. In fact, any education of Negroes was forbidden by law in some states. Today, in contrast, many Negroes have achieved outstanding success in the arts and sciences, as well as in the business and professional world. It is true that public school education at the time of the Amendment had advanced further in the North, but the effect of the Amendment on Northern States was generally ignored in the congressional debates. Even in the North, the conditions of public education did not approximate those existing today. The curriculum was usually rudimentary; ungraded schools were common in rural areas; the school term was but three months a year in many states, and compulsory school attendance was virtually unknown. As a consequence, it is not surprising that there should be so little in the history of the Fourteenth Amendment relating to its intended effect on public education.

In the first cases in this Court construing the Fourteenth Amendment, decided shortly after its adoption, the Court interpreted it as proscribing all state-imposed discriminations against the Negro race. The doctrine of "separate but equal" did not make its appearance in Court until 1896 in the case of *Plessy v. Ferguson, supra,* involving not education but transportation. American courts have since labored with the doctrine for over half a century. In this Court, there have been six cases involving the "separate but equal" doctrine in the field of public education. In *Cumming v. County Board of Education,* 175 U.S. 528, and *Gong Lum v. Rice,* 275 U.S. 78, the validity of the doctrine itself was not challenged. In more recent cases, all on the graduate school level, inequality was found in that specific benefits enjoyed by white students were denied to Negro students of the same educational qualifications. *Missouri ex rel. Gaines v. Canada,* 305 U.S. 337; *Sipuel v. Oklahoma,* 332 U.S. 631; *Sweatt v. Painter,* 339 U.S. 629; *McLaurin v. Oklahoma State Regents,* 339 U.S. 637. In none of these cases was it necessary to reexamine the doctrine to grant relief to the Negro plaintiff. And in *Sweatt v. Painter, supra,* the Court expressly reserved decision on the question whether *Plessy v. Ferguson* should be held inapplicable to public education.

In the instant cases, that question is directly presented. Here, unlike *Sweatt v. Painter,* there are findings below that the Negro and white schools involved have been equalized, or are being equalized, with respect to buildings, curricula, qualifications and salaries of teachers, and other "tangible" factors. Our decision, therefore, cannot turn on merely a comparison of these tangible factors in the Negro and white schools involved in each of the cases. We must look instead to the effect of segregation itself on public education.

In approaching this problem, we cannot turn the clock back to 1868, when the Amendment was adopted, or even to 1896, when *Plessy v. Ferguson* was written. We must consider public education in the light of its full development and its present place in American life throughout the Nation. Only in this way can it be determined if segregation in public schools deprives these plaintiffs of the equal protection of the laws.

Today, education is perhaps the most important function of state and local governments. Compulsory school attendance laws and the great expenditures for education both demonstrate our recognition of the importance of education to our democratic society. It is required in the performance of our most basic public responsibilities, even service in the armed forces. It is the very foundation of good citizenship. Today it is a principal instrument in awakening the child to cultural values, in preparing him for later professional training, and in helping him to adjust normally to his environment. In these days, it is doubtful that any child may reasonably be expected to succeed in life if he is denied the opportunity of an education. Such an opportunity, where the state has undertaken to provide it, is a right which must be made available to all on equal terms.

We come then to the question presented: Does segregation of children in public schools solely on the basis of race, even though the physical facilities and other "tangible" factors may be equal, deprive the children of the minority group of equal educational opportunities? We believe that it does.

In *Sweatt v. Painter, supra,* in finding that a segregated law school for Negroes could not provide them equal educational opportunities, this Court relied in large part on "those qualities which are incapable of objective measurement but which make for greatness in a law school." In *McLaurin v. Oklahoma State Regents, supra,* the Court, in requiring that a Negro admitted to a white graduate school be treated like all other students, again resorted to intangible considerations: "his ability to study, to engage in discussions and exchange views with other students, and, in general, to learn his profession." Such considerations apply with added force to children in grade and high schools. To separate them from others of similar age and qualifications solely because of their race generates a feeling of inferiority as to their status in the community that may affect their hearts and minds in a way unlikely ever to be undone. The effect of this separation on their educational opportunities was well stated by a finding in the Kansas case by a court which nevertheless felt compelled to rule against the Negro plaintiffs:

Segregation of white and colored children in public schools has a detrimental effect upon the colored children. The impact is greater when it has the sanction of the law, for the policy of separating the races is usually interpreted as denoting the inferiority of the negro group. A sense of inferiority affects the motivation of a child to learn. Segregation with the sanction of law, therefore, has a tendency to [retard] the educational and mental development of negro children and to deprive them of some of the benefits they would receive in a racial[ly] integrated school system.

Whatever may have been the extent of psychological knowledge at the time of *Plessy v. Ferguson,* this finding is amply supported by modern authority. Any language in *Plessy v. Ferguson* contrary to this finding is rejected.

We conclude that, in the field of public education, the doctrine of "separate but equal" has no place. Separate educational facilities are inherently unequal. Therefore, we hold that the plaintiffs and others similarly situated for whom the actions have been brought are, by reason of the segregation complained of, deprived of the equal protection of the laws guaranteed by the Fourteenth Amendment. This disposition makes unnecessary any discussion whether such segregation also violates the Due Process Clause of the Fourteenth Amendment.

Because these are class actions, because of the wide applicability of this decision, and because of the great variety of local conditions, the formulation of decrees in these cases presents problems of considerable complexity. On reargument, the consideration of appropriate relief was necessarily subordinated to the primary question—the constitutionality of segregation in public education. We have now announced that such segregation is a denial of the equal protection of the laws. In order that we may have the full assistance of the parties in formulating decrees, the cases will be restored to the docket, and the parties are requested to present further argument on Questions 4 and 5 previously propounded by the Court for the reargument this Term. The Attorney General of the United States is again invited to participate. The Attorneys General of the states requiring or permitting segregation in public education will also be permitted to appear as *amici curiae* upon request to do so by September 15, 1954, and submission of briefs by October 1, 1954.

It is so ordered.

NOTES

1. Russel R. Windes and Arthur Hastings, *Argumentation and Advocacy* (New York: Random House, 1965), 95.
2. For an account of Nazi propaganda efforts, see Randall L. Bytwerk, *Julius Streicher* (New York: Stein & Day, 1983).
3. James C. McCroskey, "A Summary of Experimental Research on the Effects of Evidence in Persuasive Communication," *Quarterly Journal of Speech* 55 (1969): 169–76.
4. Bill Carter, "Baywatch Image," *New York Times* (July 3, 1995): 41.
5. "Baywatch," *Entertainment Weekly* (May 20, 1993): 8.
6. A discussion of this division and the types of evidence is presented in George W. Ziegelmueller

and Charles A. Dause, *Argumentation: Inquiry and Advocacy* (Englewood Cliffs, N.J.: Prentice-Hall, 1975), 49–82. See also a discussion of the types of evidence in J. Vernon Jensen, *Argumentation: Reasoning in Communication* (New York: Van Nostrand, 1981), 107–37; and Douglas Ehninger, *Influence, Belief, and Argument* (Glenview, Ill: Scott Foresman, 1974), 51–66.
7. Ehninger, 52.
8. Mark Shaffer, "Raising a Stink over Horse Diapers," *Tacoma News Tribune* (September 25, 1995): A4.
9. Shelby Gilje, "Some Want July Fourth Fireworks to Fizzle," *Seattle Times* (June 28, 1987): K1.
10. Edward Sussman, "The Law School Shell Game," *POV* (May 1996): 48.
11. Christopher John Farley, "Cough Up That Cash," *Time* (March 6, 1995): 47.
12. Shari Roan, "Psychologists Rate Presidents' Personalities," *Tacoma News Tribune* (August 14, 1996): SL 13.
13. Robert P. Newman and Dale R. Newman, *Evidence* (New York: Houghton Mifflin, 1969), 95–6.
14. This research is summarized in Robert N. Bostrom, *Persuasion* (Englewood Cliffs, N.J.: Prentice-Hall, 1983), 79–81.
15. Ehninger, 61.
16. Newman and Newman, 75–6.
17. Newman and Newman, 223–4.
18. Newman and Newman, 206–7.
19. Newman and Newman, 211–3.
20. From Plato *Timaeus,* Cited in Irving Copi, *Informal Logic* (New York: Macmillan, 1986), 111.
21. University of Washington Libraries, "The Internet: An Overview & Bibliography," The Internet Series Number 1: Copyright 1994 [rev. 9/95 aez].
22. University of Washington Libraries, "WWW: The World Wide Web," The Internet Series Number 11: Copyright 1994, University of Washington Libraries. [9/95, ke & tm]
23. Jakob Nielsen, *Multimedia and Hypertext: The Internet and Beyond* (Boston: AP Professional, 1995), 160.
24. Erin E. Holmberg, ed. *CD-ROMs in Print 1996* (New York: Gale Research, 1996).
25. Information regarding many of the sources described here was taken from Robert Balay, ed. *Guide to Reference Books,* 11th ed. (Chicago: American Library Association, 1996).
26. Useful material about constructing interview schedules and conducting information-gathering interviews can be found in Charles J. Stewart and William B. Cash's *Interviewing: Principles and Practices,* 5th ed. (Dubuque, Iowa: William C. Brown, 1988).

CHAPTER 8

Reasoning: Making Inferences

CHAPTER OUTLINE

- Formal Logic and Practical Reasoning
- Reasoning as Inference Making
  - Quasilogical Arguments
  - Analogy
  - Generalization and Argument from Example
  - Cause
  - Coexistential Arguments
  - Dissociation
- Fallacies of Faulty Reasoning
  - False Analogy
  - Hasty Generalization
  - False Cause
  - Slippery Slope
- Summary
- Exercises

KEY CONCEPTS

inference
syllogism
categorical syllogism
enthymeme
disjunctive syllogism
quasilogical arguments

analogy
literal analogy
figurative analogy
generalization
argument from example
cause

183

necessary condition
sufficient condition
correlation
argument from coexistence
person/act argument
argument from authority
dissociation argument

value hierarchy
false analogy
hasty generalization
post hoc fallacy
single-cause fallacy
slippery slope fallacy

This chapter will consider the reasoning process used in arguments. As you may recall from Chapter 1, reasoning is the rational link between the evidence and the claim in the argument; it authorizes the step an arguer makes when he or she connects an argument's evidence to its claim. When we reason, we make connections, distinctions, and predictions; we use what is known or familiar to us to reach a conclusion about that which is unknown or unfamiliar. In reasoning, we might break a whole into its component parts, consider the precise way in which the parts are connected to each other, extrapolate from a situation we can see to some underlying condition, or in some other way think about the world and how it operates. Good critical thinking involves good reasoning that meets certain tests for the particular kind of reasoning being used. In this chapter, we will briefly discuss the contemporary history of the study of reasoning, describe six forms of reasoning frequently used in everyday life, and state and apply the tests for those six types of reasoning.

Competent reasoners can evaluate their own and others' reasoning, construct good arguments themselves, and identify the unstated assumptions and connections people make in their arguments. They can also analyze the arguments of other people to discover their strengths and weaknesses. As we noted in Chapter 1, reasoning, along with claims and evidence, is one of the three basic components of any argument. Chapter 6, on argument claims, focused on clearly stating the end point of an argument; Chapter 7, on evidence, emphasized the need to identify and critique the starting point of an argument and to apply standards to judge the quality of evidence offered for a claim. This chapter will concentrate on the rational connection an arguer makes between the two when she or he constructs an argument.

In moving from what is known and acceptable (the evidence) to what is unknown or controversial (the claim), arguers often state their reasoning in an *inference*. *An inference states the step one has made in linking the evidence to the claim.* Inferences can be explicit or implicit in an argument. For example, we might explicitly say "Don't play in the street *because a car might hit you.*" On the other hand, we might simply say "Don't play in the street. You might get hurt." In this case, the inference, "because a car might hit you," is unstated or implicit. In studying and analyzing the arguments of others and in detecting possible weaknesses in reasoning, it is important to be able to identify the *type of reasoning* used in the argument, even if the arguer does not state it.

When people use arguments, they employ various inference patterns that they themselves may not always be able to identify and explain. Sometimes you can "flush out" a person's reasoning by way of a challenge ("Wait a minute, how did you reach *that* conclusion, based on the information you just gave me?"). Often, the unstated inference is the weak point in the person's argument. If you can identify how the arguer connected the claim to the evidence, you will know what type of reasoning was employed. Each kind of reasoning suggests a set of tests or questions that function as standards to evaluate its quality. Knowing what type of reasoning was used and what tests to apply will improve your critical thinking skills as you become better able to analyze and critique others' arguments.

Knowing the various kinds of reasoning will not only make you a better argument critic, it will make you a better arguer yourself. If you know the various reasoning forms and the tests and standards for judging them, you will be better able to monitor the effectiveness and quality of your own reasoning which is another important critical thinking skill. Argument theorist Stephen Toulmin has observed that a "sound" argument is "one that will stand up to criticism."[1] Each of the inference types discussed in this chapter—quasilogical, analogy, generalization, cause, coexistence, and dissociation—must meet certain standards to be judged to be sound.[2] Knowing these types and the tests applicable to them will enable you to foresee possible weaknesses in your arguments and anticipate objections others might raise to them.

FORMAL LOGIC AND PRACTICAL REASONING

The contemporary study of reasoning has its roots in the field of formal logic. During the first half of the 20th century, most students studied logic in a philosophy course, where they concentrated on the forms and application of formal and symbolic logic.[3] Logic in these courses was considered to be a formal science, a type of theoretical study free from any immediate practical application. Such study reduced arguments to their basic elements and expressed relations in standardized form for purposes of comparison and analysis. The basic unit of study was the syllogism. *A syllogism is made up of three statements, includes two or three terms associated with each other throughout the statements, and draws a conclusion from a major and a minor premise.* An example of a syllogism is:

Major Premise:	Every mammal is warm-blooded.
Minor Premise:	Every whale is a mammal.
Conclusion:	Therefore, every whale is warm-blooded.

Such an "argument" could be expressed symbolically as:

Major Premise:	Every A is B.
Minor Premise:	Every C is A.
Conclusion:	Therefore, every C is B.

Formal logic as the study of syllogisms dominated the study of logic for some time. It treated reasoning forms as if they had the consistency and rigor of mathematical symbols, and as if the relationship between terms and between premises was as simple and unequivocal as in algebra and mathematics.

Unfortunately, this model was not very adequate for studying and learning the forms of practical argument. Indeed, it was very inadequate for this purpose. In the

1950s and 1960s, a number of scholars began to criticize formal logic and to propose alternatives for the study of argument. For example, Stephen Toulmin in his book, *The Uses of Argument,* criticized formal logic for a number of reasons.[4] He noted that everyday arguments could never be held to be as universally valid as the reasoning forms in a syllogism such as the one above. Since formal logical relations depend on the use of symbols ("A," "B," and "C"), they strip arguments of their everyday meanings, ambiguities, and equivocations. They therefore mislead students by assuming that the use of terms is always clear and never varies. Toulmin also said that statements in "real" arguments have more functions than three (major premise, minor premise, conclusion), and he presented his model of argument (which we will explain in Chapter 12) to show some of these other functions. Also, as Toulmin observed, substantive everyday claims are usually viewed as *probably* true rather than as *certainly* and *always* true as implied by formal logic.

While many philosophers were at first understandably cool toward Toulmin's book, teachers and scholars in the fields of speech and English were more enthusiastic about it. They had been teaching students for some time how to construct and critique arguments expressed in everyday language designed for real audiences, and they thought that Toulmin's model for analyzing arguments and his view that arguments were constructed and supported by principles in specific fields were very useful. At about the same time that Toulmin's book appeared, two European scholars, Chaim Perelman and Lucie Olbrechts-Tyteca, published the English translation of *The New Rhetoric: A Treatise on Argumentation.*[5] Like Toulmin, these two authors argued that sole reliance on formal logic to study practical argument was inadvisable. Their own approach was different from, yet complementary to, Toulmin's.

Unlike Toulmin, who was primarily concerned with a *logical* perspective on argument, Perelman and Olbrechts-Tyteca were interested in a *rhetorical* perspective. They began their work by observing how all sorts of arguers—public speakers, essayists, and even philosophers—constructed their arguments with an *audience* in mind. Arguers who wish their arguments to succeed, they said, will select the various elements that make up their arguments with an eye to their audience. They will use premises they know their audience agrees with, values they believe them to hold, examples with which they are familiar, and language they will understand. Perelman and Olbrechts-Tyteca also believed that arguers make use of *reasoning forms recognizable to their audiences.*[6]

Perelman and Olbrechts-Tyteca worked by studying arguments in use—in speeches, essays, books, and articles. They described the reasoning forms they found in these sources and, after 10 years of studying arguments, they identified 13 categories of argument forms used in practical argument.[7] In this chapter, we will adopt their category scheme. In particular, we will describe six categories of reasoning—quasilogical, generalization, causal, coexistential, and dissociation. We selected these 6 of the 13 categories because they are probably the ones most frequently used by arguers.[8] Because the first category, quasilogical argument, is based on the reasoning forms found in formal logic, we will briefly describe the syllogism. A complete discussion of formal logical forms would be quite lengthy and involved. Extensive explanations of this topic are available in other sources for those interested in studying the applications of syllogistic reasoning.[9] Our discussion here is intended merely as an introduction to the topic.

Categorical syllogisms, such as the one above on whales as mammals, essentially work by putting things into categories by means of classification and equating the categories with each other. If the statements made in the major and minor premises are true and if the form of the syllogism is correct, then the conclusion necessarily follows. For example, if it is true that all mammals are warm-blooded and that all whales are mammals, then it always follows that every whale is warm-blooded. By identifying what is called the "middle term"—mammal—with the other two terms, one can reliably connect the remaining terms together in a necessary relationship.

Two forms of the syllogism exemplify those used by arguers seeking to draw probable and not necessary conclusions from premises.[10] The first type of syllogism providing a form of argument that can be used in practical reasoning is the categorical syllogism. *The categorical syllogism draws a necessary conclusion from two premises stated as simple propositions.* Here are some examples of categorical syllogisms:

All students at this institution must pay tuition.
Mary is a student at this institution.
So, she must pay tuition.

No men are amphibious.
Smith is a man.
Therefore, he is not amphibious.

In order for arguments of this kind to be sound, two conditions must be met. First, the initial statement must be true. That is, the predicate of the statement must apply to all the persons or things named in the subject. Second, the instance named in the second or minor premise must fall within the class with which it is associated.

A second form of syllogism that provides a basis for practical reasoning is the disjunctive syllogism. Unlike the categorical syllogism in which we make a judgment about something based on its membership or inclusion in a class, a disjunctive syllogism uses a process of exclusion or elimination. *Disjunctive syllogisms set forth two alternatives in the major premise, deny one of them in the minor premise, and affirm the other in the conclusion.* For example,

That long-haired person over there is either a man or a woman.
It is not a woman.
Therefore, it is a man.

Jones said I would receive either an A or a B for the term, depending on how I did on the final exam.
I did not receive an A because I failed the exam.
Therefore, I must have received a B.

Symbolically, this reasoning form is expressed as follows:

Either *a* or *b*.
Not *a*.
Therefore, *b*.

Reasoning of this form works from two or more alternatives. One by one, each alternative is eliminated until the candidate that remains is selected in the conclusion. In order for this form of reasoning to be sound, two conditions must be met. First, all possible alternatives must be identified. If they are not, an unnoticed alternative that is not considered may turn out to be the best. During the gasoline shortages in the late 1970s, many people claimed that we must either ration gas or entirely deplete our oil reserves. As it turned out, the increased price of oil led to many energy-saving measures that made rationing unnecessary. Second, the alternatives given must be separate and distinct. Otherwise, they cannot be eliminated one by one. For example, suppose we assume that we could go either to the mountains or the seashore on vacation and that we made a choice based on that assumption. In some areas of the country, however, mountains and seashore are within a day's drive of each other, and both can be included in a single vacation, so use of disjunctive reasoning to choose between them might lead to a poor conclusion.

In addition to the syllogistic forms just described, there are other forms used to reason in everyday argument. The remainder of this chapter will focus on six categories of argument identified by Perelman and Olbrechts-Tyteca. When you can identify and discriminate between these forms, you will be in a position to develop sound inferences for your own arguments and to supply unstated inferences in the arguments you hear and read. While we will be concentrating on the *logical* dimensions and requirements of these argument forms, we encourage you to keep in mind that the purpose of any argument you use is to convince your audience, and that you should use argument forms that you believe they will recognize and accept.

REASONING AS INFERENCE-MAKING

Of the six inference types we will discuss in this section, the first five—quasilogic, analogy, generalization, cause, and coexistential—are *associative* schemes; they bring elements together and evaluate or organize them in terms of one another. They may bring the elements together in terms of equivalence, comparison, contrast, sequence, or some other connection, but the reasoning works because each part of the argument is viewed in terms of the other. The sixth form is *dissociative;* it aims to disengage or disunite elements originally considered as a unity. Dissociation is unique from the other five types but equally important.

Before we begin our discussion of the argument types, we want to remind you that some arguments may fall into more than one type. This is because *real* arguments do not possess the neatness and clarity of the forms of mathematics and formal logic. An argument might make a causal claim based on a comparison (analogy), or it might use examples to show that a causal relationship exists. This will be a problem only when you are identifying arguments by type, as in some of the examples in the exercises at the end of the chapter. In these cases, more than one correct classification of an argument may be possible. Arguments do not exist in a vacuum, and so we should remember that, as Perelman and Olbrechts-Tyteca said, "One must not believe that these classes of argumentative schemes are isolated entities. We often [can] interpret an argument in accordance with one scheme or another."[11] What is important is to correctly identify at least *one* of the reasoning forms occurring in an argument, and not to be too troubled by some overlap between the forms.

Quasilogical Arguments

Quasilogical arguments are labeled "quasi" because they appear *similar* to the syllogistic structures of formal logic. Their similarity to the formal reasoning of logic or mathematics gives quasilogical arguments a compelling air, and people often find them persuasive because of their simplicity and clarity. *Quasilogical arguments place two or three elements in a relation to one another so as to make the connections between them similar to the connections in formal logic.* It would be fair to say that quasilogical arguments can be reduced to formulas because of their simplicity and clarity. For example, one could say: "If player A beats player B, and B beats C, it follows that player A would probably beat player C." This is simply stated and formulaic, but the statement is probable and not certain like the statements in formal logic. In the section that follows, we will emphasize three types of quasilogical arguments that are quite common—transitivity arguments, incompatibilities, and arguments from reciprocity.

Transitivity arguments are structured like the categorical syllogism and function like enthymemes. They have three terms that are associated with each other through processes of classification, but the relations between the terms are probable and not certain. Nevertheless, the relations established between the terms by the arguer are so clear and simple that they seem compelling, just like formal logical relations. Consider the following example:

As a student at Big Time Private University, Mary is paying high tuition.

This could be reconstructed in the form of a categorical syllogism as:

Major Premise:	All students at Big Time Private University pay high tuition.
Minor Premise:	Mary is a student at Big Time Private University.
Conclusion:	So, Mary pays high tuition.

Notice that the middle term (students at Big Time Private University), appears in both the major and the minor premises. The middle term functions like an "equals" sign; it enables the arguer to associate the remaining two terms ("pay high tuition," and "Mary") in the conclusion of the argument.

Transitivity arguments have to meet certain tests in order to be considered cogent, and these tests generally are related to their form. First, they must contain three and only three terms. If they have four or more terms, they do not have the simple infrastructure of the categorical syllogism and thus cannot be classified as transitivity arguments. Second, their premises must be true. Since the conclusion of a transitivity argument simply combines the substance of the two premises, those premises must be true or the conclusion will be just as false as the premise with which one starts! Third, all three of the statements must be stated (or restatable) as simple classifications. If the relations are too complex ("is greater than," "leads to," "is comparable to," "represents," and so forth), then the inference is not a simple categorical inference and the argument is not a transitivity argument. Fourth, the middle term must occur in both of the premises so it can fulfill its "equals" function and make it possible to connect the remaining two terms in the conclusion.

The next type of quasilogical arguments are incompatibilities. Incompatibilities are similar to the contradiction in that they imply two alternatives between which a choice must be made. (That is, one must choose one *or* the other.) The problematic nature of the incompatibility results because both alternatives are stated at the same time. Since the two alternatives are opposite to each other and since they are being simultaneously stated, their combination is "incompatible" and implies a situation that should be resolved. Here are two examples:

> I hate all people who generalize.
>
> Wait a minute, if I want people to trust me, you're saying I have to deceive them into thinking I'm something I'm not!

Of course, the first person is making a generalization herself while at the same time claiming to hate everyone who generalizes. The second person observes that in order to obtain trust, he has to deceive others. Both are affirming mutually incompatible and conflicting ideas together. Incompatibilities, then, contain two alternatives that are incompatible and show a conceptual conflict or a conflict of interests.

Incompatibilities can be tested in much the same way as disjunctive syllogisms. First, the two terms must indeed be mutually exclusive; if they can be maintained together, then no contradiction exists. Second, they must be viewed as necessarily relevant to each other. If one of the terms can be defined as irrelevant, then the incompatibility can be resolved.

The third form of quasilogical argument to be considered in this section is argument from reciprocity. Reciprocal relations are reflected in the if/then relation of the conditional syllogism:

Major premise:	If you expect your superiors to treat you well, then you should treat your own subordinates well.
Minor premise:	Your superiors do treat you well.
Conclusion:	So, you should treat your subordinates well.

Reciprocal relations assert a hypothetical relationship between two situations or conditions and imply a mutual dependence between them: "You should treat your own subordinates as you want your superiors to treat you." Reciprocity implies symmetry; the two parts of the argument are related to each other and their equivalence is emphasized.

Reciprocity is based on our belief that individuals and situations that can be put into the same category should be treated in the same way. It emphasizes the characteristics that make situations or persons equivalent to each other. How can supervisors who treat their employees badly complain when they are mistreated by their own bosses? Employees, supervisors, and their bosses are all workers in the same company; they all likewise deserve fair and equal treatment.

Reciprocity arguments may be stated in various ways:

> If I were ever required to violate my conscience to keep the office of president, I would resign the office.
>
> How can begging be a crime in this society when charity is viewed as a virtue?
>
> What is honorable to learn is also honorable to teach.

In all of these examples, two actions or situations are treated as reciprocal. Violation of one's conscience in order to retain an office means that one should resign the office; begging and charity are viewed as symmetrical acts, as are teaching and learning. The first of these examples is stated as a conditional relation, the second as a question, and the third as a statement of equivalence.

Arguments from reciprocity generally should meet two tests. They should equate two situations, individuals, or phenomena with each other. If more than two are implied, then the argument falls into some other classification. Furthermore, the arguer should use the symmetry between the two to argue that they should be treated reciprocally. Since the claim of reciprocity arguments is that the two elements should be treated together and equivalently, the arguer must highlight the similarity between them.

Quasilogical arguments occur frequently and are commonly used in ordinary speech. People using quasilogical arguments generally attempt to simplify a situation by reducing it to a very limited number of component parts and then set those components into clear and unequivocal relations. The clarity and simplicity of these relations thereby give their arguments the same compelling nature that we find in formal logic and in mathematics. For additional examples of quasilogical arguments, see Figure 8–1.

QUASILOGICAL ARGUMENTS

- "Sort of" logical; *resemble* formal logic; limited to two or three terms
- Views two elements as *equal to, incompatible with,* or *dependent on* each other
- Relationship between the elements appears simple and clear

EXAMPLES

Transitivity: Bill's friends are my friends, and you're a friend of Bill's, so you are a friend of mine.

As Syllogism: Bill's friends are my friends.
You are Bill's friend.
So, you are my friend.

Incompatibility: The candidate says he's opposed to nepotism, but he appointed his cousin as director of the White House Travel Office. (Nepotism is hiring or appointing relatives.)

As Syllogism: No opponents of nepotism appoint their relatives.
This candidate appointed his relative.
So, this candidate is not [really] opposed to nepotism.
[And his words and actions are incompatible.]

Reciprocity: Meeting our responsibilities means doing a better job.

As Syllogism: If we do a better job, we will meet our responsibilities.
We are doing a better job.
So, we are meeting our responsibilities.

FIGURE 8–1 Quasilogical Arguments

Analogy

Like reciprocity, analogy emphasizes the similarity between two elements. *An analogy reasons that because two objects resemble each other in certain known respects, they will also resemble each other in respects that are unknown.* Analogy differs from reciprocity, however, because its purpose is different. A reciprocity argument claims that two situations should be treated alike; an analogy makes an attribution about something that is unknown. Most of our early learning occurs by means of analogy. The child who discovers that the flame of a candle is hot and can burn fingers will avoid other fires in the future. We come to expect that what has happened in the past will happen in the future, that similar situations will have similar outcomes, and that similar objects will exhibit the same characteristics. Such regularities give order and uniformity to our experience and interpretation of the world.

There are two forms of analogy. The first is the literal analogy and the second is figurative analogy. *A literal analogy compares two objects of the same class that share many characteristics and concludes that a known characteristic that one possesses is shared by the other.* The inference made in a literal analogy can be represented by Figure 8–2, and it can be stated as follows:

> Object X has attributes A, B, C, and D.
> Object Y has attributes A, B, and C.
> Therefore, Object Y will probably possess attribute D as well.

For example, if one were to argue that a ban on nonreturnable bottles and cans should be instituted in Washington State because a similar ban in Oregon worked to decrease container litter, the argument would be a literal analogy. The arguer would probably support the analogy by pointing out similarities between the two states and conclude that what worked in one state would work in the other.

> The state of Oregon has moderate beverage consumption, limited revenues for collecting and disposing of container waste, demographic characteristics similar to Washington State, and a ban on returnable bottles and cans that effectively reduced container waste.

> The state of Washington also has moderate beverage consumption, limited revenues for collecting and disposing of container waste, and demographics similar to Oregon's.

> Therefore, Washington state's proposed ban on nonreturnable beverage containers will reduce container waste.

In this analogy, the *evidence* consists of all the statements of similarity between the two states; the *claim* draws the conclusion that the ban (the unknown characteristic) will work; and the *inference* is that the two states resemble each other in all relevant respects.

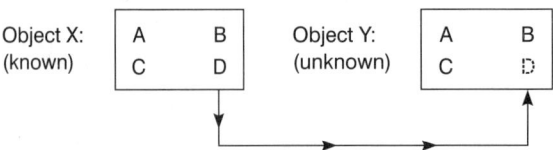

FIGURE 8–2 Structure of the Analogy

Literal analogies are subject to tests of at least three different kinds. The first has to do with the *quality of the comparison*. To have probative value, literal analogies must compare two objects that belong to the same class. In the preceding example, Washington and Oregon are clearly in the same class: Not only are both states, but they are also similar in size and demographics and located in the same region of the United States. To the extent that the compared objects are not alike in respects relevant to the conclusion of the analogy, the comparison is undermined. Differences in the classes compared affect the cogency of an analogy, since they may lead to differences or discrepancies that could undermine the comparison.

The objects compared do not have to be exactly in the same class, however. One could compare a program implemented citywide with one that is statewide; both are geographical areas although they differ in size and the compared programs would differ in scope.

The similarities cited must also be relevant to the comparison and to the claim to which it leads. In the above example comparing Washington and Oregon, some aspects (patterns of beverage consumption, facilities for waste disposal, amount of litter) are relevant to the claim about whether a bottle bill will work. Other aspects, such as the climate and natural features of the two states, could be considered irrelevant.

A second test for the literal analogy has to do with *quantity;* is there a sufficient number of similarities to support the comparison? How many are enough? Obviously, there is no unequivocal answer to this question. The larger the number of relevant similarities, the more probable the conclusion. For example, if the support of the bottle bill could demonstrate that more bottles would be returned if purchasers had to pay a deposit than would be returned through increased recycling, the analogy would be strengthened. Or, if Washington and Oregon are virtually identical in all relevant demographic details, the comparison would be stronger.

The third test for a literal analogy is related to *opposition;* are there any significant dissimilarities that would undermine the comparison? For example, in Washington state at present, citizens generally recycle container litter. They are motivated to do so by the high cost of garbage disposal because recycling is free. Oregon does not have the same costs nor the same recycling program. Since so many containers are presently recycled in Washington, the benefit from a bottle bill might be minimal. This example illustrates the importance of considering possible significant differences when one advances a literal analogy or comparison to prove a claim. For additional examples of literal analogies, see Figure 8–3.

The second type of analogy is the figurative analogy. From a logical point of view, figurative analogies do not have probative value but can be used to illustrate a point or to get listeners to see things in a different light. *The figurative analogy is a comparison between two objects of different classes in which a relation or quality within one is said to be similar to a relation or quality within the other.* Since the two objects in a figurative analogy are not truly similar, the comparison is metaphorical and illustrative rather than concrete and literal. Figurative analogies function primarily to make what is remote or poorly understood immediate and comprehensible. Speakers and public figures often use figurative analogies to focus the public's attention on the features of a situation that they want to emphasize.[12] President Reagan repeatedly referred to the Strategic Defense Initiative as a "shield," thereby causing the American public to see it as a passive barrier to be used

---

ANALOGICAL ARGUMENTS

- Assume two objects, situations, or events are similar
- One is known; the other is less known
- Assume that if the two are similar in ways that are known, they will also be similar in other ways
- Make an attribution to a comparatively unknown object, situation, or event

EXAMPLES

As it becomes easier and easier to obtain images and documents on line in the home, it is possible that people will download and copy these somewhat indiscriminately. The advent of the photocopy machine led researchers to become less discriminating and to copy articles of only marginal interest. . . . In a similar way, on-line access to full-text documents and digital images may lead people to accumulate items of only marginal interest.

> Howard Besser, "From Internet to Information Superhighway," *Resisting the Virtual Life,* ed. James Brook and Iain A. Boal (San Francisco: City Lights, 1995), 9.

Evidence: Photocopy machine led to indiscriminate copying of articles.

Inference: Online access to full text and images may lead to accumulation of marginal items.

In this fiftieth anniversary of the end of World War II, Germans remain understandably nervous about the staying power of fascism, which was largely a product of the interwar years. How much more cautious, then, should Americans be about assuming that racism and sexism—much older and more pervasive problems—have been defeated by a mere 30 years of legal and social initiatives?

> Mary Steward van Leeuwen, "The Affirmative Action Glass: Half-Full or Half-Empty?" *Books and Culture* (September/October 1995): 15.

Evidence: Germans still concerned about fascism 50 years after Holocaust.

Inference: Americans today cannot assume racism and sexism are no longer problems.

FIGURE 8–3 Analogical Arguments

only for defense. President Franklin Roosevelt compared the Lend Lease Act by which we supplied England with weapons and equipment to fight the Germans in World War II to the act of lending a garden hose to a neighbor to put out a house fire. Figurative analogies can be tested for their rhetorical effectiveness: Do they cause audiences to reshape their attitudes in the direction desired by the arguer? These analogies cannot be tested on logical grounds, however, since they compared items and objects from different classes.

Generalization and Argument from Example

In a generalization one reasons that what is true of certain members of a class will also be true of other members of the same class or of the class as a whole. As in the analogy, one begins

CHAPTER EIGHT Reasoning: Making Inferences

with what is known or familiar (the examples that have been observed) and moves to what is less well known or less familiar. Furthermore, since reasoning is usually on the basis of characteristics that are known, the same type of inference is made in the generalization as is made in the analogy. The generalization, however, involves more than two instances and often makes claims about a whole class of objects.

Generalizations move from *some* to *all* members of a class. For example,

> Because the rabbits I have seen have short tails, all rabbits must have short tails.

> We've had a dry spell during July and August for the last three years, so there must be one every summer.

The characteristics (short tails, dry spell) that have been observed are generalized and applied to the class as a whole (rabbits, summer seasons). This sort of inference is illustrated in Figure 8–4.

Generalizations occur very frequently, and we use them to make conclusions about groups of people or experiences. We also see professionally produced generalizations in the form of Gallup polls, Nielsen ratings, market surveys, clinical experimentation, and other forms of statistical sampling where the population sampled is considered to represent the general population. Generalizations are also used when an arguer has been able to observe some but not all the members of a class and wishes to make a claim about the class in general. For example, Doris explains why she monitors her child's television viewing by referring to the programs she has seen:

Doris: I never let Heather watch Saturday morning cartoons. I try to find something else to occupy her time.

Ann: Why? I surely do appreciate their babysitting potential.

Doris: Listen, have you ever watched that stuff? Crass commercialism and violence, that's all it is.

Ann: Oh, come on. You're exaggerating.

Doris: No, I'm not. I watched "She-Ra" and "Hercules" and two other adventure cartoons one morning. Over one third of the time was devoted to commercials for candy and toys. And I counted 32 violent acts in two hours of programming. I can think of better ways for my child to spend her time!

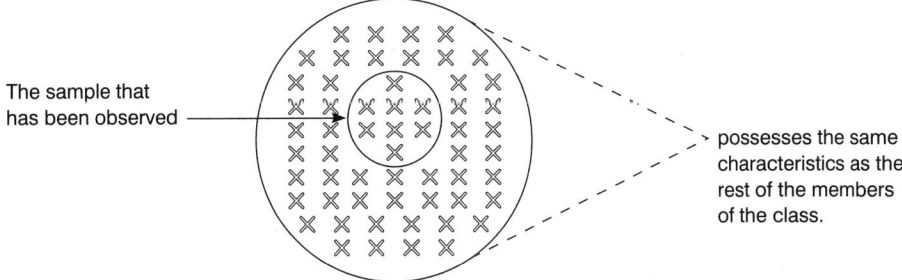

FIGURE 8–4 Structure of the Generalization

In her argument, Doris makes an inference about the programs she has not watched based on the programs she has watched. Her *evidence* is that one third of the time was devoted to commercials and that she saw 32 violent acts. Her *claim* is that these programs display "crass commercialism and violence." Her *inference* is that "She-Ra," "Hercules," and two other programs are typical of all Saturday morning cartoons.

Another form of generalization is reasoning from example. Whereas a generalization will make a general statement based on observation of a *number* of examples, an argument from example will make a general statement based on observation of just *one* example. *Argument from example seeks acceptance for some general rule or principle by offering a concrete, particular case.* Suppose Doris had said, "In one of the programs I watched, there were eight fights in 20 minutes. The characters used swords, knives, and their fists to resolve every problem. Every disagreement led to a confrontation, and every confrontation led to a fight. This program shows how continuously violent these cartoons can be." As in the discussion between Doris and Ann, Doris is trying to establish a general trend. She does this by describing in detail a single program she has seen. The form of reasoning is illustrated in Figure 8–5.

Like the analogy, arguments from generalization and example are subject to tests of *quality, quantity,* and *general opposition*. First, the example or examples cited must be *relevant* to the general claim. If the programs Doris cited were not cartoons, or if they were cartoons intended for older or adult viewers, her generalization would not be relevant to a claim about children's cartoons. Furthermore, the example or examples cited must be *typical* of the class in question. If no other Saturday cartoon has as many as eight acts of violence in a single showing, then the one Doris watched could not be considered representative of the rest of the cartoons, and her generalization would be open to question.

Second, the criterion of *quantity* (applicable only to the generalization) can be met only when Doris has cited a sufficient number of examples. There are nearly three dozen children's cartoons aired on commercial networks and cable channels on most Saturday mornings.[13] Are Doris's four examples enough to support her general claim? The cogency and persuasiveness of her claim will surely depend on the number of examples she can cite. This raises the question of how many examples are sufficient to support a generalization. There is no clear-cut answer because the requisite number of examples depends on the particular argument and the size of the available sample.

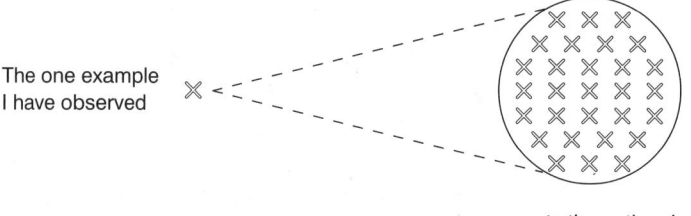

FIGURE 8–5 Structure of Reasoning from Example

There should be enough examples to satisfy the audience and to be weighed against possible counterexamples.

Third, the existence of counterexamples provides the test of *opposition* to both generalization and argument from example. Cartoons such as "Smurfs," "The Gummi Bears," and "Alvin and the Chipmunks" contain very few or no acts of violence and portray characters who cooperate peacefully with each other and have a good time. If Ann listed or described programs such as these, Doris would have to reconsider whether the characteristics of violence and commercialism really apply to *all* children's cartoons. For additional examples of generalization and reasoning from example, see Figure 8–6.

GENERALIZATION AND EXAMPLE

- Assume that what is true of one or some members of a class will also be true of others or of the whole class
- The evidence is the presentation of specific instances
- The inference is that these are representative of others

EXAMPLES

Along with reducing tax rates, we must also aggressively reduce tax rules and regulations. It's estimated that last year, alone, American taxpayers spent 1.8 billion hours filling out their tax forms. Businesses spent twice as much time sending the IRS over 1 million reports.
> Bob Dole, "Weekly Radio Address," July 13, 1996. Online, CNN Time, Allpolitics Internet, July 15, 1996. http://allpolitics.com/news/9607/13/gop.radio/transcript/shtml

Evidence: 1.8 billion hours, over 1 million business tax forms
Inference: Represent complicated tax rules and regulations

When one teaches about Marco Polo, or William of Normandy, or Goethe, or Joan of Arc, one is essentially engaging in the process of transmitting information about a cultural heritage and legacy. The names of the Africans, Ibn Battuta, or King Sundiata of Mali, or Ahmed Baba, or Yenenga, are never spoken in high school classes, and under the current curricular structure, if they were heard, would lack credibility even though they are by world standards certainly the equal of the Europeans I have mentioned in contrast.
> Molefi Kete Asanti, "Imperatives of an Afrocentric Curriculum," *Contemporary American Speeches*, 7th ed., Richard L. Johannesen, R. R. Allen, Wil A. Linkugel, eds. (Dubuque, Iowa: Kendall/Hunt, 1992), 265.

Evidence: Marco Polo, William of Normandy, Goethe, Joan of Arc
Inference: These represent the exclusion of African figures from American classrooms.

FIGURE 8–6 Generalization and Example

Cause

Arguments from cause claim that one condition or event contributes to or brings about another condition or event. Causal arguments are also arguments from succession; one event must happen before the other. But, furthermore, the causal event must *produce* or *bring about* the effect. Some general examples of causal argument are presented in Figure 8–7.

CAUSAL ARGUMENTS

- Assert that one condition or event brings about another condition or event
- "Weak" cause: first condition must be present for effect to occur
- "Strong" cause: first condition guarantees effect will occur
- Evidence is the physical presence of causes and effects
- Inference is that one brings about the other

EXAMPLES

The new beltways and interstates offered cheap access to farmland on the fringe, and the result was suburban sprawl and disinvestment in existing business districts. People are waking up to the fact that low density, auto dependent sprawl has profound consequences on our quality of life and our individual and collective pocketbooks. The Chicago region grew 4 percent in population and 40 percent in land area from 1970 to 1990.
> Preston Shiller and Hank Dittmar, "Nation of Highways Paved with Opportunities and High Costs," *Seattle Post-Intelligencer* (July 23, 1996): A9.

Cause: beltways and interstates
Effect: suburban sprawl, disinvestment in existing business districts
Cause: low density, auto dependent sprawl
Effect: consequences for quality of life, pocketbooks

A great deal of effort has gone into discovering and analyzing the ways in which humans could be exposed to radioactive materials from a [nuclear] waste repository. Dozens of scenarios have been offered. In the one that has received the most attention, waste canisters corrode, and water leaches radioactive elements . . . out of the spent fuel or vitrified high-level waste, then carries them into groundwater. People would be exposed if they used the water for any of the usual purposes: drinking, washing, or irrigation.
> Chris G. Whipple, "Can Nuclear Waste Be Stored Safely at Yucca Mountain?" *Scientific American* (June 1996): 76.

Cause: stored radioactive materials leakage into groundwater
Effect: people exposed to radioactivity

FIGURE 8–7 Causal Arguments

There are two forms of causal argument. The first, or weaker form, is the necessary condition. *A necessary condition is one that must be present for the effect to occur.* To remain alive, people must consume both fluids and food. If either of these two necessary conditions is lacking, death from dehydration or starvation will result. In order to communicate, two people must speak the same language or at least understand the same nonverbal code. Reasoning from necessary condition is a relatively weak form because the effect is not guaranteed by the cause. For example, food does not *cause* life; it is simply *necessary* for life to continue.

The second form of causal argument is the sufficient condition. *A sufficient condition for an event or effect is a circumstance in whose presence the event or effect must occur.* In other words, the presence of a sufficient condition guarantees that the subsequent effect will occur. A broken fan belt on an automobile guarantees that the engine will overheat. If lightning strikes overdry timber, a fire will result. Furthermore, a number of necessary conditions, taken together, may guarantee an effect. The presence of oxygen, combustible material, and temperatures in a certain range, taken together, constitute a sufficient condition for fire.

Causal influences are complex and frequently difficult to sort out and identify. The preceding examples of causes as necessary and sufficient were supported with examples of physical, natural, or mechanical phenomena in which causal sequences are clear and inevitable. In everyday affairs, however, causal sequences are often embedded in sets of necessary and sufficient conditions that mutually influence each other in complex relationships. Consider the following argument for increased state support of public education:

> We should increase our support for public education in our state. Rather than being a drain on our revenues, such an increase is actually a long-term investment. Increased funding will lead to a small class size, better facilities, and improved materials for use in the classroom. Students will complete their education with better skills than they now have and be more productive contributors to the work force. This, and the new industry which an improved educational system will attract to our state, will, in the long run, increase our tax base which will result in improved revenues for state government.

An arguer advancing such claims would have available data on the effects of increased state support on student/teacher ratios, capital improvements, and educational resources. These would serve as *evidence*. The arguer's *claim* would be "We should increase our support for public education in our state." The arguer's inferences are a series of causal claims: first, increased funding will lead to improved education; second, better-educated students will become more productive workers; third, increased productivity will improve the tax base and thus increase state revenues in the future. This network of causal claims is represented in Figure 8–8.

Like the other forms of reasoning, causal argument has tests to gauge its adequacy. The *quality* test deals with whether the cause is a necessary or sufficient condition for the claimed effect. The fact that the necessary (as opposed to sufficient) condition does not *guarantee* the effect suggests weaknesses in the argument. Increased funding for education might be spent hiring more administrators and bureaucrats rather than on items that directly affect students; thus, education might not necessarily be improved. Furthermore,

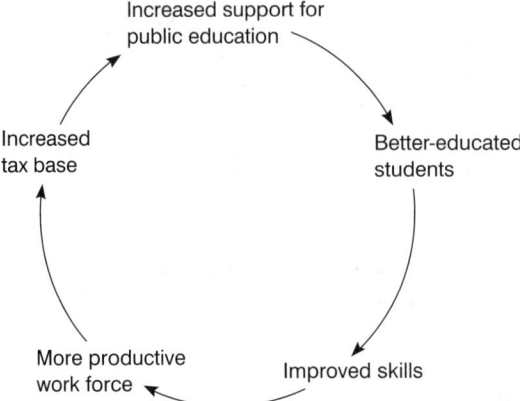

FIGURE 8–8 System of Causal Influence

if a desired effect can be attained in the absence of the purported cause, that cause is not necessary. If the schools could be improved by being reorganized, or if teachers could be trained differently without spending more money, then increased funding could not be said to be a necessary cause.

The test of *quantity* is applied to a causal argument when one considers whether the cause is sufficient to produce the effect. If increased funding alone will not measurably improve the quality of education, then funding improvement alone is not enough. Other measures, such as improvement in teacher training programs and enhanced counseling to prevent student dropouts, may also be needed.

Finally, the test of *opposition* suggests that first, the effect may have been produced by some other cause; second, the effect may be the cumulative result of many causes working together; or third, there may be some other, unanticipated cause working counter to the cause the arguer has cited. For example, increased funding for schools may not lead to improved learning because of other forces in society, such as poverty and drug use, that undermine formal education. Factors such as broken families, child abuse, and racism might cause the failure of education even when large sums of money are spent to improve the schools.

Many times, although two events are related to each other, the relationship is neither necessary nor sufficient. For an argument to meet the tests for causal reasoning, it must be fairly rigorous. Because of the many causes that can contribute to a particular effect and because of the possibility that alternative causes can intervene and reduce or eliminate the expected effect, reasoning that relies only on linear, one-to-one cause/effect relationships is risky.

A method that has proved useful in discussing the relationships among phenomena is correlation. *A correlation claims that two events or phenomena vary together; an increase or decrease in one is accompanied by an increase or decrease in the other.* For example, if a market analyst observed that improvements in the economy would be bad for bond values (because higher interest rates devalue existing bonds carrying lower rates), the analyst would be correlating economic health, higher interest rates, and bond values with each other. The arguer who wishes to show a causal relationship among phenomena is often well advised to show that a variation in one will probably contribute to a variation in the other—an argument more modest than direct causal argument but also less risky because it acknowledges the possibility of alternative and counteracting causes.

Coexistential Arguments

An argument from coexistence reasons from something that can be observed (a sign) to a condition or feature that cannot be observed. The sign or indication functions as the evidence; the existence of the condition or essence it indicates is the claim; and inferring from what we *can* observe something we *cannot* observe constitutes the inference. Coexistential reasoning is illustrated in Figure 8–9. As in analogy and generalization arguments, the inference moves from what is known (the sign) to what is unknown or less known (the condition or essence).

We frequently use signs that we can observe to infer conditions we cannot observe directly. A sore throat and runny nose are symptoms or signs of a cold. Buds on vegetation are a sign that spring is on the way. Or, consider the inference in the following conversation, for example:

Jill: You need to put oil in your car before you drive it today.

John: Why? Is the oil low?

Jill: Well, the oil light was on when I came home last night.

In this conversation, Jill's *evidence* is that the oil light came on. Her *claim* is that the oil is low. And her *inference* is that the light is a reliable indicator of the amount of oil in the car.

This example illustrates an important distinction between two forms of argument that are often confused—sign and cause. In a sign argument, the arguer intends to claim *that* a condition exists; in a causal argument, the arguer intends to explain *why* a condition exists or *how* it came about. Jill's intent is to claim that the oil is low in the car, not why or how it came to be that way. There could be an oil leak, the engine could be burning oil,

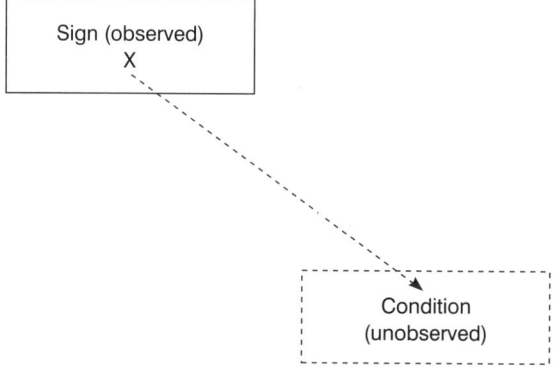

FIGURE 8–9 The Structure of Sign Argument

or oil could have been consumed through normal wear and tear: If Jill had proposed one of these factors as leading to the low oil, she would have been making a causal argument.

Sometimes the distinction between coexistential and causal reasoning is subtle and depends on how the argument is worded. Consider the following examples:

> The merchants downtown are beginning to close early and have installed iron grillwork on their windows. Crime must be becoming a serious problem in the community.

> Discrimination has existed in this country for a long time. This is shown by the Civil Rights Act, the Voting Rights Act, and the Equal Opportunity laws, all of which would have been unnecessary if discrimination did not exist.

Both of these are coexistential arguments that claim an unobserved condition—crime or discrimination—exists. In both of these examples, the arguer's intent was to show that certain underlying conditions existed, *not* to show their cause or how subsequent events came about. They could be viewed as causal arguments if the arguer had claimed that crime had *caused* the merchants to put up the grillwork or that discrimination *brought about* antidiscriminatory legislation, but then there would be a claim of a different type from the one in the above examples.

In coexistential arguments, both the sign and the condition it indicates *coexist,* or occur at the same time. Two varieties of coexistential argument are person/act argument and argument from authority. *Person/act argument reasons from a person's actions to his or her character or essence.* The act is taken as the sign; the person's character is taken as the essence.

> John turned in his last two papers late, hasn't washed his dishes in a week, and has a month's worth of dirty laundry piled up. He must be a procrastinator.

Unlike other forms of coexistential argument, person/act inferences often occur in the other direction; we reason that a person's essence or character will result in certain acts. ("Don't expect John to turn in his paper on time; he's a real procrastinator, and everybody knows it.")

Another variant of coexistential argument is argument from authority. *Argument from authority reasons that statements by someone presumed knowledgeable about a particular issue can be taken as evidence sufficient to justify a claim.* In argument from authority, the actual quote or statement functions as the evidence (sign); the claim is that whatever the quote attests is true (unobserved condition); and the reasoning is that the authority is qualified and accurate on the matter in question. Consider the following example:

> Dr. Daniel A. Lashof, senior scientist for the National Resources Defense Council, said in 1991 that "The United States cannot produce its way to energy security because it is responsible for 26 percent of the world oil consumption yet has only 3 percent of the world's oil reserves." From this we can conclude that efforts taken to increase production cannot alone solve our energy supply problems.[14]

Dr. Lashof's statement functions as the evidence in this argument; the claim is that production alone is an insufficient solution; and the inference is that a senior scientist for the National Resources Defense Council is a qualified authority to speak on this subject and that his statement should be taken as fact.

Like many other forms of reasoning, coexistential arguments must meet the tests of quality, quantity, and opposition. Sign, person/act, and authority arguments meet the test of *quality* when the relationship between the indication and the condition it indicates is constant and reciprocal. If the relation is only sporadic or intermittent, then the inference is unreliable. If a car's electrical system is shorting out, its oil light may come on even when the oil level is fine. One might see occasional grillwork on a building in an area because it is used for decoration, not protection. Making person/act ascriptions is usually a little risky because people do not invariably behave the same way all the time. (John might surprise you and actually get his paper written by the due date!) And authorities are often wrong on an issue, however compelling their credentials might be. The quality of authoritative arguments also depends on the quality of the source itself. Is the person cited truly an expert with current firsthand information relevant to the claim? The tests for authoritative opinion evidence, such as expertise, objectivity, consistency, and access, were discussed in Chapter 7.

The test of *quantity* is met when there are *enough* signs of the condition in question. We could be surer that crime was a problem in an area if there were further indications of it—a greater police presence and a higher incidence of arrests and convictions. We are more confident of claims based on authoritative statements when an arguer can cite *multiple* authorities with credible credentials on the issue.

Coexistential arguments meet the test of *opposition* when there are no countersigns that work against the arguer's claim. Frequently, the presence of a condition might be disputed because there are as many signs indicating that it does not exist as there are that it does. A common example of this is speculation about the health of the economy. In a given fiscal quarter, durable goods orders and housing starts may increase, causing some economists to announce that the country is entering a period of economic growth. Meanwhile, unemployment may rise and productivity decline, causing other experts to point to these as countersigns that indicate economic decline. This same standard may, of course, be applied to arguments from authority; we are more likely to believe authoritative arguments when there are no other equally credible authorities testifying on the side of the issue opposite to the one in question. For additional examples of coexistential argument, see Figure 8–10.

Dissociation

The last type of inference to consider is dissociation. Unlike arguments from quasi-logic, analogy, generalization and argument from example, cause, and coexistential reasons, which bring together or associate ideas, dissociation *disengages* or *differentiates between* two ideas. Furthermore, arguers using dissociation seek to assign a positive value to one of the ideas and a lesser or negative value to the other. *Dissociation arguments disengage one idea from another and seek a new evaluation of both ideas.* Most dissociations are based on the distinction between appearance and reality, with reality being what is valued. Consider the following dissociation used by Dr. Martin Luther King, Jr. in his speech "I Have a Dream":

> I have a dream that my four little children will one day live in a nation where they will be judged not by the color of their skin but by the content of their character.[15]

COEXISTENTIAL ARGUMENTS

- Claim that two things coexist
- Reason from something that can be observed (a sign) to a condition that cannot be observed
- What is known is the concrete sign; what is unknown (or claimed) is the condition
- Could reason from a person's acts to his/her character, or from an authoritative statement to an unobservable condition

EXAMPLES

The passage of the minimum wage shows what can happen when we're united, when we reach across party lines, when we work together. This can signify a new spirit of cooperation coming from Capitol Hill.
> Bill Clinton, "Weekly Radio Address," July 13, 1996. Online, CNN Time, Allpolitics. Internet, July 15, 1996. http://allpolitics.com/news/9607/13/clinton.radio/transcript.shtml

Sign: passage of minimum wage
Condition: unity, cooperation on Capitol Hill

Federal assistance to parochial schools . . . is a very legitimate issue actually before Congress. I am opposed to it. I believe it is unconstitutional. I've voted against it on the Senate floor this year.
> John F. Kennedy, "The Responsibility of the Press," *"Let the Word Go Forth": The Speeches, Statements, and Writings of John F. Kennedy,* Theodore Sorenson, ed. (New York: Delacorte Press, 1988), 126.

Sign: I voted against it
Condition: I believe it is unconstitutional; I am opposed to it.

FIGURE 8–10 Coexistential Arguments

Here the external appearance—the color of one's skin—is dissociated from the internal substance—the content of one's character—and greater value is placed on the second concept. The claims in dissociative arguments are usually implied. Here, King's claim was that "people should not be judged by the color of their skin but by the content of their character." The success of King's argument is based on society's recognition that substance is more important and more to be valued than surface appearances. In a sense, this commonly recognized and accepted distinction functions as the basis or grounds for King's argument.

Dissociations are based on value hierarchies. *A value hierarchy places one value or values above another value or values.* There are many value hierarchies that are recognized and accepted in American society: The objective is valued over the subjective, the end over the means, the unique over what is common, and the permanent over the transitory.[16] Dissociative arguments make use of these hierarchies and especially of the appearance/reality hierarchy to dissociate concepts.

To clarify how value hierarchies are used in dissociation arguments, we will consider two more examples. In the first, a frustrated voter complains:

> I'm tired of all the rhetoric in this presidential campaign. I want to see the candidates engage in some substantive debate on the real issues.

This arguer dissociates "substantive debate" (real) from the candidates' "rhetoric" (appearance). Her use of "substantive" and "real" makes it clear that it is the second idea—engaging on the real issues—that she values. Or, consider another example from a discussion on corporate takeovers.

> I don't see a takeover plan here that's going to be beneficial to the corporation. It's a one-time hit, where we get a spike in the share price, and we cash out a corporation instead of operating it as a viable entity sometime into the future.

The value hierarchy behind this dissociation is the permanent as opposed to the transitory. The "beneficial" plan, the corporation as a "viable entity" (permanent), is dissociated from the "cash out," the "one-time hit" (transitory). For additional examples of dissociation, see Figure 8–11.

The tests for dissociation arguments are much more appropriately applied from the *rhetorical* rather than the *logical* perspective. Dissociation arguments rest upon hierarchies accepted by the arguer's audience. The *quality* of a dissociation depends on the pervasiveness and strength of the value hierarchy used by the arguer. For example, during the 1992 presidential campaign, Vice President Dan Quayle repeatedly appealed to "family values" over other "life-style choices." He sought to dissociate family units made up of single parents and homosexual couples from the traditional two-parent family. His argument appealed to those audiences who believed the nuclear family unit should be valued over other kinds of families because the dissociations he sought to make depended on that hierarchy. A dissociation can meet the test of *opposition* when there are no hierarchies more pervasive and more accepted than the one the arguer is using. Quayle's dissociation was questioned by the segment of the American public that values freedom of choice over the more traditional life-style options.

FALLACIES OF FAULTY REASONING

As we have noted elsewhere, there are many ways that arguments can go wrong and thus mislead or deceive an audience. Flawed arguments, known as fallacies, can grow out of inadequate evidence, emotive language, appeals to ignorance or prejudice, or inadequate reasoning. In this section, we will discuss fallacies of the last kind, those that result when an arguer uses an inference that fails to meet the tests of quality, quantity, or opposition discussed in the preceding section of this chapter. In particular, we will discuss standard types of fallacies in arguments from analogy, generalization, and cause.[17] These three types of faulty reasoning fallacies occur very often in practical arguments.

False Analogy

A false analogy compares two things that are not alike in significant respects or have critical points of difference. You may recall from the preceding section that one of the criteria for judging the adequacy of an analogy is whether it meets the test of quality, that is, whether it

> **DISSOCIATION**
>
> - Disengages two ideas
> - Assigns a positive value to one of the two ideas and a lesser value to the other
> - Can usually be stated in a "not this ... but that" form
> - Based on accepted value hierarchies (evidence)
> - Link is to a less accepted or unrecognized value hierarchy
>
> EXAMPLES
>
> Ask not what your country can do for you—ask what you can do for your country.
> > John F. Kennedy, "Inaugural Address," *Contemporary American Speeches*, 7th ed., Richard L. Johannesen, R. R. Allen, Wil A. Linkugel, eds. (Dubuque, Iowa: Kendall/Hunt, 1992), 350.
>
> Accepted hierarchy: altruism over selfishness (not stated explicitly)
>
> Claimed hierarchy: what you can do for your country over what your country can do for you
>
> Real objectivity does NOT mean the reporter has no opinion. Anyone with a pulse has an opinion. The reporter's JOB is to have an opinion, to aggressively dig up the facts, and apply his or her carefully honed opinion to sort it all out. . . . Objectivity means the reporter is ultimately alone with the facts, and must make a SUBJECTIVE decision what to write. They must be independent of organized agendas and interest groups, not independent of their own judgment.
> > Real People for Real Change PAC, "What's Wrong with the Entertainment and New Media?" 1996. Online, Internet, July 15, 1996. http://www.realchange/org/why.htm
>
> Accepted hierarchy: objectivity over subjectivity
>
> Claimed hierarchy: a reporter's "objective" (that is, considered) opinion versus a reporter with a bias who is not objective

FIGURE 8–11 Dissociation

compares two things in the same class that share significant similarities relevant to the conclusion drawn by the arguer. Furthermore, it needs to meet the test of quantity, which requires that there be a significant number of similarities between the two things being compared. A false analogy does not meet these tests. Consider the following two examples:

> We should not teach socialism in the university any more than we should teach arson.

> The success of the 40-hour work week in making corporate America efficient and productive suggests that we should use it on farms as well.

In the first example, the arguer is comparing two things that share very few similarities. Socialism is a school of thought and political philosophy, a theory only potentially applicable to practice, whereas arson is an illegal activity. Indeed, the only way to see any similarity between the two would be to begin by assuming that socialism is patently illegal or aberrant, and there is no support for this assumption.

The second example does compare situations that are, in a sense, similar. Both corporate business and farming are lines of work that generate income and are productive for society. The question in this case is whether there are *enough* similarities to support the claim that a 40-hour work week would be equally efficient and productive on farms. Farming is quite seasonal, depends on temporary labor, and requires certain very labor-intensive actions at particular times. Someone seeking to refute this analogy might emphasize how vital the pattern and cycle of work in the two environments is to the viability of the comparison itself.

False analogies also result when someone attempts to use a figurative analogy to prove a point. Figurative analogies do not meet the test of opposition because they compare things in different classes. Their function in an argument is more illustrative and metaphorical than probative. Such comparisons enliven arguments and bring their points home. The state has been compared to an organism, the kingdom of God to a mustard seed, and life to a theatrical play. When figurative analogies are used as if they were literal comparisons, however, and are the only form of support offered for a claim, they may be fallacious.

Hasty Generalization

The adequacy of a generalization, which reasons from some to all members of a class, depends on whether enough members of the class have been observed and whether those members possess the same characteristics as other members of that class. The argument based on too few examples fails the test of quantity for a generalization, and the argument based on an atypical example fails the test of quality. *A hasty generalization draws a conclusion about a class based on too few or atypical examples.*

Drawing general conclusions from too few examples is a common error of reasoning. For example, someone might say:

> I owned two MGs—a midget and an MGB—and they gave me nothing but trouble. The choke and the batteries froze up on the "B" and the clutches went out on both cars. They were always in the shop. MGs are poorly constructed and I think they should be avoided.

This generalization is unwarranted. The arguer's experience may have resulted from the way the two cars were driven and the care they received. Maybe the arguer rode the clutches and subjected the cars to excessively cold weather. We could only place confidence in the conclusion if we had performance and maintenance records for thousands of MGs and could compare them with other classes of cars comparable to the MG. Unwarranted generalizations of this type when applied to people are called "stereotypes." Someone who believes that all Southerners are slow or that all Californians are easygoing based on an acquaintance with just a few members of either class is committing this fallacy.

Likewise, hasty generalizations can be based on observed samples that are not typical of the class about which the arguer's observation is made. Consider the following example:

> The growth and success of cottage industries in the Appalachian Mountains suggests that other impoverished areas can build small industries to raise their people out of debt.

This generalization is hasty because businesses in areas other than Appalachia are not like businesses there. The Appalachian Mountains are rural and remote, travel in portions of that area is difficult, and settled areas are widely dispersed and located some distance from shopping malls and convenience stores. These characteristics make patronage of cottage industries more likely. In other geographical areas, however, people might prefer accessible, inexpensive mass-produced goods, and cottage industries, which normally have a small profit margin, would fail.

Anyone to whom generalizations are addressed should ask the question, Are there other equally common examples that deny the conclusion? The key to discovering hasty generalizations is in discovering exceptions to the claim made. Stereotypes, for example, can always be undermined if one can cite instances of people who belong to the class in question but do not possess the characteristics attributed to the class.

False Cause

People who make causal connections between one condition or event and another are prone to two types of error—*post hoc* and single-cause fallacies. The first misidentifies a cause and the second fails the test of quantity by assuming that only one cause led to an effect when many causes, working together, might be necessary.

Post hoc comes from the Latin *post hoc ergo propter hoc,* which, literally translated, means "after this therefore because of this." *A post hoc fallacy mistakes temporal succession for causal sequence.* That is, one assumes that because two events are associated in time, one event must have caused the other. Consider four separate examples of *post hoc* reasoning:

> Serial killer Ted Bundy was found guilty of murder and executed in Florida. Before his sentence was carried out, he told an interviewer that he blamed pornography for causing his crime spree. Had it not been for pornography, he claimed, he would not have committed the crimes.

> A small university has been concerned with the increasing number of traffic accidents experienced by student drivers in university vehicles. In response to the problem, the university administration developed and administered a traffic safety program that consisted of a thirty-five-minute videotape on traffic safety and a five-question quiz on vehicle operation. To be a registered driver, the student needed to watch the video and pass the quiz. The Athletic Department registered drivers in a pilot program and then the program was extended to the entire university driving population. After one year, the program administrator wrote a memorandum to the campus community that argued the following: "Beginning with the appreciated assistance of the Athletic Department, the program, to date, has registered over 750 campus drivers and as a result, vehicle accidents have sharply decreased."

> John Hinckley shot President Reagan after seeing violent acts on TV. Therefore, violence on TV must have influenced his behavior.

> All people who have cancer drink milk. Therefore, drinking milk must cause cancer.

The arguer in each of these passages bases the claim on the assumption that some antecedent condition (pornography, driver registration, TV violence, or milk) resulted in some consequent condition (murder, decreased accidents, assassination attempt, or cancer). The connection between the antecedent and consequent, however, is temporal. In other words, the only apparent connection in each argument is that one condition followed the other, but in no argument does the advocate prove that there is a causal relationship that connects the antecedent with the consequent.

The sense in which antecedent and subsequent events in these examples are not causally connected can be clarified if one remembers the role of necessary and sufficient conditions. If a subsequent event can and often does occur without the so-called cause preceding it, then the two events are not necessarily causally related. They may be, but the information provided in the argument does not provide sufficient warrant for the claim. Do all people who see pornography act violently? Even after participating in a traffic safety program, do accidents still occur? Do people who do not watch violent television programming commit violent acts? Do people who never drink milk have cancer? If so, then the antecedent conditions cited are neither necessary nor sufficient for the effects claimed. Just because two events occur one after another in a sequence does not mean that they are causally related; they might be, but then again they might not be.

Recipients of these arguments would need to seek out additional support to confirm or deny the reasoning. For instance, does TV violence cause violence or are violent people predisposed toward violent programming? In other words, is TV violence simply a symptom and not a cause of violence in society? Do all people who drink milk get cancer? Why are there exceptions? What the argument critic needs to look for is the regularity with which the time sequence of events holds true for the argument. If there are exceptions or other unexplained conditions that might account for the conclusion, then a fallacy has probably been committed.

The second causation fallacy is single cause. *Single-cause fallacies occur when an advocate attributes only one cause to a complex problem.* There is almost never a single cause or explanation for any problem we face. Rather, most events in our complex society arise from myriad conditions and events. Yet advocates, hoping to simplify their arguments, attribute complex social problems to a single cause. This is misleading because it does not account for other, possibly important variables worth considering. Consider the following two examples:

> Low interest rates are the reason for increased housing purchases.
>
> Poor communication is the reason for the high American divorce rate.

In both cases only one cause is listed, but for an advocate to argue that there is only one cause for either housing purchases or the high divorce rate is naive at best. Increased housing purchases might be the result of a glut of houses on the market and higher individual incomes produced by a stronger economy. Financial problems and career choices may be alternative reasons for the high divorce rate. For any complex social, political, or economic problem we can think of, there is more than one cause and an arguer should take care not to oversimplify.

Slippery Slope

A frequent argument made against those who argue for change or propose a new policy is slippery slope. *The slippery slope fallacy assumes, without evidence, that a given event is the first in a series of steps that will lead inevitably to some outcome.* This sort of erroneous reasoning assumes a "domino effect"—that once one event occurs, a whole series of subsequent events or developments will occur in an uncontrollable sequence. Slippery slope is thus a fallacy of evidence use because no support is given that the subsequent events will occur. It is also a form of causal reasoning, as Edward Damer has observed:

> [The name of this fallacy suggests that] when we take one step over the edge of a slope ... we often find ourselves slipping down the slope, with no place to dig in and stop the sliding, once we start the downward movement. While this image may be insightful for understanding the character of the fallacy, it represents a misunderstanding of the nature of causal relations between events. Every causal claim requires a separate argument.[18]

In other words, to conclude that event A leads to event B, we must have substantial evidence that one cannot occur without the other and that event B will always be produced by event A. This is what constitutes a sufficient condition and thus a causal claim. In most instances of the slippery slope, however, the relationship and predicted outcome is much less certain. Consider the following example of a conversation between James and his father, Jason:

James: I was really struggling with Biology 101 and I needed to drop it. I'm sorry because I know college is expensive, but I just wasn't getting it and I was concerned about my grade point average. I went in and I spoke to the prof. She seemed to think that dropping it was a good idea because I am so far behind.

Jason: I don't care about the money as much as I care that you have dropped a class in your very first semester in college. It seems to me that once the going gets rough you're just going to quit. Is this going to be a pattern with you? Next time, will you drop the first class that is tough? I'm afraid that you might and if you keep this up you may never finish your degree.

Jason is concerned about his son's welfare. He wants him to succeed in college and he wants him to finish his degree. However, Jason commits a slippery slope fallacy. The implication here is that James will drop future classes if he is afraid of failure and that this one instance serves as a sign of a larger pattern of behavior. But Jason offers no *proof* for this claim. Instead, he discusses a particular event and reasons without evidence that it proves a larger pattern. The slippery slope is rarely accompanied by any evidence that the predicted series of events will in fact occur.

SUMMARY

This chapter defines and describes the types of reasoning used in arguments. The reasoning an arguer uses is expressed in an inference statement that links the argument's evidence with its claim. Often, arguers do not expressly state their reasoning in an inference statement. The ability to determine the nature of an unexpressed inference and its workings is an important critical thinking skill. Therefore, this chapter explains the various reasoning forms and the standards for judging them.

The first form of reasoning is quasilogical, which is based on formal logic and the syllogism. Quasilogical arguments are comprised of a limited number of statements (three or less), and state relationships between a limited number of terms (three or less). The simplicity and clarity of quasilogical arguments make them seem compelling and persuasive. This chapter describes three kinds of quasilogical arguments—transitivity, incompatibilities, and reciprocity. Transitivity arguments are based on the categorical syllogism and link terms together through a middle term that functions like an "equals" sign. Incompatibilities are based on the disjunctive syllogism and state two incompatible alternatives at the same time, thus implying a contradiction. Reciprocity arguments state two mutually dependant alternatives and imply that they should be treated equivalently.

The second reasoning form is analogy. Analogies claim that because two objects resemble each other in certain known respects, they will also resemble each other in respects that are unknown. Literal analogies compare objects in the same class, whereas figurative analogies compare relations or qualities of objects in different classes. The probability or cogency of analogies depends on the number of similarities shared by the compared objects, the relevance of those similarities to the argument's claim, and the number of dissimilarities between the compared objects.

The third form of reasoning includes generalization and reasoning from example. A generalization attributes characteristics shared by certain members of a class to the class as a whole, while argument from example reasons from a concrete, particular case to a general tendency, rule, or principle. The strength of reasoning from generalization or example depends on how typical the example or examples are of the class, whether there are counterexamples, and, in the case of generalization, whether there are sufficient examples to represent the class as a whole.

Causal reasoning is the fourth reasoning form. Arguments from cause claim that one condition or event contributes to or brings about another condition or event. Causal relations take two forms: the necessary condition for an effect is one that must be present for the effect to occur, and the sufficient condition is a circumstance whose presence guarantees the effect will occur. The cogency of causal arguments depends on whether the cited cause is alone sufficient to guarantee the effect and whether there are countercauses working against the claimed cause/effect relationship. Furthermore, relations among phenomena are rarely as linear and rigorous as causal reasoning implies. For that reason, arguers wishing to show that variations are related often use correlation rather than causation.

Coexistential arguments are the fifth form of reasoning. An inference based on coexistence reasons from something that can be observed (a sign) to a condition or feature that cannot be observed. Two of the most common types of coexistential arguments are person/act inference and reasoning from authority. In order for coexistential arguments to be cogent, the relation between the sign and the condition it indicates must be reciprocal, the number of signs indicating the condition must be sufficient, and there should be no significant countersigns.

The sixth and last form of reasoning is dissociation. Dissociation distinguishes between ideas rather than bring them together as do other forms of reasoning. Dissociative arguments disengage one idea from another and seek a new evaluation of both ideas. Dissociations connect the first idea with what the audience most values ("reality") and the other idea with what is less valued ("appearance"). They thereby break the links between the ideas and cause the dissociated idea to be more valued. The tests for dissociation arguments depend on how strongly the audience actually holds the values relevant to the argument.

Fallacies of faulty reasoning occur when arguments fail to meet appropriate tests of reasoning. A false analogy, for example, compares two objects that are not sufficiently alike to justify the conclusion drawn from the comparison. An analogy is false when there are significant differences that undermine the claim or when the two objects do not share a sufficient number of characteristics to justify the conclusion. A hasty generalization draws a conclusion about members of a class based on too few or atypical examples. The arguer who makes a hasty generalization has either failed to take into account enough members of the class or has chosen members that are not representative. Two erroneous forms of causal reasoning include *post hoc* and single-cause. A *post hoc* fallacy erroneously assumes that two events that are associated in time must be causally related as well. A single-cause fallacy oversimplifies causal relationships by mistakenly assuming that for any effect there is one and only one cause. An arguer may argue about a "slippery slope" even if the evidence and reasoning does not support a trend.

EXERCISES

For each of the following arguments:

1. Identify what type of argument it is—quasilogical, analogy, generalization or example, cause, coexistential, or dissociation.
2. Identify the evidence, claim, and inference. (Remember that the inference is often implicit. If it is not explicitly stated, supply it.)
3. Provide two questions that you might use to test the argument.

Note: It is important to remember that sometimes an argument can fall into more than one classification. The nonreturnable bottle argument in this chapter, for example, was cause and analogy. *Note, too, that you will find some of these arguments quite controversial. They should be interpreted as sympathetically as possible, i.e., in line with what the author intended.*

The three steps described are demonstrated in regard to the following argument:

> About 35 years ago, the presidents of Harvard, Johns Hopkins, Stanford, Brown, and other colleges issued a manifesto warning against federal aid to education. Their point was that federal aid inevitably meant federal control, and of course they were correct. Federal aid now means that colleges . . . have to swear up and down that they do not discriminate against women. . . . And of course there is the whole business of affirmative action, and record-keeping that, one major college has complained, takes about $1 million worth of clerical time to complete.
>
> William F. Buckley, Jr., "The Feds and College Aid," *National Review* (August 1, 1986): 46.

A. This is an argument from *cause*.

B. *Evidence:* Thirty-five years ago the presidents issued a warning. Colleges must swear they do not discriminate. One million dollars work of clerical time is spent in affirmative action record keeping.

   Claim: Federal aid means federal control.

   Inference: Federal aid and involvement causes the federal government to try to control education.

C. Might the effects of federal aid have desirable as well as undesirable consequences? Are the actions opposing discrimination the result of causes other than federal aid?

* 1. The listener should often be shown the conclusion contained in the principle. From this principle, as from the center, light shines on all parts of the work. In much the same way, a painter plans his painting so that light emanates naturally from a single source to each object. The whole work is unified and reduced to a single proposition enlightened in various ways.

   François Fénelon, *Letter to the French Academy,* Barbara Warnick, trans. (Lanham, Md.: University Press of America, 1984), 68.

2. Many of the stories depicting sexual harassment as a severe problem spring from "consultants" whose livelihoods depend upon exaggerating its extent. . . . Susan Webb, president of Pacific Resources Development Group, a Seattle consultant, says she spends 95 percent of her time advising on sexual harassment. Like most consultants, Miss Webb acts as an expert witness in harassment

cases, conducts investigations for companies and municipalities, and teaches seminars. She charges clients $1,500 for her 35-minute sexual harassment video program and handbooks.

> Gretchen Margenson, "May I Have the Pleasure . . . ," *National Review* (November 18, 1991): 37.

3. It is said by those who have examined the matter closely that the largest number of divorces is now found in communities where the advocates of female suffrage are most numerous, and where the individuality of woman as related to her husband, which such a doctrine inculcates, is increased to the greatest extent. If this be true, it is a strong plea . . . against granting the petition of the advocates of woman suffrage.

> Joseph Emerson Brown, "Against the Woman Suffrage Amendment," in *American Forum,* Ernest J. Wrage and Barnet Baskerville, eds. (Seattle: University of Washington Press, 1960), 341.

4. Any Presidential candidate who would take a holiday on a remote Caribbean island with a woman to whom he is not married and with whom he plans to spend a nonworking vacation is the biggest idiot who walked the face of the earth and for that reason alone is unqualified to be president of the United States.

> Adapted from a statement by Jeff Greenfield, "Politics, Privacy, and the Press" in *Ethics in America* television series (Corporation for Public Broadcasting, 1989).

* 5. If we burn the forests of the Amazon, we are told, our planet's lungs will give out, and we will slowly asphyxiate. Surely we have better, more practical reasons for not burning them than to stave off universal catastrophe. I can easily imagine similar arguments that would have required the interior of North America to remain empty of cities—and yet I don't think this continent is a poorer place now than it was 20,000 years ago.

> Thomas Palmer, "The Case for Human Beings," *The Atlantic Monthly* (January 1992): 88.

6. We observe here today not a victory of party but a celebration of freedom—symbolizing an end, as well as a beginning—signifying renewal, as well as change.

> John Fitzgerald Kennedy, "Inaugural Address, 1961," *Speech Criticism: Methods and Materials,* William A. Linsley, ed. (Dubuque, Iowa: William C. Brown, 1968), 376.

7. Carla Kiiskila, a resident of a section of north Wallingford that seems pretty tranquil until you try to cross the street, wrote to the Engineering Department to complain about the hazards of N. 50th Street at Sunnyside Avenue. . . . Kiiskila complains that she has several times narrowly escaped being hit and had to run for the curb to get across 50th.

   So the Engineering Department's van Gelder came out to examine the intersection. No doubt there's a danger and a problem there, he admits. [One citizen] got the Engineering folks to try crossing at the speed of an 85-year-old, and proved it was impossible. She unwittingly proved her point afterward, when she went to cross back (at normal speed) and very nearly got hit by a speeding car that spun broadside to avoid hitting her.

> Eric Scigliano, "How Can a Citizen Cross the Road?" *The Weekly* (August 27–September 2, 1986): 22.

8. 1991 statistics from the Carnegie Foundation for the Advancement of Teaching show that SAT scores are directly proportional to family income. Students from families with incomes under $10,000 score an average of 768 (combined verbal and math scores) out of a possible total of 1,200. Students from families with incomes in the $30,000 to $40,000 range have scores averaging 884. Students from families with incomes over $70,000 have scores averaging 997. Since scholastic aptitude is related to a student's position on the wealth/poverty scale, which has a lot to do with where a family lives (affluent suburb or inner-city slum), alleviating poverty would be one way of improving scholastic aptitude.

   Edd Doerr, "Whither Public Education?" *The Humanist* (November/December 1991): 41.

9. Scandal has been part of the American system from the beginning. There were allegations of sexual misconduct during the Washington presidency. The Washington cabinet almost broke up over Hamilton and Jefferson fighting with each other. These are the problems that happen in a democratic government subject to public information.

   Adapted from a statement by Rudolph W. Giulani, "Public Trust, Private Interests" in *Ethics in America* television series (Corporation for Public Broadcasting, 1989).

10. On October 11, 1985, Alex Odeh, the 41-year-old regional director of the American-Arab Anti-Discrimination Committee in Southern California, was killed by a bomb trip-wired to the front door of the ADC office. . . . Alex Odeh was a victim of the new domestic terrorism against Arab-Americans. . . .

    Shortly after major incidents in the Middle East, Arab-American students have been beaten in bars and on the streets—apparently because they looked Arab. After the announcement of the U.S. bombing in Libya, for example, ADC reports that five Arab students from Syracuse University were beaten up in a pub. A Saudi Arabian student in New Haven was assaulted outside a bar. And an Egyptian medical student required medical treatment after he was beaten in Royal Oak, Michigan. In each case, the assailants are reported to have made derogatory remarks about Arabs.

    Steve Lerner, "Terror Against Arabs in America," *The New Republic* (July 28, 1986): 22–24. Excerpted by permission of *The New Republic,* copyright 1986, Washington, D.C.: The New Republic, Inc.

* 11. Let us not seek to satisfy our thirst for freedom by drinking from the cup of bitterness and hatred. We must forever conduct our struggle on the high plane of dignity and discipline. We must not allow our creative protest to degenerate into physical violence. Again and again we must rise to the majestic heights of meeting physical force with soul force.

   Martin Luther King, Jr., "I Have a Dream," in *Speech Criticism,* 381.

12. Solvents, refrigerants, methane, and oxides—all are among the pollutants that are increasingly gathering in the atmosphere. There they are dangerously altering the natural ozone layer that protects us against harmful radiation from the sun. . . .

    Michael H. Brown, "The Toxic Cloud," *Greenpeace* (October/December, 1987): 17.

CHAPTER EIGHT   Reasoning: Making Inferences   **215**

13. The awesome power of government needs to be constantly checked by defense lawyers so that mere accusations don't inevitably turn into guilt. As Justice Brandeis said, "In order to promote liberty, we need eternal vigilance."
    Adapted from a statement by Jack Litman, "To Defend a Killer" in *Ethics in America* television series (Corporation for Public Broadcasting, 1989).

14. The deficit is a hard problem, but we know that it is not the wallet Washington lacks, it is the will! We know Washington . . . will find $500 billion to bail out banks and bankers that stole people's money. Think about it; $5 billion would allow us to reach nearly every child eligible for *head start,* and yet, we're told we don't have the resources. But when it comes to S and L's, we are ready to commit 100 times that amount. How does that make sense? Are savings and loans 100 times more important?
    Mario Cuomo, "Is Government Working?" in *Contemporary American Speeches,* 7th ed., Richard L. Johannesen, R. R. Allen, and Wil A. Linkugel, eds. (Dubuque, Iowa: Kendall/Hunt, 1992), 320.

15. The [Supreme] Court's description of the place of Roe [v. Wade] in the social history of the United States is unrecognizable. Not only did Roe not, as the Court Suggests, *resolve* the deeply divisive issue of abortion, it did more than anything else to nourish it, but elevating it to the national level where it is infinitely more difficult to resolve.
    National politics were not plagued by abortion protests, national abortion lobbying, or abortion marches on Congress, before *Roe v. Wade* was decided. Profound disagreement existed among our citizens over the issue—as it does over other issues, such as the death penalty—but that disagreement was being worked out at the state level.
    Justice Scalia, dissenting, *Planned Parenthood v. Casey,* 505 US 995. Supreme Court 1992.

16. We are much too intelligent; much too victimized by racism, sexism, militarism, and anti-Semitism; much too threatened as historical scapegoats to go on divided from one another. We must turn from finger pointing to clasped hands. We must share our burdens and our joys with each other once again. We must turn to each other and not on each other and choose higher ground.
    Jesse Jackson, "The Rainbow Coalition," given to the Democratic National Convention, July 17, 1984, in *Contemporary American Speeches,* 385.

17. The Israeli and Palestinian peoples who fought each other for almost a century have agreed to move decisively on the path of dialogue, understanding, and cooperation. We live in an ancient land and as our land is small, so must our reconciliation be great. As our wars have been long, so must our healing be swift. Deep gaps call for lofty breezes. I want to tell the Palestinian delegation that we are sincere, that we mean business.
    Shimon Peres, Foreign Minister of Israel, "Statements by Leaders at the Signing of the Middle East Pact," *New York Times* (September 14, 1993, International edition): A6.

18. [T]he first amendment to the Constitution does not protect only nice speech or only attractive speech, or only popular speech. We would not need a Constitution for that purpose. The great thing about the United States of America

is that our Constitution protects any crackpot who wants to stand on his soapbox and express any oddball point of view that pops into his mind.
John Danforth, "Against a Constitutional Amendment Banning Flag Burning," in *Contemporary American Speeches,* 334.

19. Stricter control over pesticides that affect the female hormone estrogen will be necessary if alarming findings are borne out regarding their potential harmful effects on humans and wildlife.

    Scientists from Tulane University have published findings in the journal *Science* that show worrisome effects when pesticides that have been linked to breast cancer and male birth defects are combined. . . .

    The Tulane findings came days after an international group of experts, the Work Session on Environmental Endocrine Disrupting Chemicals, warned of threats to intelligence, development, and reproductive health posed by chemicals such as dioxin and PCBs found in pesticides and plastics.

    Those chemicals, which mimic natural human and animal hormones, can "change the character of human societies or destabilize wildlife populations," they said.
    "Pesticides, Estrogen Link," editorial, *Seattle Post-Intelligencer* (July 12, 1996): A14.

✱ 20. Even uglier has been the growing number of cases where affirmative action for qualified minorities has turned into affirmative discrimination against qualified majorities and minorities. Asian Americans are denied entrance to the University of California system because of their ethnicity; white males face an almost impossible job market in academia. People with one-eighth Indian blood seek favored treatment as disadvantaged Native Americans. The misnamed Equal Opportunity Commission fined a Chicago firm for hiring too many Hispanics and too few blacks. A high school in Piscataway, New Jersey, fired one teacher because she was white in order to make room for a black teacher. And on it goes.
Doug Bandow, "A Vision Betrayed: Discrimination Is No Answer to Discrimination," *Books and Culture: A Christian Review* (September/October 1995): 13.

21. Right now, there is every indication that, as a direct result of the Gingrichites' unconscionable half-trillion dollars in cuts in Medicare and Medicaid, which will wreck every vital federal and state program that assures delivery of health care services to Americans, the nation's hospital death rates and infant mortality rates, and the death rates of the destitute elderly, disabled, chronically ill, immigrant, and homeless populations will soar. This is a predictable result, based on the fact that budget cuts will further reduce reimbursements to hospitals, thereby forcing hospitals to close.
Linda Everett and Nancy Spannaus, "Cuts in Medicare Mean Murder," *The New Federalist* (January 15, 1996): 1.

22. Let the skeptics of this peace recall what once existed among these people. There was a time when the traffic of ideas and commerce and pilgrims flowed uninterrupted among the cities of the fertile crescent. In Spain, in the Middle East, Muslims and Jews once worked together to write brilliant chapters in the history of literature and science. All this can come to pass again.
President Clinton, "Statements by Leaders at the Signing of the Middle East Pact," *New York Times* (September 14, 1993, International Edition): A6.

23. President Reagan says the nation is in recovery. Those 90,000 corporations that made a profit last year but paid no federal taxes are recovering. The 37,000 military contractors who have benefitted from Reagan's more than doubling the military budget in peacetime, surely, they are recovering. The big corporations and rich individuals who received the bulk of the three-year multibillion tax cut from Mr. Reagan are recovering. But no such recovery is under way for the least of these. Rising tides don't lift all the boats, particularly those stuck on the bottom.
    Jesse Jackson, "The Rainbow Coalition," in *Contemporary American Speeches,* 386.

24. The states (of the United States) are pitted against each other in the kind of destructive competition that we sought to move away from 200 years ago when we tore up the Articles of *Confederation.* Ironically, this is occurring just as Europe moves toward *consolidation*—uniting—in order to make themselves *stronger.* In 1992, the European Economic Community will fuse itself into the largest economy . . . in the world. They, getting stronger by uniting, *we* growing weaker—by *fragmentation.*
    Mario Cuomo, "Is Government Working?" in *Contemporary American Speeches,* 318.

25. The evidence is clear, cumulative, and robust enough to rule out dismissal or denial. And it has been accumulating for over two decades. . . . What it points to is this: Information technology, upon which we are now very dependent, has occasioned an epidemic of chronic, often crippling, workplace injuries and layoffs. It has also failed remarkably to reduce workloads or, in most cases, to boost productivity. As a result, computers have significantly raised the cost of doing business and intensified the pace of work without delivering on many of the benefits presumed, promised, or imagined to have accompanied the information age.
    R. Dennis Hayes, "Digital Palsy: RSI and Restructuring Capital," in *Resisting the Virtual Life,* James Brook and Iain A. Boal, eds. (San Francisco: City Lights, 1995), 173.

NOTES

1. Stephen Toulmin, *The Uses of Argument* (Cambridge: Cambridge University Press, 1958), 8.
2. Our typology of inferences is taken from Chaim Perelman, *The Realm of Rhetoric,* W. Kluback, trans. (Notre Dame, Ind.: University of Notre Dame Press, 1982), 53–137.
3. We include here only a brief history of logic in the 20th century. The origins of formal logic go back to Aristotle's *Prior* and *Posterior Analytics,* and early accounts of practical reasoning appear in Aristotle's *Topics, Rhetoric,* and *Sophistical Refutations,* all written in the fourth century B.C. Historical background for the study of reasoning can be found in Frans H. van Eemeren, Rob Grootendorst, and Francisca Shoeck Henkemans, *Fundamentals of Argumentation Theory: A Handbook of Historical Backgrounds and Contemporary Developments* (Mahweh, N.J.: Erlbaum, 1996).
4. Toulmin, 94–210.
5. Perelman and Lucie Olbrechts-Tyteca, *The New Rhetoric: A Treatise on Argumentation,* John Wilkinson and Purcell Weaver, trans. (Notre Dame, Ind.: University of Notre Dame Press, 1969).
6. This point is emphasized in Barbara Warnick and Susan L. Kline, "The New Rhetoric's Argument Schemes: A Rhetorical View of Practical Reasoning," *Argumentation and Advocacy* 29 (1992): 1–15.
7. Perelman explains their method of research in "The New Rhetoric: A Theory of Practical

Reasoning," in *The Rhetorical Tradition,* ed. Patricia Bizzell and Bruce Herzberg, (Boston: St. Martin's, 1990), 1077–102.

8. In a study of 622 arguments in five televised panel discussions, Warnick and Kline found that 37 percent of the arguments were quasi-logical; 22 percent were causal; 12 percent were coexistential; 5 percent were generalization or example; 6 percent were analogical; and 4 percent were dissociative. In considering these percentages, it is important to note that many arguments were classified into two or more of these categories.

9. For excellent accounts of traditional syllogistic logic, see *The Encyclopedia of Philosophy,* s.v. "Logic, Traditional"; Edward P. J. Corbett, *Classical Rhetoric for the Modern Student,* 2d ed. (New York: Oxford University Press, 1971), 50–81; Irving M. Copi, *Introduction to Logic,* 5th ed. (New York: Macmillan, 1978); and James D. Carney and Richard K. Scheer, *Fundamentals of Logic,* 2d ed. (New York: Macmillan, 1974).

10. The treatment of syllogistic forms as used in practical reasoning is based on Douglas Ehninger, *Influence, Belief, and Argument* (Glenview, Ill.: Scott, Foresman, 1974).

11. Perelman and Olbrechts-Tyteca, 192.

12. Perelman and Olbrechts-Tyteca, 385.

13. *TV Times* (supplement to *Seattle Times*), February 21, 1993.

14. Adapted from Daniel A. Lashof, "Should S.341, the National Energy Security Act, Be Approved?: Con," *Congressional Digest* (May 1991): 382.

15. Martin Luther King, Jr., "I Have a Dream," in William A. Lindsay, *Speech Criticism: Methods and Materials* (Dubuque, Iowa: William C. Brown, 1968), 382.

16. For a description of hierarchies accepted in Western society, see Gregg B. Walker and Malcolm O. Sillars, "Where is Argument? Perelman's Theory of Values," in *Perspectives on Argumentation,* Robert Trapp and Janice Schuetz, eds. (Prospect Heights: Waveland, 1990) 134–50.

17. The reasoning fallacies discussed here are included in many standard lists of fallacies. For discussions of fallacies, see C. L. Hamblin, *Fallacies* (London: Methuen, 1970), 135–76; W. Ward Fearnside and William B. Holther, *Fallacy: The Counterfeit of Argument* (Englewood Cliffs, N.J.: Prentice-Hall, 1959); and Howard Kahane, *Logic and Contemporary Rhetoric,* 4th ed. (Belmont, Calif.: Wadsworth, 1984).

18. T. Edward Damer, *Attacking Faulty Reasoning,* 2d ed. (Belmont, Calif.: Wadsworth, 1987), 94.

SECTION FOUR

Arguing Extended Cases

CHAPTER 9

Case Construction: Arguing about Propositions of Fact

CHAPTER OUTLINE

- Arguing about Facts, Values, and Policies
- Relating Facts, Values, and Policies
- Principles of Case Construction
- Stock Issues in Fact-Based Cases
  - Definition
  - Threshold
  - Application
- Principles of Refutation
- The Issues Brief
- Summary
- Exercises

KEY CONCEPTS

propositional arena
case
presumption
prima facie case
stock issues

definition
threshold
application
burden of rejoinder

We live in a society in which people are inclined to believe facts and statistics when they hear about them. Somehow, factual information has a "taken for granted" quality to it. But, as we observed in Chapter 6, there are many "facts" about which various people disagree. Chapter 3 discussed at length the question of whether John F. Kennedy was killed by a single assassin. Because this assassination actually happened, there is only one "correct" answer to the question of who killed Kennedy. Yet, for years various government agencies and other interested parties have debated about whether Lee Harvey Oswald acted alone or in concert with someone else. Other questions of fact are related to the environment. There is currently considerable debate about whether atmospheric pollution will lead to global warming and climate change and, if so, to what extent this will happen. In medicine, as well, there are assiduous debates about questions of fact. For example, to what extent do birth control pills and hormones lead to an increase in the rate of cancer among women? How harmful are elevated levels of cholesterol, and what are the most effective ways of lowering cholesterol levels? These are all potentially questions of fact, questions that might serve as the basis for extended arguments pro and con.

The questions in the previous paragraph concern historical and predictive facts. Theoretically, they are potentially verifiable by empirical facts, yet experts disagree. Being able to identify facts that are relevant to a proposition, to evaluate the accuracy and adequacy of those facts, and to apply the tests of statistical evidence to numerical analyses are important critical thinking skills. Arguing about propositions of value can provide a valuable opportunity to gain such skills. This chapter provides a mechanism for gaining experience in argument on factual matters. Since this chapter and the two that follow it concern procedures to be used in developing extended argumentative cases, we will discuss how to analyze a proposition, develop a position, and defend it in an extended argument on a question of fact. When you have completed this chapter, you will be in a better position to think, act, and respond critically to your environment and the issues that guide your decision making.

In this chapter and in Chapters 11 and 12, we will explain how to develop extended arguments supporting and opposing socially significant facts, values, and policies. This chapter will focus specifically on the process for developing, defending, and opposing fact-based propositions. Although learning to develop arguments about factual propositions is important in its own right, the principles of building extended arguments about fact propositions are vital to the deliberation of other types of propositions as well. In Chapter 6 we explained how all three types of propositions are interrelated and that each type of proposition functions in concert with the other two. Similarly, extended arguments about fact-based resolutions share similarities with extended arguments about values and policies. Therefore, this chapter will focus on the background necessary for arguing fact propositions, but the principles and techniques discussed here are also intended to lay a foundation for advocating and opposing propositions of value and policy. The concepts and terminology discussed in the following sections are parallel to the principles used for developing extended arguments with other propositions.

ARGUING ABOUT FACTS, VALUES, AND POLICIES

Propositions establish an arena for argument. *A propositional arena is the ground for dispute and includes all the issues for controversy within a given proposition.* Figure 9–1 illustrates how a proposition surrounds an arena for argument that includes many potential issues for argument. Propositional arenas contain many issues, and not all of them will be developed in an argument. The arguer's task is to analyze the proposition for the relevant issues and develop an extended argument that either supports or denies the proposition. To develop an overall position on a topic or proposition, you must know how to identify the significant and controversial issues within the field of argument. You further must know how to find the relevant evidence to support your claims through research. You need to be able to articulate your arguments and defend them against opposing points of view. You also will need to know how to select from a large number of potential arguments the ones that will be most effective with your audience.

In completing these steps, you will construct an argumentative case. *A case is an extended argument supporting or opposing a proposition.* You may recall from Chapter 6 that a proposition is the "main claim" or "overarching claim" of an extended argument. Examples would be the following:

> The federal government should significantly increase regulation of mass media advertising in the United States.
>
> Euthanasia for terminally ill patients is desirable.
>
> John Doe is guilty of murder in the first degree.
>
> Kitsap Country should enact significant growth management legislation.

Cases favoring such propositions might take the form of a speech in support of some legislation, a case for the defense or prosecution in a criminal trial, or the affirmative or negative side in a debate. Cases are characterized by a network of claims and subclaims, each supported by further argument. (See Figure 6–2 for an example.)

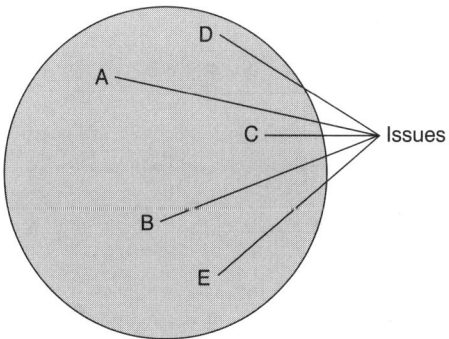

FIGURE 9–1 Propositional Arena

We make cases about fact, value, and policy-based propositions almost daily, and while value and policy cases are probably more common in public argument, cases about propositions of fact are common in many private arguments and in certain fields of argument. Some fields focus almost exclusively on fact-based propositions. Courts of law, for instance, examine historical fact propositions. For example, attorneys might argue whether:

> Chris Smith is guilty of theft.
>
> Anne Jones is guilty of reckless driving.
>
> Organization A violated export laws.

Each of these is a proposition for a case that will argue about historical facts. Lawyers, judges, and juries are then concerned with whether the case built by the prosecution is sufficient to prove the probable truth or falsity of the claim. Similarly, members of the medical field will diagnose or predict disease using factual propositions. They might argue:

> Smoking cigarettes has caused you to develop emphysema.
>
> Laser eye surgery will correct near-sightedness.
>
> Taking this prescription will alleviate your symptoms.

Other fields may also use fact propositions as a genus for discussion and deliberation. Politicians often engage in fact-finding studies to determine whether certain policies work. Scientists will use fact propositions (such as hypotheses) to argue about the nature of the world and universe. Fact propositions, as discussed in Chapter 6, can be classified in three ways: historical, relational, and predictive. Argument cases can be developed using any of these types of fact propositions.

Most of us at one time or another have had the opportunity to develop extended cases based on fact propositions. Arguers use fact propositions to help establish what was, is, or will be. Consider, for example, the following propositions that might be part of an academic assignment:

> America's massive military build-up of the '80s caused the collapse of the Soviet Union.
>
> Cutting financial aid means fewer students can attend college.
>
> Life on Earth began with living cells from Mars.
>
> Continued use of CFCs will result in the complete breakdown of the ozone layer.

RELATING FACTS, VALUES, AND POLICIES

Advocates often construct cases supporting propositions of fact, value, and policy. As we discussed in Chapter 6, these three propositions are not exclusive of one another. Rather, they are related and each implies the other. Policy claims, for instance, are based on underlying values and the existence of certain facts. We tend to decide on a course of action when we believe there is a potential benefit. The benefit (the factual outcome of the action) is measured by how valuable it is compared to any potential costs related to the same action. Our space program is an example of this:

Policy proposition: The world should work together to construct a permanently staffed space station in orbit around the Earth.

Benefits	**Costs**
Scientific knowledge	Potential lives lost—remember *Challenger*
Potential for increased world harmony	Huge amounts of money
Technological advances	Loss of autonomy in directing missions

Here the potential benefits are weighed against the potential costs, and the comparison is directly related to our value system and our assessments of the facts. After the *Challenger* disaster, many people argued that human life should always come first and scientific knowledge and technological advances should come second. In this case, the factual assessment of risk to human life and the value of human life were so high that for some individuals the costs far outweighed the possible benefits.

On the other hand, facts and values imply policies. For example, if a patient were terminally ill, in tremendous pain, and with no hope of recovery (fact arguments) then we might decide that this person should have the right to decide if the continued struggle to live was more important than making the choice to die (value argument). If everyone could agree that certain forms of euthanasia were justified and desirable in certain circumstances, then lawmakers would enact legislation making those forms of euthanasia legal (policy argument). The reason that there is so much variation in abortion laws in different states is that there is no fact consensus about when life begins and no value consensus between pro-choice and pro-life factions in various parts of the country.

Although facts, values, and policies are tied to each other, the types of claims and evidence used in policy and fact arguments are different from those in value arguments. In selecting policies, people make decisions about what action to take based on their assessment of the risks involved and the potential benefits to be obtained. Most people choose an action when the benefits are perceived to be greater than the costs or disadvantages of taking action. For example, a stockbroker might propose that her client invest heavily in the stock market. In support of this proposition, the broker could cite market trends, projections of growth in the economy, and our competitiveness in foreign trade. These are all empirical economic facts, and in the end the broker places her faith in them and decides that the stock market *probably* will continue to rise. The broker's client weighs the broker's arguments and the facts and statistical projections she has cited and decides whether to invest. This process of risk analysis allows decision makers to decide in favor of polices and courses of action that appear to offer the greatest utility or benefit.[1]

Policy arguments therefore concern action to be taken in the future, and they are based on empirical facts and on trends and projects. Value arguments, on the other hand, are usually based on the present and rely on social agreement concerning values. In Chapter 6, we defined values as positive or negative attitudes toward certain end states of existence or broad modes of conduct. Examples of values are freedom, equality, self-respect, and family security. When we express our values, we express our own conceptions of the worth of objects or ideas. Values, then, regulate our orientations toward the objects and experiences in our lives.

We do not take action unless we are convinced that such action is valuable and based on certain verifiable premises—facts. Similarly, we tend not to value things that have no basis or grounding in facts. Therefore, constructing an extended argument about fact, value, or policy claims does not exclude other types of cases; each proposition implies the existence of the other. Policy claims are based on underlying values; we only choose an action when we have determined that it is beneficial, and "benefit" is often measured by the value the action fulfills. Advocates often construct cases supporting claims of fact, value, and policy.

PRINCIPLES OF CASE CONSTRUCTION

The process of decision-making occurs in courtrooms, legislatures, board rooms, and voting booths. Ideally, decisions are reached because of argumentation by informed persons who support various positions on an issue. Argumentation and decision making are the processes we use in our society to reach reasonable consensus about the problems we face. To some extent, the nature of our problems and the issues that we consider significant change over time. In some years, concern about the economy, joblessness, inflation, and interest rates dominate our discussions. In other years, wars and concern for world peace occupy our thoughts. Different issues and concerns emerge each year as the contexts for argument change and evolve.

Issues such as abortion, capital punishment, environmental protection, and crime control are continuing sources of disagreement and debate in our society. If you wish to become seriously involved in the discussion of topics such as these, you will need to know how to construct argumentative cases about them. Whether your case is oriented toward facts, values, or policies, there are certain recognized principles exemplified in legal briefs, legislative proposals, speeches, and academic debates that you should know. Before we discuss the specific methods of case construction, therefore, we need to pause to discuss the general principles of case construction.

The first principle is that the person advocating a change in value or policy has the *burden of proof* and must overcome the *presumption* in favor of what currently exists or is accepted. Burden of proof is the obligation of the arguer advocating change to overcome presumption with argument. As we explained in Chapter 6, the presumption "preoccupies the ground" of the controversy and will continue to do so until it is successfully challenged by some new belief, value, or action. *Presumption, then, is the belief that current thinking, attitudes, values, and actions will continue in the absence of good arguments for their change.* Essentially, presumption can be understood using the aphorism "if it ain't broke, don't fix it" (because you may end up making it worse than when you began). Therefore, the function of the burden of proof for the advocate is to prove that the risks inherent in change can be overcome by the benefits of change.

Copernicus, for example, once made the argument that the Earth revolved around the Sun. Because his claim was not accepted by the church or majority of scholars at the time, he had the burden to prove his argument. The existing framework of beliefs (that the Sun revolved around the Earth) had the presumption. Once the world came to accept (over a period of time) that his argument was correct, then a new reality—that the Earth revolved around the Sun—was presumed to be correct, and any new subsequent interpretation of the facts would have the burden of proof.

It is important to note that people are predisposed to favor what they currently believe and what exists.[2] In other words, people are by nature conservative when it comes to making decisions based on argument; they will be persuaded to support a change only if they come to believe it is a good idea. The convention of presumption in argument thus does not imply that the present system of value *should* be favored; it only implies that an arguer should recognize the necessity of overcoming this conservative predisposition if he or she expects to make an argument effectively. In the field of law, for instance, the concepts of burden of proof and presumption form the foundation for much legal argument. An accused is presumed innocent unless proven guilty. In the absence of substantial argument that proves beyond a reasonable doubt that a defendant is guilty, to ensure a fair trial we will presume that the person is innocent.

There are times when it is unclear which side of an issue has the presumption and which side has the burden of proof, because facts, values, and polices may be inconsistent or not fully determined. On the topic of capital punishment, for example, different researchers dispute whether it deters crime. Some argue that people do not commit capital offenses because they fear the death penalty. Others contend that people who commit such crimes are not driven by concern for possible penalties but by their passions or disregard for the law. Studies that have been done on whether capital punishment deters crime conflict with each other. Furthermore, public attitudes on capital punishment do not lie clearly on one side or the other of the issue. In the case of a topic such as this, the location of the presumption may be less important, and the convention of argument is that whoever asserts a position has the burden of proof for that argument.[3]

A second important principle of case construction is that the central claims advanced by an advocate should address the proposition's major issues. In Chapter 6, an issue was defined as a point of potential disagreement viewed as significant by parties to an argument. For example, if the main proposition of a fact-based dispute was that "Watching violence on television causes violence in children," certain issues are likely to come to mind (i.e., what is violence? Are children who watch violence predisposed toward being violent in the first place? Can we demonstrate that increases in violence on television are associated with increases in violence in children?). These issues must be addressed because audiences would expect to hear about them whenever media violence is discussed.

Assume that this topic was a value proposition: "Restricting violence in children's television is desirable." A somewhat different set of issues is suggested. Are these "restrictions" to be total or partial? What standards or criteria should be used to determine whether restrictions are desirable? What values would be fulfilled or furthered by restricting children's programming? How do current social values relate to a restriction on violence in television?

If the topic were a policy proposition, the kinds of issues argued would change again because the audience would expect different types of arguments to prove the proposition. Consider the proposition "The federal government should ban all violence on television." Not only does this proposition assume prior discussion of relevant facts and values, it suggests an action to address the concerns developed in our assessment of facts and values. In this case, audience members would probably ask: What are the problems associated with violence on television? Are there less restrictive means available to manage any problems? Will this solution actually cure the problem? Do the benefits of this solution outweigh the costs (e.g., potential loss for First Amendment rights and freedoms)?

An arguer who initiates discussion of a topic by proposing a change must present what is called a *prima facie* case. A prima facie *case "on its face" presents good and sufficient arguments for adopting the viewpoint or action proposed by an advocate.* Cases are considered *prima facie* when their supporters satisfactorily address all of the major issues a reasonable audience would expect to see addressed. The issues that need to be addressed depend on the proposition and on what the audience knows about it. *Stock issues depend on the type of proposition and are the issues recipients expect to see addressed in order for the arguer to meet the burden of proof.* For example, on the question of whether research funding should be granted for the investigation of AIDS, an advocate would probably not need to prove that there is a problem. If the arguer could prove that increased funding of a particular research application would dramatically reduce the incidence of AIDS, his or her case would be *prima facie*. Therefore, in the absence of opposition or significant questions regarding a proposal, it should be adopted.

Arguers should keep their audience's attitudes and expectations in mind when they construct cases. If there is a clear presumption in favor of existing policy or in favor of a certain value orientation on a topic, advocates must take that presumption into account as they construct a case. Furthermore, they should be familiar with the major issues related to a topic and make sure they address them. If the case is based on a reasonable proposal and if the major claims relevant to a proposal are supported to the satisfaction of the audience, then the case will be *prima facie*. The general principles of case construction discussed in this chapter are based on reasonable audience expectations and the conventions of argument. Advocates who carefully take them into account will find that the cases they present will be persuasive and compelling to the audience for which they are intended.

STOCK ISSUES IN FACT-BASED CASES

When we argue about fact propositions, there are certain stock issues that must be addressed. These issues are the reasonable questions recipients have about the nature of any given fact proposition. Although there are many issues that can be used to develop fact-based cases, generally we can group the primary stock issues for fact cases into three categories: issues of definition, threshold, and application. This section will develop each of these stock issues in detail, enabling you to identify and build arguments supporting each type. To illustrate how these issues work, imagine the following conversation between a student and her advisor:

Student: I took the Art course to satisfy the University's Art requirement. I don't understand why it doesn't count for that requirement.

Advisor: The University only counts certain Art courses. The one you took is Art 351 and the Art requirement is for any Art course number in the 100s or 200s—not the 300s or 400s.

Student: So what you are telling me is that not all Art courses satisfy the Art requirement? Only some do?

Advisor: Sorry, but the catalog is not always very clear about what counts and doesn't count. But as you can see here, it does make a distinction about what kinds of courses count for the Art requirement.

University catalogs, along with most contracts or agreements are often rich sources of factual argument. Different parties may read the same documents and come to very different conclusions about what they mean. In this case, each of the primary stock issues of fact disputes is present.

Definition

Definition is the first of the fact stock issues. Before advocates can seek to interpret the meaning of a particular fact or set of circumstances, the nature of the facts must be clearly defined. The fact advocate must clearly define the facts of the case and explain their relevance to the proposition. *The stock issue of definition can consist of statements of historic fact, causal relationships, and predictive facts* as was discussed in Chapter 6. The attorneys and judges in the field of law proceed by defining the relevant laws and then determining whether the issues in the case fit the laws of definition. Courts of law examine historical facts in which alleged crimes occurred. In the initial example, the student and advisor needed to clearly define which courses met the Arts requirement and which courses did not. According to the University catalog only courses numbered in the 100s or 200s met the requirement.

Definition is a part of any fact-based argument. If we argue about the existence of life on other planets, we need to define what we mean by "life." Are we talking about intelligent life or microbes? If we argue that corporal punishment increases discipline and learning in schools, we need to decide if "corporal punishment" is physical punishment (such as a spanking), emotional punishment (such as humiliation), or some other form of punishment. Without a clear sense of definition, the arguers will not know how to develop the argument case. The stock issue of definition, then, provides a clear end point for the case. In other words, if the advocate can prove that some case meets the requirements of the definition, then the proposition is proven true or correct.

Threshold

The issue of threshold is closely related to the issue of definition. Because much of life and social action is not precise, there are many degrees of behavior and degrees of interpretation. *The issue of threshold establishes the acceptable limits of definitions.* A word or phrase can be defined in many ways. The definition of "life," for example, has been subject to much debate for decades. Does life start at the moment of conception? Does it start at birth? Does life end when brain activity ends? Or does it end when the heart stops beating?

When we argue about the limits of a definition, we are arguing about its threshold. While we know that a 20-year-old, healthy, active, college student is alive, we might debate the point at which life begins or ends. Beyond the threshold, we know life exists. The problem for advocates, however, is being able to argue at which point does life start or end. In the case of the student, the threshold was any Art course numbered 100 to 200. The student could take multiple courses in that range and could take upper-division courses in addition to the lower-division ones, but the threshold was any one course of lower-division work.

Threshold issues are common in our daily lives and in the workplace. If, for instance, you were planning to buy a new game for your personal computer, you would encounter the issue of threshold on the side of the game's package. The package might say:

Minimum requirements include:
IBM compatible 586
Windows 95
8X CD-ROM drive
16 megabytes memory
8 megabytes hard drive storage
Color SVGA monitor

Each of these requirements are threshold requirements. If the machine is an older 486 or if it is not an IBM compatible, then the threshold is not met and the software will not run. Your machine may far exceed the threshold, but unless it at least meats the minimum requirements set forth in the threshold, purchasing the software would not be wise.

Similarly, employers use threshold issues in developing want ads. Recently a newspaper ran an ad for the following position:

> Wanted: Public relations consultant. Must have a BA in Communication or closely associated area. Must have five years experience in public relations. Knowledge of computers is essential. Must know *Microsoft Office* products. Must be able to travel for work-related projects for periods of up to two weeks. Should be good team player and self starter. Salary competitive.

In this case, the organization is looking for a public relations consultant. For the organization, the threshold for an acceptable candidate centered on the degree earned, experience in the field, knowledge of computers, and travel. Candidates need to meet each of these requirements before they could be considered for the position.

Application

The third stock issue of application focuses on whether the example or phenomenon under consideration meets the requirements of definition and threshold. *Application is the illustration that the case examined is sufficient proof to verify the definition and its threshold.* In other words, application is the argument that some case or phenomenon meets the threshold for the definition. Suppose an applicant for the want ad mentioned earlier submitted a resume that highlighted the following abilities:

- Bachelor's degree in Speech Communication, University of Washington
- Six years experience in public relations and marketing
- Microsoft Office Trainer for current employer

This person has submitted an application—an argument that she or he meets the minimum threshold requirement for the position. The application is simply the argument that some instance—the applicant in this case—does or does not meet the requirements set forth in the threshold and definition arguments.

WHICH CAREERS HAVE THE MOST POTENTIAL?

When we argue about fact propositions we sometimes look at different interpretations of history or current relationships. And sometimes we attempt to make predictions about the future. For example, what 10 careers have the most and least potential for the next 10 years? This was the question asked by *Point of View* essayist Eva Pomice.[4] According to her essay, the following career choices are the best and worst for the next decade:

Best Prospects	Worst Prospects
10. Physical Therapist	10. Corporate Middle Manager
9. Interactive Advertising Executive	9. Librarian
8. Priest, Rabbi, Minister	8. College Professor
7. Intellectual Property Lawyer	7. Bartender
6. Management Consultant	6. Real Estate Agent
5. Family Doctor	5. Factory Worker
4. Industrial Environmentalist	4. Telephone Operator
3. Mutual Fund Money Manager	3. Government Bureaucrat
2. Online Content Producer	2. Bank Teller
1. Computer Animator	1. Accountant

If you were asked to produce a list of the 10 careers with the most potential, best or worst, would your list match this one? Probably not. What careers appear on the list is determined by an important step in designing a fact-based argument. Specifically, what are the threshold requirements that help define a career with potential from one that has no potential? In this case, Pomice used the following thresholds:

- 10-Year Job Growth. How fast can each profession be expected to grow? For example, Interactive Advertising Executives (people who design on-line, interactive ads) has a current work force of 5000 and is expected to grow 400 percent during the next decade. College Professors, on the other hand, will experience almost no growth in positions available and Bartenders will decrease by 7 percent.

- Starting Salary. What is a reasonable expectation for an initial salary? On-Line Content producers (people who write material for web pages and on-line publications) can expect an initial salary of about $40,000 per year with a five year salary of $80,000 and a potential salary of $150,000. Corporate middle managers will tend to start with a much lower initial salary and long-term job prospects are not as positive.

- Coolness Factor. This is Pomice's view of how prestigious a job is. A librarian has a very low "coolness factor," whereas an Interactive Advertising Executive has a high level of prestige.

- Burnout. Does the job have long-term potential before the employee needs a change? Some careers have a high level of burnout. For example, she rates an intellectual property lawyers as having a burnout factor of 7, whereas a family doctor has a factor of 4.

- Getting There. This is the measure of how hard it is to attain the credentials for the career desired. Some careers require a significant investment of time, energy, and money. A physician, for example, must have a B.A., M.D., three-year residency

> program, and board certification. A computer animator, however, requires a degree in animation for a two- or four-year program.
>
> Pomice drew these standards from experts she interviewed and the Bureau of Labor Statistics. However, her decision about which standards to use was based on her analysis of what the definition of "potential" was. Other standards could just as easily have been used and might have yielded significantly different results.

The student's academic record from the initial example provides another illustration of how an application might be argued. In considering her case, the advisor asks the question: "Did her record meet the requirements of the University?" To answer that question, the advisor could compare her transcript to the threshold to determine whether her performance met the definitional requirements. In other words, the advisor could examine her course, Art 351, to see whether it met the threshold requirements. It does not. Suppose, however, that her course had been Art 101. In that case, the course clearly would have met the threshold requirement because it was numbered in the 100-to-200 range, which in turn would have met the definitional requirement to complete one course of lower-division Art. The same process could be used in buying software for a computer. If the computer meets all the threshold requirements to run the software, then the software in question should work.

PRINCIPLES OF REFUTATION

Anyone who opposes a *prima facie* case, once presented, has the burden of rejoinder. *The burden of rejoinder is the requirement that those who oppose a proposal respond reasonably to the issues presented by the original advocate.* For example, in a murder case, the state has the burden to prove beyond a reasonable doubt that the defendant committed the crime. The defense has a burden of rejoinder to refute the arguments presented by the state. And the defendant has the presumption of innocence until the burden of proof has been met by the state.

Meeting the burden of rejoinder means that the arguer must engage systematically in refutation of an opponent's case. Refutation is the process of discrediting someone's argument by revealing weaknesses in it or by presenting a counterargument. Refutation can be divided into kinds or types along two lines. First, refutation can be classified into case-level refutation (aimed at the opponent's whole case or extended argument) or specific refutation (aimed at individual arguments). Second, refutation can be classified as destructive (aimed at tearing down the opponent's arguments as presented), constructive (aimed at providing counter arguments to be weighed against the opponent's), or bargaining (aimed at providing a middle ground or compromise between the case and any potential counterarguments).

Case-level refutation can be designed in three ways—direct refutation, counteradvocacy, or a combination of the two. Direct refutation moves down the opponent's case through his or her main claim, principle subclaims, and sub-subclaims; refutes each one; and then synthesizes these individual responses into a rationale for rejecting the opponent's proposal. In effect, this strategy shifts the burden of proof back to the original advocate. Counteradvocacy involves offering an alternative proposal of either policy or value to be weighed in comparison with the original proposal. Counteradvocacy more nearly reflects real-life decision-making, in which various alternative proposals compete with each other, than it does direct refutation, which assumes merely a "yes/no" decision. Refuting through counteradvocacy however, means that the refuter, like the original advocate, assumes a burden of proof to support and defend the counterproposal. The most commonly used method of refutation is a combination of direct refutation and counteradvocacy in which the opponent attacks the arguments of the other person and at the same time offers an alternative proposal.

We will provide more specific suggestions for case-level refutation in Chapters 10 and 11, where we discuss propositions of value and policy. There we will indicate possible arguments that can be used by arguers seeking to refute value and policy proposals at the case level. It is important to remember that when you design case-level refutation, you must decide on an overall strategy, develop a response that is coherent, and communicate your overall approach or philosophy to the audience.

In the remainder of this section, we will discuss specific refutation that is directed at individual arguments within an opponent's case. The five strategies discussed here, taken together, constitute a repertoire of approaches that can be used to indict the arguments of an opponent and to defend your own position. In a debate, skilled arguers can use a variety of these strategies in combination to keep their opponents on the defensive. For purposes of illustration throughout this discussion, let us assume that the opponent has presented an argument for handgun control. The argument to be refuted asserts that in the past decade, over 200,000 people have been killed in handgun fire, that criminals and unstable people have legal access to handguns, and that a waiting period for handgun purchases will help to address these problems.

The first strategy for refutation is called "exploratory refutation." Use of this technique involves asking a number of questions or raising a number of objections designed to cause opponents to take a stand on issues an advocate hopes to refute. Exploratory refutation is analogous to drawing opponents out into the open so they can be fired upon. In response to the handgun argument, one might ask a number of questions. How many of the 200,000 handgun deaths were due to the lack of a waiting period? How long will the waiting period be? How will the mere existence of a waiting period ensure that criminals and unstable people cannot get guns? Exploratory refutation is especially effective when one's opponents have limited speaking time, because such questions often take a good deal of time to answer. Exploratory refutation is effective only when refuters pursue and critique claims made by their opponents in answer to their questions.

A second effective refutation strategy is to note contradictions or inconsistencies in the opponents' arguments or use of evidence. For example, assume that the supporters of handgun control stated that students shot in a high school had been wounded and killed by handguns. This argument could be refuted if one could show that a waiting period could not prevent such incidents because the handguns obtained in this incident were purchased legally by persons with no criminal record or history of mental instability. The advocates' original analysis of the problem could then be shown to be inconsistent with their call for a waiting period to screen out "undesirable" gun purchasers.

The third strategy is to apply the tests of evidence described in Chapter 7 to the opponents' evidence. Evidence may be biased, outdated, irrelevant, inexpert, inconsistent, unreliable, inaccurate, or inaccessible. Criticizing opponents' evidence is usually not as damaging as some of the other refutation strategies and should not be overused. However, when biased or inexpert evidence is used repeatedly, pointing out inadequacies in evidence can be very damaging. Opponents of gun control often cite the National Rifle Association for support, but this lobbying group is very biased on the topic.

The fourth refutation strategy is to attack opponents' reasoning by applying the tests of reasoning in Chapter 8 to their inferences, or by detecting fallacies as treated in Appendix D in their arguments. The refutation may charge that analogies were made between dissimilar phenomena; that generalizations were based on nonrepresentative samples; and/or that *post hoc* relationships were mistaken for causal relationships. The argument for a waiting period in obtaining handguns is based on a series of causal links: that the lack of a waiting period enables criminals and mentally unstable people to get guns, that these people substantially contribute to the number of handgun deaths, and that instituting a waiting period will therefore prevent the deaths. These causal links could be successfully refuted if it could be shown that most handgun deaths are accidents, suicides, or caused by people who know each other. The opponents of handgun control could show that merely instituting a waiting period will not substantially decrease gun deaths, because the presence or absence of a waiting period is neither a necessary nor sufficient condition causing handgun deaths.

Attacking opponents' evidence and reasoning and showing inconsistencies in their arguments are all forms of destructive refutation; they attempt to dismantle or undermine the arguments being refuted. The fifth refutation strategy is constructive. Here the opponent presents counterevidence and counterarguments to be weighed against the arguments being refuted. Opponents of a waiting period might argue that increased restrictions on the legal sale of handguns will not decrease those handgun deaths that are caused by "undesirable" handgun purchasers. The *real* cause, they might argue, is the ease of illegally obtaining guns through sources supported by organized crime. They might then refute the waiting period by arguing with evidence that handgun deaths and injuries are largely the result of illegal firearms and that a waiting period will not control illegal possession of firearms.

The experience of preparing refutations of others' arguments and of anticipating others' refutations of our own arguments can contribute substantially to the development of critical thinking ability. Our arguments often seem quite strong and airtight until they are attacked by people who are skeptical of our viewpoint. By carefully considering objections that might be raised against our arguments, we can improve our reasoning and become more discriminating in our use of evidence.

THE ISSUES BRIEF

Writers on argument have recently pointed out that familiarity with multiple views on an issue improves one's own arguments as well as one's ability to anticipate and respond to others' views. As Josina Makau has observed, "the quality of deliberation on controversial issues depends, in large measure, on the arguers' ability to thoughtfully consider as many alternative perspectives as possible."[5] Many people who first approach a topic think they have their minds made up. As they conduct research on the topic and read the opinions of various authorities, they begin to see that the situation or the solution is not as readily apparent as they first thought. Often in the process of researching for a speech or debate, students will actually shift their opinions to the side opposite to the one they had favored in the beginning!

Researchers on critical thinking tell us this is a good thing. They have found that novice thinkers seek quick closure on a topic, neglect audience attitudes and possible objections, and fail to take into account obvious weaknesses in their own arguments. Experienced thinkers, on the other hand, withhold their opinions until they have gathered relevant information, begin by analyzing and interpreting the problem, study the attitudes of their potential audience, and develop a broad range of lines and types of arguments to support a claim.[6]

To assist you in becoming an "expert thinker" of the latter type, we recommend that you construct an "issues brief" on your proposition. An issues brief is a synthesis of opposing views on the stock issues of a proposition. The weakness of the issues brief is that it appears to assume that there are only two polarized sides, one supporting the proposition and one opposing it. Of course, on many controversial topics people's attitudes are more complex than that. For example, a person might oppose the death penalty in some cases and yet support it in others. We might favor some statements and positions of a politician and oppose others. Most often people do not take extreme positions on any given issue but instead admit exceptions or recognize the middle ground. In any case, while issues briefs are useful in showing the range of arguments available to an advocate, arguers should remember that there may be positions not reflected in a two-sided brief.

Nevertheless, the issues brief allows the advocate to consider more than one viewpoint, and that is its value. What follows is a brief about the difficulty level and rigor of the curriculum in America's universities that articulates arguments on all the stock issues discussed in the previous section. Actually, the term *brief* is a misnomer, because a fully developed brief can be quite long. When examining this brief, you should realize that each of the arguments is a claim that would need to be supported by further arguments and/or evidence and reasons.

Are America's Universities tough enough? Jeffrey Walling does not think so. In his article "Colleges Should Change Course," he claims that standards for college graduates have declined so much as to make the value of a University education questionable. He says, for example,

> A 1993 survey by the National Center for Education Statistics showed that half of 5,000 college graduates . . . could not read or interpret a simple bus schedule. Forty-four percent could not determine the contrast in a newspaper article featuring two opposing views. Seven out of eight could not figure the cost of carpeting a room (even with a calculator).
>
> Is it any wonder that, in a Roper survey conducted this year, 84 percent of college seniors couldn't say who was U.S. president at the start of the Korean War (President Harry S. Truman), and only 8 percent knew the source of "government of the people, by the people and for the people" (Lincoln's Gettysburg Address)?[7]

His conclusion is that America's schools have lost their rigor. They need to become much tougher. Included in Figure 9–2 are the principle claims related to the proposition that American Universities are not sufficiently difficult.

I. A "sufficient" curriculum should meet the following requirements. (definition)
  A. Curriculum and instruction should be rigorous and intensive to provide students with a needed discipline of learning.
  B. Curriculum and instruction need to provide a standardized knowledge base for our students.
  C. Students must be continually challenged—there should be no "easy" or "fluff" courses.
II. Minimally, a student should expect the following from a university education. (threshold)
  A. Mandatory, core courses should provide students with a general education and common base of knowledge.
  B. All students who hope to compete in the 21st century need to be equipped with knowledge of science and math.
  C. Students should be required to be physically present in class for their education.
  D. We should be looking for ways to increase classroom education time.
III. American universities are not adequately preparing our students. (application)
  A. Over the past 100 years the number of mandatory or core courses has declined from 36% to 7%.
  B. Over the past 100 years the number of colleges requiring science courses have declined from 86% to 34%.
  C. Over the past 100 years the number of days students spend in a classroom has declined from 204 to 156.
  D. No university has looked for ways of increasing days in class, rather each has looked for ways to reduce the total time spent in class.
	I. These definitions are wrong.
	  A. Curriculum and instruction should be rigorous but rigor does not necessarily mean a common curriculum or time in class.
	  B. Standardization implies one way of thinking and education should be about many ways of thinking.
	  C. All courses should challenge students, however, students with different abilities find some courses easy and others difficult.
	II. The standards set up to determine a sufficient education are wrong—they are very dated.
	  A. Traditional core course model is Eurocentric and does not emphasize diversity of understanding.
	  B. Technical skills for the 21st century include many other disciplines in which students take course work such as computer science, technical communication, and engineering.
	  C. Classroom time should not be equated with learning, which includes many other things such as internships, study abroad, and service learning.
	  D. We should look for ways to increase education, not time in a chair.
	III. University students are better prepared now than ever before.
	  A. Mandatory, core courses have been replaced with a superior, diverse curriculum.
	  B. Students are selecting courses emphasizing critical thinking over rote knowledge.
	  C. Number of days spent in a classroom does not determine educational success.
	  D. Overall, student test scores and abilities are increasing.

FIGURE 9–2 Proposition: Curriculum and instruction in American universities are insufficient to educate our students.

The task of the advocate is to present each of the stock issues as clearly and articulately as possible. Each argument should include the relevant evidence and reasoning in support of the claims such that the audience is able to understand its meaning and relevance to the proposition. The opposition to the argument needs to do the same with the exception that the opposition needs only to successfully refute a minimum of one stock issue. The reason for this is simply that if the opposition to a case can disprove any one of the stock issues, the case is rendered non–*prima facie,* which means it is no longer valid.

SUMMARY

Our society has a tendency to believe that if something is factual it must be beyond the scope of debate. This chapter had two goals. First, it illustrates how facts are often central to many different controversies. And second it focuses on general principles of case construction and refutation that can help guide an arguer through the development of cases for different types of propositions.

Although facts are considered to be verifiable elements of our environment, experts and arguers often disagree about their nature, causes, or meaning. These are the subjects of arguments about propositions of fact. When we argue about propositions of fact—as well as propositions of value and policy we begin by isolating the propositional area. The propositional area is the area in which the issues for any given dispute exist. Arguers analyze the issues within the area to determine which issues are most relevant and important for a proposition and the audience for the argument. From their analysis of the issues and their construction of arguments about the proposition, arguers begin the process of developing extended arguments about the proposition. These extended arguments are called "cases."

When arguers build cases about propositions, they should be aware that each type of proposition is related to each other type—they are not exclusive of one another. Rather, policy propositions tend to assume certain facts and values. Similarly, facts exist within our interpretive frameworks of what is valuable or not. And values have implications for policy and tend to assume certain facts.

Case construction focuses on the process we use to build a *prima facie* argument for the proposition. Central to the concept of case construction are two principles: the burden of proof and presumption. The burden of proof means that advocates have the responsibility to prove that a case and all of its associated risks is warranted beyond the current system. Presumption is the belief that current thinking, attitudes, values, or actions should continue to exist in the absence of compelling arguments to change them.

Advocates have presented a *prima facie* case when they have met their burden of proof. Generally, *prima facie* cases are comprised of arguments that develop all of the stock issues for a proposition. While the stock issues vary by proposition type, they are defined as the issues the recipients expect to see addressed in order for the arguer to have met the burden of proof.

With propositions of fact, there are three stock issues that recipients generally ask to have addressed. These are definition, threshold, and application. The stock issue of definition describes the major fact elements of the proposition. It focuses on what the end point of the case will be by offering a clear and concise definition of the terms in the proposition. The stock issue of threshold establishes what the limits or parameters are for the definitions. Threshold is intended to provide a clear way of distinguishing between what is included and excluded by the definitions. Finally, the stock issue of application is the argument that the phenomenon or example under consideration is included or excluded by the threshold arguments.

Once advocates have fulfilled the burden of proof and presented a satisfactory case for change, their opponents have the burden of rejoinder to respond reasonably to the issues raised in the case. In responding, the opponents engage in refutation.

Refutation is the process of discrediting someone's argument by revealing weaknesses in it or by presenting a counterargument. Refutation can be divided into case-level (aimed at the opponent's case as a whole) or specific (aimed at individual arguments).

When refuting cases, opponents have three options. First, they can use direct refutation in which they tear down each of the arguments and the whole taken together. Second, they can employ counteradvocacy, by offering an alternative point of view. Third, they can employ a combination of direct refutation and counteradvocacy by attacking the advocates' argument and at the same time offering alternatives of their own.

Specific refutation, which is directed at individual arguments, can be implemented through five strategies that can be used singly or in combination. First, refuters can use exploratory refutation; they can raise a number of questions and objections to draw out their opponents and make them take positions on issues on which their opponents might be vulnerable. Second they can note contradictions and inconsistencies in their opponents' case. Third, they can indict their opponents' evidence, showing it to be biased, outdated, irrelevant, inexpert, or unreliable. Fourth, refuters can attack reasoning by revealing fallacies and mistakes in their opponents' inferences. Fifth, refuters can produce arguments and evidence of their own that can be weighed against the arguments their opponents have made. Knowing these strategies of refutation and anticipated objections and criticism of one's arguments can contribute substantially to critical thinking ability and to the skills of advocacy.

Finally, this chapter presented an issues brief as one way of understanding the process of advocacy. The issues brief is a way of examining two contrasting points of view and the arguments for and against a proposition. It provides a way for advocates to learn about and understand multiple views on a proposition, which is central to the process of developing critical thought.

EXERCISES

Exercise 1 Take any of the following propositions of fact and construct an issues brief. For the purpose of this exercise, the issues brief need contain only the claims that one might expect an arguer to make.

1. Computer skills increase grade point averages.
2. Strict vegetarian diets harm a person's health.
* 3. Third-party candidates cause diversity in the political process.
4. The welfare system makes people not want to work.
* 5. Leif Ericson discovered America.
6. Restrictions on tobacco products in the United States have resulted in the export of tobacco products to lesser-developed nations.
7. Low-cost air-ticket prices have caused airline safety to decrease.
8. The Social Security system will be bankrupt in 20 years.
9. An asteroid caused the extinction of the dinosaurs.
10. Take-home tests improve student retention of subject matter.

Exercise 2 This chapter discussed different ways of refuting argument cases. First, we discussed strategies for refutation. These included the following:

- Case-level refutation, which is aimed at the entire case
- Specific refutation, which is aimed at individual arguments within the case

CHAPTER NINE   Case Construction: Arguing about Propositions of Fact   **239**

Second, we talked about styles of refutation, which included:

- Destructive refutation, which is aimed at tearing down the opponent's arguments
- Constructive refutation, which is aimed at offering alternatives through counter-arguments
- Bargaining refutation, which attempts to provide a negotiated or compromise argument

Consider the following outlines for a fact-based case argument. Develop a refutation strategy for these cases:

CASE 1

Proposition: Banning handguns saves lives.

Case Arguments	Refutation
I. Definitions	
A. Handguns are personal weapons.	
B. A ban would prohibit private ownership.	
II. Threshold	
A. We are talking about private guns, not guns owned by military or police.	
B. Handguns include any weapon that can be reasonably concealed on a person.	
III. Application	
A. Thousands die each year from the intentional discharge of private, concealed weapons.	
B. Thousands die from the unintentional use of handguns.	
C. Countries that have banned handguns have been successful at saving lives.	

CASE 2

Proposition: Sex education prevents teen pregnancy.

Case Arguments	Refutation
I. Definitions	
A. Sex education is instruction about human reproduction and birth control.	
B. Teen pregnancy is the unintentional pregnancy in people aged 13–19.	

Case Arguments	Refutation

II. Threshold

  A. We are talking about instruction in middle and high schools.

  B. Instruction must include information about biology and birth control.

  C. Instruction is accompanied by access to birth control.

III. Application

  A. In countries where there is intensive sex education, teen pregnancy has decreased.

  B. Teen pregnancy has decreased in schools where there is instruction in this country.

Exercise 3 In the decision, *Gideon v. Wainwright*, the U.S. Supreme Court decided that defendants without the funds to pay for an attorney should be granted a court-appointed attorney. The decision is an argument in favor of a proposition of fact—that indigent defendants are entitled to an attorney. Following is the decision written by Justice Black. As you read the decision consider the following issues:

1. What is the source for most of the definitions in the decision?
2. How does the Court define the grounds for the decision?
3. What are the threshold issues discussed in the decision?
4. How are the facts of the case related to the discussion of definitions?

Petitioner was charged in a Florida state court with having broken and entered a poolroom with intent to commit a misdemeanor. This offense is a felony under Florida law. Appearing in court without funds and without a lawyer, petitioner asked the court to appoint counsel for him, whereupon the following colloquy took place:

The COURT: Mr. Gideon, I am sorry, but I cannot appoint Counsel to represent you in this case. Under the laws of the State of Florida, the only time the Court can appoint Counsel to represent a Defendant is when that person is charged with a capital offense. I am sorry, but I will have to deny your request to appoint Counsel to defend you in this case.

The DEFENDANT: The United States Supreme Court says I am entitled to be represented by Counsel.

Put to trial before a jury, Gideon conducted his defense about as well as could be expected from a layman. He made an opening statement to the jury, cross-examined the State's witnesses, presented witnesses in his own defense, declined to testify himself, and made a short argument "emphasizing his innocence to the charge contained in the Information filed in this case." The jury returned a verdict of guilty, and petitioner was sentenced to serve five years in the state prison. Later, petitioner filed in the Florida Supreme Court this habeas corpus petition attacking his conviction and sentence on the ground that the trial court's refusal to appoint counsel for him denied him rights "guaranteed by the Constitution and the Bill of Rights by the United States Government."

Treating the petition for habeas corpus as properly before it, the State Supreme Court, "upon consideration thereof" but without an opinion, denied all relief. Since 1942, when *Betts v. Brady*, 316 U.S. 455, was decided by a divided Court, the problem of a defendant's federal constitutional right to counsel in a state court has been a continuing source of controversy and litigation in both state and federal courts. To give this problem another review here, we granted certiorari *370 U.S. 908.* Since Gideon was proceeding *in forma pauperis*, we appointed counsel to represent him and requested both sides to discuss in their briefs and oral arguments the following: "Should this Court's holding in *Betts v. Brady*, 316 U.S. 455, be reconsidered?"

I

The facts upon which Betts claimed that he had been unconstitutionally denied the right to have counsel appointed to assist him are strikingly like the facts upon which Gideon here bases his federal constitutional claim. Betts was indicted for robbery in a Maryland state court. On arraignment, he told the trial judge of his lack of funds to hire a lawyer and asked the court to appoint one for him. Betts was advised that it was not the practice in that county to appoint counsel for indigent defendants except in murder and rape cases. He then pleaded not guilty, had witnesses summoned, cross-examined the State's witnesses, examined his own, and chose not to testify himself. He was found guilty by the judge, sitting without a jury, and sentenced to eight years in prison. Like Gideon, Betts sought release by habeas corpus, alleging that he had been denied the right to assistance of counsel in violation of the Fourteenth Amendment. Betts was denied any relief and, on review, this Court affirmed. It was held that a refusal to appoint counsel for an indigent defendant charged with a felony did not necessarily violate the Due Process Clause of the Fourteenth Amendment, which, for reasons given, the Court deemed to be the only applicable federal constitutional provision. The Court said:

> Asserted denial [of due process] is to be tested by an appraisal of the totality of facts in a given case. That which may, in one setting, constitute a denial of fundamental fairness, shocking to the universal sense of justice, may, in other circumstances, and in the light of other considerations, fall short of such denial.

316 U.S. at 462. Treating due process as "a concept less rigid and more fluid than those envisaged in other specific and particular provisions of the Bill of Rights," the Court held that refusal to appoint counsel under the particular facts and circumstances in the *Betts* case was not so "offensive to the common and fundamental ideas of fairness" as to amount to a denial of due process. Since the facts and circumstances of the two cases are so nearly indistinguishable, we think the *Betts v. Brady* holding, if left standing, would require us to reject Gideon's claim that the Constitution guarantees him the assistance of counsel. Upon full reconsideration, we conclude that *Betts v. Brady* should be overruled.

II

The Sixth Amendment provides, "In all criminal prosecutions, the accused shall enjoy the right . . . to have the Assistance of Counsel for his defence." We have construed this to mean that, in federal courts, counsel must be provided for defendants unable to employ counsel unless the right is competently and intelligently waived. Betts argued that this right is extended to indigent defendants in state courts by the Fourteenth Amendment. In response, the Court stated that, while the Sixth Amendment laid down no rule for the conduct of the States, the question recurs whether the constraint laid by the Amendment upon the national courts expresses a rule so fundamental and essential to a fair trial, and so, to due process of law, that it is made obligatory upon the States by the Fourteenth Amendment.

316 U.S. at 465. In order to decide whether the Sixth Amendment's guarantee of counsel is of this fundamental nature, the Court in *Betts* set out and considered

> [r]elevant data on the subject . . . afforded by constitutional and statutory provisions subsisting in the colonies and the States prior to the inclusion of the Bill of Rights in the national Constitution, and in the constitutional, legislative, and judicial history of the States to the present date.

316 U.S. at 465. On the basis of this historical data, the Court concluded that "appointment of counsel is not a fundamental right, essential to a fair trial." *316 U.S. at 471*. It was for this reason the *Betts* Court refused to accept the contention that the Sixth Amendment's guarantee of counsel for indigent federal defendants was extended to or, in the words of that Court, "made obligatory upon, the States by the Fourteenth Amendment." Plainly, had the Court concluded that appointment of counsel for an indigent criminal defendant was "a fundamental right, essential to a fair trial," it would have held that the Fourteenth Amendment requires appointment of counsel in a state court, just as the Sixth Amendment requires in a federal court.

We think the Court in *Betts* had ample precedent for acknowledging that those guarantees of the Bill of Rights which are fundamental safeguards of liberty immune from federal abridgment are equally protected against state invasion by the Due Process Clause of the Fourteenth Amendment. This same principle was recognized, explained, and applied in *Powell v. Alabama*, 287 U.S. 45 (1932), a case upholding the right of counsel, where the Court held that, despite sweeping language to the contrary in *Hurtado v. California*, 110 U.S. 516 (1884), the Fourteenth Amendment "embraced" those "fundamental principles of liberty and justice which lie at the base of all our civil and political institutions," even though they had been "specifically dealt with in another part of the federal Constitution." *287 U.S. at 67*. In many cases other than *Powell* and *Betts*, this Court has looked to the fundamental nature of original Bill of Rights guarantees to decide whether the Fourteenth Amendment makes them obligatory on the States. Explicitly recognized to be of this "fundamental nature," and therefore made immune from state invasion by the Fourteenth, or some part of it, are the First Amendment's freedoms of speech, press, religion, assembly, association, and petition for redress of grievances. For the same reason, though not always in precisely the same terminology, the Court has made obligatory on the States the Fifth Amendment's command that private property shall not be taken for public use without just compensation, the Fourth Amendment's prohibition of unreasonable searches and seizures, and the Eighth's ban on cruel and unusual punishment. On the other hand, this Court in *Palko v. Connecticut*, 302 U.S. 319 (1937), refused to hold that the Fourteenth Amendment made double jeopardy provision of the Fifth Amendment obligatory on the States. In so refusing, however, the Court, speaking through Mr. Justice Cardozo, was careful to emphasize that immunities that are valid as against the federal government by force of the specific pledges of particular amendments have been found to be implicit in the concept of ordered liberty, and thus, through the Fourteenth Amendment, become valid as against the states, and that guarantees "in their origin . . . effective against the federal government alone" had, by prior cases, been taken over from the earlier articles of the federal bill of rights and brought within the Fourteenth Amendment by a process of absorption, *302 U.S. at 323, 325, 326*.

CHAPTER NINE Case Construction: Arguing about Propositions of Fact

We accept *Betts v. Brady's* assumption, based as it was on our prior cases, that a provision of the Bill of Rights which is "fundamental and essential to a fair trial" is made obligatory upon the States by the Fourteenth Amendment. We think the Court in *Betts* was wrong, however, in concluding that the Sixth Amendment's guarantee of counsel is not one of these fundamental rights. Ten years before *Betts v. Brady,* this Court, after full consideration of all the historical data examined in *Betts,* had unequivocally declared that "the right to the aid of counsel is of this fundamental character." *Powell v. Alabama,* 287 U.S. 45, 68 (1932). While the Court, at the close of its *Powell* opinion, did, by its language, as this Court frequently does, limit its holding to the particular facts and circumstances of that case, its conclusions about the fundamental nature of the right to counsel are unmistakable. Several years later, in 1936, the Court reemphasized what it had said about the fundamental nature of the right to counsel in this language:

We concluded that certain fundamental rights, safeguarded by the first eight amendments against federal action, were also safeguarded against state action by the due process of law clause of the Fourteenth Amendment, and among them the fundamental right of the accused to the aid of counsel in a criminal prosecution, *Grosjean v. American Press Co.,* 297 U.S. 233, 243-244 (1936), And again, in 1938, this Court said:

> [The assistance of counsel] is one of the safeguards of the Sixth Amendment deemed necessary to insure fundamental human rights of life and liberty.... The Sixth Amendment stands as a constant admonition that, if the constitutional safeguards it provides be lost, justice will not " still be done."

Johnson v. Zerbst, 304 U.S. 458, 462 (1938). To the same effect, see *Avery v. Alabama,* 308 U.S. 444 (1940), and *Smith v. O'Grady,* 312 U.S. 329 (1941). In light of these and many other prior decisions of this Court, it is not surprising that the *Betts* Court, when faced with the contention that "one charged with crime, who is unable to obtain counsel, must be furnished counsel by the State," conceded that "[e]xpressions in the opinions of this court lend color to the argument...." *316 U.S. at 462-463.* The fact is that, in deciding as it did—that "appointment of counsel is not a fundamental right, essential to a fair trial"—the Court in *Betts v. Brady* made an abrupt break with its own well considered precedents. In returning to these old precedents, sounder, we believe, than the new, we but restore constitutional principles established to achieve a fair system of justice. Not only these precedents, but also reason and reflection, require us to recognize that, in our adversary system of criminal justice, any person haled into court, who is too poor to hire a lawyer, cannot be assured a fair trial unless counsel is provided for him. This seems to us to be an obvious truth. Governments, both state and federal, quite properly spend vast sums of money to establish machinery to try defendants accused of crime. Lawyers to prosecute are everywhere deemed essential to protect the public's interest in an orderly society. Similarly, there are few defendants charged with crime, few indeed, who fail to hire the best lawyers they can get to prepare and present their defenses. That government hires lawyers to prosecute and defendants who have the money hire lawyers to defend are the strongest indications of the widespread belief that lawyers in criminal courts are necessities, not luxuries. The right of one charged with crime to counsel may not be deemed fundamental and essential to fair trials in some countries, but it is in ours. From the very beginning, our state and national constitutions and laws have laid great emphasis on procedural and substantive safeguards designed to assure fair trials before impartial tribunals in which every defendant stands equal before the law. This noble ideal cannot be realized if the poor man charged with crime has to face his accusers without a lawyer to assist him. A defendant's need for a lawyer is nowhere better stated than in the moving words of Mr. Justice Sutherland in *Powell v. Alabama:*

> The right to be heard would be, in many cases, of little avail if it did not comprehend the right to be heard by counsel. Even the intelligent and educated layman has small and sometimes no skill in the science of law. If charged with crime, he is incapable, generally, of determining for himself whether the indictment is good or bad. He is unfamiliar with the rules of evidence. Left without the aid of counsel, he may be put on trial without a proper charge, and convicted upon incompetent evidence, or evidence irrelevant to the issue or otherwise inadmissible. He lacks both the skill and knowledge adequately to prepare his defense, even though he has a perfect one. He requires the guiding hand of counsel at every step in the proceedings against him. Without it, though he be not guilty, he faces the danger of conviction because he does not know how to establish his innocence.

287 U.S. at 68–69. The Court in *Betts v. Brady* departed from the sound wisdom upon which the Court's holding in *Powell v. Alabama* rested. Florida, supported by two other States, has asked that *Betts v. Brady* be left intact. Twenty-two States, as friends of the Court, argue that *Betts* was "an anachronism when handed down," and that it should now be overruled. We agree.

The judgment is reversed, and the cause is remanded to the Supreme Court of Florida for further action not inconsistent with this opinion.

Reversed.

NOTES

1. Vincent Follert, "Risk Analysis: Its Application to Argumentation and Decision Making," *Journal of the American Forensic Association* 18 (1981): 99–108.
2. Richard Whately, *Elements of Rhetoric*, Douglas Ehninger, ed. (Carbondale, Ill.: Southern Illinois University Press, 1963), 112–3.
3. For further discussion about burden of proof and presumption in advocacy, see Gary Cronkhite, "The Locus of the Presumption," *Central States Speech Journal* 17 (1966): 276; and Barbara Warnick, "Arguing Value Propositions," *Journal of the American Forensic Association* 18 (1981): 112–5. Permission to draw material from the latter article was granted by the American Forensic Association.
4. Eva Pomice, "Annual Picks of 10 Career Fields to Get into—and 10 Career Fields to Dump," *Point of View* (May 1996): 52–63.
5. Josina M. Makau, *Reasoning and Communication* (Belmont, Calif.: Wadsworth, 1990), 142.
6. Joanne G. Kurfiss, *Critical Thinking: Theory, Research, Practice, and Possibilities,* ASHE-ERIC Higher Education Report No. 2 (Washington, D.C.: Association for the Study of High Education, 1988), 25–34.
7. Adapted from Jeffrey Walling, "Colleges Should Change Course," *USA Weekend* (September 20–22, 1996): 4–6.

CHAPTER 10

Arguing about Values

CHAPTER OUTLINE
- Values and Value Systems
- The Process of Value Change
- Values and Argumentation
- Stock Issues for Value Arguments
  - Definition
  - Field or Perspective
  - Criteria
  - Application
  - Hierarchies
- The Issues Brief
- Summary
- Exercises

KEY CONCEPTS

value system
instrumental values
value redistribution

value emphasis
value restandardization
value object

Read the situations described in Figure 10–1. If you discuss what should be done in each of these situations with your friends and fellow students, you will probably find that they disagree with each other and that their differing opinions arise from their differing values. In these situations, values such as privacy, honesty, trust, altruism, freedom, and marital fidelity come into conflict with each other. While most people might generally agree that such values are *important,* disagreement and thus argumentation arise when they must *choose between* them. Such choices are not confined to our personal lives. Our leaders and legislators often must make similar choices between incompatible values when they decide on public policy or government spending. For example,

- Should we prohibit logging in our national forests and preserve the environment, or should we permit logging and preserve jobs and the regional economy?
- Should we cut back on Medicare and Medicaid to cut the deficit, or should we continue to fund these programs and provide health care for the poor and elderly?

Deliberating about such choices requires critical thinkers who see the value in premises and assumptions that differ from their own, who can critique their own deepest prejudices, biases, and misconceptions, and who can develop well-grounded criteria for choosing among competing values.[2]

VALUES AND DECISION-MAKING: WHAT WOULD YOU DO?

SITUATION 1:
You are on your way to class, and you are running late. As you hurry down the street, a homeless woman approaches you and asks you for a dollar, "to buy some food," she says. Her clothes are tattered and she looks poor.
—What do you do?

SITUATION 2:
Nancy and Bob, a married couple you have known for years, are your best friends. You frequently go out with them to various activities and social events. You've recently heard from a third party that Bob has been seeing someone else, and you believe that this is true. Should you tell Nancy? Or have a talk with Bob? Or do nothing?
—What do you do?

SITUATION 3:
You have just finished your midterm exam in your communication theory course. You and your study group worked very hard studying for this exam, preparing sample answers for items on the review sheet and discussing them. During the exam, you notice that one group of students appears to be cheating and using "crib notes" to write their answers. You are concerned that they will make high scores on the exam and that your grade will suffer.
—What do you do?

FIGURE 10–1 Values and Decision Making

CHAPTER TEN   Arguing about Values   **247**

The purpose of this chapter is to acquaint you with the basic dynamics of value controversy. The first section will explain how choices are evaluated, how values are prioritized by individuals, and how and why values change over time. The second section will explain the relationship between values and argumentation and the bases for value arguments. The third section will orient you to the basic kinds of issues that arise in value argumentation, and the last section will describe specific procedures for constructing cases supporting and opposing value propositions. The formats suggested in this last section are particularly useful for essays, speeches, and debates in which extended cases for or against value claims must be composed. But value disputes also occur in conversations, discussions, and other argumentative situations. Because such disputes revolve around issues similar to the ones we discuss, our strategies for constructing cases should be useful in other communication situations as well.

VALUES AND VALUE SYSTEMS

Values are pervasive both in the life of society and the life of the individual. Milton Rokeach, who researched American values for the past three decades, made some important distinctions about the nature and types of values. He noted that each person has values organized into a value system. *A value system is an enduring organization of beliefs concerning preferable modes of conduct or end states of existence along a continuum of relative importance.*[3] By this, Rokeach meant that each of us has values that are organized into hierarchies. *A value hierarchy is an ordering of values such that some are ranked more highly than others.* For example, people who want to prohibit logging in our national forests value environmental preservation over jobs and economic growth.

A value is a particular kind of belief. Rather than being descriptive or capable of being true or false, a value is prescriptive; it helps us to judge whether an action or state of being is desirable or undesirable. Rokeach divided values into two main categories—instrumental and terminal. *Instrumental values concern modes of conduct or the means for fulfilling other values. Terminal values concern desirable end states of existence.*[4] We get an education (instrumental value) so that we can find a rewarding career (terminal value). We work hard (instrumental value) so that we can have a comfortable life (terminal value). Examples of instrumental values are educational opportunity, leisure time, and economic prosperity. Instrumental values have a means/end relationship with certain terminal values such as family security, an exciting life, a sense of accomplishment, and self-respect. Rokeach estimated that, whereas an individual possesses a limited number of terminal values—somewhere between one and two dozen—the total number of instrumental values may be several times that number because we use many avenues or instruments to reach our objectives or terminal value states.

Values can also be divided into personal and social values. Personal values such as self-esteem, salvation, and social recognition are self-centered and intrapersonal in nature, whereas social values such as world peace, family security, and altruism are society-centered or socially centered.[5] Objects and actions are thus valuable because they fulfill our intellectual, biological, or spiritual needs at either the personal or social level.

From the 1960s through the 1980s, Rokeach conducted extensive studies of American value systems. Narrowing the list of terminal values to 18, he surveyed large samples of the American public to discover how these 18 terminal values were ordered. Results from his studies in 1968 and 1981 are reported in Table 10–1. Three observations about this rank ordering of values are particularly noteworthy. First, American values appear to be quite stable across time. Although there are some changes, the same high- and low-ranked values in 1968 were ranked high and low in 1981. Concerning this stability, Rokeach and his coauthor noted that "such highly stable findings would seem to suggest that there is little, if any, value change occurring in American society, at least in the thirteen-year period under consideration. Many social scientists would probably interpret such findings as confirming the widely shared view that human values are deep-lying components of collective belief systems and are thus inherently resistant to change."[6]

Second, these value orderings are somewhat similar for men and women and for blacks and whites. In contrast to the stereotype that men value achievement and intellectual pursuits while women value love, affiliation, and the family, Rokeach found that these values were similarly ranked by Americans of both sexes. In regard to race, the rank orderings of blacks and whites were similar *with the exception of the value of equality,* which was ranked second by blacks and twelfth by whites. Furthermore, when Rokeach matched blacks with the whites in his survey according to education and socioeconomic status, the differences between the two races in value rankings either disappeared or became minimal, again with the exception of the different rankings of equality.[7]

Third, this ranking of terminal values was specific to American culture. Rokeach gathered information on value rankings from Australians, Canadians, and Israelis and

Rank Order of Terminal Values (1968)[3]

Males (All races)	Females (All races)	Blacks	1981 Survey[6]
1. a world at peace	1. a world at peace	1. a world at peace	1. family security
2. family security	2. family security	2. equality	2. a world at peace
3. freedom	3. freedom	3. freedom	3. freedom
4. a comfortable life	4. salvation	4. family security	4. self-respect
5. happiness	5. happiness	5. a comfortable life	5. happiness
6. self-respect	6. self-respect	6. self-respect	6. wisdom
7. a sense of accomplishment	7. wisdom	7. happiness	7. a sense of accomplishment
8. wisdom	8. equality	8. wisdom	8. a comfortable life
9. equality	9. true friendship	9. salvation	9. salvation
10. national security	10. a sense of accomplishment	10. true friendship	10. true friendship
11. true friendship	11. national security	11. a sense of accomplishment	11. national security
12. salvation	12. inner harmony	12. inner harmony	12. equality
13. inner harmony	13. a comfortable life	13. national security	13. inner harmony
14. mature love	14. mature love	14. mature love	14. mature love
15. a world of beauty	15. a world of beauty	15. social recognition	15. an exciting life
16. social recognition	16. pleasure	16. a world of beauty	16. a world of beauty
17. pleasure	17. social recognition	17. pleasure	17. pleasure
18. an exciting life	18. an exciting life	18. an exciting life	18. social recognition

TABLE 10–1 Rank Order of Terminal Values, 1968 and 1981

found sizable differences between cultures. Israelis ranked national security second, whereas it was never ranked higher than tenth by Americans. Canadians ranked happiness, mature love, and true friendship much more highly than Americans. Seymour Lipset, who has done extensive cross-cultural comparisons between Americans and Canadians, has noted that Americans are more religious, more patriotic, more populist and antielitist, and more socially egalitarian than Canadians and citizens of other developed countries. America is also more "antistatist" (distrustful of centralized government) than all other developed nations and thus is exceptional in the low level of support it provides for its poor in welfare, housing, and medical care. Lipset reports that among the developed nations, the United States has the highest proportion of its people living in poverty.[8] These studies of American values indicate that the orderings and priorities we place on various terminal values are culture-specific. As we noted in Chapter 2, people of different cultures and ethnicities will perceive and respond to value arguments in different ways. They will view as important those values that concern them most directly. The question of which values are ranked most highly by one's audience should always influence the design of one's value argumentation.

THE PROCESS OF VALUE CHANGE

In any society that is not experiencing violent domestic upheaval or social change, there will be many commonly accepted core values. As noted in Table 10–1, "a world at peace," "family security," and "freedom" are three central accepted and acknowledged values in American society. Nicholas Rescher, a scholar who has researched value-oriented reasoning, has observed that "there unquestionably exists (and will continue to exist) a prominent value consensus in America."[9] In our own society and in others, however, certain values are unstable and fluctuate in their importance and in the extent to which people adhere to them.[10] Because these fluctuations affect the hierarchies used in argumentation, advocates should be sensitive to them.

Values change in three different ways. One type of value change occurs when a value that was held by a minority becomes more widely disseminated and becomes a majority value. Rescher has labeled this *value redistribution, which is a process in which a value becomes more and more widely diffused throughout a society until virtually all its members adhere to it.* In the period of the Vietnam war protests, for example, peace activists staged marches, rallies, draft card burnings, sit-ins, and other forms of protest against the war. The existence of peace logos, signs, and symbols along with speeches and rallies gradually raised the consciousness of the general population about peace as a value so that it came to be more widely held. Ultimately, American sentiment against the war was a major factor influencing political figures to bring an end to our involvement in Vietnam.

Rescher observes that in the normal course of events, values come to be emphasized or deemphasized; that is, they come to be more or less important to the people who hold them. *In value emphasis, values move upward in a value hierarchy. In value deemphasis, they move downward.* This increase or decrease in the extent of our adherence to values can be brought about by new information or by changes in our social or economic environment. For example, new information about the causes of cancer, heart attack, and stroke has noticeably changed Americans' awareness of good health in prolonging life. This increased emphasis on good health has changed our attitudes and behavior regarding exercise, smoking, and salt and cholesterol intake. Changes in the economic environment in the early 1980s and the early 1990s led to a dramatic decrease in the number of professional jobs available to college graduates. As a result, college students came to value their education in terms of its "marketability" and sought degrees in business, engineering, and computer science in increasing numbers.

Rescher cites value restandardization as a third factor affecting the way in which values are applied within a society. *Value restandardization is a process in which standards used to measure whether a value is being met increase or decrease.* For example, the criteria to measure whether one has an adequate standard of living have changed over the years. In the late 1940s and early 1950s, costs and inflation were low; most families had only one car; and mortgages were well within the reach of middle-class income. Today, in many areas even modest homes are expensive; cable television and telephones are considered basic utilities; life-styles often require that most families have two cars; and many other costs have risen. Standards for an adequate income and life-style have changed dramatically over the past 40 years.

In addition to cultural variations in value rankings, values vary in response to changing social conditions. As time passes, certain values may become more widely diffused in a society, may increase or decrease in importance, or be restandardized. Value advocates should consider what factors—new information, technological development, or economic fluctuation—might affect the values they are discussing. Also, when incompatible values conflict, advocates should determine what standards audiences are likely to use to choose between them. As we shall see in the remaining sections of this chapter, audience adherence plays a major role in establishing basic premises in a value argument.

VALUES AND ARGUMENTATION

To support fact and policy claims, arguers can refer to truths and to facts that are verifiable and recognized by the audience. For example, if someone were to claim that "capital punishment deters crime," that person could use studies of the relationship between existence of the death penalty and the incidence of first-degree murder and other capital crimes. But if the claim was that "capital punishment is justified," a different strategy would be required. Here, the advocate would have to draw upon value hierarchies and the relationship between values recognized in society to provide justification for capital punishment.

This is why the research findings of Rokeach and others who have studied American values are so important to value argument. When people disagree about values, a choice must be made, and one criterion for deciding between competing values is their relative status in the larger society. Rokeach's findings reported in Table 10–1 tell us which terminal values are viewed as the most important by the American public, and his and others' studies provide resources that indicate which values should be favored.[11]

Another researcher who has studied values in Western society is Chaim Perelman. Perelman and his coauthor Lucie Olbrechts-Tyteca have identified particular value hierarchies that seem to be widely accepted in Western cultures and that are therefore used as a foundation for value claims.[12] First is the hierarchy of *quantity*—whatever produces the greatest good for the largest number of people at the least cost is to be preferred. This hierarchy, which values more over less and judges alternatives based on effects and outcomes, comes from utilitarianism. ("We should subsidize health care cooperatives to provide affordable health care for all citizens of the country.") Second is the hierarchy of *quality,* which values what is unique, irreparable, or original. Human life is often viewed from this perspective, as are great works of art. ("The Sistine Chapel is worth restoring, even at great cost, for the works of Michelangelo cannot be replaced.") Third is the hierarchy of *the existent,* which values the concrete over the possible. ("You should accept that job offer you have now rather than waiting for another one that might not materialize.") Fourth is the hierarchy of *essence,* which values what is at the core of a group or class rather than what is on the fringes. ("Free enterprise is central to what this country is all about, and we should do whatever we can to preserve free enterprise.") The fifth hierarchy, that of *the person,* values the dignity and autonomy of the person over all competing values.[13] ("Euthanasia allows a person death with dignity, and a dignified death is more important than life for a terminally ill person.") The hierarchies of quantity (more over less), quality (the unique over the common), the existent (the concrete over the merely possible), essence (the central over the peripheral), and the person (individual dignity and autonomy over all else) are very commonly accepted throughout society and can be used as a basis for value claims.

Perelman and Olbrechts-Tyteca remind us that "when a speaker wants to establish values or hierarchies or to intensify the adherence they gain, he may consolidate them by connecting them to other values or hierarchies."[14] In the examples above, such things as affordable health care, the restoration of the Sistine Chapel, free enterprise, and euthanasia were said to be preferable because of their association with the values higher in these five pervasive hierarchies. Each of these five hierarchies is common and used frequently in arguments.

The theorists whose work we have discussed, then, have suggested principles that can be quite useful in constructing arguments about values:

1. Generally, terminal values should be viewed as more significant and important than instrumental values.

2. When one is choosing between competing instrumental values (that is, choosing the most effective means to an end), the value that best meets the particular needs of the situation should be preferred.

3. In choosing one value over others, one should consider the hierarchies of quantity, quality, the existent, essence and the person if they are applicable to a particular choice or course of action.

4. The results of Rokeach's value survey of terminal values indicate a rather stable value system that is accepted by the American public and that can be used to support value preferences.

5. Values are not entirely fixed, however. Because values tend to change slowly, the advocate should consider the possibilities of value redistribution, value emphasis, and value restandardization as described by Rescher.

When a choice must be made between competing values, or when an arguer seeks to defend a particular value hierarchy, these five principles can provide the means for justifying a shift or change in values or for opposing value orderings proposed by other arguers.

STOCK ISSUES FOR VALUE ARGUMENTS

As we observed in Chapter 6, propositions of value support a value orientation toward some value object. *A value object is an idea, practice, event, policy, or state of affairs that is to be judged by means of an evaluation.* In the proposition "euthanasia is desirable," euthanasia is the value object; in the proposition, "required sex education in the public schools is justified," required sex education is the value object. To argue successfully for a particular orientation to a value object, value advocates must address certain stock issues. *Stock issues are questions that must be asked and answered to construct a satisfactory case on a proposition.* Both policy and value propositions imply certain stock issues, and they are called "stock" issues because they are standard; they are the issues audiences expect to see addressed and resolved before they will accept a policy or value case. In Chapter 11, we will discuss the stock issues for policy cases; here we will discuss stock issues for supporting propositions of value.[15] These include definition, field, criteria, application of criteria, and hierarchies.

The role of stock issues will be illustrated through examples from supporting and opposing arguments on the topic "euthanasia is desirable." Euthanasia, generically defined as a means for producing a gentle and easy death, is a controversial topic in America today. The law holds that patients have the right to refuse medical treatment and that patients with living wills can be allowed to die without specific measures (hydration, feeding tubes, resuscitation) to preserve their lives. However, when a patient becomes comatose and has not expressed preferences regarding treatment, the course of action to be taken is much less clear. Furthermore, laws applying to doctor-assisted death (induced death) are also inconsistent, particularly in regard to penalties for assisted suicide. The public is aware of highly publicized cases in which an immediate family sued to have a relative removed from life-support mechanisms, or severely deformed infants were allowed to die, or spouses and other loved ones ended the lives of suffering patients. Euthanasia dramatizes the conflicts between our religious beliefs, our humanitarian instincts, our legal codes, and our medical practices. As such, it is a highly appropriate topic for value controversy.

Definition

The first issue on which advocates and opponents of value claims are likely to clash is that of definition. The value advocate must clearly define the value object, as well as any other controversial terms related to the topic. By defining terms, the arguer establishes his or her own views of the basic concepts on which controversy will turn. Some objects, practices, policies, and other phenomena may be readily understood, whereas others are more complex. With euthanasia as the value object, arguers supporting the claim that the practice is desirable might provide a definition that includes only passive euthanasia—the withholding or removal of life-sustaining treatment from patients who are dying and have no hope of recovery.[16] Their opponents might challenge this definition by arguing that it is insufficiently inclusive. "Euthanasia" is often said to include measures that bring about death ("mercy killing"). If opponents of euthanasia present an alternative definition, they must show why it is better than the original definition. One cannot just arbitrarily redefine the value object without showing the inadequacies of the original definition.

There are many methods that can be used to define terms. For example, one may provide actual examples of the value object with which the audience is familiar. (The removal of a feeding tube from the comatose Nancy Beth Cruzan is such an example.) The history of the status of the value object in society is another source for definitions. (One could cite a number of court cases and other situations in which euthanasia has occurred.) The term's etymology or derivation is another source. ("Euthanasia" comes from the Greek *eu* = happy; *thanatos* = death.) The opinions of authorities and experts who have studied the topic may function as a useful source for definitions. Finally, ordinary usage based on dictionary definitions can serve as a basis for definitions.

Proponents of a value claim should avoid defining terms in ways that are incompatible with the values they are advocating. For example, those supporting passive euthanasia because it allows dying patients freedom of choice would not want to stipulate situations in which euthanasia must take place. This would deprive patients of freedom of choice by requiring actions mandated by the situation. The characteristics of the value object that are identified should be compatible with the field of analysis and the values that are applied within it.

Field or Perspective

A second stock issue for value argument is the field or perspective within which the value object will be evaluated. In Chapter 3, we defined argument fields as contexts for argument commonly accepted by participants in a dispute. Fields such as law, medicine, physics, and economics suggest standards of proof and evidence useful in making evaluations. The priorities, practices, and conventions in certain fields determine what values are important and how judgments are to be made. If two fields are applied in evaluating the same value object, the standards and rules drawn from each of them may be in conflict. For example, at certain times in certain jurisdictions, the legal definition for death was "irreparable cessation of spontaneous cardiac and respiratory activity," while the medical definition was cessation of brain activity as indicated by a flat electroencephalograph. Furthermore, legal decisions are based on the letter of the law and precedent in similar court cases, while medical practice is based on medical ethics, which obligate a physician not to do anything that makes the patient worse. Clearly, the fields of law and medicine have very different definitions, standards, and procedures for guiding decisions in euthanasia cases.

Advocates using a multilogical approach to value argument could argue from perspectives other than fields, so long as they make the source of their assumptions and standards clear to the audience. Perspectives could include religions (Judaism, Buddhism, Christianity, Islam, etc.), cultures (systems of meaning expressed in symbolic form), or academic disciplines (literature, normative ethics, social psychology). What is important in an argumentation setting is to be aware that the source or basis for one's values cannot be taken for granted but must itself be subject to open discussion and examination just as other perspectives are. Also, the perspective chosen must be suitable to the topic and to the values of the audience. For example, euthanasia probably cannot be successfully justified from an economic perspective. Although an increase in the frequency of euthanasia would save a great deal of money, most people in our society would find the idea of putting a financial value on human life repugnant. Given the attitudes and predispositions of Americans, selecting economics as the field of evaluation for euthanasia would be inappropriate.

Criteria

In addition to their definitions, value advocates should carefully select the criteria by which they will evaluate the value object. *Criteria are field- or perspective-dependent standards to be used to decide whether the value object fulfills certain values.* Criteria are the measures, norms, or rules used to judge whatever is being evaluated. For example, if we say "this ice cream is good," we must have in mind certain criteria or standards (creaminess, good taste, natural ingredients) by which we will judge the ice cream. Here the value would probably be pleasure or enjoyment; if the value object meets or measures up to the standards, it fulfills the value in question; if not, then it must be judged negatively.

The standards advocates select should be taken from the field or perspective they have presented for evaluation. Advocates supporting the desirability of euthanasia could select individual ethics as their field and argue that the greater good of the individual is its purpose. Within this framework, they could defend the values of physical well-being, self-respect, and freedom of choice. Therefore, the standards these values suggest are that physical pain and suffering should be minimized or avoided, that those affected should be able to maintain dignity and avoid degradation, and that those affected should be able to make free choices concerning what happens to them. If the advocates can establish these three standards, they then only need to prove that euthanasia enables those standards to be met in order to establish their case.

Their opponents could argue for an alternative field and a different set of criteria. For example, they could argue that social ethics should be the field for evaluation rather than just what is good for the individual. On a social level, alternative standards might come into play. In opposition to the three criteria above, opponents might argue that the weak and the old should be protected, that life (the highest value) should be preserved, and that the medical profession should uphold its responsibility to preserve human life.

Both advocates and opponents of the desirability of euthanasia must validate their criteria through further argument, especially when those standards are questioned or challenged. Three strategies are available for establishing criteria. First, one can link them to more generally accepted and unquestioned standards and argue that because the more general standard is accepted, the audience should also accept the particular standard the advocate is supporting. For example, we put suffering animals out of their misery; why can we not allow a human being who is suffering to die? Or, we show compassion to strangers but refuse to allow our loved ones to end their own misery. Second, the standards can be justified by showing that no other standards take precedence over them. For example, in this country we believe that freedom of choice is more important than life itself. ("Live free or die" was a central motto of the colonial period, and Patrick Henry's "Give me liberty or give me death" is well known.) Third, advocates can show the logical consequences of failing to apply the standards they advocate. Advances in medical technology have made it possible to "keep alive" individuals who are brain dead by artificially stimulating respiration and heartbeat. Once the machines have been activated, doctors are afraid to discontinue them because they fear malpractice suits and even criminal charges. The logical consequences of a complete refusal to sanction euthanasia would be the continued existence of thousands of patients who could only be said to be "alive" in a technical sense.

Application

The fourth stock issue deals with the application of the criteria the advocates have established. That is, does the value object meet the standards for fulfilling the values in question? Here is where factual information and experience can be used for evidence. Supporters of euthanasia should be able to show that passive euthanasia enables patients to avoid suffering and to die with dignity. The extent to which the criteria apply and the number of patients affected by the criteria are significant here. How many patients are terminally ill and on life-support mechanisms? What proportion of these patients are likely to be affected by the euthanasia practices the advocates favor? If the proportion is small or the use of passive euthanasia likely to be infrequent, the advocates' argument may lack significance.

On the other hand, opponents of euthanasia would have at least two options open to them on this stock issue. First, they might argue that the supporters' criteria do not apply. If many terminally ill patients are not sustained by life-support mechanisms, then passive euthanasia would not diminish their suffering. Furthermore, if most terminally ill patients are comatose and unable to express their wishes, then passive euthanasia would not provide death with dignity for those patients. Second, opponents might refer to the alternative criteria they have proposed and argue that applying those criteria better fulfills certain values. For example, if opponents of euthanasia established as a criterion that doctors should be able to uphold their responsibility to preserve life, then asking them to disconnect life-support mechanisms would work against that standard.

Hierarchies

In any extended value case, a certain value hierarchy is implied because in defending any value orientation, advocates implicitly favor one value or certain values over other values. The hierarchy applicable in any evaluation may become explicit only when that evaluation is challenged and contrasted to an alternative hierarchy. Therefore, explicit defense of a particular hierarchy may not be required when a value case is presented initially. Should the case be challenged by opponents with different values, however, opposing hierarchies will usually become a major issue in the controversy.

Supporters and opponents of euthanasia would quite naturally support different value hierarchies. Those supporting euthanasia would be likely to support freedom of choice and self-respect for the individual, whereas opponents might support the sanctity of human life and social responsibility. In defending their respective hierarchies, advocates of each position attempt to intensify their audience's adherence to and appreciation for the values at the top of their hierarchies. In other words, they attempt to persuade their listeners to rank order values in the same way that they do. In defending a certain hierarchy, the value advocates can make use of the resources provided in the previous section: the distinction between terminal and instrumental values, the needs implied in the situation, Perelman's study of Western hierarchies, Rokeach's value survey, and Rescher's account of value change. In addition, advocates can seek out other studies of American values and value hierarchies.[17]

Opponents of a value proposition can also reorder the audience's hierarchies by showing that the evidence and arguments the supporters used to support their own hierarchies were questionable. If euthanasia supporters argued that their own values were highly ranked by Americans, their opponents could respond that this is merely a form of argument *ad populum*. Keep in mind that just because the majority of the people *believe* that something is right does not mean that it *is* right. Many Americans in the South favored school segregation at one time, but it was not morally "right." Perhaps the values currently ranked highly by most Americans reflect excessive self-interest and ought not to be the ones most valued. Euthanasia opponents could argue that the social welfare field they advocate is based on the idea that we should be more concerned with long-term consequences for the whole society than we are with the immediate interests of particular individuals.

THE ISSUES BRIEF

Writers on argument have recently pointed out that familiarity with multiple views on an issue improves one's own arguments as well as one's ability to anticipate and respond to others' views. As Josina Makau has observed, "the quality of deliberation on controversial issues depends, in large measure, on the arguers' ability to thoughtfully consider as many alternative perspectives as possible."[18] Many people who first approach a topic think they have their minds made up. As they conduct research on the topic and read the opinions of various authorities, they begin to see that the situation or the solution is not as readily apparent as they first thought. Often in the process of researching for a speech or debate, students will actually shift their opinions to the side opposite to the one they had favored in the beginning!

Researchers on critical thinking tell us that this is a good thing. Richard Paul notes that experienced critical thinkers know how to clarify the values and standards relevant to a situation, compare the values embedded in competing perspectives and interpretations, and question deeply their own framework of thought.[19] Living as we do in a multicultural, diverse society requires us to understand and appreciate value orientations that differ from our own and to respect and incorporate the perspectives of individuals who come from religious and cultural backgrounds and personal experiences dramatically different from our own. Experience in value advocacy can enable many arguers to do this.

As a means of assisting you to incorporate divergent perspectives into your argument, we recommend that you construct an "issues brief" as we initially discussed in Chapter 9. The potential weakness of the issues brief is that it appears to assume that there are only two polarized sides, one supporting the proposition and one opposing it. Of course, on many controversial topics people's attitudes are more complex than that. On the topic of euthanasia, for example, some people might feel that euthanasia is not justified under any condition, whereas others believe a terminal patient ought to have the final say in controlling the manner and timing of his or her death. There are also people who believe that some forms of euthanasia may be justified in some circumstances. In other words, they hold neither absolutely positive nor absolutely negative views on the topic but rather more complex ones that take circumstances into account.

What follows is a brief on the euthanasia topic that articulates arguments on all the stock issues discussed in the previous section. When examining this brief, you should realize that each of the arguments is a *claim* that would need to be supported by further arguments and/or evidence such as the opinions of authorities or facts or statistics. What is included in Figure 10–2 are the principal claim (the proposition), the

Proposition: Euthanasia is desirable.

Issue 1: Definition. How should the value object and other terms important to the topic be defined?

I. Euthanasia will be defined as passive—withholding or removing life support systems from moribund patients.

    A. "Life-support systems" include equipment that provides basic life functions—respiration, heartbeat, etc.—through artificial means.

    B. "Moribund" patients are people with no possibility of recovery who will die in the normal course of events.

    C. This definition is supported by etymology and the opinion of experts.

I. This definition is overly restrictive and should include active euthanasia.

    A. Active euthanasia has traditionally been included in the term.

    B. Some "moribund" and comatose patients have, in fact, recovered consciousness.

    C. *Webster's Dictionary*, eighth edition, defines euthanasia as "the act of killing individuals who are hopelessly sick or injured."

Issue 2: Field. In what field or from what perspective should the value object be evaluated?

II. Euthanasia will be evaluated within the field of normative ethics.

    A. Normative ethics promotes the best quality of life possible for the individual.

    B. Normative ethics is appropriate because it overrides the letter of the law and the requirements of technology.

II. Euthanasia should be evaluated in the field of societal welfare.

    A. Societal welfare considers the moral fiber and well-being of society as a whole.

    B. Societal welfare is appropriate because it presumes that the quality of a society is measured by its ability to protect the weak and the old.

Issue 3. Criteria. What standards should be applied to determine whether the value object fulfills the desired values?

III. To be beneficial, euthanasia should meet certain standards.

    A. Euthanasia should allow free choice concerning the manner and timing of a person's death.

    B. Euthanasia should prevent needless suffering and futile prolongation of life.

    C. Euthanasia should prevent hardship for the families of terminally ill patients.

III. Other standards are more important.

    A. Treatment of the terminally ill should protect and preserve life.

    B. Treatment of the terminally ill should enhance the will to survive.

    C. Treatment should not undermine the general respect for life in our society.

FIGURE 10–2 Issues Brief with Definition, Field, Criteria, and Application

---

Issue 4: Application. Do the proposed standards in fact apply to the value object?

IV. Euthanasia is beneficial and desirable.
   A. It preserves freedom and dignity of the individual.
   B. It ends patients' suffering.
   C. It gives families a say in patients' treatment.

IV. Euthanasia is harmful to society.
   A. It puts pressure on terminally ill patients and undermines the will to survive.
   B. In the absence of active euthanasia, patients will continue to suffer anyway.
   C. Families can be distressed and torn apart by the responsibility to make these decisions.
   D. Society's attitudes toward the preservation of life will be negatively affected.

Issue 5: Hierarchies. What values and what rank ordering of values should apply to this value object?

V. Euthanasia preserves and promotes personal freedom, comfort, and self-respect.
   A. Freedom, comfort, and self-respect are three of the eight top-ranked values in Rokeach's value survey.
   B. Freedom of choice and dignity are the essence of what it means to be human.

V. Euthanasia undermines our respect for life which should be the highest value.
   A. If life is not preserved and protected, all other values are moot.
   B. Our Christian belief tells us that life is a gift, not ours to do with as we please.
   C. A human life is unique and irreplaceable.
   D. A society that does not value life becomes degraded and immoral.

FIGURE 10–2 *continued*

major subclaims, and the sub-subclaims that constitute the two cases supporting and opposing the proposition.

In his *Rhetoric* written over 2000 years ago, Aristotle defended the art of speaking persuasively on issues. He wrote, "we must be able to employ persuasion, just as strict reasoning can be employed, on opposite sides of a question, not in order that we may in practice employ it in both ways (for we must not make people believe what is wrong), but in order that we may see clearly what the facts are, and that, if another man argues unfairly, we on our part may be able to confute him."[20] Aristotle recognized that matters that are subject to argument are never so straightforward and simple that they can be quickly resolved. (If they were, they would not be the subject of argumentation.) Rather, when we deliberate about policies or values, the issues we consider are difficult and nettlesome. An issues brief such as we have just presented can help the advocate weigh the various positions and arguments on an issue and produce a reasonable and considered argument in support of a proposition.

SUMMARY

This chapter was intended to provide a systematic approach to value argument. Although some people have expressed the view that values are basically subjective and irrational, many contemporary theorists of argument have successfully provided the means for developing a rational approach to supporting value claims. They have recognized that many arguments in fields such as law and medicine are based on values and provide the grounds for making decisions and taking action. These theorists have explained how value arguments are structured, how they can be assessed, and how advocates can construct extended arguments supporting value claims.

Values are generally organized into value systems. A value system is an enduring organization of beliefs concerning preferable modes of conduct or end states of existence along a continuum of relative importance. Rokeach's surveys of American values have shown that Americans value family security, a world at peace, freedom, and self-respect over many other values and that these values are relatively stable and do not change dramatically over time. Surveys of value systems are important to the value advocate, who must gauge his or her argument to suit the values and attitudes of an audience. Furthermore, when individuals or groups of people disagree about values, it is because their value systems are ordered differently. The values ranked as most important by one are ranked as less important by the other.

In any society, value hierarchies are subject to fluctuation and change. Values may become more widely held because a persistent minority successfully argues for their importance. Because of new information or changes in the social or economic environment, values may become more or less emphasized. The standards that are applied to determine whether a value has been met may become more or less stringent. Because audience adherence is a vital factor in establishing the basic premises in a value argument, advocates should be aware of factors that may bring about changes in the importance and pervasiveness of values in society.

An arguer supporting a particular value proposition must advocate some orientation toward a value object. A value object is an idea, practice, event, policy, or state of affairs that has to be measured in an evaluation. To successfully support a value proposition, the value advocate must address five stock issues. First is definition: How is the value object and terms important to the topic to be defined? Second is the field for evaluation: In what field or from what perspective should the value object be evaluated? Third is criteria: What standards should be applied to determine whether the value object fulfills the desired values? Fourth is application: Does the value object in fact meet the standards that have been proposed by the advocate? Fifth is the value hierarchy: What values and what rank ordering of values should be applied to this value object? The chapter concluded with an issues brief on the topic of euthanasia to illustrate how these five stock issues function in a value controversy.

EXERCISES

* *Exercise 1* What follows is an excerpt from a Supreme Court decision on flag burning (*Texas v. Johnson* 491 U.S. 397 [1989]). In this case, a man named Johnson participated during the 1984 Republican National Convention in Dallas, Texas, in a political demonstration to protest the policies of the Reagan administration and some Dallas-based corporations. After a march through the city streets, Johnson burned an American flag while protesters chanted. He was convicted of desecration of a venerated object in violation of a Texas statute, and the State Court of Appeals upheld the conviction. However, the Texas Court of Criminal Appeals reversed the ruling, holding that the State could not punish Johnson for burning the flag in this situation because his action was expressive conduct

protected by the First Amendment provisions protecting freedom of expression. The decision was appealed to the U.S. Supreme Court, which ruled in favor of Johnson. Below are excerpts from the majority opinion, which was authored by Justice William Brennan. In regard to his value-based argument, answer the following questions:

1. What values does Justice Brennan affirm in this opinion?
2. What values does Brennan view as opposed to his position?
3. What criteria for evaluation does Brennan apply in the decision?
4. What is your own value position in regard to Brennan's specific argument here?

The State asserts an interest in preserving the flag as a symbol of nationhood and national unity. . . .

Johnson was prosecuted because he knew that his politically charged expression would cause "serious offense." If he had burned the flag as a means of disposing of it because it was dirty or torn, he would not have been convicted of flag desecration under this Texas law: Federal law designates burning as the preferred means of disposing of a flag. . . . The Texas law is thus not aimed at protecting the physical integrity of the flag in all circumstances, but is designed instead to protect it only against impairments that cause serious offense to others. . . . Whether Johnson's treatment of the flag violated Texas law thus depended on the likely communicative impact of his expressive conduct.

Texas argues that its interest [is] in preserving the flag as a symbol of nationhood and national unity. . . . Quoting extensively from the writings of this Court chronicling the flag's historic and symbolic role in our society, the State emphasizes the "'special place'" reserved for the flag in our Nation. . . . The State's argument is not that it has an interest simply in maintaining the flag as a symbol of *something,* no matter what it symbolizes; indeed, if that were the State's position, it would be difficult to see how that interest is endangered by highly symbolic conduct such as Johnson's. Rather, the State's claim is that it has an interest in preserving the flag as a symbol of *nationhood* and *national unity.* . . . According to Texas, if one physically treats the flag in a way that would tend to cast doubt on either the idea that nationhood and national unity are the flag's referents or that national unity actually exists, the message conveyed thereby is a harmful one and therefore may be prohibited.

If there is a bedrock principle underlying the First Amendment, it is that the government may not prohibit the expression of an idea simply because society finds the idea itself offensive or disagreeable. . . .

Texas' focus on the precise nature of Johnson's expression, moreover, misses the point of our prior decisions: their enduring lesson, that the government may not prohibit expression simply because it disagrees with its message, is not dependent on the particular mode in which one chooses to express an idea. If we were to hold that a State may forbid flag burning wherever it is likely to endanger the flag's symbolic role, but allow it wherever burning a flag promotes that role—as where, for example, a person ceremoniously burns a dirty flag—we would be saying that when it comes to impairing the flag's physical integrity, the flag itself may be used as a symbol—as a substitute for the written or spoken word . . . we would be permitting a State to "prescribe what shall be orthodox" by saying that one may burn the flag to convey one's attitude toward it and its referents only if one does not endanger the flag's representation of nationhood and national unity.

We are tempted to say, in fact, that the flag's deservedly cherished place in our community will be strengthened, not weakened, by our holding today. Our decision is a

CHAPTER TEN   Arguing about Values   **261**

reaffirmation of the principles of freedom and inclusiveness that the flag best reflects, and of the conviction that our toleration of criticism such as Johnson's is a sign and source of our strength. Indeed, one of the proudest images of our flag, the one immortalized in our own national anthem, is of the bombardment it survived at Fort McHenry. It is the Nation's resilience, not its rigidity, that Texas sees reflected in the flag—and it is that resilience that we reassert today.

The way to preserve the flag's special role is not to punish those who feel differently about these matters. It is to persuade them that they are wrong. . . . We can imagine no more appropriate response to burning a flag than waving one's own, no better way to counter a flag burner's message than by saluting the flag that burns, no surer means of preserving the dignity even of the flag that burned than by—as one witness here did—according its remains a respectful burial. We do not consecrate the flag by punishing its desecration, for in doing so we dilute the freedom that this cherished emblem represents.

Exercise 2   Below are two arguments—one supporting Affirmative Action in higher education admissions and the other opposing it. These arguments are taken from the "pro" and "con" briefs of Ramona Hunter and Kaidren Winiecki, who presented a debate on Affirmative Action in their University of Washington argumentation course on December 7, 1995. The adaptations presented here are used with their permission. Construct an issues brief of the two arguments using the value analysis format discussed in this chapter. Your issues brief should look like the one on euthanasia in this chapter, that is, organized according to the opposing positions on the definition of the value object, selection of the field for evaluation, choice of criteria for judgment, application of criteria, and the respective opposing value hierarchies.

Argument Supporting Affirmative Action in Higher Education Admissions

Affirmative Action, according to the *Cassell Dictionary of Modern Politics,* 1994 ed., refers to policies designed to promote the incorporation of minority or disadvantaged groups into political, social, and economic institutions, and to promote equality of employment opportunity. Affirmative Action is intended to correct historical imbalances which have resulted from discrimination. It was first used in the 1960s in the U.S. when President Lyndon B. Johnson ordered contractors to "act affirmatively" to employ workers without discrimination.

We are evaluating Affirmative Action from the perspective of educational benefit to students. That which is educationally beneficial should contribute to the students' enlightenment through education, promote student learning, and enhance dialogue and diversity in institutions of higher learning.

Affirmative Action does indeed promote the values of educational enlightenment and diversity. It promotes enlightenment because it gives students a chance to receive an education that exposes them to a plethora of ideas, without denying them their basic constitutional rights. As Catherine Jay Didion, the Executive Director of the Association for Women in Science, wrote in a 1995 article for the *Journal of College Science Teaching,* "Affirmative Action, properly applied, can benefit faculty and students by fostering a dialogue with those who speak in different accents, come from a variety of heritages, and represent many regions of the United States. A diverse student and faculty population can result in a strong, more dynamic higher education community."

Affirmative Action promotes diversity because it provides educational opportunities for minority and disadvantaged students who otherwise would not have access to higher education. Without pro-active steps on the part of admissions officials, the percentage of African American and Hispanic students in our nation's colleges and professional schools would be greatly reduced, as statistics have shown.

Those who argue against Affirmative Action will say that it is not "fair" to non-minority students. We can see, however, that most of the standardized test measures used in college admissions are not "fair" to low income students, who consistently score lower on such tests than higher income, non-minority students. We also see that many studies have shown that such tests are not reliable predictors of student performance once they are admitted to schools and colleges.

Argument Opposing Affirmative Action in Higher Education Admissions

According to *A Critical Dictionary of Educational Concepts,* 2nd edition, 1990, Affirmative Action, also known as positive discrimination, secures preferential treatment for a particular group on the grounds that the group in question has hitherto suffered disproportionately.

Applying the standards of normative ethics, in particular the principle of fairness, Affirmative Action admissions goals are not fair in higher education because the program is unfair to students not targeted for preferential treatment. Fairness means having or exhibiting a disposition that is free of favoritism or bias, impartial, just to all parties, equitable. We are taught this value from the time we are infants, acknowledging its importance to ourselves and others to ensure a peaceful environment.

Affirmative Action procedures at many universities result in policies and practices that are biased in favor of minority students. For example, at the University of Texas Law School, the files of minority students who did not initially meet the criteria for admission were color-coded and sorted by ethnicity when the applications were reviewed. They were then reviewed again, and many times were accepted. The courts decided that these admissions procedures violated the Constitution because they failed to afford each individual applicant with a comparison with the entire pool of applicants, not just those of the applicant's own race.

At UCLA and also at Berkeley, black students were admitted with SAT scores below those of whites. Governor Pete Wilson said in a September 1995 *ABA Journal* article that, "if the UC admissions system were given a grade for fairness, it would get an F."

We should find a way to provide equal educational opportunities to all students, but there are other ways to do this than Affirmative Action. We could improve the pre-college preparation of students in the schools so that they can be admitted on the same criteria as other students and not continue to be disadvantaged as they begin their college education. In that way, we will have an educational system that is truly "fair," rather than one that discriminates against some groups to benefit other groups.

NOTES

1. The first two examples are adapted from Lisa H. Newton, *Ethics in America: Study Guide* (Englewood Cliffs, N.J.: Prentice-Hall, 1989), 53–7.
2. Richard W. Paul and Gerald M. Nosich, "A Model for the National Assessment of Higher Order Thinking," in A. J. A. Binker, ed., *Critical Thinking: What Every Person Needs to Survive in a Rapidly Changing World* (Santa Rosa, Calif.: Foundation for Critical Thinking, 1992), 85; and Richard W. Paul, "The Critical Thinking Community," *The Center and Foundation for Critical Thinking,* January 24, 1996: online, Internet, July 5, 1996. http://loki.sonoma.edu/Cthink/
3. Reprinted with the permission of The Free Press, a Division of Simon & Schuster from *The Nature of Human Values* by Milton Rokeach. Copyright © 1973 by The Free Press.

4. Rokeach, 7–8.
5. Rokeach, 7–8. Another theorist who divided values along these lines is Donald Walhout, who made a distinction between social values (political stability, equality, freedom, etc.) and individual values (social participation, friendship, proper self-love). See his *The Good and the Realm of Values* (Notre Dame, Ind.: University of Notre Dame Press, 1978), 45–6.
6. Milton Rokeach and Sandra J. Ball-Rokeach, "Stability and Change in American Value Priorities," *American Psychologist* 44 (1989): 777.
7. Rokeach, 57–9 and 66–72.
8. Seymour Lipset, *Continental Divide: The Values and Institutions of the United States and Canada* (New York: Routledge, 1990), 37–9.
9. Nicholas Rescher, *Introduction to Value Theory* (Englewood Cliffs, N.J.: Prentice-Hall, 1969), 115.
10. The account of value change in this section is drawn from Rescher, 111–118.
11. For other studies of American values, see Gail M. Inlow, *Values in Transition: A Handbook* (New York: John Wiley, 1972); and Ben J. Wattenberg, *The Good News Is the Bad News Is Wrong* (New York: Simon & Schuster, 1984). Many studies of contemporary American values are available.
12. Chaim Perelman and Lucie Olbrechts-Tyteca, *The New Rhetoric: A Treatise on Argumentation,* trans. John Wilkinson and Purcell Weaver (Notre Dame, Ind.: University of Notre Dame Press, 1969), 83–99. In addition to the hierarchies stated here, these authors noted the hierarchy of order—that the cause or that which comes first should be valued over that which comes later.
13. For further explanation of these hierarchies, see Gregg B. Walker and Malcolm O. Sillars, "Where Is Argument? Perelman's Theory of Values," in *Perspectives on Argumentation,* Robert Trapp and Janice Schuetz, eds. (Prospect Heights, Ill.: Waveland, 1990), 143–5.
14. Perelman and Olbrechts-Tyteca, 83.
15. The stock issues suggested here are taken from Paul W. Taylor, *Normative Discourse* (Englewood Cliffs, N.J.: Prentice-Hall, 1961): 14–103. An earlier version of this explanation appeared in Barbara Warnick, "Arguing Value Propositions," *Journal of the American Forensic Association* 18 (1981): 109–19. Many points in the euthanasia example appeared in Stainislaus J. Dundon, "Karen Quinlan and the Freedom of the Dying," *Journal of Value Inquiry* 4 (1978): 280–91. This journal has many useful articles on value-oriented issues such as abortion, euthanasia, and human rights.
16. Richard Worshop, "Assisted Suicide," *CQ Researcher* 2 (1992): 148.
17. Other studies of American values were cited in note 9.
18. Josina M. Makau, *Reasoning and Communication* (Belmont, Calif.: Wadsworth, 1990), 142.
19. Paul and Nosich, 101.
20. Aristotle, *Rhetoric* 1355a.

CHAPTER 11

Arguing about Policies

CHAPTER OUTLINE

- Policy Arguments and Policy Systems
- Stock Issues in Policy Arguments
  - Ill
  - Blame
  - Cure
  - Cost/Benefits
- Issues Brief
- Alternative Formats for Arguing Policies
  - Comparative-Advantages Case
  - Goals Case
- Alternative Formats for Refuting Policy Arguments
  - Strategy of Defense of the Present Policy System
  - Strategy of Defense of the Present Policy System with Minor Repairs
  - Strategy of Counterproposals
- Summary
- Exercises

KEY CONCEPTS

systems perspective
ill
qualitative significance
quantitative significance
blame

structural blame
structures
attitudinal blame
cure
plan of action

265

agent
mandate
effects
cost
benefits
needs-analysis case

direct refutation
comparative advantages
goals argument
defense of the present policy system
minor repairs
counterproposal

We make policy decisions daily. We might decide to study instead of going to the movies or we might decide to live off-campus instead of in a dorm. Or, depending on our individual values and personal convictions, we might decide to buy shares in an oil company or support stronger environmental protection laws. Our daily decisions affect us personally, socially, economically, nationally, and internationally.

The decision to act or not to act involves a process of policy argumentation. For example, consider the following three claims:

> All U.S. citizens should be subjected to mandatory AIDS screening.
>
> I should study tonight.
>
> Politicians should be subjected to twelve-year term limitations.

These statements are policy propositions that focus arguments around specific choices and actions. Each asks the recipient to behave or cooperate in certain ways and, presumably, if the arguments supporting the claims are sufficient, then the recipient will fulfill the expected action.

This chapter examines how policy arguments work and how arguers construct and refute extended policy cases. When you have finished reading this chapter, you should be able to recognize, write, and respond to policy arguments and extended policy cases.

Policy arguments are different from the fact and value arguments discussed in Chapters 9 and 10. If we argue that U.S. citizens should be tested for AIDS, we are advocating some future action. If we say that we should study tonight, we are also advocating future action. And if we support term limits, we promote a future action. Policy arguments are future-bound. Because historical policies and actions cannot be directly changed through argument alone, when we make policy proposals we focus on what *should* be done from this time forward. We could argue that we should have had AIDS testing, or we should have studied, or we should have had term limits, but because all of these fall into the past, arguing about them is more like speculation than advocacy because there is no opportunity to change what has happened. Policy propositions look toward what has not yet happened, but should. The "future action" nature of policy arguments is fundamentally different from value arguments because fact and value arguments can examine and evaluate whether current and past conditions were true, justified, or reasonable. In a value-oriented discussion, we can say:

> Testing all U.S. citizens for AIDS is justified.
>
> Studying would have been a good thing for me to do.
>
> Term limitations are justifiable.

In a fact-oriented discussion we could argue:

> Testing for AIDS is widespread in the United States.
>
> When I have studied in the past I have received good grades.
>
> Term limitations have reduced the number of career politicians.

Fact and value propositions can study what currently is, what should have been in the past, or even what facts and values we would hold as true or reasonable in the future because the focus of such argumentation is definition or evaluation—not action. We can evaluate the past and present to learn, but we cannot act differently in the past. Policy propositions are bound to future actions.

Because the future is uncertain, and no one can know precisely what will happen, policy arguments ask hearers to act based on a prediction of what will work or what will not work. We have only a tentative idea of what probably will *occur*.[1] Therefore, accepting a policy proposition commits a hearer to a future call to action. The decision to act, in turn, depends on the listener's assessment of how successful or reasonable an argument *probably* is.

POLICY ARGUMENTS AND POLICY SYSTEMS

Policy arguments take a variety of forms. When Congress considers a bill, the hearings and debates about the bill take the form of policy argumentation. When the president argues in favor of a budget proposal, the argument is a policy argument. However, policy arguments are not reserved exclusively for passing legislation or for argumentation in formal or established forums. Often, extended policy arguments are developed without a large public audience and even without an explicitly stated proposition. Consider the following exchange between Dave and Jason:

Dave: I've had it with studying. My brain isn't working right anymore. I think we should take a break and go see a movie or something.

Jason: Are you crazy? We both have finals in the morning, and I don't know about you, but I've put off studying way too long. As it is, I don't think I'll get any sleep tonight.

Dave: Well, even if we don't have a couple of hours to get out and see a movie, I think we should at least take a half-hour out to go up to the store and get some snacks.

In this discussion, Dave and Jason are arguing about a policy. Should they take a break from studying? Policy arguments often occur in personal and interpersonal contexts. We use policy arguments daily to help make decisions at many levels—personal, local, regional, national, and international. We often argue with our family, friends, and colleagues about decisions we want to make and actions we want to take. Such arguments may range from where to live, what job to take, whether to study or take a break, or whom to vote for in an upcoming election.

This section will examine how policy arguments function as part of a system. We take the position that extended policy arguments function systematically, which means that as we seek to change one part of the system through our arguments, we change the overall nature of the system. Such changes carry with them both benefits and costs that arguers should understand and consider.

It is not always clear how policy arguments affect our lives. Obviously, we make decisions about how our lives will be conducted, but we may not always be aware of the short- and long-term consequences and benefits of the actions we take. *A systems perspective recognizes that the world is a complex and interconnected set of relationships between and among component parts that compose a whole and that one change in any part of the system changes the other elements of the system.* This means, then, that a system is a set of parts that are interrelated with one another to form a whole unit.[2]

At its most basic level, a system has five defining characteristics.[3] First, systems possess objects or parts. When Dave and Jason argued about whether to study or take a break, both individuals and the subjects they studied serve as objects or parts of the system. Each plays a role and performs a particular function: Dave and Jason studied together, and studying is the focus of the discussion. Second, each object in the system has attributes. Attributes are the characteristics inherent in the objects or parts. Dave feels the need to take a break; Jason is concerned about how much time he has to prepare for finals. Third, the objects within a system are interrelated. This means that there is a relationship that binds Dave, Jason, and studying together. Their discussion would have been meaningless unless they both were studying. If their relationship changed or their tests had been completed, so too would the argument. Fourth, systems operate within an environment. This means that systems have a context that supports and gives meaning to the activity within the system. The environment for Dave and Jason consists of a campus community that has midterm examinations and finals. Fifth, systems have boundaries. A boundary is a definitional line that separates the system from its environment. The only people involved in the decision to study or take a break are Dave and Jason. The ultimate decision rests with them. Boundaries enable us to define who or what constitutes the system and who or what does not.

Understanding the nature of systems enables arguers to appreciate the complexity and consequences of policy arguments. Consider the growth in online courses. More and more students are able to engage in "distance learning" and attend classes by way of VCR and e-mail. Students who could not otherwise go to school are able to take course work and complete their degrees from home. Many colleges and universities have begun to offer such electronic courses. Colorado State University, for instance, offers an electronic MBA program. George Washington University offers electronic Masters degrees in a variety of areas. Students read the same texts as their in-class counterparts but office hours with professors are conducted over e-mail and lectures are broadcast over satellite or taped for later viewing.

By some estimations as many as 4 million American students are now involved with electronic education. More than 75 universities and colleges now offer some online degree programs, and the number is increasing each year. The tuition for the courses is typically half of the regular tuition and the flexible time allows more people to have access to high education.[4]

Electronic education functions within the educational system. The objects or parts of the system are the colleges and universities involved, the teachers, the students, and the subject matter. Their attributes or characteristics include their abilities to leave the house for an education, their schedules that permit or do not permit them to attend regularly scheduled courses, their family commitments, and their abilities as students. The environment is higher education in America. The environment includes issues such as attitudes about students who earn degrees even if they have never set foot on the campus and the way courses are taught when face-to-face interaction between student and teacher is not present. The relationships are the connections among students and faculty. Distance learners have less contact and build fewer connections than students who attend classes on campus. Finally, the boundaries are what separates students from nonstudents and a university from its environment. Typically, university boundaries are tied closely to their physical boundaries. As online programs grow, the physical boundary separating a university from its environment is diminished. More people are able to take courses even if they have not been on the physical campus. The boundary expands to cover more students with a virtual education.

What affects one part of the system can be felt throughout the system. Any policy decision carries benefits and costs for the entire system. People act in contexts, and the actions we take affect our contexts. Even something as simple as asking a question in class affects all the members of the class, including the teacher and the question-asker. If the student asking the question does so over e-mail after the lecture, its potential impact will not be as immediate or influential as the same question asked in class so that all the students could share in the discussion.

When we take actions in a system, we experience both benefits and costs. The benefits are all the advantages associated with the decision and the costs are all the associated disadvantages. Electronic learning, for instance, has the advantage of providing access to education for millions of students who could not otherwise earn a degree. It helps break down barriers for nontraditional students in terms of both cost and ability to attend classes. There are also costs associated with electronic learning. Those same students do not receive the benefits of working with other students or professors. Their education will not be as rich as it might have been if they were on campus. The quality of the relationships among faculty and students is not as good, and resources devoted toward distance learning may take away from other educational programs for on-campus students.

When we evaluate whether we should engage in a particular action, we evaluate the likelihood of the benefits as well as the likelihood of the costs throughout the system. Presumably, most people act when the net benefits are perceived to be greater than the net costs or disadvantages associated with an action. This process of decision making is called "risk analysis" and was introduced in Chapter 9.

STOCK ISSUES IN POLICY ARGUMENTS

When a policy is proposed, it must address certain issues. These issues are the reasonable questions recipients have about the validity of any action and they were introduced in Chapter 10 as stock issues—questions that must be asked and answered to construct a satisfactory case on a proposition. Although many issues may serve as stock issues for policy analysis, we can generally group them into four categories: ill, blame, cure, and cost/benefits.[5] This section will develop each of these stock issues in detail, enabling you to identify and build arguments supporting each type. Imagine for a minute the following conversation between two roommates:

Juli: I think we should go to Alaska and work in a fish cannery. While that might sound like a strange idea, I've always heard that there is a lot of money to be made and they are always looking for people to work there.

Nancy: Wait a minute! That's an awfully long way from home. Why don't we just find something around here for the summer instead of making such a long trip? I know of two or three fast food places that are hiring.

Juli: I'm out of money and I need to find a good paying job for the summer. Otherwise I'm just not going to be able to stay in college. Besides, we've decided that we want to work together this summer, right?

Nancy: Right. But still, can't we just stay around here—it would be more fun and we know people.

Juli: We could, but I have a friend who said in her first summer up there she made more than $7,000 and that is much more than we could ever hope to make around here. Besides, it would be fun to get away for a summer.

Nancy: Maybe, but I've heard jobs up there are difficult to get.

Juli: Not unless you know someone, and I do. She said we could get hired without any problem.

The conversation between Juli and Nancy presents an extended policy argument the friends can either accept or reject. The proposition advanced by Juli is that the roommates should work in Alaska. In support of this, she said she has heard that a lot of money can be made there and that jobs are always available.

However, consider the order of the questions and answers. Juli began with a proposition for going to Alaska to work. It was phrased as a declarative sentence and Nancy did not need to respond—so why did she answer the sentence with a question? Her reason is the same as any listener's reason might be. People often do not accept propositional statements without asking for specific supporting arguments from the speaker. Nancy pointed out that they could find jobs nearby, so what made Juli think they needed to travel to Alaska? She also said that a few places were hiring. A correct answer to each question was important: If Juli had not thought her plan through sufficiently, or if her answers were unsatisfactory, Nancy would have rejected her idea because it would not have been *prima facie* (acceptable at first glance).

This conversation is typical of many policy arguments. The advocate needs to be aware of the stock issues and prove them reasonably before a recipient can be expected to take action.

Ill

When Nancy asked Juli what was wrong with their current plan for summer work, she was asking Juli to supply an argument proving the stock issue of ill. *An ill is a current wrong or harm the advocate is trying to resolve.* When Russian President Boris Yeltsin announced in June 1992 that Soviet authorities may have held as many as 2800 American prisoners of war captured during the Cold War, the United States launched an immediate investigation of his claim, including an inspection tour of Russian prison camps. If the Russians were holding American prisoners of war, then an ill existed. This is why American investigators looked for any evidence to support Yeltsin's claim to prove that in fact a wrong was present. If there must be a reason for people to act, this involves proving an argument of ill.

Before people are persuaded to act, they look for a significant ill. Most people do not act without some significant cause. For example, we might drive by litter scattered along a road. Although most of us agree that litter is a problem (an ill), we would probably not stop to pick it up and dispose of it properly; however, if the litter found its way into our front yard, we would be more inclined to do something. It is a question of significance. If the ill is seen as significant for us, we are more likely to act.

The difficult question to answer is whether an arguer is presenting an ill that is significant enough to warrant the type of action proposed. Significance can be either qualitative or quantitative. *Qualitative significance is related to the intensity of the effect; we assess something as significant to the extent that it strengthens or diminishes life.* Evaluating qualitative significance usually requires comparative consideration of values. An example of a value conflict of this type was shown during the hearings involving the Iran/contra arms deal during President Reagan's administration. Should Congress be systematically excluded from knowledge of covert operations in the interest of national security? Which is more important—the confidentiality and security of operations by the Central Intelligence Agency and the National Security Council, or public control (via Congress) of U.S. foreign policy? The significance of these two factors is qualitative and value-based; it cannot be reduced to quantitative terms.

Quantitative significance is related to the scope of the effects claimed; how many people will be affected and how frequently? Quantitative significance is often more easily evaluated than qualitative significance because it simply involves statistical comparison. As long as the evidence available is reliable and accessible, quantitative significance can usually be more easily weighed than qualitative significance. For example, if Juli argued that going to Alaska for two months would yield $10,000, the quantitative comparison of $10,000 to $3,000 at any other summer job is easier than evaluating the effect of such income on their life-styles.

Is it significant if one person's financial future is diminished? If one person becomes ill? If a hundred people become ill? The answer to these questions is difficult because a great deal depends on the context of the proposed policy. An ill is generally considered significant enough to warrant action if life or the quality of life is threatened. Of course, significance is a relative term and it depends on how we value life and quality-of-life issues. (A complete discussion of value and value hierarchies can be found in Chapter 10.) For example, preserving a right to free speech or association has value only to the extent that it helps or hurts people.[6] Or, when we express outrage against animal testing for cosmetics, we argue that it unnecessarily destroys the quality of animal life. But what happens in a case in which animal experimentation is necessary for human survival? In 1992, for example, a baboon liver was transplanted into a human being to save the person's life. Is a human life worth more than a baboon's life? These qualitative issues can be difficult questions to answer, but generally, they involve the use of a value hierarchy. One of the ways of measuring the significance of an ill is by its impact on living beings.

Blame

We assume that most people in the world are relatively honest and caring and would not intentionally allow an ill to exist. If it is true, for instance, that prisoners of war exist in Russian prisons, we would assume that U.S. officials as well as Russian officials would try to bring these people home unless there was some compelling reason to leave them. But if there truly are POWs in foreign prison camps, why haven't the Russians returned them already? Although we may attempt to avoid ills and we may strive to overcome them, we continue to allow significant ills to exist. We allow people to starve in Ethiopia even though U.S. farmers produce a surplus of food each year. We have a tax system that is viewed by many to reward the wealthy at the expense of the middle class and indigent. We allow people to die for lack of adequate medical care.

The stock issue of blame helps explain why people are unable to resolve or diminish ills. Put simply, *blame is the attribution of an ill to causes within the present policy system.* Blame points to the person, people, or agencies responsible for the ill. For the ill to be corrected, the blame must be removed. If the blame for Juli's and Nancy's lack of money is lack of jobs, then they must find good summer jobs to provide them with income and to alleviate the ill. If Food and Drug Administration rules are written in such a way as to encourage animal testing, then they must be rewritten to overcome the ill. With the case of Juli and Nancy, once they take jobs in Alaska, they could make enough money to stay in school for the next year.

There are two types of blame that act as barriers to resolving ill: structural and attitudinal. *A structural blame is the result of a defect that is an integral part of the nature of the current policy system.*[7] Understanding a structural blame requires understanding a structure. *Structures are the fixed elements or features of a policy system.* Examples of structural elements of policy systems are laws, contracts, treaties, rules, and orders. Taken as a whole, structures reflect the formally accepted rules governing our society and political system. Such structures are "fixed" because they can be removed only by means of formal action taken to replace them with other structures. In 1973, Congress passed a law that lowered the maximum speed on U.S. highways from 65 mph to 55 mph. Then, again in 1990, Congress replaced the 55 mph speed limit law with a new and limited 65 mph speed limit law. When the U.S. Supreme Court prohibited a woman from using an abortion-inducing drug, RU-486, that had been prescribed to her while she was in Europe, a formal structure was introduced into the U.S. political and legal system that overrode the previous FDA rule that exempted such drugs from regulation provided they were for personal use. A formal action such as congressional legislation or a Supreme Court decision or other formalized rule requires a policy proposal for the removal or alteration of a structure.

In 1896, the issue of racial discrimination was before the Supreme Court, and it ruled in *Plessy v. Ferguson* that separate but equal facilities did not discriminate. Consequently, separate white and black lavatories, schools, and restaurants were seen as fair and just so long as the facilities were provided equally. In 1954, however, over the issue of equal educational opportunity, the case of *Brown v. Board of Education* was brought before the Supreme Court. This case charged that because of the "separate but equal" rule established in *Plessy*, an ill of educational discrimination existed and that black students were unfairly deprived of educational opportunities. The Supreme Court found for Brown on the ground that separate was inherently unequal.[8] The Court noted: "We conclude that in the field of public education the doctrine of 'separate but equal' has no place. Separate educational facilities are inherently unequal."[9] The blame for our inability to provide equal educational opportunity was attributed to a fixed structure—the Supreme Court decision in *Plessy v. Ferguson*. To correct the problem of discrimination, the decision had to be overturned—the structure had to be removed.

A second type of blame is attitudinal. *Attitudinal blame arises from people's beliefs and values rather than from a law or some other structure of the present system.* Typically, we assume that good people would not allow unnecessary evils to exist. We assume that if Juli and Nancy could, they would have enough money without traveling or working hard hours. We assume that if other countries hold American POWs, the soldiers will be returned. However, if an ill is allowed to exist because of prevailing beliefs or value hierarchies, then an attitudinal blame has been identified. Attitudinal problems may result in defective structures or failure to adequately support good structures within the system. For example, people smoke even though they know it will damage their health and eventually kill them. The blame does not rest in some law or structure forcing them to smoke, rather it rests in their attitudes toward smoking. Similarly, although the United States adopted civil rights legislation in 1964, attitudes continue to perpetuate *de facto* segregation in some regions.

With the *Brown* decision, the structural barrier preventing equal educational opportunity was removed. It seems reasonable, then, that once the structural blame was gone, educational equality could exist. However, apart from structural problems, resistance among administrators or influential community members may perpetuate the ill regardless of the presence or absence of a structure. The problem may not be in the structure at all, but could lie with the attitudes and value hierarchies of the people administering the system. In such cases, the structure is only a reflection of underlying attitudes that cause ills to exist.

Cure

Being able to isolate and attribute blame for a given ill is not particularly useful unless the advocate has some way of resolving the problem. This is the role of cure. Cure is the third stock issue for policy cases and is the one asked for by Nancy when she said she heard that jobs in Alaska were difficult to get. *Cure demonstrates that some course of action can work to solve the ill.* In other words, if Juli and Nancy go to Alaska, will they find jobs? If we send food to Ethiopia, does it cure starvation? How much of the ill does it cure—all, some, or none? If we mandate desegregation in the schools, do we alleviate discrimination?

Cures consist of two parts: a plan of action and its effect on the ill. *A plan of action is the specific program advocated in support of the proposition.* Examples include Juli's plan to work in Alaska and the government's plan to bus students to schools to overcome segregation. When advocates specify direct and definite courses of action, they are specifying plans of action.

Some plans of action are formal whereas others are much less so. Minimally, however, we expect anyone advocating change to offer a plan that describes both an agent and a mandate. *An agent is the person, group, or agency responsible for implementing the policy program.* For example, if Juli and Nancy decide to work in Alaska, they will have to contact Juli's friend and apply for jobs. *A mandate is the specific action the agent will undertake.* For example, school boards across the nation began developing plans for busing programs to ensure integration following the *Brown* decision. Such programs constituted a mandate for schools ("You will have busing programs") overseen by school boards.

Plans of action can be very detailed or very simple. Almost any legislation passed by Congress from the budget to foreign assistance programs involves extremely detailed plans of action that specify almost every action associated with the legislation. These plans can often take many volumes and thousands of pages to describe. On the other hand, Juli's plan for Nancy and her to work in Alaska is very simple and largely informal. Unlike Congress, her plan is not a law nor is it a contract; it is simply an informal agreement between two people to take a particular action to alleviate an ill.

Having a plan, however, does not mean it will work. Juli says working in Alaska will give her enough money to stay in school, but she needs to advance arguments to prove her claim that her plan will work. This is the role of effects. Effects is the argument that the plan of action can solve or cure the ill. In other words, what effect does the plan have on the ill? Too often, people assume that if a plan is designed to address an ill, it will automatically work. For example, busing was designed to alleviate the ill of school segregation, but it didn't entirely work. Aside from creating its own myriad problems, the plan did nothing to reduce segregated neighborhoods, differences in socioeconomic status, or any of the other variables that contribute to and perpetuate segregation. It addressed a symptom. *Effects is the argument presented about the relative effectiveness of a plan.* If the plan worked a little, is that preferable to nothing? The problem that remained beyond the structure of segregation was the attitude of segregation. If the plan of action cannot overcome prejudiced attitudes, then the ability of the plan to affect the ill is diminished because the social system will seek to undermine it.

Cost/Benefits

Recognizing that policies are adopted within a larger system is an important step in understanding cost. *The cost is the problems or disadvantages associated with taking a policy action.* The assumption is a simple one: For any action we take, we give up or pass by other actions or cause systematic changes that may not be beneficial. Therefore, the issue of cost asks, "What are the negative consequences of this action?" If Nancy and Juli decide to go to Alaska, their costs might be giving up social activities and friends at home or they may get homesick. If school boards are forced by the *Brown* decision to bus students, the cost is that schools now need to spend money on transportation concerns instead of classroom issues. Also, many students will need to be bussed to schools further from home, which means that students have the cost of time, that they are not in their community schools, and that their friends all live further away.

Benefits are the positive consequences of policy action. There are many examples of how enacting some policy will result in positive outcomes.[10] For example, busing will provide greater cultural diversity in the classroom. Students will have an educational opportunity that is superior on average because of a greater mix of teachers, students, and facilities. The worth of the benefits depends on the value structure—how much value do we place on the benefits and how much value do we place on the cost? If integrating the U.S. educational system is a highly placed value, then the benefits of busing probably outweigh the associated cost.

Cost and benefits are interrelated. When we make decisions, we examine both sides of the system and consider the cost and benefits of competing system alternatives. On the one hand, we look at the cost and benefits associated with the present system. On the other hand, we look at the cost and benefits associated with the proposed system. Whichever system has the greatest net benefits will, presumably, be the system we will support. Cost and benefits act as a fulcrum on which policy decisions are weighed. Arguers use this fulcrum to decide which system is most beneficial.

ISSUES BRIEF

As observed earlier, policy advocacy may occur in many settings—conversations, discussions, debates, editorials, etc. The advocate may have extended time for speaking and for presenting a case, or may have only intermittent speaking times and may have to develop a policy argument in several sections at different times. The situation may have an effect on how the policy argument is developed, structured, and presented. Regardless of situational constraints, policy advocates persuade their audiences that the benefits of their proposal outweigh its cost by showing the consequences of action and inaction through the development of extended arguments. This section will introduce and explain how a needs-based policy argument can be developed and refuted. While other approaches to arguing policies will be developed in the following section, the needs-based approach is the most commonly used means of advocating policy decisions. This section will introduce you to needs-based policy arguments and will illustrate how such arguments can be refuted.

On occasion, an advocate will find a problem that is caused by a defect in the current system that can be resolved. When such is the case, a needs case is appropriate. *A needs-analysis case claims that the ill existing in the current system cannot be corrected within the present system but can be cured by the advocate's policy proposal.*[11] Needs arguments are very common in persuasive speeches as well as more extended debates because the format and requirements for the argument are simple and straightforward. All that is required of an advocate is proof that a significant ill exists, that it is caused by some feature of the present system, and that it can be resolved through the proposed plan of action.

An extended needs argument is developed in two distinct clusters of arguments. The first establishes a significant ill and blame. The ill and blame are developed together to reveal that the present system suffers a significant problem that cannot be resolved for structural or attitudinal reasons. The second cluster presents a plan of action and proves that the proposed plan can cure the ill presented.

Often, needs-based cases will develop a third cluster of arguments that focus on the benefits of the plan. Although the plan achieves benefits by reducing the ill and overcoming the blame, it may also have additional benefits. For instance, busing students will have the effect of curing (at least in part) racially segregated schools. This functions as a benefit. However, there are additional benefits that are not related to the ill or the blame but occur as a natural consequence of changing the system. For instance, beyond integration, students will have the benefits of learning from a diverse group of teachers. These "spin-off" benefits add to the desirability of the plan of action, although they are not necessarily related to the ill as identified.

In response, an arguer who opposes the proposal may use the strategy of direct refutation. Although other refutational strategies will be discussed later, direct refutation is a common and effective means for an opponent to respond to proposals. *Direct refutation is an approach used by policy opponents that is designed to argue and disprove at least one of the stock issues in the proposal.* In using a direct refutation approach to a proposal, opponents attack it on one or more of the stock issues of ill, blame, cure, and cost/benefits. Because any policy proposal minimally must succeed in proving each of the stock issues, if an opponent can successfully defeat any one of the stock issues, the proposal is no longer *prima facie*. Direct refutation does not require the opponent to support any current or proposed policy system, only to argue against the one presented. Essentially, with direct refutation, the advocate takes the position "I am not going to defend any policy system but I will challenge everything my opponent has said and show the case to be insufficiently proven."

Fundamentally, arguers using this strategy take advantage of the issue of presumption. Because audiences are naturally predisposed to favor the current, known policy system, arguers using direct refutation simply must show that the policy proponents have failed to fulfill their burden of proof on one or more stock issues to show that the proposed plan should not be adopted.

Arguers using the strategy of direct refutation generally parallel the case they oppose in organization and argumentation. If the case presents significant ills, the advocate claims that these ills are caused by certain attitudes or structures, that a certain plan will correct the ills, and that it will produce certain benefits; then the person using direct refutation would attempt to show that the ills do not exist or are insignificant, that the causes for them have been misidentified, that the proposed plan is flawed and unworkable, that it will not correct the ill, and that the claimed benefits will not be produced. Figure 11–1 is an outline of how a needs case can be developed and opposed.

The emphasis with the needs-based organizational pattern is how well the plan of action can cure the ill. The stock issue of cost/benefits is not readily apparent in this format. Although the opposing side argues for specific costs, the benefits in the case are inherent in the plan's ability to cure the ill. This means that if the case is true, then the benefits will be realized when the plan works and the significance of the ill is diminished and a blame is removed.

Direct refutation presents a clear counterargument for each of the significant arguments developed in the case being opposed. Although the example on the next page shows refutation against every case argument, a solid refutation may be conducted with less detail and breadth. Minimally, the advocate needs to disprove any one of the stock issues because in doing so one of the elements of a *prima facie* case is disproved. Notice too that beyond simply answering the case argument, an opponent would also offer the cost associated with a system change.

CHAPTER ELEVEN   Arguing about Policies   **277**

I. There is a need for a new system.
   A. There are significant ills.

   B. The present system is to blame.

II. There is a plan that can solve the problem.
   A. This plan of action will resolve the ill.
      1. What agent should act?

      2. What mandate should be given to the agent?
   B. This plan will have the effect of curing the ill.

III. In addition to solving the ill, the following benefits will accrue (optional).
   A. Benefit 1

   B. Benefit 2

I. There is no need for a new system.
   A. The ills are insignificant or do not exist.
   B. The present system is capable of handling any ills should they arise.

II. The plan should not be adopted.
   A. The plan is unneeded or won't work.
      1. This agent is incapable or unqualified to act.
      2. This mandate won't work to cure the ill.
   B. Even if this plan worked, it cannot cure the ill.

III. This plan will receive no benefits.
   A. Benefit 1 won't come true.
      1. The benefit is exaggerated.
      2. The plan of action does not get this benefit.
   B. Benefit 2 won't come true.

IV. The case will accrue many costs.
   A. Cost 1
   B. Cost 2

FIGURE 11–1 Needs Case as Developed and Opposed

Consider an employee asking for a raise. The employee might begin by saying, "I am unhappy because my current pay is not enough to motivate me to do my best work. The problem is that the pay system does not recognize individual merit or responsibility and has not kept up with my abilities." Here the worker has isolated a problem ("I am unhappy") and placed the blame on the structure of the pay system. The next step is to present a plan ("I deserve another two dollars an hour"). And finally, the employee needs to offer the employer the effects of the plan ("If you give me the extra money, I will be happy and more productive; a happy employee is a good employee"). Beyond this, the employee may offer additional benefits ("I would be willing to work more overtime, take on additional responsibilities"). If the employee is successful and receives a raise, the original pay structure has been replaced with a new one because of a significant need.

The employer, on the other hand, could use a direct refutation strategy to counter the employee's case. For instance, the employer could say "I don't care if you are happy or not as long as you get the job done, and if you can't do your job there are many more people who would be more than happy to." This response mitigates the importance of the ill because, in essence, the employer is responding that the ill is unimportant. Similarly, the employer could point to cost ("If I give you a raise, I would have to give everyone a raise. This company cannot afford such an expenditure in recessionary times and we would go bankrupt. As much as you may deserve a raise, at least this way the company can remain solvent and in business."). The employer's argument in this case is that the cost, going out of business, outweighs the employee's harm of being unhappy.

There are many significant issues that require policy action that might use a needs-based approach. For example, consider the problem of tobacco. Since the Surgeon General first warned us about the dangers inherent in smoking, the tobacco industry has been attacked and increasing regulations have been placed on smoking—how old people have to be, where they can smoke, and increased insurance premiums for those who do smoke. Is it fair?

Most of the evidence we have suggests that smoking is very dangerous. Smoking increases the risk of getting various types of cancer, including throat and lung cancers. Because it increases the heart rate by 10 to 25 beats per minutes or up to about 36,000 beats a day, smokers risk heart disease and heart attack as well as stroke. Smoking constricts the blood vessels in the arms and legs and leads to a greater risk of amputation. On average, therefore, every cigarette costs smokers between 5 and 20 minutes of life and tobacco is the underlying cause of more than 420,000 deaths each year.

Smoking is deadly. It kills the equivalent of three Boeing 747 planeloads of people each day, which is 17 times more people each year than are victims of homicide for all of the United States and 50 times more than die from illegal drugs. In addition, smoking contributes to up to 40,000 nonsmoker deaths from heart disease and lung cancer. More than one third of the people who die in cigarette-related house fires are nonsmokers whose cigarette did not cause the fire. All tolled, smoking costs the United States about $50 billion each year in medical costs.[12]

For years the federal government has struggled over what to do about tobacco. In 1996 the federal government moved to regulate it as a drug and placed it under the jurisdiction of the Food and Drug Administration (FDA). Yet, smoking continues to increase among 15-to-30-year-old people and has its highest growth rate among young women. Tobacco is a $45 billion industry and it is fighting to at least maintain its grip on the market share of the United States as well as other nations.

The case argument in Figure 11–2 is fairly simple. A problem exists (smoking) that has a clear and direct solution (a ban). The important feature of this argument is that the plan of action must cure the ill and the blame. If the ills cannot be cured, then the plan is irrelevant. While this might seem obvious, often advocates offer plans that will only partly solve a problem or only partly overcome the blame. In such cases, the need is only partially satisfied and the significance of the case is reduced.

It is important to note in this issues brief that we have outlined only claims. Each of these claims is part of an argument and the advocates on both sides of the proposition

I. Thousands of people are dying every day. (ill)	I. The estimates of death and dying are exaggerated.
A. Cancer and heart disease is on the rise.	A. Cancer and heart disease come from many sources and tobacco is only one of them.
B. Nonsmokers are being severely harmed.	B. The evidence supporting the harms to nonsmokers is suspect.
II. Current efforts are not adequate to solve the problem. (blame)	C. Consumption is beginning to decrease.
A. People want to smoke and circumvent the laws. (attitudinal)	II. Current efforts are reasonable.
B. Individual state efforts are fragmented and inadequate to reduce the consumption of tobacco. (structural)	A. The laws as they exist effectively protect children.
C. Current federal and state laws are inadequate to stop tobacco consumption. (structural)	B. Adults should be able to make their own choices.
III. A ban on the sale and consumption of tobacco products will eliminate the problem.	III. The proposed cure will not work.
A. The federal government should render all tobacco products illegal. (plan of action)	A. We have tried prohibition before without success.
B. A ban will prevent the consumption of tobacco products and eliminate the harms. (effects)	B. Historically, prohibition has resulted in an increase in consumption.
	C. People will still find a way to smoke because the plan of action does not overcome the attitudinal barriers.
IV. The benefits to this action are tremendous. (benefits)	D. Tobacco growers will find other markets in Asia and the harms will just be transferred elsewhere.
A. Because of reduced medical expenditures related to smoking, the health care system will be saved.	IV. The costs associated with the plan outweigh any potential benefits.
B. We have the potential to save thousands of lives each year.	A. The tobacco industry will fold and many workers will be unemployed.
1. Nonsmokers will be saved.	B. All people lose their freedoms when we lose our ability to choose options relating to personal health.
2. Smokers will be saved.	

FIGURE 11–2 Proposition: The United States should ban the sale of all tobacco products.

would need to produce supporting arguments, reasons, and evidence to prove their claims true. Also, there are many other possible arguments in support of the claims. Advocates may choose as many or as few as they perceive are necessary to support the proposition and persuade the recipients.

The viability of a needs case rests on the advocate's ability to identify correctly an ill within the present system, to locate the features within the present system that cause the ill, and to remove the deficiencies in the present system through a plan of action that will work. In other words, the needs analysis rests on the premise that the present system has important defects that contribute to a significant ill. The needs approach offers a clear analysis of each stock issue and presents beneficial alternatives for the present policy system. The focus of a needs case is that the current system is unsatisfactory and the best solution is to adopt the advocate's course of action.

Because the needs case seeks to replace the current structure, an arguer should use it when the ill is particularly significant and can clearly be cured through an alternative to the current system. Needs cases must overcome a greater presumption than other types of cases because they are a new system that seeks to replace the old system. Therefore, the evidence and reasoning supporting the cure (that the effect of the plan will be to cure the ill) is particularly important. This means that the role of the opponent is to cast as much doubt on the proposal as possible. Unless the benefits of the plan (through curing the ill as well as additional benefits) are sufficient to overcome the risk inherent in changing systems, the case will probably not be adopted by the audience.

ALTERNATIVE FORMATS FOR ARGUING POLICIES

In the previous section, you were introduced to a particular case format, the needs case. Needs arguments are based on the premise that the current system is a failure because it has been either unwilling or unable to redress a significant ill. On occasion, however, the present system is attempting to address a problem or is addressing a problem in a way that, in the advocate's view, is inappropriate. Such situations may require the use of alternative argument formats. This section will introduce and explain two alternate approaches to presenting and supporting policy propositions: comparative advantages and goal. While other approaches are possible, these two are commonly used and widely adaptable for many different situations. How they are used in policy argument will depend on the nature of the topic being discussed and the situation in which the argument is made.

Comparative-Advantages Case

Often, there are problems that have no clear-cut or easy solutions. Sometimes, the present system is already attempting to cure the ill and there is no obvious deficiency in the way the system is dealing with a problem. In such cases, an advocate may want to argue for a new system that is superior to the present system. The case argument that is developed compares the advantages and disadvantages of two competing system alternatives and, hence, is called a comparative-advantages case.

The comparative-advantages argument develops the position that in comparison with the current system, the proposed system has more benefits. Instead of isolating a problem and offering a cure (as with the needs case) the focus of a comparative-advantages argument is to argue that the advocate's proposal is comparatively stronger or more beneficial than the current system.

In a comparative-advantages argument, the ways stock issues are developed are different from a needs argument and the systems approach underlies the logic of the case. For instance, in a needs argument the ill was a harm that the current system could not cure. But if the present system has already identified the problem and is trying to cure it, then such an analysis would be redundant because both sides would agree that such an ill exists. For example, there is probably agreement that discrimination exists and that school segregation is bad. The present system is already attempting to solve the problem through mandatory busing and other programs designed to integrate education. An advocate wanting to cure discrimination would probably not have to prove that discrimination is bad because the current system already embraces that view. With a comparative-advantages case, however, the advocate would argue that there are more effective ways to reach a goal and address problems than those in the present system. With school busing, then, the advocate might claim that there are better ways to achieve equal educational opportunity than busing. In a comparative-advantages case, the ill is interpreted as inadequacies in existing plans and policies. The blame in such an argument rests on the way the current system seeks to cure the ill; the cure is the alternative.

Cost and benefits become an important argument in a comparative-advantages case. Whereas the needs case proved benefits by alleviating the ill, in a comparative-advantages case, the advocate makes the argument that there are many benefits associated with the proposed system and costs associated with the current system. Comparative-advantages cases seek to be accepted because they are better than the current system. This approach does not attempt to identify a single ill or set of ills or their causes; rather, it emphasizes the policy proposed and its effects in comparison to the present system.[13] This means that even if the proposal is not perfect and cannot entirely remove the blame or cure the ill, it is *comparatively* better than the present system.

An advocate using a comparative-advantages approach would cluster arguments in the following areas:

    I. Plan of Action
        A. Agent: Who should act?
        B. Mandate: What action should be taken?
    II. Benefit 1
        A. The scope and effectiveness of the present system is limited. (ill)
        B. The present system cannot remedy the ill. (blame)
        C. The proposed plan of action will solve the problem. (effect)
    III. Benefit 2

A comparative-advantages case fulfills its burden of proof by successfully arguing that the proposed plan is an improvement over the present system and can be favorably compared with other competing systems. To understand how this works, consider a conversation between two college roommates, Lucas and George.

Lucas: I think it is time to move off-campus. I hate living in the dorms and I hate eating cafeteria food. In general, I hate living on campus. So many freshmen, so much noise.

George: Yes, but living on campus has many benefits. If we move into an apartment, who will cook our meals? Who will clean the bathrooms? Who will we socialize with? It seems to me that what we are doing now is the best alternative.

Lucas: You're wrong. Look at it this way—if we move off-campus, we will save a lot of money. In fact, I figure that our housing cost will drop by about a third. Besides, the freedom to come and go without worrying about dorm rules and regulations far outweigh any reason to stay in the dorms. Besides, I like the idea of just having time to get away from campus and relax.

George: Well, I hadn't thought of it like that. I especially hadn't thought about the cost savings and I suspect that between you and me, we can cook better than the cafeteria. Let's move!

In this conversation, Lucas develops a comparative-advantages argument. Both Lucas and George want a comfortable place to live, they want to save money, and they want freedom. But Lucas points out that living off-campus will achieve these ends better than living in the dorm. Even though the present policy system, living in dorm rooms, was not bad *per se,* changing policy systems, living off-campus, produced more net benefits than net cost.

On a broader scale, consider the argument for reducing ozone depletion. During the 1980s and 1990s, ozone became an international concern. Ozone is the protective layer that shields the earth from the sun's ultraviolet rays. Without the ozone layer, people exposed to sunlight would develop much more severe sunburns and ultimately skin cancer. There is a great deal of consensus on this issue. Most researchers who have looked at the issue of ozone depletion have found that with a damaged ozone layer, the food chain in the oceans will be destroyed, that up to 3 million people will die of skin cancer by 2075, and that our forests will begin to die. In short, if the ozone goes away, so do most forms of life. Most also agree that human beings have contributed significantly to the problem with the use of CFCs (chlorofluorocarbons), which are found in refrigerators, air-conditioning systems, and aerosol cans, to name a few.

The question is, and remains, how can we deal with this problem? Many governments, including the United States, recognize the severity of ozone depletion and have begun to adopt programs to correct it. For instance, an international agreement, known as the Montreal Protocol on Substances that Deplete the Ozone Layer, has been continually strengthened and adopted by many nations. It includes a program to phase out dangerous CFCs and other substances that deplete ozone. At the same time, the United States has worked to phase out the use of CFCs and U.S. trade policies have placed restrictions on governments that fail to limit CFCs. In general, the United States recognizes a problem—as does most of the rest of the world—and is working to reduce that problem.

There is a problem that the current system recognizes should be addressed. Furthermore, there is a program that is designed to alleviate the ill imposed by that problem. Does this mean that an advocate has no ground on which to argue about CFCs or ozone depletion? Clearly a needs case wouldn't be appropriate here because the current system is not to blame—it is attempting to do something. There are programs designed to solve the problem. The broader question, however, is "Is there a better solution?" If there is a better alternative than the present system's, then a comparative-advantages approach is justified and might take the following form:

I. The United States should ban CFCs now. (plan of action)
   A. Congress should enact a policy. (agent)
   B. The policy should eliminate the use and production of CFCs. (mandate)
II. This plan of action will help preserve the ozone layer. (benefits)
   A. Current efforts to diminish ozone depletion only postpone the end of life on earth. (ill)
   B. Present policies are too little too late. (blame)
      1. The Montreal Protocol is ineffective and unenforceable. (structural blame)
      2. The U.S. policies have so many loopholes that they are ineffective. (structural blame)
   C. A complete ban will preserve the ozone better than all of the current policies. (cure)

With this example, the case contrasts what is being done currently with what could be done—the comparison of alternative systems. The ill analysis in the benefits focuses on a deficiency in the current system. It would be inappropriate to argue that ozone depletion is bad because both sides would agree and the argument is simply a restatement of common ground. Instead, the ill focuses on the deficiency of the present system. The blame, then, becomes the reason why the present system is unable to remedy its own ill and the cure is the proof that the alternative will overcome the systemic defects identified in the ill and blame.

Goals Case

Extended policy arguments using a goals approach have a focus that is very different from either the needs or comparison approaches discussed earlier. *The goals argument presents a significant goal and the case revolves around a comparison of systems attempting to achieve the goal.*[14] This means that an advocate using a goals approach must identify and defend a specific goal that is or should be a focus in the current system. This goal is something that is or should be highly valued in the context of the policy system (see Chapter 10 for more detail on how values function). For example, a goal of the legal system is justice. A goal of the Supreme Court is to uphold the Constitution. A goal of families is to provide a comfortable life for one another. There are many different goals that operate from a social, and/or political, and/or economic level.

The goals approach functions on the premise that a particular goal is not being met because of a structure or attitude (blame) in the present system. Therefore, the proposal in a goals case seeks to eliminate factors that prevent the system from achieving the goal.

The goals case should prove that the present system cannot achieve the goal because of structural or attitudinal blames. The argument progresses by presenting a plan of action that overcomes the blame and better achieves the goal than the present system. This approach makes the assumption that eliminating inconsistencies between important goals and policies is a sufficient warrant for change.[15]

Generally, a goals argument develops in the following organizational pattern:

I. An important goal exists.
II. Flaws in the present system are to blame for its inability to achieve the goal.
III. There is a plan of action that will better achieve the goal.
IV. The proposed plan of action will better meet the goal.

With this format, the ill takes the form of an unmet goal. The case does not argue that the present system is bad *per se* but that it is missing an opportunity by failing to achieve an important objective. The blame argues that some feature or flaw in the present system prevents it from achieving the goal. The cure is a plan that removes the barrier to the goal and the benefits are the ability of the plan to better meet the goal. The case argument may also offer additional benefits from altering the present system.

Identifying the appropriate goal, however, can be difficult. The goal must either be accepted by the parties of the dispute or the advocate must argue that it should be an important goal. In our complex system of values and policies, it is not uncommon for different values to overlap and conflict. There are many instances in which individual rights conflict with social rights. Consequently, what has value and is an important goal for one person might be unimportant or a bad goal for another. It is important, therefore, to recognize that what is a reasonable goal for a given audience is largely dependent on the field used for the argument. (Refer to Chapter 3 for a description of fields and how they influence arguments.)

Different groups of people often have goals that conflict. For several years the goal of environmental protection has clashed with the goal of economic development and this has been a particularly heated issue with regard to the spotted owl controversy. The spotted owl is indigenous to the old-growth forests of the Pacific Northwest. It is an endangered species that does not appear to nest in newer forests. For it to survive, according to many environmentalists, we need to protect the ancient forests. On the other hand, people in the logging industry argue that placing the old-growth forests off-limits to harvesting could result in up to 700,000 jobs lost and will have the effect of destroying many small Washington, Oregon, Idaho, and Montana towns. Which value is more important? The protection of the spotted owl or the protection of jobs? This can be a difficult issue to resolve and President Bush, faced with deciding how to proceed, in 1991 called upon a group of investigators called the "God Squad" to determine whether logging should be allowed even at the expense of the owl. Logging won. In this case, the goal of protecting U.S. economic interests outweighed the goal of protecting species.

If we wanted to construct a goals argument, there are two ways we could proceed. First, we could argue that the goal of economy over species is an important goal but that the present system is unable to meet that goal because of some blame. In fact, this was the argument made by many loggers who claimed that the owl's status as a threatened species prevented the United States from achieving important economic goals. An alternative way of arguing this issue would be to prove that another goal is superior and should be supported. Such a case might be organized as follows:

I. Protecting species should be our most important goal.
   A. Species diversity guarantees our own survival.
   B. We don't have the moral right to justify the extinction of a species.
II. The present system is allowing the spotted owl to die. (blame)
III. We should guarantee the right of owls and other protected species to live. Congress (agent) should eliminate the "God Squad" and place biodiversity as our highest priority. (mandate)
IV. Such a program has many advantages. (benefits)
   A. The spotted owl will survive.
   B. We set a much more reasonable precedent.
   C. We help our economy become more diverse with less reliance on logging as the sole industry of many towns.

With the goals case, the present system's inability to meet the goal serves as the ill. The blame is the barrier that prevents the system from meeting the goal. The cure is the plan of action and its effects in guaranteeing better species diversity, and the benefits are the positive consequences associated with acting and better meeting the goal.

ALTERNATIVE FORMATS FOR REFUTING POLICY ARGUMENTS

As there are many approaches for supporting policy proposals, there are also many approaches for opposing them. As we noted in Chapter 9, listeners who choose to respond to the issues presented by the original advocate assume a burden of rejoinder. In other words, they must address the central stock issues as originally presented and provide a sufficiently strong reason for rejecting the case as originally presented. The central question guiding the response is, Why do we reject policy systems? You have already been introduced to one strategy—direct refutation—based on the premise that the proposal is incoherent or inadequate in itself. It may have flaws or it may fail to address all the stock issues adequately.

Beyond direct refutation, an opponent may employ three other macro-level strategies to counter an extended policy case. These strategies are defense of present policy, minor repairs, and counterproposals. The remainder of this section will describe each of these options and illustrate how each can be used to oppose policy cases.

Strategy of Defense of the Present Policy System

When advocates elect to defend the present policy system, they commit themselves to the argument that the present policy has greater systemic benefits than the proposal. *Defense of the present policy system rests on a comparison of the proposal and the present system and argues that the present system is superior.* Opponents of a proposal who use this strategy take the position that "compared with the proposed alternative, the present system is more beneficial." Arguers using this approach focus primarily on the issues of ill and blame and argue that present structures and attitudes are sufficient to cure the ill identified in the proposal.

Defense of present policies can be effective for any case approach. As with the strategy of direct refutation, it parallels the organization of the extended case and seeks to disprove at least one of the stock issues. The difference between this approach and direct refutation is that the utility and benefits of the current system become arguments against the proposal. In a sense, what is good about the present system is a reason not to replace it, such as the cost of the proposed system.

Respondents defending the current policy system will show that the present system is adequate and that any deficiencies have been erroneously identified or exaggerated by those advocating change. After all, any change involves risk and may result in disadvantages that outweigh the supposed benefits of correcting an ill or problem. As with those who use direct refutation, advocates of present policies take advantage of the presumption in their favor. It is advisable to assume that most audiences would prefer to stay with known policies than to assume the risk of adopting an untested policy unless the present policy is proven to be inadequate or problematic.

Recall the argument about exporting hazardous waste to underdeveloped countries. An arguer using defense of current policies would focus the refutation on the ability of current mechanisms and restrictions to cure the ill. Furthermore, the arguer would offer cost associated with changing systems that the present system does not accrue.

Defending current policies requires the arguer's commitment to support structures as they exist and currently function. When an arguer chooses to defend current policies, a commitment is made to adopt a consistent and systemic view of the argument. With direct refutation any responsive argument could be made; with support of present policies the answers should not contradict present policies. This approach should be used when the systemic benefits of the present system are greater than the benefits of the proposed system.

Strategy of Defense of the Present Policy System with Minor Repairs

Occasionally, people opposing policy proposals may recognize that the current policy, if left unaltered, cannot correct the ill or solve the problem. They believe, however, that if minor flaws such as inadequate funding, lack of information, or improper administration were corrected, the present policy could be made adequate. The premise of this strategy is that "the present system is basically fine, but it could be streamlined and improved with minor additions or changes that don't involve wholesale systemic changes." *The defense of present policies with minor repairs strategy offers small changes to existing policies to improve their effectiveness and efficiency in meeting the needs.*

Minor repairs are by definition minor. As such, they should not involve significant structural or attitudinal changes to the policies or their administration. To do so involves a fundamental change in the nature of the policy system and means that the arguer is no longer defending the present system but a new and different system. Advocates using this strategy should defend the integrity of the present system. Offering minor repairs means that the essential characteristics of the present policy must remain intact.

For example, consider the case for preserving ozone. Perhaps the present system's failure lies in the cost of implementing programs and not in the programs themselves. An advocate using minor repairs might argue to reprioritize funding so that the current structures are allowed to work. The system is not changed, just its implementation.

The strategy of defending present policies with minor repairs focuses on the blame issue. If the respondent can prove that minor system changes can accomplish the same objective as the proposed case, there is no reason to act. The present system cannot be held accountable for shortcomings if it has the capacity to adapt to new challenges and ills. The minor-repairs approach argues for a flexible system.

Defense of present policies with minor repairs is advisable when you believe that the blame has been exaggerated and that the change proposed by the opponents is greater than what is needed to correct the ill. Making minor modifications in an existing policy, it can be argued, is surely less risky than implementing an entirely new policy system.

Strategy of Counterproposals

If a respondent analyzes the proposition and the case presented and discovers that the opponent's indictments of the current policy system is justified, then a different strategy is needed because defending the present system is no longer an option. *A counterproposal is an alternative plan of action presented by the policy opponent that is different from both the present policy and the plan proposed by opponents.* An arguer presenting a counterproposal accepts that an ill exists and that the present system is unable to cure it. But the arguer maintains that the opponent's case is still invalid because either the case misunderstands the nature of the problems and a different solution is needed, or there is a better plan of action to solve the ill and blame as identified in the case.

The strategy of counterproposal argues that the alternative presented should supersede the proposed policy. Consequently, an arguer presenting a counterproposal develops an extended case independent of the original case argued. For example, with the case of hazardous waste exports, an arguer could argue that the wastes are bad but then so is a complete ban. Therefore, the advocate might offer a counterproposal of international regulation. Perhaps the United States and other industrialized nations should agree on international regulations such that underdeveloped countries can still reap the economic benefits of waste disposal but be protected by regulations and safeguards sanctioned by the international community.

The counterproposal does not disagree with the needs and blame analysis presented in the original proposal. Instead, the argument not only centers on the relative ability of the two systems to achieve the benefits but also diminishes the ill and blame. If the counterproposal is better able to cure the ill and overcome the blame than the original proposal, then it should be adopted instead.

When should a counterproposal be used? A counterproposal does not enjoy the same presumption of strategies using present policies because it offers a new plan of action. As with any new plan of action, there is risk involved with change. Therefore, when you put forward a counterproposal, you assume the burden of proof to demonstrate the proposed counterpolicy system can cure the ill and blame better than the originally proposed system.

In sum, the purpose of a counterproposal is to provide a competing policy system to compare with the advocated policy system. It should provide an argument for rejecting the proposition because it provides greater benefits with less cost than does the proposed system.

The three macro-level argument strategies for refutation presented in this section are not mutually exclusive. Nor do any of these case-level arguments preclude using direct refutation. Depending on the respondent's analysis of the proposal, it may be appropriate to use two or more of the strategies in combination. Each offers different options for the arguer and each addresses different issues. The objective of the respondent is to provide an argument against adoption of the proposed policy system. As long as using multiple strategies does not lead the arguer to contradict his or her own arguments, a combination of approaches is useful.

SUMMARY

This chapter examined how to construct and refute extended policy arguments. It began by discussing the nature of extended policy arguments and important policy concepts.

Extended policy arguments are composed of subsidiary claims supporting a policy proposition and the reasoning and evidence that support them. Policy arguments, unlike other types of argument, ask audiences to make decisions about future actions based on their expectations of what is probable or likely to occur. When we decide between different policy alternatives, we base our decisions on our assessment of net benefits and net cost associated with a system.

Understanding systems is important because policy arguments seek to change the complex nature of our social, economic, and political systems. A systems approach to policy argumentation begins with the assumption that policies are interconnected and that changes in one part of a system have effects in other parts of the system. When we examine the relative merits of any particular policy system, we need to assess not only the policy but also the extended system of changes it represents and the system it is designed to replace. No action occurs in a vacuum and advocates as well as listeners need to be aware of the consequences of action or inaction.

Before listeners are likely to accept extended policy arguments, they expect certain issues to be addressed. Stock issues are issues that must be addressed adequately before a listener will accept a proposition. With policy propositions, we can discuss four categories of stock issues: ill, blame, cure, and cost/benefits. The ill is a current wrong or harm associated with the present system that the advocate is trying to resolve. The blame is the attribution of the ill to some deficiency in the present system, and blame may be both structural and attitudinal. The cure demonstrates that some course of action can work to solve the ill and consists of a plan of action and its effects. The cost is the problems or disadvantages associated with taking an action, and the benefits are the positive consequences of action.

When an advocate constructs an extended policy argument, all these issues must be addressed. However, depending on situational variables of audience and proposition, the advocate may choose to focus on different aspects of the proposition. This chapter discussed three different strategies for arguing in favor of policy propositions: needs, comparative advantages, and goals. A needs case maintains that the current system is unsatisfactory and the best solution is to adopt a new system to replace the defective one. The comparative-advantages approach argues that the proposed system can achieve greater advantages than the current system. The goals approach claims that the elimination of blame precluding the attainment of important goals is a warrant for change.

This chapter also discussed four possible strategies that can be used to oppose extended policy arguments: direct refutation, defense of present policies, defense of present policies with minor repairs, and counterproposals. The strategy to be chosen depends on the nature of the topic, the characteristics of the case to be opposed, and the beliefs and attitudes of the audience. The first strategy, direct refutation, does not involve defending any particular positions but instead tests each of the significant arguments presented in the opponent's case. Defense of present policies, however, defends existing structures and proves that such structures are of greater utility and benefits than the plan of action proposed in the case. When existing policies have minor flaws that prevent them from functioning correctly, a respondent may offer a defense of present policies with minor repairs. The minor repairs are intended as modifications designed to overcome minor problems in existing policies. Finally, advocates may use counterproposals. Counterproposals are an effective strategy if the opponent's case fails to understand the nature of the problem or if the respondent has a better proposal for curing the problem.

Taken as a whole, policy arguments are an important element in our daily lives. We decide whether or not to take action based on individual assessment of the cost and benefits derived from different extended policy arguments. This chapter was intended to help describe and systematize a process familiar to all of us and fundamental to the process of our decision-making.

EXERCISES

Exercise 1 For each of the following propositions, outline a needs case, a comparative-advantages case, and a goals case using the formats discussed in this chapter:

   A. Proposition: I should buy a new car.
   B. Proposition: I should live with my parents until I have established myself in a career.
   C. Proposition: The federal government should provide more student financial aid.
✱ D. Proposition: I should attend a different school.

Exercise 2 Select two of the affirmative cases you constructed in Exercise 1. For each of them, construct a negative case. Use a different negative strategy for each of the propositions: direct refutation, defense of present policies, defense of present policies with minor repairs, and counterproposal. After you have completed your outlines, explain how each of them differs from the other. What are the advantages of each and in what type of situation would each be most appropriate?

✱ *Exercise 3* Below is a set of scrambled claims supporting the proposition "The federal government should legalize the sale, possession, and use of marijuana." Some claims could be used to outline an extended argument using needs analysis, others could be selected to construct a comparative-advantages case, and still others could be used to make up a goals case. Organize the scrambled statements to make up a needs-analysis case, a comparative-advantages case, and a goals case. Note that some of the statements will be used in all three cases, others twice, and some only once.

1. A benefit of regulating marijuana will be to decrease the youth smoking problem.
2. A great deal of money is wasted enforcing present laws; hundreds of millions of dollars are spent and only 10 percent is confiscated.
3. Funds will no longer be spent needlessly enforcing an unenforceable law.
4. The plan will be financed by reallocating money presently spent for marijuana control.

5. There is a significant need to change marijuana laws in this country.
6. Legalization of marijuana will be beneficial.
7. A major goal of our society is to eliminate illegal drug use.
8. One fourth of all marijuana users are under the age of 17.
9. By regulating marijuana, present laws divert law enforcement officials from pursuing and prosecuting hard drug traffickers, and thereby undermine our efforts to control hard drugs.
10. Marijuana sale and consumption will be regulated by the Food and Drug Administration.
11. Harmful substances such as paraquat will be eliminated, protecting consumers.
12. By focusing enforcement efforts on harder drugs, the proposed plan would enable us to better meet our goals of eliminating use of hard drugs.
13. The possession, sale, and use of marijuana will be legalized.
14. Experts estimate that marijuana regulation will prevent a significant percentage of the 10 million underage smokers from trying marijuana.
15. These problems are caused by present marijuana laws that are vaguely worded and inconsistently enforced.
16. Monitoring and regulating of marijuana sales are the only ways to decrease youth consumption.
17. Some of the illegally sold marijuana contains paraquat, which causes physiological damage.
18. Young people will no longer be affected by marijuana and other harmful side effects.
19. The following plan of action should be adopted.
20. Decreasing usage has significant beneficial effects.

Exercise 4 Below are two sets of scrambled claims for cases opposing legalization of marijuana. The first is a direct refutation opposing the needs-analysis case included in Exercise 3. The second set of statements develops a counterproposal. Unscramble the claims in each case and construct an outline from them.

Direct Refutation

1. The plan to legalize marijuana won't work.
2. Two thirds of high school seniors oppose marijuana use.
3. Reallocating present enforcement funds will not provide sufficient revenue to support the plan.
4. There is no need to change marijuana laws.
5. Young people who wish to experiment with marijuana will still be able to obtain it after it has been legalized.
6. Use among young people is decreasing.

7. Because marijuana is not physically or psychologically harmful or addictive, regulating its use will provide no benefits.
8. Funds spent on marijuana enforcement are insignificant; only four percent of drug arrests are for marijuana violations.
9. No benefits will result from the plan.
10. Paraquat is no longer used to destroy marijuana plants.
11. Personnel and funding to regulate and control marijuana distribution are unavailable.

Counterproposal

1. The counterproposal is a better proposal than legalization of marijuana.
2. It is true that there is a significant need to change marijuana laws.
3. Revenue collected from these fines will be given to law enforcement agencies for control of hard drugs.
4. Under decriminalization, we no longer need to use resources and time prosecuting people for a minor, victimless offense.
5. People found to possess marijuana in small amounts for personal use will be subject to minimal fines.
6. Decriminalization allows redirection of funds to areas in which enforcement is most needed.
7. Decriminalizing marijuana continues to indicate society's disapproval of substance abuse.
8. Instead of legalizing marijuana, we should decriminalize its use through the following proposal.

NOTES

1. Jerome R. Corsi, "The Continuing Evolution of Policy System Debate: An Assessment and Look Ahead," *Journal of the American Forensic Association* 22 (1986): 158.
2. Ludwig Bertalanffy, "General System Theory—A Critical Review," *General Systems* 12 (1962): 1–20.
3. Steven W. Littlejohn, *Theories of Human Communication,* 3d ed. (Belmont, Calif.: Wadsworth, 1989), 46–8.
4. Mary Lord, "Cyber-Education," *U.S. News and World Report* (October 30, 1995): 92–3.
5. George W. Ziegelmueller and Charles A. Dause, *Argumentation: Inquiry and Advocacy* (Englewood Cliffs, N.J.: Prentice-Hall, 1975), 32–7.
6. William L. Benoit, Steve R. Wilson, and Vincent F. Follert, "Decision Rules for the Policy Metaphor," *Journal of the American Forensic Association* 22 (1986): 141.
7. Austin J. Freeley, *Argumentation and Debate: Critical Thinking for Reasoned Decision Making,* 6th ed. (Belmont, Calif.: Wadsworth, 1986), 167.
8. Richard Kluger, *Simple Justice: The History of Brown v. Board of Education and Black America's Struggle for Equality* (New York: Vintage Books, 1975), 781–2.
9. *Brown, et al. v. Board of Education of Topeka, Shawnee Co., Kansas,* 347 U.S. 483 (1954).
10. Many authorities have examined the nature of policy benefits and advantages. For more information see Russel R. Windes and Arthur Hastings, *Argumentation and Advocacy* (New York: Random House, 1965), 229.
11. Freeley, 184.

12. Michael Castleman, "A Life in Smoke: How Cigarettes Work on Your Body as They Destroy It," *Mother Jones* (May/June 1996): 57–8.
13. W. Scott Nobles, "Analyzing the Proposition," in Douglas Ehninger and Wayne Brockriede, *Decision by Debate,* 2d ed. (New York: Harper and Row, 1978), 169.
14. John D. Lewinski, Bruce R. Metzler, and Peter L. Settle, "The Goal Case Affirmative: An Alternative Approach to Academic Debate," *Journal of the American Forensic Association* 9 (Spring 1973): 458.
15. Lewinski, Metzler, and Settle, 458.

SECTION FIVE

Analyzing Arguments

CHAPTER 12

Argument Analysis and Criticism

CHAPTER OUTLINE

- Benefits of Argument Analysis
- A General Model for Argument Analysis
  - Analysis of Simple Arguments
  - Analysis of Other Structural Patterns
  - An Application
- The Toulmin Model
  - The Nature and Background of the Toulmin Model
  - Six Parts of the Model
  - Difficulties in Applying the Model
  - Argument Chains and the Toulmin Model
- Comparison of the Two Models
- Summary
- Exercises

KEY CONCEPTS

simple argument
complex argument
chain argument
compound argument
data

warrant
backing
qualifier
reservation

In our daily lives, we are constantly the target of persuasive appeals and in a position to judge the arguments of others. Campaign speeches, product advertising, editorials, business proposals, and even personal decisions require that we understand and evaluate arguments. In this process, it is useful to be able to tell a good argument from a bad one. In particular, judging others' arguments involves receptive critical thinking skills, such as understanding arguers' intended meanings, isolating their claims, deciding whether those claims are adequately supported by evidence, making unstated inferences explicit, knowing how those inferences work, pinpointing unstated assumptions, and detecting fallacies and erroneous reasoning.

In the preceding chapters of this book, we have focused largely on the nature and contexts for argument and on constructing arguments. In this chapter, we will provide the tools for argument analysis and criticism that enable you to identify an argument's parts and how they are related to each other. Argument analysis enables you to accurately identify an arguer's point of view, supply assumptions and inferences that may not be stated, and evaluate the adequacy of the argument as a whole. These are important critical thinking skills that will be valuable to you as you assess the messages you hear and read.

In Chapter 1, we introduced a simple model of argument. In that model, an individual argument was said to have three components—a claim (expressed opinion); evidence (facts, beliefs, or premises supporting the claim); and reasoning (the inference or link between the evidence and the claim). While arguments generally state or imply these three components, they often are more complicated, possessing many kinds of statements and a complex structure. In this chapter, we will extend and expand our Chapter 1 model by showing how to represent pictorially the workings of all kinds of arguments. These pictorial representations show how the parts of an argument are related to one another and are called argument diagrams.

These diagrams show how the statements comprising arguments support or reinforce each other. In this capacity they function like blueprints or wiring diagrams and have many of the same uses and advantages.[1] Many methods for constructing diagrams of arguments have been proposed by philosophers and argumentation theorists. This chapter will present two models for diagramming—a general model and the Toulmin model. Both models break arguments down into certain components and indicate how those components are to be arranged in diagrams. This chapter will outline these procedures; enable you to construct argument diagrams of your own; and thereby assist you in comprehending, criticizing, and refuting arguments.

BENEFITS OF ARGUMENT ANALYSIS

Too often students (and other critics and recipients of arguments) attempt to refute arguments or to criticize them without having undertaken the necessary preparation. Criticism requires that one correctly understand an argument and carefully interpret it *before* attacking it or responding to it. One "correctly understands" an argument and interprets it accurately when one can provide an account of the argument that squares with its author's intended meaning and with the interpretations of other recipients of the argument. The need for systematic understanding and interpretation will become more apparent if we consider two of the principal benefits of argument diagrams.

One benefit of argument analysis is that it helps us better understand the arguments we encounter. Many arguments are not readily understandable when we first hear or read them. By diagramming and interpreting an argument, we come to a well-grounded comprehension of its language and structure. As an example, consider Daniel Webster's 1833 refutation of John C. Calhoun. Calhoun had earlier taken a strong "states rights" position, arguing that the federal Constitution was a compact between states, not an instrument of "we the people," and that each sovereign state should retain its power to judge the constitutionality of an act of Congress. Webster strongly objected to Calhoun's interpretation, claiming that it attributed too much power to the states, and he questioned Calhoun's wording as follows:

> The first resolution declares that the people of the several states *"acceded"* to the Constitution.... The natural converse of *accession* is *secession;* and, therefore, when it is stated that the people of the States acceded to the Union, it may be more plausibly argued that they may secede from it.... *Accession,* as a word applied to political associations, implies coming into a league, treaty, or confederacy, by one hitherto a stranger to it, and *secession* implies departing from such league or confederacy. The people of the United States have used no such form of expression in establishing the present government. They do not say they *accede* to a league, but they declare that they *ordain* and *establish* a Constitution.[2]

A thorough consideration of this argument would lead us to ask the following questions: What is Webster's major claim in this portion of his address? Is it implied or explicitly stated? What basic premises does he state for his argument? How are they tied together? Answering such questions leads us to an understanding of the basic thrust of Webster's argument and an identification of the statements and inferences pivotal in tying his premises to his claim. (We will answer these questions and show how Webster's argument is diagrammed later in this chapter.)

The second benefit to argument diagrams is that they enable the recipient to judge and evaluate the argument. They enable one to identify the premises and evidence, ascertain the reasoning used by the arguer, and consider how these two forms of support are linked to the claim. Diagramming is thereby an intermediate step to testing an argument's evidence and reasoning, as our critique of various arguments in this chapter will illustrate. Diagrams also isolate secondary claims on which the primary claim depends, show how the premises are linked to support the claim, and reveal statements that are tangential or irrelevant to the claim. One can therefore avoid wasting time attacking incidental remarks or unimportant premises and go to the heart of the argument—its central inference—by noting the roles of vital subsidiary claims and essential premises. We will now introduce diagramming by means of two models—the general model and the Toulmin model.

A GENERAL MODEL FOR ARGUMENT ANALYSIS

The general model for analyzing arguments discussed in this section has for a long time been used by philosophers to portray the structure of practical arguments. In a rudimentary form, this model was introduced by Monroe C. Beardsley in his book *Practical Logic* in 1950. Beardsley used his model to identify the skeleton of an argument—the pattern in which its premises and claims were related to each other.[3] Variations of this model have recently appeared in books by Michael Scriven and Irving Copi, whose procedures we have adapted to a description of argument diagramming.[4]

Our variation of the general model divides arguments into four types or classifications. Arguments are classified according to the degree of complexity in their structure. By "complexity of structure," we mean how many statements there are in the argument and how they are linked together. This ranges from the simplest arguments (Type I), which are comprised of only one premise and one claim, to the most complicated (Type IV), which are comprised of many premises and many claims linked together in numerous ways. In addition, this section will explain five steps in analyzing arguments and constructing diagrams and illustrate them with examples.

Analysis of Simple Arguments

The best way to become acclimated to argument analysis is to begin with simple arguments. *A simple argument consists of one premise and a claim that follows from it.* The inference connecting the two may be stated or implied. The first task is to recognize a text as an argument and not some other kind of communication event. The definitions and descriptions offered in Chapter 1 are helpful here. Unlike other kinds of communication, arguments advance a claim, offer support for it, and are made in a context of disagreement.

It is important to note that statements function as premises and as claims *relative to each other*. No statement in isolation is either one or the other:

> Because it's going to rain today, you should take your umbrella.
>
> Because you are taking your umbrella, it's probably not going to rain today.

In both statements, the presence or absence of rain is claimed to be causally connected to the presence of an umbrella (although the second argument is facetious and an example of *post hoc* reasoning). However, the fact that either clause can function as premise or as claim in relation to the other illustrates the point. "Premise" and "claim" are relative terms like "employee" and "employer."[5] They function as they do only in context and in relation to each other.

The problem, therefore, is to be able to tell in any simple or complex argument which statements are premises and which are claims. There are two clues that can help one to do this. One is that the premises are generally *the most readily verifiable and least arguable statements in the argument*. In the first example above, the prediction that it's going to rain can probably be supported through reference to a weather report or conditions outside, and the arguer expects the arguee to agree that it will rain. In the second example, the arguee very likely has an umbrella in hand, a fact that can be observed by both parties. The most accepted statement, the one least likely to be questioned, then, serves as the premise of the argument.

The second kind of clue arises from the wording of the passage in which the argument occurs. Arguers often provide contextual cues called "conclusion indicators" and "premise indicators" to help recipients follow their arguments, and these can assist the analyst in structuring statements in the argument text. *Premise indicators* are words like "because," "since," "for," or phrases like "the fact that," "by considering," or "as shown by," and they indicate that what follows is to be relied upon as a base for drawing a claim. *Conclusion indicators* include "therefore," "so," "consequently," "it follows that," and so forth, and introduce statements by relating them to other, less-arguable statements. Such transitional words or signposts should be noted, for they indicate how the arguer intended that recipients relate statements within the argument to each other.

You may recall that in Chapter 8 we extensively discussed a third component of arguments—the reasoning linking the premises and the claim. This component is often implicit and not expressly stated in the argument. If it is stated, it is stated in the form of an inference. In the general model of argument being discussed here, an inference is not categorized as a separate or unique type of statement. Instead, it is simply treated as a linking statement or subsidiary claim to be placed between the premise and the final claim. How this occurs in diagrams will become clear when complex and compound arguments and argument chains are considered later in this chapter.

For now, let us apply the diagramming procedure to the simplest possible form—the argument with one premise and one claim. As our example, we will again use a passage from Webster's reply to Calhoun:

> Where sovereign communities are parties, there is no essential difference between a compact, a confederation, and a league. They all equally rest on the plighted faith of the sovereign party.[6]

We will now explain the five steps in argument analysis according to this general model and apply them to this simple argument. The five steps are ascertaining the meaning, numbering the statements in the argument, identifying the argument's final claim, constructing a diagram, and criticizing the argument.

The first step is to figure out what the arguer means. This step is important because many arguments hinge on definitions of terms and some arguments use technical or archaic language that is not readily understandable. The above argument, for example, is expressed somewhat archaically and relies on a defining characteristic of agreements between governments. Reference to a dictionary reveals that "to plight" means "to pledge"; "faith" means "allegiance" or "duty"; and a "sovereign community" is an independent government of some kind.[7] So, restated in contemporary language, the argument would say:

> Where independent governments are parties [to an agreement], there is no essential difference between a compact, a confederation, and a league. They all equally rest on the pledged duty and allegiance of each government.

Checking on and verifying the meaning in this way helps the analyst to understand the argument and to discover whether there was the kind of slippage in the use of terms or equivocal use of language that we discussed in Chapter 5.

When longer arguments are involved, the analyst should begin by reading the entire argument straight through once or twice to grasp its overall meaning, then look up any specialized, technical, or archaic words. There are two things to keep in mind about interpreting the language of the argument during this step. First, one should interpret the argument in a way that is fair to the arguer. For example, Webster in his argument is not claiming that compacts, confederations, and leagues are exactly alike, only that they share the characteristic of pledge of duty and allegiance. If the analyst interpreted the argument's claim to be that the three types of agreement were exactly alike, he or she would overstate Webster's claim (and thus make the argument easier to criticize). When interpreting an argument, one should define terms as the arguer intended them to be defined, make the strength of the claim proportionate to the author's intention, and otherwise give the argument a fair and sympathetic reading. To do otherwise would be unfair to the arguer. Second, one should not prematurely evaluate or criticize the argument but instead should seek to understand it. If one moves to evaluation and criticism too quickly, there is a danger that the argument and the arguer's intent will be misconstrued and that the evaluation will be concerned with a claim other than the one the arguer intended.

The second step in analysis is to number the statements in the argument. Numbers should be assigned consecutively in the order in which statements occur in the text of the argument, like this:

> ① Where sovereign communities are parties, there is no essential difference between a compact, a confederation, and a league. ② They all equally rest on the plighted faith of the sovereign party.

The question of what counts as a statement to be numbered and what does not will invariably arise during this step. Different analysts may number statements in a given argument in different ways, and such variations are not a problem as long as the diagrams are clear and useful in displaying the structure of the argument.

Two guidelines are useful in numbering statements because they lead to diagrams that display the thoughtline of the argument clearly and increase the effectiveness of subsequent analysis. First, one should assign numbers only to complete thought units, not to partial thoughts. A "complete thought unit," whether it is a sentence, an independent clause, a noun phrase, or a participial phrase, will be expressible as a complete and fully formed idea. In the example we have been using, the phrase "where sovereign communities are parties" is not a complete thought unit because it depends on the rest of the sentence for its meaning. Any statement that is not understandable when it stands alone is a thought fragment and not a complete thought unit. Therefore, it should not be numbered separately. However, some phrases occurring in sentences are capable of being expressed as complete ideas with only minor changes and should be separately numbered. This is illustrated in the following argument:

> Despite the pessimism of the doomsayers, ① the economy will continue on the upswing this year. With ② low interest rates, ③ decreased energy prices, and ④ a booming stock market, ⑤ it's hard to visualize any cause for a slowdown.

The three noun phrases in the second sentence could easily be expressed as complete thoughts ("interest rates are low, energy prices are decreasing, the stock market is booming"). They should therefore be numbered separately.

The second guideline for numbering statements in arguments is also illustrated by the above argument. Rhetorical flourishes, editorial asides, repetitions, and other extraneous material should not be numbered. The phrase "despite the pessimism of the doomsayers" sets up the statement rhetorically but does not function as either premise or claim. It should not be included because it has no argumentative function and would detract from the clarity of the diagram. Any statement that is made merely to "set the stage," reinforce other statements, or digress from the main thoughtline of the argument should not be numbered because it is not a part of the central thoughtline of the argument taken as a whole.

CHAPTER TWELVE   Argument Analysis and Criticism   **301**

The third step in analysis is to identify the argument's main claim. If there is more than one main claim, then there is more than one argument. The number of independent conclusions in a passage determines the number of arguments it contains.[8] This situation will be more fully discussed in the next section of this chapter. If there are conclusion indicators present, circling them may assist in diagramming the argument. In this third step, it is advisable to consider the possibility that the argument's primary claim has not been explicitly stated. If the preliminary interpretation of the argument in step one indicated that the arguer left the principal claim unstated, it should be supplied now. The analyst should explicitly state the claim and supply it with a number in parentheses (to show the claim is implicit) prior to diagramming.

The fourth step in the analysis is to diagram the argument. Circled numbers representing the thought units and statements in the argument can be used. Those representing basic premises are placed at the top, and the diagram flows downward to the final or main claim. When diagrammed, Webster's argument looks like this:

The second statement in the argument was the premise, and the first was the claim. Webster's conclusion that there is no essential difference between a compact, a confederation, and a league rested on the premise that the three share a common characteristic—the "plighted faith" (pledged allegiance) of a "sovereign party" (independent government). Thus, the second statement is placed at the top of the diagram and the first statement at the bottom.

It should be noted that here we have placed starting points or premises at the *top* of the diagram and the claims at the *bottom*. The argument model we introduced in Chapter 1 placed evidence or premises to the left below the level of dispute, while the claim was on the right above the level of dispute. We are now asking that you rotate that model so that evidential statements are placed at the *top* of the diagram and the structure flows *downward* to the final claim. This keeps our presentation of the general model in line with its presentation by other authors. As you will see, in the second model presented in this chapter, the starting point of an argument is again placed on the left of the diagram instead of at the top. This should not present a problem as long as the analyst is consistent in the use of any given model.

The fifth and final step is to criticize the argument. Now that the argument's parts and their relation to one another have been identified, we are in a position to critique the argument's evidence and reasoning. In regard to the evidence, we can begin by observing that Webster cites no source for his observation that compacts, confederations, and leagues all rely on the pledged allegiance of the parties that agree to join them. Since Webster has cited no source other than what he thinks his audience already believes, some of the tests of evidence in Chapter 7 cannot appropriately be applied to his argument. It would not make sense to consider whether Webster's citation is accurate (since he worded it himself), or whether it is recent (since this historical citation was worded when Webster gave the speech). It would, however, make sense to ask whether this "fact"—that all three alliances rest on a voluntary agreement—is *relevant* to his argument about the Constitution. It would be very worthwhile, too, to consider whether Webster's observations about various forms of government are *consistent* with the observations of other political figures of his day and with scholarship on government and politics of that time. The tests of evidence applied to an argument, then, should be appropriate to the context and use of the evidence in that argument.

Criticism also involves testing the arguer's reasoning. Here Webster emphasizes the similarity between compacts, confederations, and leagues; all rely on the voluntary actions of their members. Further, he argues that there is "no essential difference between" the three. The tests of quality, quantity, and opposition described in Chapter 8 could be applied to Webster's comparison. Clearly, the three objects compared are all forms of consensual agreement and thus are in the same class, so Webster's argument meets the test of quality. But Webster cited only one similarity between the three forms of agreement; he could have cited more. Confederations, compacts, and leagues are formed voluntarily by parties of somewhat equal status who share a common purpose. Citing more similarities would certainly have strengthened Webster's argument and better met the test of quantity.

Diagramming and criticizing arguments using the general model for argument analysis therefore involves five steps. First, after identifying a statement as an argument with premises and claims, the analyst should carefully examine its terms and phrases to ascertain what the argument means. The resulting interpretation should be fair in recapturing its author's intended meaning and should refrain from evaluation and criticism. Second, the thought units in the argument should be assigned numbers in the order of their occurrence. Only sentences and phrases expressible as complete thoughts should be numbered, and tangential statements and digressions should not be assigned numbers. Third, the argument's main claim or primary conclusion should be identified. If implicit, it should be expressly stated and assigned a number in parentheses. Fourth, the argument's structure should be laid out in a diagram beginning with the most accepted or easily verifiable premises at the top and flow downward to the main claim. Fifth, the argument should be criticized and evaluated by using the tests of evidence and reasoning described in Chapters 7 and 8 of this book.

Analysis of Other Structural Patterns

The foregoing illustration of argument analysis has made use of the simplest form of argument in which only one claim is stated and supported by a single premise. As might be expected, most arguments have a more complicated structure than this. Four categories or types of argument structure are illustrated in Figure 12–1. We have already explained Type I (simple) arguments. The remainder of this section will explain and illustrate the other three types.

Type II (complex) arguments have two or more premises supporting a single claim. The following argument is a good example of this pattern:

① Constitutionality aside, setting the minimum [drinking] age at 21 has been a practical disaster.

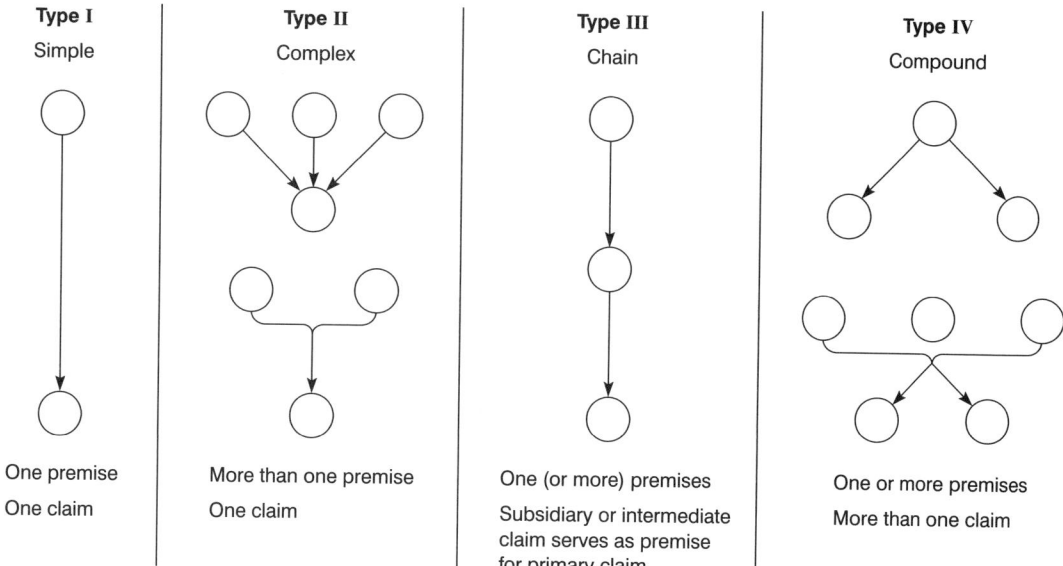

FIGURE 12-1 Diagrams of Argument Structure

> Designed to attack drunken driving on the part of teenagers, ② it discriminates against a whole category of people, many of whom drink only moderately. ③ It penalizes female teenagers, whose DWI convictions are below the national average. ④ Furthermore, clandestine drinking has created mini-prohibition on college campuses.⁹

This argument makes a claim about the harmful practical effects of setting the drinking age at 21, and its premises describe three conditions resulting from the 21-year-old minimum. There are therefore three premises and one main claim, so the diagram would look like the one in Figure 12–2.

There are two characteristics to note about this argument. First, the phrase "designed to attack drunken driving on the part of teenagers" provides background information and does not support the argument's conclusion, so it should not be numbered. Second, each premise supports the conclusion *independently* of the others. If one or perhaps even two of the premises were removed, the remaining premise(s) would still be sufficient to support the claim.

A second variation of Type II arguments is one in which premises work *in combination* to support the claim. In this pattern, the premises are interrelated and cooperate with each other. The following argument illustrates this pattern:

> ① Skier attendance figures on a national level have reached all-time highs during the past five years. Unfortunately, ② Washington state has not enjoyed the increase in market share over the past 15 to 20 years that other Western states have. ③ During the late 1960s, Washington enjoyed 18 percent of all skier visits in the Western states. ④ This has declined steadily to a current 6 percent of that market.¹⁰

Here the author's premises are interconnected. He claims that overall skier attendance is up and simultaneously that the percentage of this market patronizing ski areas in

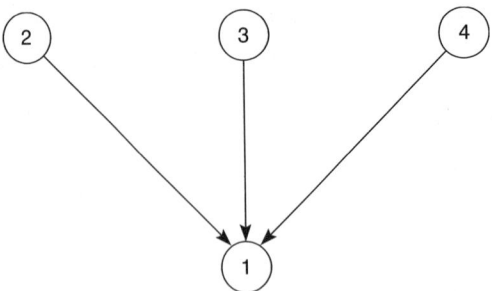

FIGURE 12-2 Type II (Complex) Argument—three premises independently support one main claim

Washington State has declined. The overall market has increased while Washington's share in it has decreased. If one disregards the information about the national increase *or* the premises stating Washington's decline in the share, the conclusion is inadequately supported. To indicate the interdependence of the premises in the diagram, one can supply a brace or bracket to connect them as in Figure 12-3.

This clearly shows that the claim that Washington has not enjoyed an increase in its share of the market is dependent on *both* a statement of the overall increase *and* an indication that the individual state share has declined.

Type III arguments are also called argument chains. As we defined them in Chapter 1, chains use proven claims as evidence for unproven claims. Initial premises or evidence are used to support a claim that, once it is established and falls below the level of dispute, can itself be used to support a further claim. A simple example of an argument chain is the following:

> ① The weather's been warming up and ② there are buds coming out on my shrubbery. ③ These are signs I'll have to start mowing the lawn soon, so ④ I'd better get the lawn mower serviced.

When diagrammed, the argument's structure would look like that of Figure 12-4.

This is a simple chain because the first two premises independently support a single intermediate claim that lawn mowing will soon be in order. Once supported, the claim

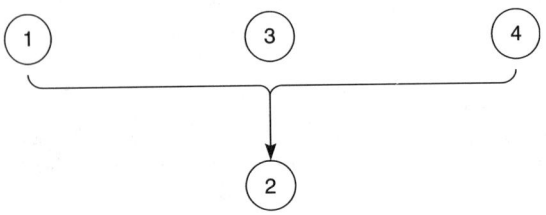

FIGURE 12-3 Type II (Complex) Argument—three premises work in combination to support a claim

CHAPTER TWELVE   Argument Analysis and Criticism

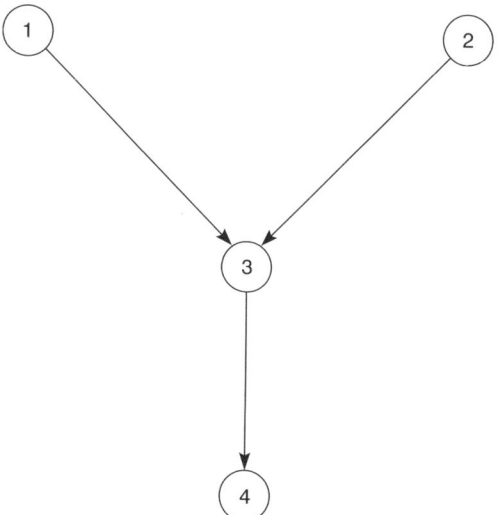

FIGURE 12–4 Type III (Chain) Argument—one or more subsidiary claims support the primary claim

that the lawn needs to be mowed is moved below the level of dispute and can in turn be used as a premise to support the main claim that the mower must be serviced. In Chapter 6, we called intermediate statements such as this "subsidiary claims" and noted their importance in linking together extended arguments. We will further discuss chains and subsidiary claims later in this chapter when we discuss another argument model. When chains and subsidiary claims play a role in the structures of arguments, the resulting diagrams take the form of tree diagrams. Tree diagrams display the linkages between thought units in the form of branching and intersecting lines flowing from the top to the bottom of the diagram. In the tree diagrams illustrated here, subsidiary or intermediate claims appear in the middle of the diagram between the basic premises and the main claim.

The most complicated argument structure is a Type IV or compound argument. *Compound arguments use one or more premises to support more than one conclusion.* Earlier in this chapter, we noted that the number of claims or conclusions in a text indicates the number of arguments present and that if there are, for example, two claims, there are therefore two arguments. This is *generally* true, but Type IV arguments are exceptions to this rule. (Type IV arguments occur infrequently, but as a class they occur often enough to be considered as an exception.)

In a compound argument such as Type IV, one single premise leads to more than one claim or to a group of interdependent premises, which, taken together, lead to two or more further claims. Because the various premises cannot be isolated and assigned separately to individual claims, the argument must be considered as a whole. Here is an example of the simplest kind of Type IV argument:

① When asked on a recent survey what is most important to them on a job, teachers usually cite an opportunity to use their minds and abilities and a chance to work with young people. ② The vast majority of teachers are in their profession not for money but for all the reasons we hope they are. ③ Perhaps we should stop comparing teachers so quickly to high-priced professionals.[11]

The first statement, containing survey results about teacher attitudes, contains the evidence in this argument and states its premise—that teachers value aspects of their jobs other than salary. From this single premise, two conclusions are drawn—first, that teachers are not in their profession for money, and second, that they are not comparable to high-priced professionals. The argument when diagrammed, then, would look like Figure 12–5.

The second variation of a Type IV argument groups a number of premises together and uses them in concert to support multiple conclusions. Here is a simple example of this type of compound argument from the same article on teaching:

As it stands now, ① teachers under nine-to-ten-month contracts who earn $25,000 have salaries slightly below the median for males with four or more years of college who are working full-time year-round. ② That $25,000 is in the top quarter of salaries paid to college-educated women working full-time year-round. ③ Teachers no longer fare so badly in the marketplace. ④ Their salaries and nine-to-ten-month teaching year make an attractive professional option.[12]

The first premise taken alone does not support either conclusion. Only when both of the first two statements as premises are combined does one get a complete picture of the situation for the entire teaching profession. Furthermore, teachers' status in the marketplace and the attractiveness of teaching as an option are two separate, although related, conclusions. This compound argument would therefore be diagrammed as in Figure 12–6.

Up to this point, this section of the chapter has described the general model for argument analysis, explained the steps to be followed in diagramming and criticizing simple arguments, and introduced three additional types of argument structures—the complex argument, the argument chain, and the compound argument. In order to bring

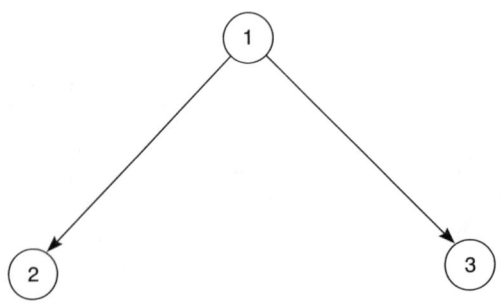

FIGURE 12–5 Type IV (Compound) Argument—a single premise leads to more than one claim

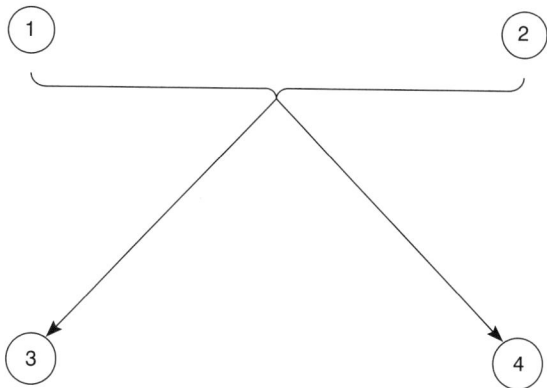

FIGURE 12–6 Type IV (Compound) Argument—multiple premises work in concert to support multiple conclusions

the whole process together, let us consider the application of the five steps to an argument chain that includes complex arguments.

An Application

Because of its economy and flexibility, the procedure for argument analysis just outlined is useful in displaying and understanding the structure of long, complicated arguments. Let us return to Daniel Webster's lengthy argument cited at the beginning of this chapter to see whether argument analysis can assist us in understanding, interpreting, and criticizing it. Recall that the argument was stated as follows:

> The first resolution declares that the people of the several states *"acceded"* to the Constitution. . . . The natural converse of *accession* is *secession;* and, therefore, when it is stated that the people of the States acceded to the Union, it may be more plausibly argued that they may secede from it. . . . *Accession,* as a word applied to political associations, implies coming into a league, treaty, or confederacy, by one hitherto a stranger to it; and *secession* implies departing from such league or confederacy. The people of the United States have used no such form of expression in establishing the present government. They do not say they *accede* to a league, but they declare that they *ordain* and *establish* a Constitution.

The steps for analyzing this argument are as follows:

1. *Ascertain the meaning.* To ensure an accurate interpretation of Webster's argument, we could check its context and the definitions of any terms that might be unclear. If we did this, we would discover that Webster is refuting John C. Calhoun's interpretation of the Constitution as summarized in three resolutions being considered by the Senate. Webster seems most concerned by the use of the term "accede" in Calhoun's first resolution. His concern grows out of the implications for using this particular term. On

the whole, Webster opposes the use of the term "accede" for two reasons: First, "to accede" means "to freely give consent to" and implies, by means of its opposite, that "to secede," parties that have "acceded" to an agreement can withdraw from it at will; and second, no such term was used when the Constitution was established, so Calhoun's interpretation cannot be historically justified.

2. *Number statements in the argument.* All of Webster's statements appear to be straightforward and relevant to his claim. The conclusion indicator, "therefore," in the second sentence should be circled, and all thought units stated in sentences or independent clauses should be numbered separately in the order in which they appear in the paragraph:

> ① The first resolution declares that the people of the several states *"acceded"* to the Constitution.... ② The natural converse of *accession* is *secession;* and (therefore) ③ when it is stated that the people of the States acceded to the Union, it may be more plausibly argued that they may secede from it.... ④ *Accession,* as a word applied to political associations, implies coming into a league, treaty, or confederacy, by one hitherto a stranger to it; and ⑤ *secession* implies departing from such a league or confederacy. ⑥ The people of the United States have used no such form of expression in establishing the present government. ⑦ They do not say they *accede* to a league, but ⑧ they declare that they *ordain* and *establish* a Constitution.

3. *Identify the argument's primary claim.* A consideration of each of the statements in this paragraph reveals that none of them articulate a claim or thesis that ties all the ideas together, so the claim must be implied. From the context, we know that Webster is attempting to refute Calhoun's strong states rights position and his use of the term *accede*. Considering the thrust of Webster's statements in the paragraph, we are justified in supplying the following conclusion:

> The use of the term *accede* in Calhoun's first resolution should not be accepted.

The claim should be added and assigned the parenthetical number (9).

4. *Construct a diagram.* The first three statements in the argument can be grouped together because they are all related to the implications of the term *accede* and its opposite *secede*. Furthermore, the first two statements are coupled together to support their conclusion, which then in turn serves as a premise for the final (implied) claim. Statements ④ and ⑤ that respectively define the terms "accession" and "secession" should be taken together to support statement ② that one is the converse of the other. Statements ⑦ and ⑧ are again coupled together (the people do not say "accede" but instead say "ordain" and "establish") to support the subclaim that no such expression was used. Therefore, the overall argument should be diagrammed as in Figure 12–7.

This diagram illustrates many of the important features of Webster's argument. By examining it we know that the claim in the first complex argument (that, if Calhoun's interpretation is accepted, people will find it easier to argue for secession) rests on two interdependent premises. Furthermore, we know that Webster's claim is implied, not stated, and that it rests on four more or less independent premises. Therefore, if a critic or opponent of Webster's argument successfully undermined only one of the premises, the argument as a whole would still hold up.

CHAPTER TWELVE   Argument Analysis and Criticism   **309**

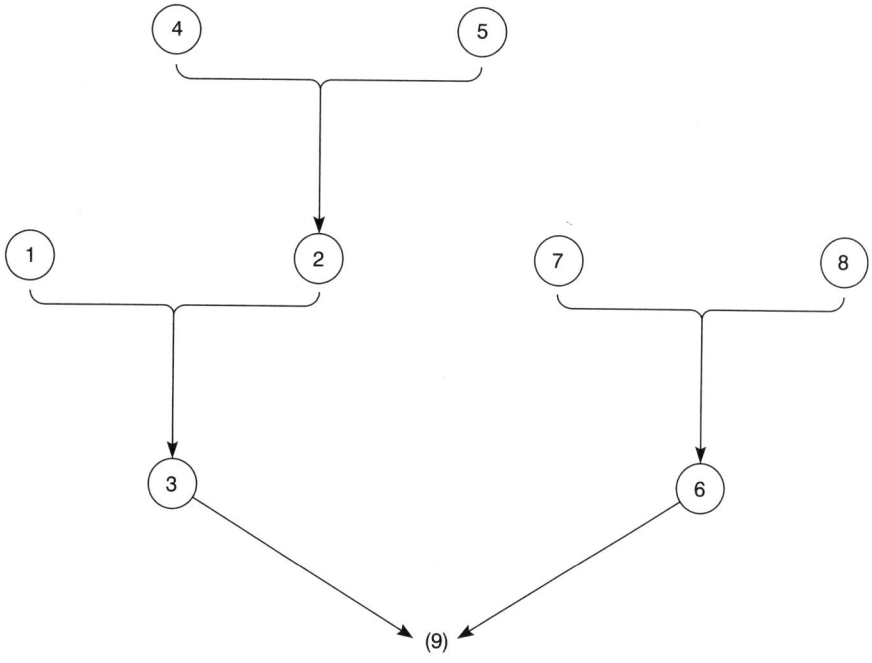

FIGURE 12–7 Type IU (Compound) Argument—premises join to support claims which chain to support a final (implied) claim

   5. *Criticize the argument.* Webster's argument rests on his definition of the terms *accede* and *secede* and on whether his interpretation of the intent of the authors of the Constitution is accurate. To test his evidence and premises, we might ask such questions as:

- Does Calhoun actually use the word *accede* in his first resolution?
- In the language of 1833, did the two terms *accede* and *secede* have the meanings Webster assigns to them?
- When the government was established, was any such term as *accede* used?
- Were *ordain* and *establish* the only words used in writing the Constitution?

Webster's reasoning in this argument is subtle but hinges on two unstated inferences: that use of a word implies its opposite, and that present interpretations of the Constitution should be governed by the intent of its authors. So, one might ask:

- *Does* the use of a word imply its opposite? What is the factual or cultural basis for this principle?
- How does Webster's argument about the intent of the authors differ from the fallacy of argument from tradition?
- Are the "people" referred to in statement ⑥ adequate authority on this matter?

Diagramming the argument has enabled us to identify the aspects that should be evaluated. For example, if the claim in statement ③ that use of a term implies its opposite can be undermined, then the argument as a whole is questionable. Does use of a term *always* imply its opposite? If someone retreats from a position, could he or she as easily advance on it? If someone requires someone else to do something, could he or she as easily free that person from any obligation? Furthermore, by allowing us to identify the starting points of Webster's argument, the diagram reminds us that his account is an *interpretation* of the intent of the Constitution's authors and must be corroborated by considering all the language they used.

Tree diagrams are useful for discovering the pattern of claims and supporting statements in an argument. Tree diagrams help someone who wants to understand, criticize, or respond to an argument because they identify subarguments that relate to the conclusion and that link statements pivotal in supporting the claim. This approach is purely descriptive and analyzes the argument in terms of what is explicitly stated.

However, because it emphasizes only the premises that are stated explicitly, there is information this approach does *not* provide. As we observed in Chapter 1, inferences and vital assumptions are left unstated in arguments more often than not. The analyst using a purely descriptive approach has no occasion to look for statements left unsaid that may be essential to a complete understanding of the argument. The general model's usefulness will become clearer as we compare it with another model of argument analysis—the Toulmin model.

THE TOULMIN MODEL

Another method for diagramming arguments—the Toulmin model—requires the analyst to supply unstated inferences and the principles supporting them, and makes other contributions to argument comprehension as well.

The Nature and Background of the Toulmin Model

In Chapter 3, we introduced the notion of a field of argument taken from Stephen Toulmin's *Uses of Argument*.[13] Following Toulmin, we noted that certain fields such as law, ethics, medicine, and science provide the various contexts for argument. Fields influence the forms of argument, the types of inferences used, the principles on which those inferences are based, the criteria applied to arguments, and the language in which they are expressed. Toulmin's model, which we are about to discuss, is based on the principle that the means for supporting and judging arguments are frequently an outgrowth of the fields in which they occur—they are field-dependent.

Toulmin believes that an argument is like an organism.[14] Its individual parts each have a different function in relation to the claim. If an argument "works" (that is, is acceptable within the field it is used by those to whom it is addressed), it is because all its parts perform their functions and work together to form an organic whole. Toulmin's model identifies the ways in which each statement in an argument bears on the claim and does justice to all the things an argument ought to do in order to be cogent. If important parts of the argument are implied or omitted, the Toulmin model directs the analyst to determine what they are and to supply them.

Six Parts of the Model

The Toulmin model contains six parts that are defined primarily by their function in an argument. The six parts are data, claim, warrant, backing, qualifier, and reservation.

The data function as the grounds for the claim and are synonymous with the evidence as we defined it in Chapter 1—"facts or conditions that are objectively observable, beliefs or premises accepted as true by the audience, or conclusions previously established." As has already been defined in Chapter 1, *the claim consists of the "expressed opinion or conclusion that the arguer wants accepted."*

The warrant expresses the reasoning used to link the data to the claim. According to Toulmin, if the data answer the question "What have you got to go on?" then the warrant answers the question "How did you get there?"[15] Warrants may take the form of rules, principles, or conventions particular to certain fields. Or they may be explicit statements of one of the patterns of reasoning identified in Chapter 8. In other words, warrants may state quasilogical, analogical, generalized, causal, coexistential, dissociative, and other types of relationships. They function very much like inferences as we defined them in Chapter 8. In the general model explained earlier in this chapter, the warrant may be the linking or pivotal statement in the argument. (Such statements are not *always* warrants, however; they may be intermediate claims in an argument chain.) What is important to remember about the warrant is that it expresses the reasoning that enables us to connect the data to the claim. If the warrant is not explicitly stated in an argument, it must be supplied when the argument is diagrammed using the Toulmin model.

Let us pause here to identify these first three parts of the model in an argument before going on to the other three parts. Consider the following argument:

> Twelve hours ago, the patient fell from a motor scooter and had a severe blow to the head accompanied by a deep scalp wound. He is pale, dizzy, lethargic, and has a low fever. The treatment strongly recommended includes flushing and stitching up the wound, administering antibiotics, and bed rest. Clinical experience has shown that without such treatment infection will set in within approximately 48 hours. Penicillin is most effective unless the patient is allergic to it.

What functions as data or evidence in this argument? Clearly, the circumstances of the accident and the patient's symptoms are readily knowable or observable facts and function as the starting point of the argument and the grounds for the claim. The claim—the conclusion or end point of the argument—is the specific recommended treatment. The warrant, or reasoned connection linking the data to the claim, is a causal prediction about what will happen to the patient if measures to prevent infection are not used. This predictive principle arises out of the field of medicine and is based on prior experience with patients in similar conditions and circumstances.

The Toulmin model is set out in a spatial pattern that is intended to show how the statements in the argument are linked to each other—what supports what and what leads to what. Generally, the first three parts are displayed as in Figure 12–8.

This arrangement indicates that the data lead to the claim and that the step made from one to the other is supported by the warrant. The data, warrant, and claim of the specific argument we've been considering would therefore be diagrammed as in Figure 12–9.

Figure 12–9 demonstrates how the Toulmin model is useful in identifying each statement's function in the argument. It indicates that the data serve as the argument's

FIGURE 12–8 Toulmin Model for Data, Claim, and Warrant

grounds and starting point; the claim as its end point; and the warrant as its rational support.

The remaining statements in this argument also each have a function in the Toulmin model. The statement that previous clinical experience has demonstrated that infection will set in is the backing. *The backing consists of further facts or reasoning used to support or legitimate the principle contained in the warrant.* Backing often consists of accepted principles or facts arising from the field in which the argument takes place. For example, the field of medicine universally accepts the principle that treatment regimens should be based on what has proven effective in prior clinical practice. This principle, as backing, supports the warrant in very much the same way that data support a claim.

Another portion of this argument to which the Toulmin model directs our attention is the qualifier. *The qualifier is a colloquial adverb or adverbial phrase that modifies the claim and indicates the rational strength the arguer attributes to it.*[16] When arguers make claims, they attribute greater or lesser degrees of strength to them. Some warrants authorize an unequivocal acceptance of the claim, whereas others may have much weaker force. The person making the diagnosis of the head wound recommends certain treatment "strongly." Other qualifiers frequently used to modify claims are "probably," "certainly," and "possibly." When they occur in arguments, qualifiers fulfill an important function because they indicate the degree of certainty that arguers feel regarding their claims.

Sometimes there are exceptions or limitations that invalidate the application of the warrant. Toulmin includes these in his model as the reservation. *The reservation states the circumstances or conditions that undermine the argument.* It is the "exception to the

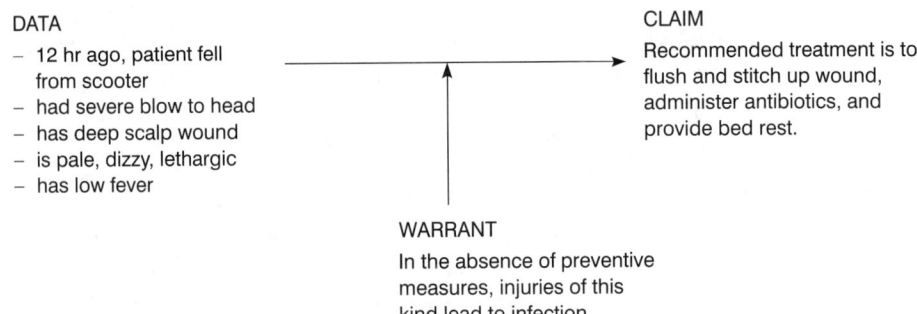

FIGURE 12–9 Toulmin Model Applied for Data, Claim, and Warrant

rule" expressed in the warrant. In the example argument, the arguer says that penicillin is recommended unless the patient is allergic to it. An allergic reaction, then, is a condition that would invalidate the recommendation that antibiotics be administered. In the Toulmin diagram, the qualifier and reservation are linked because, to the extent that circumstances or conditions restricting the claim exist, the strength of the claim is limited.

Toulmin recommends that the six parts of the model should be set out so as to show their interrelationships as in Figure 12–10. When the additional three parts are added to the diagram, we can see more clearly how they function in the argument. The backing undergirds or supports the warrant. The qualifier modifies the claim by showing the strength the arguer attributes to it. And the qualifier is related to any reservations that express exceptions to the claim by stating conditions which undermine the force of the argument.

Applying the model to the example we have just discussed yields the diagram in Figure 12–11. The elegance and usefulness of the model becomes clear when we consider how the functions of the various statements in the argument are revealed through the diagram. As we have observed, the diagram reveals that the existence of previous clinical experience "backs up" the prediction made in the warrant. Furthermore, we can see that penicillin is recommended "strongly" but not "absolutely." The recommendation is tempered by the reservation "unless the patient is allergic to penicillin" and is thus functionally connected to the qualifier because it limits its strength.

This argument from the field of medicine was relatively straightforward and easily comprehended. To test the capacity and usefulness of the Toulmin model, let us consider this more complex argument from the field of law:

> On the thirteenth day of August, 1880, George R. Falls made his last will and testament in which he gave small legacies to his two daughters, Mrs. Smith and Mrs. Phillips, the plaintiffs in this case, and the remainder to his grandson, John E. Falls. The testator, at the date of his will, owned a farm and considerable personal property. He was a widower

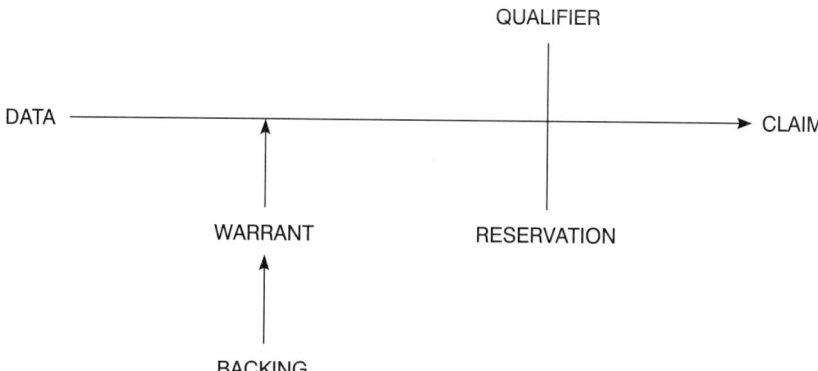

FIGURE 12–10 Toulmin Model with All Elements Displayed: data, warrant, backing, qualifier, reservation, and claim

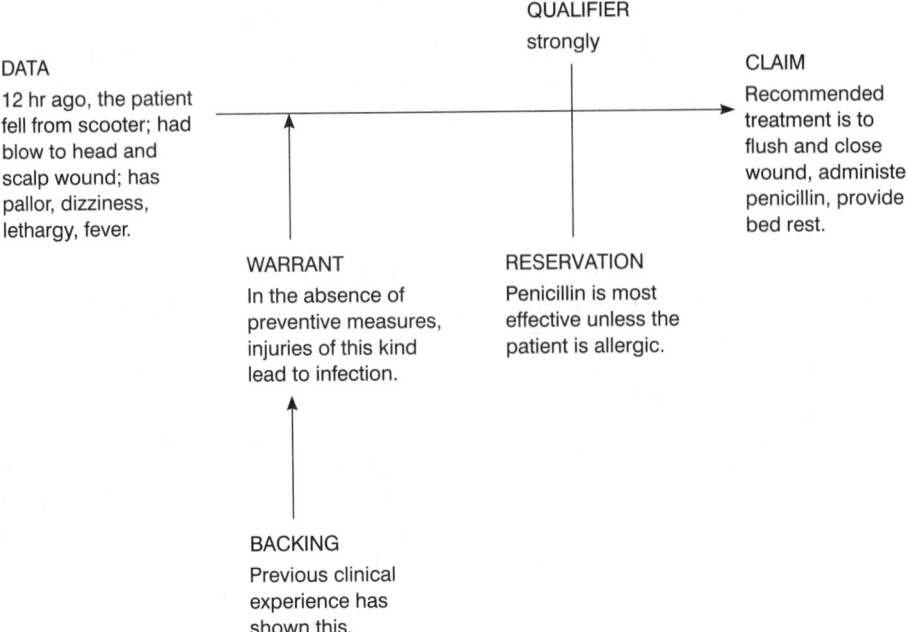

FIGURE 12-11 Toulmin Model Displays the Six Elements of an Argument

and thereafter, in June 1902, he was married to Mrs. Jones. At the date of the will, and subsequently to the death of the testator, his grandson lived with him as a member of his family.

At the time of his grandfather's death, John was 16 years old. John knew of the provisions made in his favor in the will. To prevent his grandfather from revoking such provisions, which his grandfather had manifested some intention to do, and to obtain speedy possession of his grandfather's property, John murdered his grandfather by poisoning him. John now claims the property, and the sole question for our determination is, can he have it?

It is quite true that statutes regulating the making, proof, and effect of wills and the devolution of property, if literally construed, and if their force and effect can in no way and no circumstances be controlled or modified, give this property to the murderer. It was the intention of the lawmakers that the donees in a will should have the property given to them. But it never could have been their intention that a donee who murdered the testator to make the will operative should have any benefit under it. It is a familiar canon of construction that a thing which is within the intention of the makers of a statute is as much within the statute as if it were within the letter; and a thing which is within the letter of the statute is not within the statute unless it be within the intention of the makers.[17]

The *data* in this argument are stated by the judge before he states his decision. Briefly, they include the following: The deceased left small legacies to two daughters and the remainder of his estate to his grandson; he remarried; he was considering changing his will; he was poisoned by his grandson; the grandson now claims the estate. The *claim*, or end point of this argument, does not seem to be explicitly stated but clearly would take the form of the judge's decision in the case. Because the entire passage justifies denial of the property to the donee, we can safely assume that the implied claim is "The donee in this case shall not have the property that has been willed to him." In the Toulmin model, as in the tree diagram general model introduced earlier, if the claim is not explicitly stated, the diagrammer should supply it. To indicate that it is implicit, the diagrammer using the Toulmin model encloses the implied claim in dashed lines, as in Figure 12–12.

In seeking out the warrant linking the data and claim in this argument, we must discover the reasoning that would link the data and the claim together. In this particular argument, the warrant is explicitly stated in the judge's opinion: "It never could have been [the lawmakers'] intention that a donee who murdered a testator to make the will operative should have any benefit under it." The judge believes this to be a statement of principle inherent in the American legal tradition and, if there is a precedent for it, he can thereby justify his decision that the property will be denied to the murderer. It is important to note that this warrant, like the one in the medical example given above, is *field-dependent*. It arises from the principle that legal statutes should be applied in ways congruent with the intentions of the lawmakers who proposed and approved them.

Only one remaining part of the Toulmin model is expressly stated in this argument. It is the *backing*; the principle that undergirds the warrant is expressly stated in the decision ("A thing which is within the letter of the statute is not within the statute unless it be within the intention of the makers"). The judge alludes to this as a "familiar canon of construction," which would be common knowledge among legal professionals. Because of its status as knowledge, this statement can function as support for the warrant. The finished diagram—which contains four of the Toulmin model's six parts—is shown in Figure 12–13.

Difficulties in Applying the Model

The Toulmin model's attention to the function that statements have within an argument makes it a complex model to apply to specific arguments. While most analysts can readily identify the data and claim, they have more difficulty isolating and identifying the warrant and the backing that supports it. The following points may therefore be helpful in diagramming arguments using the Toulmin model.

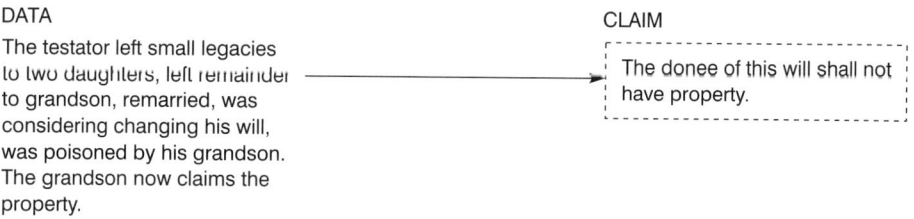

FIGURE 12–12 Toulmin Model, with Implied Claim Indicated in Dashed Lines

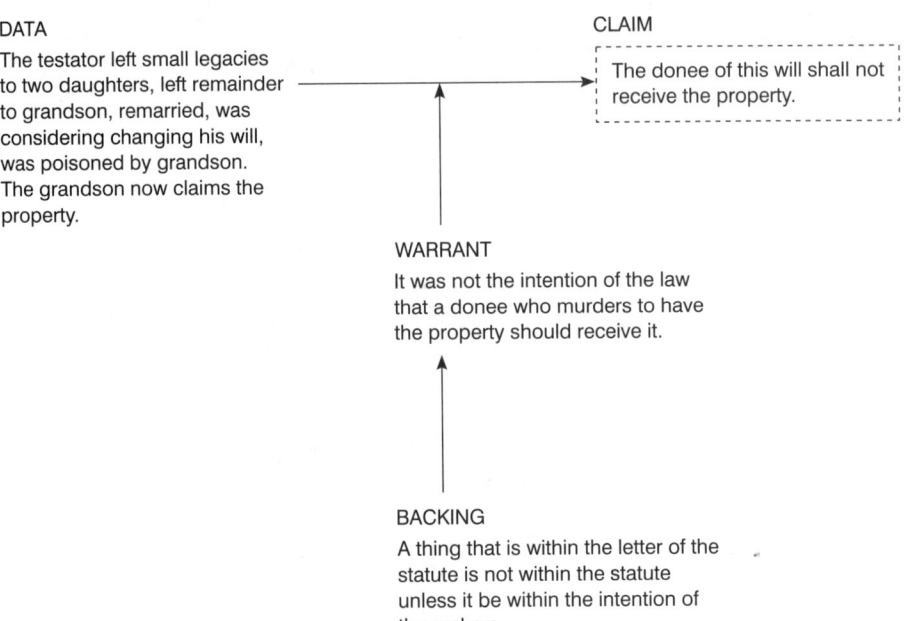

FIGURE 12–13 Toulmin Model Displaying Four of Six Possible Elements of an Argument

1. *Many arguments explicitly state only the data and claim, leaving the warrant implicit.* However, one must articulate the warrant in order to judge the reasoning contained in the argument. Therefore, every Toulmin diagram should include at least three parts—data, claim, and warrant. The warrant may be one of the reasoning forms explained in Chapter 8—quasilogical, analogy, generalization, cause, coexistence, and/or dissociation. It may also be stated as a field-dependent rule, principle, law, custom, or accepted procedure. It is best to begin by attempting to locate a warrant in the argument as stated. If one is not stated, then the analyst should determine what kind of step links the data to the claim and express the warrant explicitly.

2. *The data and the warrant are often confused.* Most statements, taken in isolation, are not identifiable by their grammar or form as warrants. A warrant is a statement linking the data to the claim and functions as such within the context of the argument. Once the most readily verifiable statements—the data—and the end point of the argument—the claim—have been identified, the analyst should examine the remaining statements to see whether any of them expresses reasoning that connects the data-statements with the claim.

3. *The backing is frequently confused with the data.* This is understandable because they are often both stated in the form of verifiable facts. One way to distinguish between them is to realize that, while the data are almost always explicitly stated and function as the starting point or grounds for the argument as a whole, the backing has a limited function. It is intended only to support the inference made in the warrant. In the court opinion cited above, the backing legitimized the legal principle applied in the judge's decision; in the medical diagnosis, the backing authorized the clinical prediction, which

justified treatment. Whereas backing is often stated only when the warrant is challenged, the data are nearly always explicitly stated in the argument.

4. *There is frequently more than one acceptable way to diagram an argument using the Toulmin model.* If the argument is very subtle or complex, different analysts may articulate the warrant differently or assign various warrants depending on how they interpret the data and the claim. (There are certain standards of correctness in analyzing arguments, however. The data and the claim are not interchangeable, and the warrant should not be confused with the data.)

Argument Chains and the Toulmin Model

The Toulmin model, like the general model of analysis, can be applied to argument chains. What serves as a claim for the initial data is then displayed as data for a further claim. If warrants are not explicitly articulated in the argument, they can be supplied, thereby providing information about the forms of reasoning used to link together the arguments in the chain. Adaptation of the Toulmin model to chains can be illustrated by using the same argument chains we used earlier to illustrate the general model.

A simple chain is evident in the following argument:

> The weather's been warming up and there are buds coming out on my shrubbery. These are signs I'll have to start mowing the lawn soon, so I'd better get the lawn mower serviced.

The data, of course, are the signs of spring readily observable in the physical environment. They are used to make a predictive claim in the second sentence that in turn becomes data for action that the arguer must take. No warrant is stated for the second inference, but the first subargument is from sign and the second is based on causal reasoning. (A serviced lawn mower will be a more effective solution for the growing grass than one which is not serviced.) So, supplying one implicit warrant would result in a Toulmin diagram of the chain that looks like Figure 12–14.

A more complicated chain as contained in Webster's indictment of Calhoun cited earlier in this chapter is illustrated in Figure 12–15. The data, warrant, qualifier, and claim of Webster's first subargument are explicitly stated. But only the data and warrant of the second subargument are supplied. The analyst must fill in the claim of the second subargument, the final claim, and the warrant supporting the final claim.

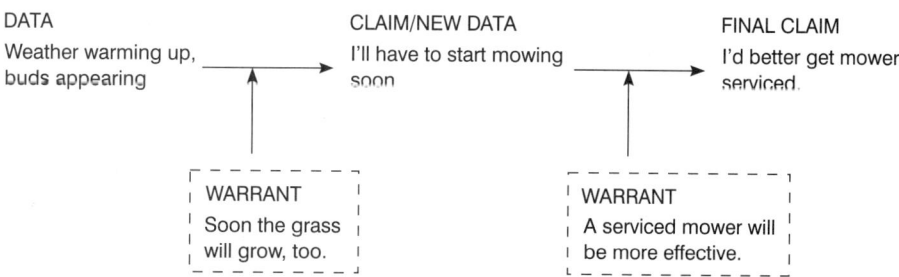

FIGURE 12–14 Toulmin Model Displaying Five Elements

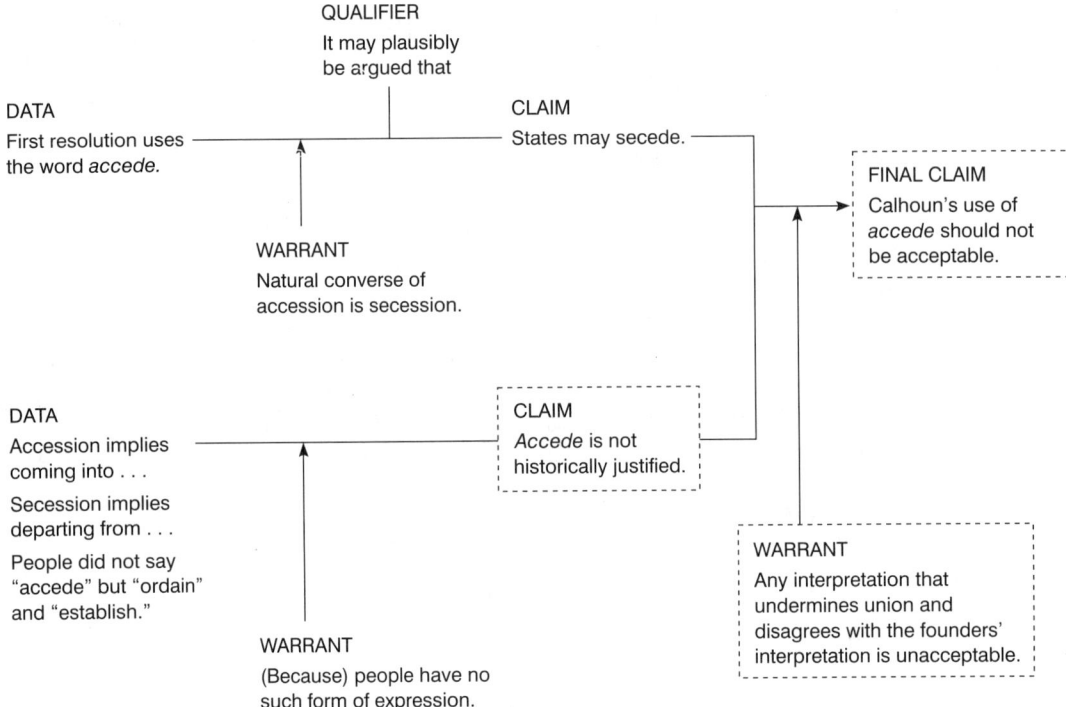

FIGURE 12-15 Toulmin Model of Argument with Explicit and Implied Components of Argument

COMPARISON OF THE TWO MODELS

The Toulmin diagram of the chain in Webster's argument illustrates some of the advantages that Toulmin diagrams have over other argument models. First, the Toulmin model explicitly indicates the degree of cogency the arguer attributes to the claims made. By drawing attention to the qualifier in Webster's first subargument, the Toulmin diagram reminds us that Webster inferred that it was only "plausible" that people might secede as a result of Calhoun's interpretation. Evidently, Webster himself thought his argument was weak and did not attribute a high degree of cogency to it.

Second, the Toulmin model calls on the analyst to supply unstated warrants. As a result, we see that the relationship of Webster's second subclaim to the final claim depends on a warrant growing out of the principle, which Webster accepts, that interpretations of the Constitution should be based on the intent of those who wrote it.

Third, the Toulmin model emphasizes the roles and functions of each statement rather than merely shows how they relate to each other. Because a statement expressing the data in an argument should be assessed by different criteria from a statement expressing the warrant, one needs to know the difference between the two. People frequently acknowledge conditions and circumstances that limit the cogency of claims, and the Toulmin model, by way of the reservation, allows such statements to be diagrammed and expressly linked to the qualifier. This allowance for counterevidence and restrictions on the claim within the model recognizes the two-sided nature of most argument.

Fourth, as previously indicated, the Toulmin model recognizes the field-dependent nature of many forms of argument. Although many arguments are based on the field invariant categories of inferences discussed in Chapter 8 (quasilogical, analogy, generalization, cause, coexistence, and dissociation), many are not. Arguments that occur in specific fields frequently rely on conventions, principles, or rules particular to a specific field or area. The Toulmin model takes into account the role of such guidelines in generating the inferences on which claims are based.

Fifth, the Toulmin model portrays any particular argument as an organic whole. In the model, data function as data only in relation to a claim; the degree of cogency expressed by the qualifier is limited by reservations that modify or restrict the warrant. In the Toulmin model, a diagram of an argument as an integrated unit displays that its persuasiveness depends on how it functions as a whole rather than as a series of detachable statements.

The general model introduced at the beginning of the chapter also has its own advantages, however. Because the general model requires less to be supplied in order to construct a diagram, it is simpler to use. Because one can allow the diagram to conform to the structure of the argument rather than structure the argument to fit the diagram, the general model is more descriptive. The absence of a preset diagram format such as one has with the Toulmin model allows the analyst using the general model to work with the argument on its own terms. Finally, the general model shows *how* premises are related to each other—whether they work independently or together to support the claim. Working with *both* models to diagram a particular argument will often be beneficial because each model reveals different characteristics and aspects of an argument.

SUMMARY

Argument analysis can be used to understand, evaluate, and refute the arguments one hears and reads. By interpreting an argument's language and discovering how the statements within it are related to each other, one can identify equivocation, isolate the argument's primary claim, articulate implicit inferences, locate secondary claims, disregard irrelevant statements, and perform other operations that lead to effective argument criticism and refutation.

Arguments can be categorized into four types. Simple arguments (Type I) consist of one premise and a claim that follows from it. Complex arguments (Type II) have two or more premises supporting a single claim. These premises can support the claim independently or in concert with one another. Argument chains (Type III) use one or more premises to support claims that, once proven, become premises for further claims. Compound arguments (Type IV) use one premise or two or more premises in concert to support more than one conclusion.

Having identified a statement as an argument, the analyst can use five steps to interpret and diagram it. These steps include determining what the argument means, assigning numbers to individual thought units in the argument, identifying the main or primary claim, displaying the argument's structure in a tree diagram, and evaluating the argument by using the tests of evidence and reasoning. During analysis, one should take into account the argument's context and the arguer's probable intent so as to render a fair interpretation of the argument.

Unlike the general model of argument discussed in the first half of the chapter, the Toulmin model assigns specific functions to each statement in the argument. The data function like evidence and premises on which the argument is based. The claim is the argument's end point or conclusion. The warrant states the reasoning used to move from the data to the claim and functions like an inference. The backing consists of facts or information used to support the inference made in the warrant. The qualifier modifies the claim and indicates the rational strength the arguer attributes to it. The reservation states circumstances or conditions in which the claim would not be true.

The Toulmin model often provides more information than the general model of argument analysis, and it is also more difficult to use. An analyst using the Toulmin model often encounters difficulties such as misidentifying unstated warrants, confusing the data and the warrant, confusing data and backing, and applying incorrect standards to diagrams of complex or subtle arguments.

The Toulmin model offers many advantages, however. It draws attention to how the arguer qualifies the argument, directs the analyst to stated implicit references, recognizes the field dependence of arguments, and emphasizes the functional nature of argument. The general model of analysis also has advantages. Because it does not have a preset structure to impose on an argument, the general model is simpler to use and more accurately reflects the way premises and claims are related to each other.

EXERCISES

Diagram each of the following arguments using both the general model of argument and the Toulmin model of argument. (It might be helpful for you to review the steps described under "An Application" and the pointers for the Toulmin model under "Difficulties in Applying the Model" in this chapter before beginning.) (See Figure 12–16.)

Then, criticize each argument by applying the tests for reasoning described in Chapter 8 and by making explicit the unstated assumptions in the argument that might be explicitly challenged. At times, the tests of evidence discussed in Chapter 7 might be useful as well. The arguments are arranged in order of difficulty, with the simplest at the beginning and the most complex at the end. For example:

Capital punishment for murderers is widely supported by the general population. A Harris poll in 1975 reported 59 percent of the public in favor of capital punishment, and that proportion reportedly was increasing. Another poll in 1978 asked the question, "Are you in favor of the death penalty for persons convicted of murder?" The results showed 66 percent of the populace in favor of the death penalty.

General Model

1. Capital punishment for murderers is widely supported by the general population.

2. A 1975 poll reported 59 percent of the public in favor of capital punishment.

3. That proportion of people favoring capital punishment was increasing by 1975.

4. A 1978 poll asked if people favored the death penalty for convicted murderers.

5. Sixty-six percent favored the death penalty.

CHAPTER TWELVE   Argument Analysis and Criticism

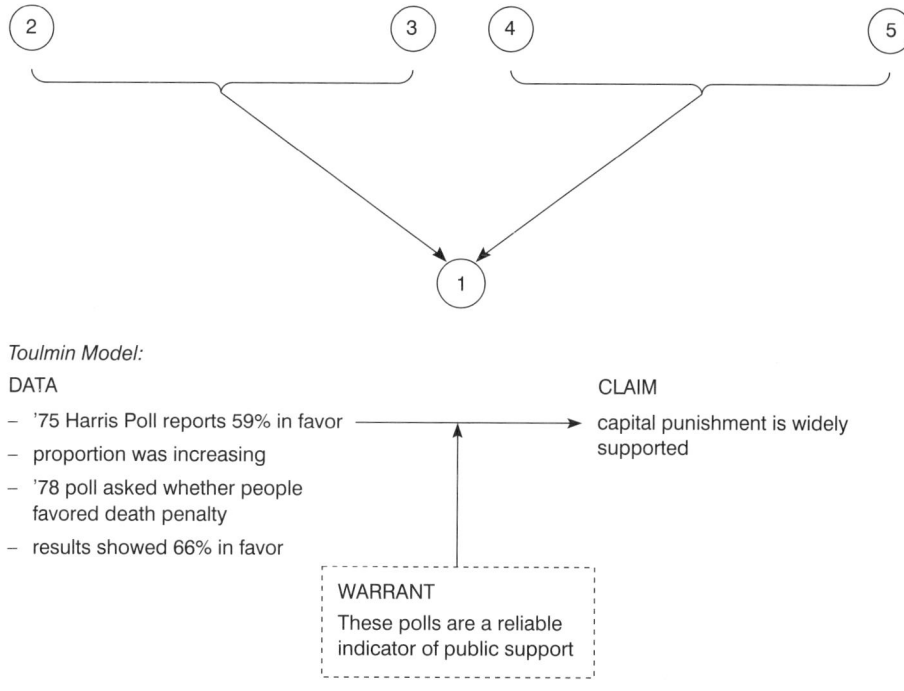

FIGURE 12–16 Comparison of the General Model and the Toulmin Model

Criticism:

The polls are outdated. Perhaps pubic opinion has shifted since the 1970s. Besides, this is a form of *ad populum* argument that assumes that because the public supports something, it should be favored. Furthermore, the arguer does not report the source of the statistics or the method used to collect them. How large was the sample surveyed? Was the sample representative of the general population? Do other surveys and polls on this question (particularly those gathered since the mid-1970s) agree with the two polls cited here?

Arguments for Analysis and Criticism

1. It is the chemical firms that release the most troubling types of molecules into the environment. In Baton Rouge, according to company data, an Exxon chemical plant was leaking 560,000 pounds of benzene yearly, while just south of there, according to a survey by the Sierra Club, eighteen plants in and around St. Gabriel and Geismar dumped about 400 billion pounds of toxic chemicals into the air during the first nine months of 1986.
    Michael H. Brown, "The Toxic Cloud," *Greenpeace Magazine* (October–December 1987): 17.

2. But it was when Abbado had the orchestra to himself in the Tchaikovsky *Marche Slave* that the real magic showed. This hackneyed piece was treated with respect, and Abbado built it steadily to one final climax rather than playing each eruption as a show-stopping event.

3. [Mountain goats] were trucked in from the Cascades by game wardens in the 1920s. After a few years the animals began to flourish, and now they're doing well. Too well, in fact. The park's mountain-goat population has nearly doubled in the past several years to 1,200 animals. Problem is, they're hard on the wilderness. They destroy the grass and other vegetation in fragile alpine meadows. They cause serious erosion by pawing and rolling in the dirt. They interfere with the park's natural ecosystem.

   "Problem in the Olympics," *The Seattle Times* editorial (August 31, 1986): A18. Used by permission.

4. [T]he data show that, if current trends continue, Social Security won't live to see another 60 years.

   The demographic trends that helped make Social Security so successful in its early years—plenty of workers paying in to support a few retirees—have started to work against it.

   In 1945, there were 42 workers for each Social Security beneficiary. Today, that figure is 3.3 workers. By 2030, it drops to two to one, according to the program's annual report.

   At current tax rates, Social Security starts to lose money by 2013—right around the time waves of baby boomers will start retiring.

   The deficits mount quickly. By 2070, annual Social Security shortfall will be more than $7 trillion.

   John Merline, "Should Social Security Retire? Public System Can't Stack Up to Market Returns," *Business Daily* (August 14, 1995): A1.

5. Is it not the great defect of our education today . . . that although we often succeed in teaching our pupils "subjects," we fail lamentably on the whole in teaching them how to think: they learn everything except the art of learning. It is as though we had taught a child mechanically and by rule of thumb, to play "The Harmonious Blacksmith" upon the piano, but had never taught him the scale or how to read music; so that, having memorized "The Harmonious Blacksmith," he still had not the faintest notion how to proceed from that to tackle "The Last Rose of Summer."

   Dorothy L. Sayers, "The Lost Tools of Learning," *National Review* (January 19, 1979): 91.

6. It's not too late. We can act. Today there are some 500 million women in the Third World who have told the World Fertility Survey that they want no more children. Most of them didn't want their last child, but they lacked the knowledge and the means to do something about it—whether it happens to be the three condoms for a penny that the United Nations Population Fund buys and distributes, or a cycle of oral contraceptives which the United Nations buys for 15 cents a cycle, or whether it's Norplant or vasectomy equipment.

   Werner Fornos, "The Environmental Crisis: A Humanist Call for Action," *The Humanist* (November/December 1991): 31.

7. The lunacy of modern city life lies first in the fact that most city dwellers who can do so try to live outside the city boundaries. The two-legged creatures have

created suburbs, exurbs, and finally rururbs (rurbs to some). Disdaining rural life, they try to create simulations of it. No effort is spared to let city dwellers imagine they are living anywhere but in a city: patches of grass in the more modest suburbs, broader spreads in the richer ones further out; prim new trees planted along the streets; at the foot of the larger back yards, a pretense to bosky woodlands.

> Henry Fairlie, "Or the Cow's Revenge: The Idiocy of Urban Life," *The New Republic* (January 5 & 12, 1987): 21. Excerpted by permission of *The New Republic* © 1987, The New Republic, Inc.

8. 1991 statistics from the Carnegie Foundation for the Advancement of Teaching show that SAT scores are directly proportional to family income. Students from families with incomes under $10,000 score an average of 768 (combined verbal and math scores) out of a possible total of 1,200. Students from families with incomes in the $30,000 to $40,000 range have scores averaging 884. Students from families with incomes over $70,000 have scores averaging 997. Since scholastic aptitude is related to a student's position on the wealth/poverty scale, which has a lot to do with where a family lives (affluent suburb or inner-city slum), alleviating poverty would be one way of improving scholastic aptitude.

> Edd Doerr, "Whither Public Education?" *The Humanist* (November/December 1991): 41.

9. Dieting is an urban obsession. Country dwellers eat what they please, and work it off in useful physical employments, and in the open air, cold or hot, rainy or sunny. Mailmen are the healthiest city workers. When was your mailman last ill for a day? If one reads the huge menus that formed a normal diet in the 19th century, you realize that even the city dwellers could dispatch these gargantuan repasts because they still shared many of the benefits of rural life. Homes were cold in the winter, except in the immediate vicinity of the hearth or stove. Cold has a way of eating up excess fat. No wonder dieting is necessary in a cosseted life in which the body is forced to do no natural heavy work.

> Henry Fairlie, "Or the Cow's Revenge: The Idiocy of Urban Life," *The New Republic* (January 5 & 12, 1987): 23. Excerpted by permission of *The New Republic* © 1987, The New Republic, Inc.

✱ 10. Ladies make excellent teachers in public schools; many of them are every way the equals of their male competitors, and still they secure less wages than males. The reason is obvious. The number of ladies who offer themselves to teach is much larger than the number of males who are willing to teach. . . . The result is that the competition for positions of teachers to be filled by ladies is so great as to reduce the price; but as males can not be employed at that price, and are necessary in certain places in the schools, those seeking their services have to pay a higher rate for them.

> Joseph Emerson Brown, "Against the Woman Suffrage Amendment," in *American Forum* (Seattle: University of Washington Press, 1960), 339.

11. Stricter control over pesticides that affect the female hormone estrogen will be necessary if alarming findings are borne out regarding their potential harmful effects on humans and wildlife.

Scientists from Tulane University have published findings in the journal *Science* that show worrisome effects when pesticides that have been linked to breast cancer and male birth defects are combined. . . .

The Tulane findings came days after an international group of experts, the Work Session on Environmental Endocrine Disrupting Chemicals, warned of threats to intelligence, development, and reproductive health posed by chemicals such as dioxin and PCBs found in pesticides and plastics.

Those chemicals, which mimic natural human and animal hormones, can "change the character of human societies or destabilize wildlife populations," they said.

"Pesticides, Estrogen Link," editorial, *Seattle Post-Intelligencer* (July 12, 1996): A14.

12. For children uninstructed in the way television "frames reality," TV today is no longer simply a benign distraction—but something actually "hostile" to learning.

Neil Postman, who has researched the subject, observes that: "The great educators—from Cicero on down—have all taught that the purpose of education and schooling is to free children from the tyranny of the present, to help them see beyond the immediate. TV works just the other way."

Because TV reduces complex thoughts and ideas to mere images, because its sole operational criterion is "entertainment value"; because it demands no historical background as a key to understanding; and finally, because *it* does the thinking for passive viewers—TV is "by its very nature opposed to what education is all about."

Adapted from Robert Marquand, "Teach Children How to See TV," *Christian Science Monitor* (December 26, 1986): 19. Reprinted by permission from *The Christian Science Monitor* © 1986, The Christian Science Publishing Society. All rights reserved.

13. [For this dialogue, there are two arguments—Professor Smith's and Professor Jones's. The general model requires two separate diagrams, while the Toulmin model requires only one, because Professor Jones's objections can be included in the reservation.]

Professor Smith: There is probably too much cheating going on in our department, and our faculty should do something about it.

Professor Jones: I haven't noticed any evidence of cheating in my classes. What makes you say it's widespread?

Professor Smith: Well, I'm sure you remember that our colleague Adams found a lot of plagiarism on the course papers turned in to him last spring. Whole paragraphs were reproduced in more than one student paper. Then, of course, our graduate student proctors often have taken up crib sheets in the 100 course exam. And I've observed students during my own tests sharing information with each other. These are signs of a pervasive problem throughout the department. Every time our faculty, teaching assistants, and proctors look for wrongdoing, they seem to find it.

	Professor Jones:	I think you're exaggerating the extent of the problem; these are the behaviors of a small group of male students in their various courses who take pride in finding ways to "get around" the system.

14. So much of the male behavior that puts women at risk—multiple partners, bisexuality, reluctance or refusal to wear condoms—cannot be changed by women alone. And so many of the attitudes that pervade societies about women's worth and place and men's rights make effective prevention campaigns extremely difficult to achieve. . . . Even when informed of the risk, women too rarely have the power to protect themselves. In every society, women are subservient to men. Depending on the degree of pressure on her to be submissive in sexual and social matters, a woman who tries to use information to prevent infection may become the target of mockery, rejection, stigmatization, economic reprisal, violence, and death.

Marcia Ann Gillespie, "HIV: The Global Crisis," *MS. Magazine* (January/February, 1991): 17.

(The following two arguments are excerpted from a group discussion on the right to die. Assume that all the participants are working together to construct *one* argument and are pursuing a shared thoughtline.)

✱ 15. Anne: Technology has affected every single part of the program.

Carrie: Yes, technology is a big one.

Anne: I don't really feel technology is just the mechanical aspect. It's chemical, biological, physical, everything. The advances in technology have gone so far that it can prolong life, yeah, but when you get in the position of an irreversibly comatose-type state, it's out of step with what man is. You know, should he be prolonged just to vegetate? Are they prolonging ill health or are they prolonging life? Technology has reached the outer limits where it's gone beyond what man is.

Carrie: It's gone beyond the purpose for which medical technology was originally intended. Its goal was to enhance human life, whereas now it just prolongs death, dying, and pain.

16. Steve: The Hippocratic Oath, which states doctors must do everything within their power to keep the patient alive, is also a problem.

Carrie: But the idea of the Hippocratic Oath is a problem. It says: "So far as power and discernment shall be mine, I will carry out the regimen for the benefit of the sick and will keep them from harm and wrong." Now the doctors or the law, . . . someone should explain the Hippocratic Oath to everyone, what exactly those words mean.

Anne: But it's an archaic document. I mean, it talks about Greek gods. . . .

Leigh: It's so ambiguous. It doesn't have to do with today's society.

Steve: It's been outgrown by technology.

NOTES

1. Irving M. Copi, *Informal Logic* (New York: Macmillan, 1986), 19.
2. Daniel Webster, "The Constitution Not a Compact between Sovereign States," in *American Forum: Speeches on Historic Issues, 1788–1900,* Ernest J. Wrage and Barnet Baskerville, eds. (Seattle: University of Washington Press, 1960), 136–7.
3. Monroe C. Beardsley, *Practical Logic* (New York: Prentice-Hall, 1950), 18–25.
4. See Michael Scriven, *Reasoning* (Point Reyes, Calif.: Edgepress, 1976). Copi's model is the simpler of the two and does not emphasize the interpretation and criticism of arguments as much as does Scriven's. To adjust our treatment of analysis to chapter length, we have eliminated steps Scriven recommends such as formulating unstated assumptions and considering related arguments. The reader interested in a more complete and extensive treatment of analysis should consult the works of both these authors.
5. Copi, 7.
6. *American Forum,* 139.
7. *Webster's New Collegiate Dictionary,* s.v. "plight," "faith," and "sovereign."
8. Copi, 20.
9. Adapted from "More Big-Brotherism," *National Review* (December 31, 1986): 18.
10. Adapted from a letter to the editor, "New Destination Ski Resorts Could Boost Clean Industry," by Mel Borgersen, *The Seattle Times* (December 21, 1986): A15. Used by permission of Mel Borgersen.
11. Adapted from Emily Feistritzer, "Balancing Act: Love and Money," *The Seattle Times* (August 31, 1986): A16.
12. Adapted from Feistritzer, A16.
13. Stephen Toulmin, *The Uses of Argument* (Cambridge: Cambridge University Press, 1969), 94–145.
14. Toulmin, 94.
15. Toulmin, 98.
16. Stephen Toulmin, Richard Rieke, and Allan Janik, *An Introduction to Reasoning,* 2d ed. (New York: Macmillan, 1984), 86.
17. Adapted from *Riggs vs. Palmer,* 115 N.Y. 506 (1889), 22 N.E. 188.

APPENDIX A

Intercollegiate Debate

One of the most enjoyable and challenging forums for practicing argumentation is intercollegiate debate. Intercollegiate debate brings together many of the ideas and activities discussed in this book. For instance, it includes gathering and using evidence, analyzing topics, constructing cases, presenting persuasive arguments, and criticizing others' arguments. In addition, intercollegiate debate offers speakers an opportunity to refute, challenge, and respond to the arguments of others.

Debate can be a highly competitive and motivating activity. It hones an individual's analytic and speaking abilities and many classes using this book may have one or more classroom debates as assignments in the course. This appendix is intended to assist instructors and students in planning and carrying out such debates.

Many topics that would be germane to such an assignment have been discussed elsewhere in this book, and they will not be repeated here. These including conducting research (Chapter 7); using reasoning (Chapter 8); detecting flaws in opponents' arguments (Chapter 12 and Appendix D); and constructing and refuting cases on topics of fact, value, and policy (Chapters 9, 10, and 11). This appendix will focus on the practical application of competitive intercollegiate debate and present alternative formats for debating.

The Nature of Intercollegiate Debate

Debate occurs frequently in American society. Most of us are familiar with political debates in which various candidates for the presidency or other political offices speak in opposition to each other about governmental policies. These debates are aired by the media and, although there is no single judge rendering a decision about them, media commentators and the electorate respond by means of criticism and voting behavior. In Congress and state legislatures, floor debates occur between senators and representatives on issues prior to voting. In law courts, the attorneys argue to a judge about the merits of a case and attempt to convince the judge or jury of the merits of the case. Community forums also provide speakers with an opportunity to debate about whether some action should be taken. While these debates are less formal in structure than legal or political debates, they are still debates—extended cases are made in an attempt to persuade a person or group of people. Academic debate provides students with the opportunity to learn this important skill of citizenship. Skilled debaters are people who have a power to influence decision-making and persuade audiences about appropriate courses of action. While classroom debates offer one venue for learning academic debate, intercollegiate debate provides students with an intensive and exciting method for developing their debating skills and critical thinking abilities.

Typically, formal debates in general, and intercollegiate debates in particular, involve third parties that serve as judges. Just as in a court of law, the judge or jury has the power to decide the merits of arguments presented by lawyers, in intercollegiate debates and other formal debates, third parties ultimately decide which side won. This means that in a formal debate, advocates do not speak to or try to convince each other but instead address a third party, or judge, who is expected to render a decision about who won the debate or who did the best job of debating. The presence of the third party distinguishes formal debates from informal debates and other types of speaking situations.

Debate has been used to teach the skills of analysis and reasoning in educational forums since ancient times. In Greece, debate was conducted in the academies. In medieval and Renaissance universities, it was used to teach disputation. And in modern England and the United States, debate has been a major form of interscholastic rivalry. In the United States, intercollegiate debating began in the late 19th century, and in 1947 the U.S. Military Academy began the National Debate Tournament (NDT) at West Point. The competitors at that tournament debated the proposition "Resolved: That labor should be given a direct share in the management of industry." The NDT was important for several reasons. First, it provided a national, standardized model for intercollegiate debating. For example, students worked as members of two-person teams. The teams were assigned to be either affirmative (in favor of the proposition) or negative (opposed to the proposition), and each side presented two constructive speeches and two rebuttal speeches. Second, the NDT served to provide a national model for tournaments. The NDT had eight rounds of preliminary competition and each two-person team debated four times on each side of the proposition—affirmative and negative— which meant that students had to prepare to debate comprehensively on a proposition. Furthermore, the 16 teams with the best win-loss record advanced into the elimination rounds and through single elimination continued to advance to the final debate round. Third, the NDT standardized competition on a single, national proposition. The NDT proposition is released in the summer and every student in the nation who participates in the NDT researches and competes on the national proposition for an entire academic year. The NDT proposition is a policy proposition. The NDT was not the first tournament to offer many of these features, but it did act as a national model that was copied by many other tournaments and it served to standardize many of the practices associated with academic debate.

Intercollegiate debate grew rapidly throughout the country, and in 1972 a new organization developed that provided an alternative format to NDT debate. The Cross Examination Debate Association (CEDA) retained many of the same elements as the NDT but added or changed other elements. First, CEDA debate was originally intended to focus on an audience-centered philosophy. Whereas NDT style debate had become highly specialized and evidence-intensive, CEDA was initially designed for audiences. Second, CEDA debate added the element of cross-examination in which each speaker stands for questions by the opposition following each constructive speech. Cross-examination gave students the chance to interact with one another in a debate. This feature of CEDA proved so popular that it was later adopted by the NDT and became a standard component of competitive debate formats. Third, CEDA debate introduced different types of propositions. While students debated the same proposition for the entire academic year, fact, value, and policy propositions were used in different years. CEDA experimented with this format and for several years had two different propositions each year: fall and spring topics. CEDA returned to the single-proposition format in 1996–97. And finally, CEDA did not have a national tournament until 1986. Instead, the CEDA organization tracked national sweepstakes points that awarded a school's performance for an entire year of debating and then gave the top schools sweepstakes awards.

CEDA- and NDT-style debates have both evolved into highly prepared, researched, and specialized forms of debate. Over a period of several years, both formats became increasingly similar until 1996 when both organizations agreed to share topics and formats for the most part. However, many schools became concerned with the high "entry barriers" associated with academic debate. The amount of time and money required for extensive NDT and CEDA research as well as traveling competitive teams nationally meant that many students were not able to participate effectively in either organization. In response, parliamentary debate became an option and the National Parliamentary Debate Association and American Parliamentary Debate Association developed. These organizations stress audience-centered debate, in which speaking and arguing are the focus and research and evidence are stressed less.

Parliamentary debate is extemporaneous debate. As with CEDA and NDT, students compete at tournaments against other students in two-person teams, but the format and topics for debate are very different. In parliamentary debate, the propositions are given to the teams just before the debate round and students have a short period of time (usually 15 minutes) to construct and organize their case arguments. Prepared materials (such as issue briefs) are not permitted in the debating chamber. Consequently, students draw on their education and background for evidence as opposed to extensive on topic library research. Parliamentary debate was developed as a model of a parliament. Therefore, instead of affirmative and negative sides, in parliamentary debate the team in favor of the proposition is called the "government" side and the team opposed to the proposition is the "opposition."

NDT, CEDA, and Parliamentary debate focus on two-person debate teams, and these are the dominant forms of debate in college. Many high schools across the country also participate in interscholastic debate, and they typically engage in one of two types. The first type of high school debate is policy debate that focuses, much like NDT-style, on two-person teams and policy propositions. In addition, many high schools engage in Lincoln-Douglas–style debate that focuses on individual competitors as opposed to two-person teams and on value-orientated propositions.

Intercollegiate debate extends classroom and campus debates beyond individual institutions and provides students with the opportunity to argue against members of other colleges and universities. Each year, more than 400 colleges and universities in the United States participate in some form of intercollegiate debate and attend various tournaments throughout the nation and the world.

Intercollegiate Debate Propositions

Just as we have discussed in this book, debate proposition is central to the practice of intercollegiate debate. However, in contrast to the types of propositions we have discussed elsewhere in the book, the intercollegiate debate proposition is usually stated in more general terms. The debate teams, then, have some latitude in which to choose their interpretation of the proposition. Some recent NDT propositions have been:

Resolved: That the Commander-in-Chief power of the President of the United States should be substantially curtailed.

Resolved: That the federal government should substantially change rules and/or statutes governing criminal procedure in federal course in one or more of the following areas: pretrial detention, sentencing.

Resolved: That the United States government should substantially increase its security assistance to one or more of the following: Egypt, Israel, Jordan, Palestinian National Authority, Syria.

These topics are relatively broad and contain many issues and many potential case areas. CEDA debate propositions are similar to NDT propositions. The primary difference is that while NDT debate focuses on policy propositions, CEDA debate has used different types of propositions including:

Resolved: That the welfare system exacerbates the problems of the urban poor in the United States.

Resolved: That the United States should significantly increase the development of the earth's ocean resources.

Resolved: That the national news media in the United States impair public understanding of political issues.

CEDA propositions can be fact, value, or policy, and some CEDA propositions involve comparisons between two alternative values or actions. Parliamentary propositions, however, are very different from either CEDA or NDT propositions. The most obvious difference is that parliamentary propositions are announced immediately before the debate begins and the debaters have little time to develop their arguments. The other difference is in the propositions themselves. Whereas some parliamentary propositions are direct, others are analogic—they are designed to be compared to concrete cases and examples. For instance, the following are direct parliamentary propositions:

This house believes that higher education was intended for the intellectual elite.

This house believes that the United States is a good world "policeman."

This house believes that there ought to be a better way to choose a president.

Direct parliamentary propositions may be of any type: fact, value, or policy. Direct propositions specify the particular cases or actions to be debated. Indirect or analogic propositions require debaters to apply a case study or extended example to the proposition. In other words, the proposition serves as a figurative analogy for the case argued by the debaters. Some examples include:

This house believes that the truth is out there.

This house believes that what costs little is of little worth.

This house believes in love at first sight.

These propositions are very broad and open to interpretation. In these instances, the parliamentary debater would need to figure out what case studies or examples would prove the proposition true or false.

The following sections examine how propositions are interpreted and how they guide academic debates. These are only some issues that debaters grapple with but they are important for understanding how to develop a reasonable interpretation of a proposition.

Topicality

Topicality refers to whether a case fits inside or outside the proposition. If a case fits outside the proposition, it fails to provide *prima facie* support for the proposition and the side in favor of the proposition loses because it did not prove the proposition true. The wording of the proposition creates a boundary that defines what is considered "topical" and what is considered "nontopical." In other words, any given proposition defines what is a relevant issue for discussion and what is an irrelevant issue. For example, if we were discussing the proposition "Resolved: That euthanasia should be legal," the topic would include issues of right to die, death with dignity, patients with terminal illnesses, and whether doctors should knowingly allow people to die. Yet, the topic also excludes issues such as foreign policy, whether Democrats are better than Republicans, or any other irrelevant issue. Therefore, if a team argued a case that proved a college education should be mandatory for everyone, the case would fall outside the proposition and the case would be nontopical.

The dividing line between what is relevant and what is irrelevant is called a "parameter." *A parameter is the boundary or barrier that defines what is included in the relevant set of issues so that advocates can understand what issues are relevant and what issues are irrelevant for a given proposition.* For example, consider the following proposition:

Resolved: The United States should adopt a national health care program.

The wording of this topic creates an area of issues. In other words, we know that the status of health care in the United States is an issue. We know that the insurance industry and fee-for-service medical care are all issues. And we know that a lack of health insurance is an issue. All of these issues fall within the parameter of the topic—these are issues that the propositional area contains.

At the same time, we know that there are some issues that are irrelevant for this proposition. The term *United States* for example constrains us to proposing a program that is in the United States and not some other country. We are also constrained by the term *health care,* which excludes issues such as life or car insurance, military expenditures, and the like. And we are constrained by the term *national,* which means that whatever the affirmative case proposes, the plan of action must have a national scope. If the affirmative advocates argue for propositions or plans of action that fall outside the topic, they are considered nontopical and irrelevant to the discussion. Consequently, a nontopical case does not support the resolution (because it falls outside the parameter of the topic) and an advocate arguing for a nontopical case should lose the debate.

Although the proposition indicates the general nature and direction of the affirmative's position on the topic, the case offers a specific interpretation of how the proposition should be enacted. For example, the proposition might call for a significant increase in federal government support for health care. The affirmative case should then identify specific problems with the health care delivery system in the United States and present a plan for solving the problems—through support of health maintenance organizations, subsidies to private health insurance companies, or some other means. Similarly, a value proposition states a general value orientation, but an affirmative team's case on the proposition will specify what value hierarchies to apply as well as the criteria to be used to make the evaluation. And, if the proposition was fact-based, the affirmative team's case must identify the definitions and threshold to be applied.

Topicality deals with whether the affirmative's specific case is a legitimate application of the general proposition for debate. The affirmative case should adhere to the letter and spirit of the meaning implied in the proposition. Affirmative teams, because they lose sight of the central issue of the proposition or because they wish to surprise their opponents, often (but by no means always) offer cases that depart from the proposition in some way. When this happens, the negative should demonstrate that the case is not propositional through reasoning and explanation.

Jurisdiction

Just as a judge in a court of law must have the jurisdiction to decide a legal case, so a debate judge must have jurisdiction to decide a debate. For example, if in a court of law a prosecutor wanted to try a defendant in Portland, Maine, for a crime committed in Los Angeles, California, the court in Portland would not have the right to decide the case because it does not fall within its jurisdiction (unless the appropriate procedures for change of venue or extradition were followed).

Similarly, in a debate, the judge must either vote affirmative in favor of the resolution or negative against the resolution. This means that if the affirmative case fails to adequately address all of the resolution or defends a resolution that is different from the one agreed on by the participants, then the affirmative has not justified the resolution and the judge has no jurisdiction to vote for it.

Consider, for instance, the following proposition:

> Resolved: That the welfare system has exacerbated the problems of the urban poor in the United States.

If an affirmative argued that the welfare system adversely affects the lives of poor people in the United States, the affirmative's argument would ignore the term "urban"; although the case may fall within the parameter of the resolution and be topical, by ignoring or minimizing the significance of one of the defining terms of the proposition, the affirmative would not have justified the topic as it was written. Instead, the affirmative has justified a different proposition, that the welfare system has exacerbated the problems of the poor in the United States.

Affirmative cases are limited by the proposition. They must prove the proposition and present a reasonable and *prima facie* argument in support of it. If the affirmative omits relevant terms or substantively alters the proposition, then the affirmative has not justified the initial proposition that both teams came prepared to debate.

Generalization

When deciding how to approach the analysis of a debate topic, affirmative speakers are faced with a decision. Can the affirmative adequately argue all of the proposition, or must the affirmative focus on a case that represents a subset or example of the proposition? This decision is an important one and depends on the nature of the proposition.

Consider the following proposition:

Resolved: That the tuition at our school should be increased 6 percent for next year.

In this example, the resolution is focused and narrow, which means that an arguer is tightly constrained with regard to how the topic can be interpreted. The plan of action is a simple one: raise tuition.

On the other hand, consider this proposition:

Resolved: That the United States should significantly increase its foreign military commitments.

Contrast this proposition with the previous one and the difference becomes apparent. While the first proposition specified a singular and concrete plan of action, the second proposition allowed an affirmative advocate to examine many different plans of action. In fact, it is difficult to imagine any one plan of action that would address all of the topic's subject matter. Increased military commitments could involve hundreds of different plans. Since time limits and research ability prevents a team from addressing all of this proposition (because of its breadth), the affirmative case may select a single, representative example that proves the resolution. For example, the United States could increase its aid to Somalia, Russia, or China. The United States could send troops to Europe or sell aircraft to Saudi Arabia. There are many possible plans of action.

Because many possible plans are available, the advocate, when dealing with a broad proposition, will typically select a subset of the topic—an example—and argue that the example (perhaps placing nuclear missiles abroad) is typical of the entire proposition and therefore warrants the entire proposition. If, however, the affirmative example is not typical because the case is a hasty generalization or the sample is not representative of other important military concerns, then the negative would argue that the affirmative's case represented an invalid generalization.

Debate Pragmatics

Successfully conducting a debate involves handling practical matters such as note taking, speaker order, and time limits. Methods for dealing with such matters have evolved

Taking Notes

Skill in refutation requires you to keep track of the arguments introduced and developed by both sides in a debate. Most people have learned to take notes in a linear format. For instance, in classroom lectures, we learn to begin at the top of the page and work our way to the bottom. Such a system does not work well in debate because the arguments do not remain static—they are dynamic. In debate, arguments are introduced, refuted, extended, refuted again, and summarized. Keeping track of arguments as they develop over time, then, can be challenging and requires the use of two-dimensional note-taking, which is called "flowing." *A flow sheet is a two-dimensional representation of all the arguments presented in a debate by both teams.* It is similar to a balance statement of a business's financial status in that it provides an overall picture of the status of arguments in a debate.

Debaters use flow sheets to keep track of arguments. Each speech is summarized in a separate column on the flow sheet, and responses to specific arguments are connected horizontally across the page. The flow sheet for the first four speeches in a debate on limiting firearms in the United States is represented in Figure A–1. As you read vertically in each column, you will see how each speech developed and what its contents were. As you read horizontally across the page, you will see what responses each speaker made to the arguments of the preceding speaker. For example, under blame, an issue raised by the first negative speaker, you will see that she argued that people will not comply with gun control because they do not believe in it. The second affirmative speaker responded that most people favor gun control as shown in public opinion polls conducted since 1963. The second negative speaker attempted to contradict this evidence by presenting her own poll that showed overwhelming opposition to gun control. This is an example of horizontal tracking of a particular argument across the flow sheet.

Developing note-taking skills in flow sheet form requires practice. You must listen closely and take rapid, accurate notes. Debaters often develop a system of abbreviations to facilitate this task, such as ↑ for "increase," ↓ for "decrease," # for "number," "hi" for "high," etc. A clear, orderly flow sheet enables a debater to see at a glance the status of important arguments in the debate. The debater can note which arguments were granted, ignored, and dropped in the round so as to remind the judge that his or her own position on them is unchallenged. When there is a response from the other team, the flow sheet enables a speaker to see quickly what the response was and to plan his or her own responses before speaking.

Debate Formats

In political and parliamentary debates, many types of formats are used. *A debate format is a statement of the order in which participants in a debate will speak and the length of speaking time allocated to each speech or question/answer period.* Debate formats are prearranged

APPENDIX A Intercollegiate Debate

RESOLVED: THAT THE FEDERAL GOVERNMENT SHOULD INITIATE AND ENFORCE A PROGRAM THAT WOULD SIGNIFICANTLY LIMIT THE USE OF FIREARMS IN THE UNITED STATES

1st Affirmative, Constructive	1st Negative Constructive	2nd Affirmative, Constructive	2nd Negative Constructive
Firearms injure thousands each year (Ill) —There are 55 mil. handguns in circ. —↑ by 2 mil. per yr. —10,000 people killed per yr. —250,000 people wounded per yr. *Current efforts are ineffective (ill)* —1986 Gun Control Act last legislation enacted —Patchwork quilt of 25,000 state/local laws re. guns —No formal screening process —Of 2,000 people who applied, 187 were felons	—Not quantitatively significant —26,000 people killed in drunk driving accidents —24,000 killed in falls, drowning, fires *Their plan of action does not support the proposition* 1. 21 day waiting period not a "signif" change 2. Proposition calls for fed'l enforcement, not state	—IS significant —since '63, more Ams. killed by handguns than died in WWII —10,000 per year is signif. —77% killed by family member or acquaintance Like 55 mph speed limit which is state enforced	—Auto deaths kill 10X more people —Aff. plan will channel funds away from drunk driving DROPPED
Plan 1. National gun regis. prog. 2. 1 yr. jail term + $500 fine for noncompliance 3. Nonsporting handguns banned 4. Dealer lic. fees ↑ to $500. 5. 21 day waiting period bet. applying & obtaining gun 6. Admin. by Fed'l Bureau of Alcohol and Firearms 7. Enforced by states	—Courts will not enforce stiffer penalties —Jail terms do not deter; prisons overcrowded How much will this cost? How will you provide financing?	 1. ↑ in lic. fee to $500 2. gun regis. fee of $50 3. Fines for non-enforcement by states	

FIGURE A–1 Sample Flow Sheet

1st Affirmative, Constructive	1st Negative Constructive	2nd Affirmative, Constructive	2nd Negative Constructive
			How will checks be run on firearm purchasers during waiting period? How many dealers will be deterred by increase in fee? How many violators will be sent to jail?
	Attitudinal Inherency Many people do not believe in gun control. Many people believe they have a "right to bear arms" Criminals will circumvent plan through smuggling, etc.	2/3 of American public have favored greater controls since '63	Poll showed —337,000 against 7,000 favor
This plan will work (cure) '82 pilot study in DC —guns banned in '77 —in '74 there were 174 killings —in '78 there were 112 killings	—Poor study with flawed methodology —Overall DC crime actually ↑ during this period How can you guarantee this result?	—W. Germany & other countries do show rel'ship bet. guns & gun deaths —crime went up generally during this period	
There are many benefits 1. # of dealers ↓ because dealer fees ↑ # of guns & gun deaths ↓	Increase can easily be made up through lucrative sales —No correlation between # of guns and # of homicides —6 states with strictest laws have highest homicide rates	—These 6 states had "unusually high" homicide rates before gun laws enacted —Gun laws not the causal factor —Present system allowed example of John Hinckley —He had been arrested before —He had psychiatric problems —Yet he bought a gun from a pawn shop and shot the President	—How does your waiting period ensure such people won't get guns? —How can psychiatric disorders be detected in your plan? *Costs* 1. When handguns unavail., people resort to long guns— more deadly 2. Enforcement means violation of civil liberties to locate gun 3. Plan too financially burdensome —overcrowded prisons —enforcement costly
2. ↓ # of felons with guns because of waiting period	—Present system already has waiting period		

FIGURE A–1 *continued*

APPENDIX A   Intercollegiate Debate   **337**

before the debate—either because of agreement by participants or because of conventions or rules governing the practice of debate in a particular forum. For example, the League of Women Voters sets the format for many presidential debates, whereas parliamentary debates are governed by the rules of parliamentary practice.

In intercollegiate debate, certain formats are standard. Generally, each speaker in a debate speaks twice, and the sides (affirmative and negative) alternate in speaking turns. Initial (or "constructive") speeches are longer than refutation (or "rebuttal") speeches. Parliamentary debate is an exception. In a parliamentary debate, each side presents one rebuttal speech. Figure A–2 shows the speeches and times for each form of debate we have discussed this far.

Affirmative speakers begin the debate because they present the initial case for a change that gets the debate under way. Because they have the burden of proof, the affirmative is also allowed to speak last. Although being first and last speaker may seem advantageous for the affirmative, it does have a disadvantage. That is the uninterrupted negative speaking block of thirteen minutes in the middle of the debate. During this

NDT	**CEDA**	**Parliamentary**
First affirmative constructive, 9 minutes	First affirmative constructive, 8 minutes	Prime minister constructive, 7 minutes
Second negative cross-examination of the first affirmative speaker, 3 minutes	Second negative cross-examination of the first affirmative speaker, 3 minutes	
First negative constructive, 10 minutes	First negative constructive, 8 minutes	Leader of opposition, 8 minutes
First affirmative cross-examination of first negative speaker, 3 minutes	First affirmative cross-examination of the first negative speaker, 3 minutes	
Second affirmative constructive, 10 minutes	Second affirmative constructive, 8 minutes	Member of government, 8 minutes
First negative cross-examination of second affirmative speaker, 3 minutes	First negative cross-examination of second affirmative speaker, 3 minutes	
Second negative constructive, 10 minutes	Second negative constructive, 8 minutes	Member of opposition, 8 minutes
Second affirmative cross-examination of second negative speaker, 3 minutes	Second affirmative cross-examination of second negative speaker, 3 minutes	
First negative rebuttal, 5 minutes	First negative rebuttal, 5 minutes	Leader of opposition rebuttal, 4 minutes
First affirmative rebuttal, 6 minutes	First affirmative rebuttal, 5 minutes	Prime minister rebuttal, 5 minutes

FIGURE A–2 Speaking Order and Times for NDT, CEDA, and Parliamentary Debate

time, the second negative constructive speaker ordinarily presents broad arguments against the case such as disadvantages (cost) or objections to the affirmative value. The first negative rebuttalist responds to the second affirmative constructive speaker's attacks on his or her first speech. In any case, the first affirmative rebuttalist obviously has the challenging task of responding to two negative speeches in only 5 minutes. If question/answer periods or cross-examination are used in an educational debate, they are usually interspersed with the earlier speeches in which affirmative and negative cases are initially presented.[2]

An alternative to the traditional two-person team debate format is Lincoln-Douglas–style (LD) debate. LD debate takes its name from the famous senatorial debates between Abraham Lincoln and Stephen Douglas, and instead of involving two people on each side of the proposition, it uses only one person on each side. LD debates typically take the format shown in Figure A–3.

To fit classroom debates into available time, your instructor may use some variation of these formats. Occasionally time is allowed to both teams for between-speech preparation and consultation for rebuttals. Whatever the format for a debate may be, it is necessarily adjusted to the circumstances and conditions under which the debate is presented.

Affirmative constructive	6 minutes
Negative cross-examination of affirmative speaker	3 minutes
Negative constructive	7 minutes
Affirmative cross-examination of negative speaker	3 minutes
Affirmative rebuttal	4 minutes
Negative rebuttal	6 minutes
Affirmative rebuttal	3 minutes

FIGURE A–3 Speaker Order and Time Limits in Lincoln-Douglas–Style Debates

Conclusion

This appendix was designed to provide you with basic information needed to participate in a classroom or intercollegiate debate. As noted earlier, debate provides a challenging and stimulating forum for practicing the argumentation skills discussed in this book. Although novices often find their first debate assignment intimidating and frustrating, they also quickly recognize the fact that debating develops many valuable and essential skills—critical listening, analytical thinking, proficiency in reasoning, research, use of evidence, and, as one author noted, courage![3] Should a debate assignment be a part of your argumentation course, we hope that knowledge of debate stock issues and formats will assist you as you speak in competition with other members of your class and other schools.

NOTES

1. See Austin J. Freeley, *Argumentation and Debate,* 6th ed. (Belmont, Calif.: Wadsworth, 1986), 16–8; Douglas Ehninger and Wayne Brockreide, *Decision by Debate,* 2d ed. (New York: Harper, 1978), 110–6; James Edward Sayer, *Argumentation and Debate: Principles and Applications* (Sherman Oaks, Calif.: Alfred, 1980), 341–2 and 307–17; Carolyn Keefe, Thomas B. Harte, and Laurence E. Norton, *Introduction to Debate* (New York: Macmillan, 1982), 41–59; J. W. Patterson and David Zarefsky, *Contemporary Debate* (Boston: Houghton Mifflin, 1983), 94–7 and 222–6; and Russell T. Church and Charles Wilbanks, *Values and Policies in Controversy* (Scottsdale, Ariz.: Gorsuch Scarisbrick, 1986), 4–6 and 338–44.
2. Space limitations preclude a discussion of cross-examination strategies in this appendix. Should you engage in cross-examination in a debate, you should consult the explanations of question/answer strategies in Freeley, 294–9; Sayer, 345–53; Patterson and Zarefsky, 256–81; and Church and Wilbanks, 217–29.
3. Freeley, 25–6.

APPENDIX B

Answers to Selected Exercises

Chapter 1
Exercise 1

1. This is not an argument because the speaker, Yeltsin, is stating his intentions—that everyone will be punished, will be made answerable, etc. There is no claim stated, nor is there any support offered.

5. This is an argument. The claim is that "Social Security won't live to see another 60 years." Support for the claim comes in the form of the statement of demographic trends that will change as there are progressively fewer workers to support ever-increasing numbers of older people. The predictions made by the author all lead up to his conclusion, which also supports the claim: that the shortfall will be $7 trillion by 2070 if policies are not changed in the meantime.

10. This is clearly an argument. The claim is the "nuclear power is uneconomical and unreliable. . . ." The support comes from the examples of accidents in the past and the Nuclear Regulatory Commission's predictions about a core meltdown.

Chapter 2
Exercise 1

2. This is not an example of the quasilogical style, since no claims are made and no hard evidence is presented. It is not analogical style, either, because that style makes use of narrative. The style here is presentational, the author uses a series of rhetorical questions that keep the reader engaged and thinking about what the answers might be. The passage also lists a series of synonyms that are intended to provoke comparison without reaching a specific conclusion. The effect is not closure, as with an argument, but the passage will still be thought-provoking and might lead the reader to question some assumptions and to rethink his or her perspective on virtuality.

The author's values are hard to identify, since he is raising questions and trying to provoke thought rather than making claims. He does appear to be somewhat skeptical about technology and virtual experience, rather than enthused about them.

5. This passage is in the quasilogical style. Clinton reassures the listener that he has "worked with Congress to craft legislation that replaces welfare with work," and he gives a series of examples of what his administration has done and what the *New York Times* has said about it.

    Clinton here seems to favor the work ethic and to believe that getting people off welfare and putting them to work is a good thing. These values are compatible with the views of political conservatives who think that people should work hard and not "live off the government."

9. This passage is in quasilogical style. The author points to a "revealing pattern" (claim). He says that this pattern is evident in massaging of data, minimalization of death tolls in other genocides, claims that those deaths were wartime casualties or the result of natural causes. This list of actions functions as evidence for the claim.

    This author seems to be committed to the "facts" and to the idea that people exaggerate certain elements of a situation in order to support their own biases. Opposing values might support the view that the Holocaust was unique because of its nature as a preplanned, technically implemented strategy of mass genocide.

Chapter 3

Exercise 1

- What kinds of grounds do medical doctors use . . . ?
  The medical profession in general and doctors specifically ground their arguments in many different ways. These include patient case studies, patient charts, and laboratory experiments. Generally, the medical profession uses evidence that is verifiable and observable and tends to generalize from specific cases or experiments to understand how different diseases or injuries affect people.

- What constitutes acceptable evidence for medical arguments?
  Medical evidence needs to be verifiable. In other words, if one doctor conducts a study and finds evidence of a cure for AIDS, other professionals will attempt to verify those results through replications. Much medical research makes use of "double-blind" studies, in which a large number of people receive a medicine or a placebo and then their subsequent condition is studied. Also, long-term studies of particular populations reveal whether a given treatment has been effective.

- In what spheres do medical doctors operate?
  Doctors operate in all three of the spheres discussed in the text. When medical professionals brainstorm ideas about treatment or discuss in relatively informal settings how their cases have gone, they are arguing in the personal sphere. When

they discuss experimental evidence or debate the merits of various treatments, they are making arguments in the technical sphere. And when they talk with a patient's family members about the costs and benefits of a particular treatment, they adapt their arguments to a public sphere so they can be better understood.

- What are the audience expectations of this field?
  Patients want doctors to be correct. Because much of the medical profession is mysterious and frightening to patients, doctors need to be reassuring and speak from experience and knowledge. Patients, then, want their doctors to know what the appropriate answer is.

- What are some conventions or rules followed by doctors?
  There are many. Typically, doctors advise their patients to get second opinions. They look for strong empirical support for conclusions. They consult with the family members and patient about the proper methods of treatment. And they live by the Hippocratic Oath, which governs the medical profession's ethics.

Chapter 4
Exercise 2

1. Lamkin cites the author Rosabeth Moss Kanter to give credibility to her own claim that women must work to gain organizational power. By focusing on the specific sources and methods of gaining power, Lamkin keeps her audience interested in her topic. She emphasizes a feminist perspective by citing a female authority when addressing an all-female audience.

   Because of her lively content, similarity in attitudes with the audience, and focus on a topic the audience is probably interested in, Lamkin will probably be able to hold audience attention and win acceptance for her ideas.

5. First and foremost, Ms. Crooks stresses her long and intensive experience with the topic. She stresses the American value of consensus-building through open exchange—a value her audience shares.

   One problem with this treatment is that the author's purpose is vague. Her audience may wonder what her point is and lose interest in what she has to say.

Chapter 5
Exercise 1

PO	Four score and seven years ago
RH	our fathers brought forth on this continent a new nation, conceived in liberty, and dedicated to the proposition that all men are created equal.
CO & RH	Now we are engaged in a great civil war, testing whether that nation, or any nation so conceived and so dedicated, can long endure.

PH	We are met on a great battlefield of that war. We have come to dedicate a portion of that field, as a final resting place for those who here gave their lives, that that nation might live. It is altogether fitting and proper that we should do this.
PO & RH	But, in a larger sense, we cannot dedicate—we cannot consecrate—we cannot hallow—this ground. The brave men, living and dead, who struggled here have consecrated it, far above our poor power to add or detract.
ME	The world will little note, nor long remember what we say here
RH	but it can never forget what they did here. It is for us, the living, rather, to be dedicated here to the unfinished work which they who fought here have thus far so nobly advanced.
PO & RH & EM	It is rather for us to be here dedicated to the great task remaining before us—that from these honored dead we take increased devotion to that cause for which they gave the last full measure of devotion—that we here highly resolve that these dead shall not have died in vain—that this nation, under God, shall have a new birth of freedom—and that government of the people, by the people, for the people, shall not perish from the earth.

Lincoln relies most frequently on the poetic and rhetorical language functions. Rather than emphasizing his own feelings through the emotive function or informing his audience through the use of cognitive language, he wishes to eulogize the fallen troops and urge the country to rededicate itself to preservation of the union, freedom, and democracy. Lincoln's poetic and rhetorical uses of language have been widely admired and praised by his contemporaries and successors. The Gettysburg Address is considered a classic of English prose style and rhetorical effectiveness.

Chapter 6

Exercise 1

1. Noncontroversial. This is a factually true statement.
5. Double-barreled. Whether a practice is "desirable" and whether it is "necessary" are two different issues. Here they have been combined in one claim.
14. May or may not challenge the present system. Whether or not this claim is well formulated will depend on the jurisdiction in which it is made. If there are legal limitations on abortion availability—parental consent, or limitation on trimester, for example—the claim would challenge the present system. But if abortion is generally available, it would not challenge the system.

Exercise 2

1. Past fact

Chapter 7
Exercise 1

1. *Expertise:* Is Kause an expert? What are his credentials? Neither his title nor his position is cited.

   Statistical method: No information is given about the size or representativeness of the sample or the method used.

5. *Relevance* and *Accuracy of citation:* Is Kennedy's quotation relevant to the military draft? In what context was it made? The crucial part of this argument—that the country is in a military force crisis—is not supported by any evidence.

   Non sequitur: Kennedy's claim (in his inaugural address) was made in relation to volunteer service. Since he was not calling for mandatory service (which is just the opposite of his point), the claim here is unsupported by the quote cited because the quote is irrelevant to it.

10. *Expertise:* Who is Dr. Harvey Brenner? His credentials are not given.

    Recency: This study was conducted in 1975. It is questionable as to whether it applies to current conditions.

    Relevance: The argument assumes a causal connection between unemployment and death, but the evidence does not state a causal relation, only a correlation.

Chapter 8

1. *Analogy*

   Evidence: A painter paints his painting so that light shines on all parts of the work.

   Claim: The listener should . . . be shown the conclusion contained in the principle.

   Inference: (implied) [The speaker's task is like the painter's.]

   Questions: Is writing a composition or giving a speech like painting a picture in this sense?

   —How is aesthetics like composition?

5. *Analogy*

   Evidence: North America did not remain empty of cities; the continent is not a poorer place now than 20,000 years ago.

   Claim: We have more practical reasons for not burning Amazon forests than to stave off natural catastrophe.

   Inference: (implied) [The forests of the Amazon are like the natural state of the North American continent 20,000 years ago.]

   Questions: Were the original North American forests as essential to environmental preservation as Amazon forests?

   —Have conditions changed in 20,000 years such that destruction of Amazon forests would have more impact now?

11. *Dissociation*

   Evidence: We could act through bitterness and hatred; we could allow our protest to degenerate into violence.

   Claim: We must struggle on the high plane of dignity and discipline; we must meet physical force with soul force.

   Inference: (implied) [Effective response to oppression need not be violent; it can be dignified yet forceful.]

   Questions: Should not oppression, which is a form of violence itself, be responded to by violence?

   —Are not bitterness, hatred, and violence justified in such circumstances?

20. *Generalization*

   Evidence: Asian Americans denied entrance; impossible job market in academia; people seek treatment as disadvantaged minorities; Chicago firm fined; white teacher fired.

   Claim: Affirmative Action for qualified minorities has turned into affirmative discrimination. . . .

   Inference: (implied) [The instances cited are representative of a general pattern of reverse discrimination.]

   Questions: What about the issue of underrepresentation in certain schools and occupations; how is this to be corrected? Are the instances cited atypical instances?

Chapter 9

Exercise 1

Item 3
Third-party candidates cause diversity in the political process.

   I. Definitions
      A. Third parties are parties that field presidential candidates for the presidential election.
      B. Third parties are not Democrats or Republicans.
      C. Diversity means multiple points of view.
      D. Diversity means focus on many issues.
   II. Threshold
      A. At a minimum, the third parties must be beyond the existing two parties.
      B. At a minimum, the issues must be outside the mainstream issues of the two parties.
   III. Application
      A. The Green Party is outside the Republican and Democratic sphere.
      B. The Green Party contributes many unique issues related to environmentalism.

APPENDIX B   Answers to Selected Exercises **347**

Item 5
- I. Definitions
  - A. Definitions of discovery
    1. He must have landed on North American soil.
    2. He must have been the first nonnative to land.
    3. He must have recorded the incident.
  - B. Definitions of America
    1. This refers to the North American continent.
    2. This refers to the mainland only.
- II. Threshold
  - A. The minimal requirement is to have landed somewhere in North America.
  - B. The minimal requirement is to have provided some lasting record of the discovery.
- III. Application
  - A. Leif Ericson landed in what is now Maine in North America.
  - B. Leif Ericson recorded the discovery in his ship's logs.

Chapter 10

Exercise 1

Values affirmed by Brennan: freedom of expression, inclusiveness of all ideas

Values opposed to Brennan's position: loyalty to the country first and foremost, patriotism

Criteria for Evaluation:

- to respect legal principles for treatment of the flag
- to avoid offense to others
- to protect any behavior construed as "communication"
- to preserve the principles on which the nation was founded
- to preserve free expression
- to allow various views to be heard
- to preserve the dignity of the flag

Chapter 11

Exercise 1D

First proposition: I should attend a different school.

Needs Case

- I. My personal situation is such that I should transfer to another college.
  - A. Northeast Exclusive College no longer meets my needs.

1. It does not offer a program in my chosen major.
2. The high tuition is causing me to go into debt.
B. The prospects of getting the education I want here are dim.
1. No curriculum changes in my interest area are planned.
2. The high tuition will force me to drop out of school.
II. Transferring to another college seems the best plan.
A. My parents and I will discuss my options during spring break.
B. Next fall I will probably transfer to State University.
C. This action will allow me to stay in school in my chosen major.
III. A transfer to another college will be beneficial.
A. It will save thousands of dollars in tuition.
B. It will broaden my educational experience.
C. It will allow me to enroll in a major department that is highly ranked nationally.

Comparative Advantages Case

I. Transferring to another college next year is my plan.
A. I will consult my parents about the decision.
B. I will transfer to State University next year.
II. The transfer will be economically beneficial.
A. I will save $4,000 in tuition next year alone.
B. Neither my parents nor I will have to go into debt to finance my last two years of college.
C. $4,000 is a significant proportion of my family's annual income.
D. Only a transfer will avoid indebtedness since I do not qualify for financial aid or scholarships.
III. The transfer will be educationally beneficial.
A. State University offers the major program I've selected.
B. This major is exciting to me and offers excellent career opportunities.
C. Northeast Exclusive College does not offer this major and has no plans to do so.

Goals Case

I. My goal is to obtain a Bachelor's degree in dental hygiene in a quality program at reasonable cost.
II. Northeast Exclusive College does not offer this program and its tuition is very high.
III. Transfer to State University seems advisable.
A. I will discuss this with my parents during spring break.
B. I will transfer into the hygiene program at State University next fall.
IV. In two years, I will receive a degree in a field with good career opportunities.

APPENDIX B   Answers to Selected Exercises

Exercise 3

Needs Case

I. (5)
   A. (2)
   B. (8)
   C. (15)
   D. (17)
II. (19)
   A. (4)
   B. (10)
   C. (13)
III. (6)
   A. (1)
   B. (3)
   C. (11)

Comparative Advantages Case

I. (19)
   A. (4)
   B. (10)
   C. (13)
II. (6)
   A. (3)
   B. (11)
III. (1)
   A. (14)
   B. (16)
   C. (18)
   D. (20)

Goals Case

I. (7)
II. (19)
   A. (4)
   B. (10)
   C. (13)
III. (9)
IV. (12)

Chapter 12

Note: There is often more than one correct way to diagram an argument using either model. Since there may be individual variations in the way various analysts number and connect statements in the general model and supply principles as warrants in the Toulmin model, there are often two or three correct ways to diagram an argument. There are, however, incorrect diagrams. The claim should not be mistaken for data, for example. The following diagrams are therefore suggestive. Further refinements should be made through class discussion and consultation with your instructor.

1. ① It is the chemical firms that release the most troubling types of molecules into the environment. ② In Baton Rouge, according to company data, an Exxon chemical plant was leaking 560,000 pounds of benzene yearly, while just south of there, ③ according to a survey by the Sierra Club, eighteen plants in and around St. Gabriel and Geismar dumped about 400 billion pounds of toxic chemicals into the air during the first nine months of 1986.

General Model:

```
    2           3
     \         /
      \       /
       v     v
          1
```

Toulmin Model:

DATA
– Exxon chemical plant leaked 560,000 pounds
– Eighteen plants dumped 400 billion pounds

CLAIM
It is the chemical firms that release the most troubling molecules.

WARRANT
These examples represent the problem.

Criticism:

The argument seems too ready to indict chemical plants as the main source of the problem. The evidence focuses on only two examples, and one of those is water and the other air pollution. What other sources of pollution (such as nonpoint pollution) might there be? Have the various possible sources been compared as to their impact?

10. ① Ladies make excellent teachers in public schools; many of them are every way the equals of their male competitors, and still they secure less wages than males. ② The reason is obvious. ③ The number of ladies who offer themselves to teach is much larger than the number of males who are willing to teach. . . . ④ The result is that the competition for positions of teachers to be filled by

APPENDIX B Answers to Selected Exercises **351**

ladies is so great as to reduce the price; but ⑤ as males cannot be employed at that price, and ⑥ are necessary in certain places in the schools, ⑦ those seeking their services have to pay a much higher rate for them.

General Model:

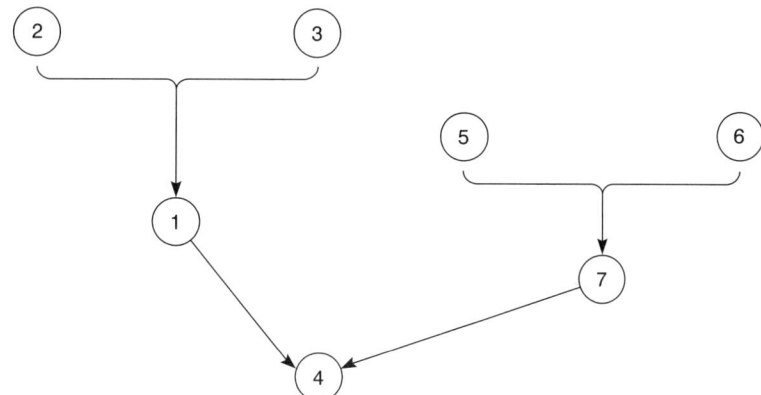

Toulmin Model:

DATA
– Number of ladies larger than number of males.
– Males cannot be employed at that price.
– Males are necessary.

CLAIM
Competition for positions by ladies reduces price.
Males receive higher rate.

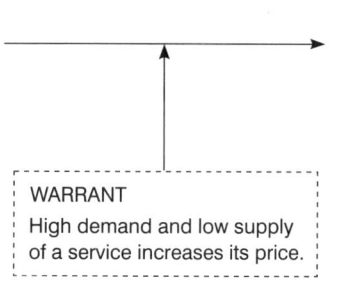

WARRANT
High demand and low supply of a service increases its price.

Criticism:

The argument rests on a "supply/demand" relationship: that a larger supply of a commodity (in this case, female teachers) decreases its value. First, for the argument to hold up, the assumptions made by its author must all be true: Male teachers must be "necessary" in certain places, and there must be a much larger supply of females competing for positions than there are males. Second, other causes (rather than supply/demand) are not considered. For example, females might simply be willing to accept lower pay than males, or the pay differential might be the result of systematic discrimination.

15. Anne: ① Technology has affected every single part of the program.
    Carrie: Yes, technology is a big one.
    Anne: ② I don't really feel technology is just the mechanical aspect. ③ It's chemical, biological, physical, everything. ④ The advances in technology have gone so far that it can prolong life, yeah, but when

you get in the position of an irreversible comatose-type state, it's out of step with what man is. ⑤ You know, should he be prolonged just to vegetate? ⑥ Are they prolonging ill health or are they prolonging life? ⑦ Technology has reached the outer limits where it's gone beyond what man is.

Carrie: ⑧ It's gone beyond the purpose for which medical technology was originally intended. ⑨ Its goal was to enhance human life, whereas now it just prolongs death, dying and pain.

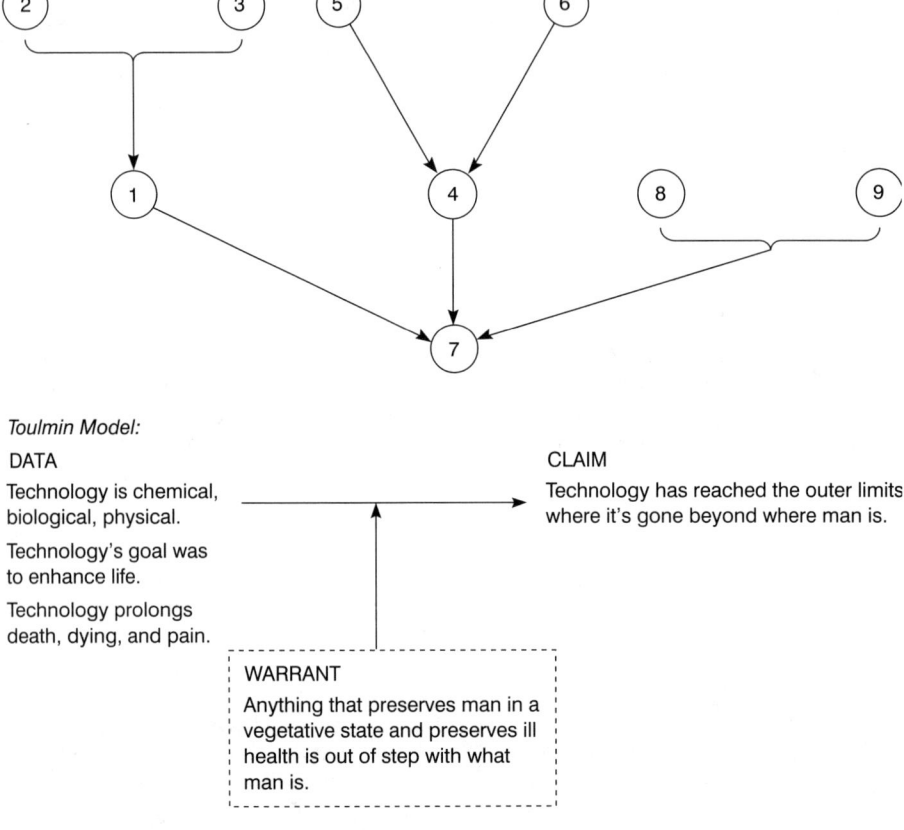

General Model:

Toulmin Model:

DATA
Technology is chemical, biological, physical.
Technology's goal was to enhance life.
Technology prolongs death, dying, and pain.

CLAIM
Technology has reached the outer limits where it's gone beyond where man is.

WARRANT
Anything that preserves man in a vegetative state and preserves ill health is out of step with what man is.

Criticism:

Part of the evidence here is that technology's original goal was to enhance human life. That may or may not be the case, but is technology intended to "enhance life" in the immediate situation, or to enable research and conditions that would enhance life in the long run? Furthermore, the group is applying its own conception of what "life" is (not vegetative, but something to be enhanced and enjoyed). This conception should perhaps be questioned and not merely assumed and accepted.

APPENDIX C

Glossary

abstraction   Refers to the degree to which relevant characteristics are omitted in language.

accessibility   Depends on whether or not someone offering an opinion is or has been in a position to observe firsthand the matter being disputed.

ad hominem   Fallacy that launches an irrelevant attack on the person or source originating an argument instead of responding to substantial issues raised in the argument.

ad populum   Fallacy that occurs when the substance of an argument is avoided and the advocate appeals instead to popular opinion as a justification for the claim.

agent   The person, group, or agency responsible for implementing the policy program.

amphiboly   Exploits ambiguity in grammatical structure to lead to a false or questionable conclusion.

analogical style   Makes its claims by calling to mind stories or fables known in the culture that imply principles and ideas favored by the arguer.

analogy   Reasons that because two objects resemble each other in certain known respects, they will also resemble each other in respects that are unknown.

appeal to tradition   A fallacy that occurs when someone claims that we should continue to do things the way we have always done them simply because we have always done them that way.

application   The illustration that the case examined is sufficient proof to verify the definition and its threshold.

argument   A set of statements in which a claim is made, support is offered for it, and there is an attempt to influence someone in a context of disagreement.

argument chain   Uses a proven argument as evidence for an unproved claim.

argument fields   Sociological contexts for arguments marked by patterns of communication that participants in argumentative disputes can recognize.

argument from authority   Reasons that statements by someone presumed knowledgeable about a particular issue can be taken as evidence sufficient to justify a claim.

argument from coexistence Reasons from something that can be observed (a sign) to a condition or feature that cannot be observed.

argument from example Seeks acceptance for some general rule or principle by offering a concrete, particular case.

argument occasion Refers to the rhetorical situation of the argument.

argument occasions Consist of the specific fields and situations in which arguments arise.

argument style Refers to cultural preferences in the arrangement of arguments and the methods for developing extended arguments.

argumentation The process of making arguments intended to justify beliefs, attitudes, and values so as to influence others.

artifacts Physical evidence that helps to prove an argument. An artifact is simply a physical object that a speaker might use to prove a point.

attitudinal blame Arises from people's beliefs and values rather than from a law or some other structure of the present system.

backing Consists of further facts or reasoning used to support or legitimate the principle contained in the warrant.

balance The requirement that the issues for and against a proposition be included equally in the propositional field.

begging the question A fallacy that assumes as a premise or as evidence for an argument the very claim or point that is in question.

benefits The positive consequences of policy action.

bias An unreasoned distortion of judgment or a prejudice on a topic.

blame The attribution of an ill to causes within the present policy system.

burden of proof Obligates arguers to provide good and sufficient reasons for changing what is already accepted.

burden of rejoinder The requirement that those who oppose a proposal respond reasonably to the issues presented by the original advocate.

case An extended argument supporting or opposing a proposition.

categorical syllogism Draws a necessary conclusion from two premises stated as simple propositions.

cause Arguments that claim that one condition or event contributes to or brings about another condition or event.

chain argument Also called Type III arguments, are arguments in which one or more subsidiary claims support the primary claim.

challenge Means that an arguer's claim confronts recipients' existing values, beliefs, or behaviors.

claim An expressed opinion or a conclusion that the arguer wants accepted.

claim of historical fact Rests on the strength of probable evidence to which we have access.

clarity Refers to how well a claim focuses arguments on a particular set of issues.

cognitive function Function of language used to inform.

comparative advantages A type of case that develops the position that in comparison with the current system, the proposed system has more benefits.

complex argument Has two or more premises supporting a single claim.

compliance The use of rewards and punishments by a powerful source to get recipients to believe or act in a certain manner.

compound argument Uses one or more premises to support more than one conclusion.

connotative meaning The subjective meanings a given individual holds of symbols used in a particular situation.

controversiality States a position that is not currently accepted or adhered to by the audience.

correlation Claims that two events or phenomena vary together; an increase or decrease in one is accompanied by an increase or decrease in the other.

cost The problems or disadvantages associated with taking a policy action.

counterproposal An alternative plan of action presented by the policy opponent that is different from both the present policy and the plan proposed by the opponents.

critical thinking An investigation whose purpose is to explore a situation, phenomenon, question, or problem to arrive at a hypothesis or conclusion about it that integrates all available information and that therefore can be convincingly justified.

culture System of shared meanings that are expressed through different symbolic forms such as rituals, stories, symbols, and myths that hold a group of people together.

cure Demonstrates that some course of action can work to solve the ill.

data Function as the grounds for the claim.

defense of the present policy system A refutational strategy that rests on a comparison of the proposal and the present system and argues that the present system is superior.

definition Stock issue can consist of statements of historic fact, causal relationships, and predictive facts.

denotative meaning The objective meaning held by language users in general.

derived credibility Results from what is said in the message—the quality of the claims and evidence used and the ways arguers employ their own expertise to get their claims.

direct refutation An approach used by policy opponents that is designed to argue and disprove at least one of the stock issues in the proposal.

disjunctive syllogism Sets forth two alternatives in the major premise: deny one of them in the minor premise, and affirm the other in the conclusion.

dissociation argument Disengages one idea from another and seeks a new evaluation of both ideas.

double-barreled Claims that advance two or more claims simultaneously and, as with ambiguous terms, often lead arguers in separate directions because the relevant issues for each part of the claim are different.

effects The argument presented about the relative effectiveness of a plan.

emotive function Function is used to express and convey the feelings, attitudes, and emotions of the speaker.

emotive language Manipulates the connotative meaning of words to establish a claim without proof.

enthymeme A rhetorical syllogism that calls on the audience's existing beliefs for one or both of its premises.

equivocation Exploits the fact that a word has more than one meaning so as to lead to a false conclusion.

ethics The study of what is morally right or just.

euphemism A linguistic device for replacing words and phrases that carry a negative connotation with words and phrases that carry a positive connotation.

evidence Consists of facts or conditions that are objectively observable, beliefs or statements generally accepted as true by the recipients, or conclusions previously established.

exigence Can be defined as "an imperfection marked by urgency; it is a defect, an obstacle, something waiting to be done, a thing that is other than it should be."

expertise The possession of a background of knowledge and information relevant to the subject matter under discussion.

external consistency The agreement of evidence with sources of information other than the source being used.

factual claims Make inferences about past, present, or future conditions or relationships.

fallacy An argument that is flawed by irrelevant or inadequate evidence, erroneous reasoning, or improper expression.

false analogy Compares two things that are not alike in significant respects or have critical points of difference.

field-dependent standards The rules, norms, and prescriptions guiding the production of arguments in a particular field.

field-invariant standards Apply generally, regardless of the field of argument.

figurative analogy A comparison between two objects of different classes in which a relation or quality within one is said to be similar to a relation or quality within the other.

generalization Where one reasons that what is true of certain members of a class will also be true of other members of the same class or of the class as a whole.

goals argument Presents a significant goal and the case revolves around a comparison of systems attempting to achieve the goal.

hasty generalization Draws a conclusion about a class based on too few or atypical examples.

identification The influence that occurs because people find a source attractive and wish to enhance their own self-concepts by establishing a relationship with the source.

ill The current wrong or harm an advocate is trying to resolve in a policy argument.

inference   States the step one has made in linking the evidence to the claim.

initial credibility   Based on an arguer's credentials, status, and reputation as known to recipients before they hear or read the message.

instrumental values   Concern modes of conduct or the means for fulfilling other values.

internal consistency   The absence of self-contradiction within information provided by a source.

internalization   A process in which people accept an argument by thinking about it and by integrating it into their cognitive systems.

issues   Points of potential disagreement.

issues brief   A synthesis of opposing views on the stock issues of a controversial topic.

language   The systematic coordination of grammar and vocabulary used to convey meaning.

level of dispute   Level or imaginary line that separates what is accepted by the audience from what is not accepted.

literal analogy   Compares two objects of the same class that share many characteristics and concludes that a known characteristic that one possesses is shared by the other.

mandate   The specific action the agent will undertake in a policy case.

metalingual function   Comments on language use itself rather than on objects or ideas in the world.

minor repairs   The defense of present policies with this strategy offers small changes to existing policies to improve their effectiveness and efficiency in meeting the needs.

necessary condition   Must be present for the effect to occur.

needs-analysis case   A policy case format that claims the ill existing in the current system cannot be corrected within the present system but can be cured by the advocate's policy proposal.

non sequitur   Fallacy that contains a claim that is irrelevant to or unsupported by the evidence or premises purportedly supporting it.

objectivity   Refers to a source's tendency to hold a fair and undistorted view on a question or an issue.

person/act argument   Reasons from a person's actions to his or her character or essence.

phatic function   Used socially to reinforce the relationship among parties to a communicative exchange.

plan of action   The specific program advocated by an arguer in support of a policy proposition.

poetic function   Emphasizes the structure and artistry of expression in a message.

policy claims   Call for a specific course of action and focus on whether a change in policy or behavior should take place.

post hoc **fallacy**   Mistakes temporal succession for causal sequence.

predictive claim   Based on the assumption that past relationships and conditions will be repeated in the future.

presentational style   Takes its model from poetry, sweeps the recipient along through a rhythmic flow of words and sounds, parallel clauses, and visual metaphors and moves the audience through aesthetic appeal.

presumption   The predisposition to favor an existing practice or belief until some good reason for changing it is offered. The belief that current thinking, attitudes, values, and actions will continue in the absence of good arguments for their change.

***prima facie* case**   "On its face" presents good and sufficient arguments for adopting the viewpoint or action proposed by an advocate.

primary source   The original source of the evidence.

propositional arena   The ground for dispute and includes all the issues for controversy within a given proposition.

propositions   Overarching or main claims, which serve as the principal claim of an extended argument.

qualifier   A colloquial adverb or adverbial phrase that modifies the claim and indicates the rational strength the arguer attributes to it.

qualitative significance   Related to the intensity of the effect; we assess something as significant to the extent that it strengthens or diminishes life.

quantitative significance   Related to the scope of the effects claims; how many people will be affected and how frequently?

quasilogical arguments   Place two or three elements in relation to one another so as to make the connections between them similar to the connections for informal logic.

quasilogical style   Takes its model from formal logic, relates claims to each other deductively, and makes use of "logical connectives" such as "thus," "hence," and "therefore."

reasoning   Constructs a rational link between the evidence and the claim and authorizes the step we make when we draw a conclusion.

relational claim   Attempts to establish a causal relation between one condition or event and another.

reliability   Has been proven to be correct many times in the past.

reluctant testimony   Testimony made by sources who speak against their own vested interest.

representative sample   Possesses all the characteristics of the larger group from which it is drawn.

reservation   States the circumstances or conditions that undermine the argument.

rhetorical function   Aims to direct or influence thoughts and behaviors.

rhetorical situation   A natural context of persons, events, objects, relations, and an exigence that strongly invites arguments.

sample   A population or group of people or objects that researchers survey when a study is conducted.

secondary source   Compiles, analyzes, or summarizes primary sources.

simple argument   Consists of one premise and a claim that follows from it.

single-cause fallacy   Occurs when an advocate attributes only one cause to a complex problem.

slippery slope fallacy   Assumes, without evidence, that a given event is the first in a series of steps that will lead inevitably to some outcome.

source credibility   Refers to an arguer's ability to be believed and trusted by recipients.

statistics   Facts and figures that have been systematically collected and ordered so as to convey information.

stock issues   Depend on the type of proposition and are the issues recipients expect to see addressed in order for the arguer to meet the burden of proof. Questions that must be asked and answered to construct a satisfactory case on a proposition.

strategies   Means used to adapt arguments and make them appealing to audiences.

straw arguments   Fallacy that attacks a weakened form of an opponent's argument or an argument the opponent did not advance.

structural blame   The result of a defect that is an integral part of the nature of the current policy system.

structures   The fixed elements or features of a policy system.

sufficient condition   A circumstance in whose presence the event or effect must occur.

syllogism   Made up of three statements, includes two or three terms associated with each other throughout the statements, and draws a conclusion from a major and a minor premise.

systems perspective   Recognizes that the world is a complex and interconnected set of relationships between and among component parts that compose a whole and that one change in any part of the system changes the other elements of the system.

terministic screen   A linguistic filter through which human beings perceive their world.

threshold   Issue establishes the acceptable limits of definitions.

trustworthiness   Depends on whether people believe the arguer is motivated to tell them the truth.

value claims   Assess the worth or merit of an idea, object, or practice according to standards or criteria supplied by the arguer.

value emphasis   Values move upward in a value hierarchy.

value hierarchy   Places one value or values above another value or values.

value object   An idea, practice, event, policy, or state of affairs that is to be judged by means of an evaluation.

value redistribution   A process in which a value becomes more and more widely diffused throughout a society until virtually all its members adhere to it.

value restandardization A process in which standards used to measure whether a value is being met increase or decrease.

value system An enduring organization of beliefs concerning preferable modes of conduct or end states of existence along a continuum of relative importance.

values Fundamental positive or negative attitudes toward certain end states of existence or broad modes of conduct.

warrant Expresses the reasoning used to link the data to the claim.

APPENDIX D

Fallacies

In Chapters 6, 7, and 8 we discussed in depth the various tests of claims, evidence, and reasoning. At that time, we also introduced the fallacies associated with evidence and reasoning. As a general rule, if an argument's evidence or reasoning is somehow flawed because it fails one of these tests, the argument is most likely fallacious. Because each of the primary fallacies has been discussed in different sections of the book, this appendix will not try to repeat them here. Rather, the purpose of this appendix is to provide in a single place a typology of fallacies that might be useful in analyzing and criticizing arguments. We will emphasize again, however, that flawed evidence or reasons usually lead to a flawed argument. If a study cited in support of a claim is based on an unrepresentative or inadequate sample or weak methodology, its conclusions should be doubted and careful analysis may reveal one or more fallacies. If a source citation is inaccurate, secondhand, or taken out of context, it should be questioned. Arguments are only as good as the evidence and reasons on which they are based, and as recipients and critics of arguments, we should always examine evidence and reasoning carefully.

The fallacies in this appendix are divided into four groups: fallacies of faulty reasoning; fallacies of grounding that stem from a lack of evidence or poor use of evidence; fallacies related to audience that focus the audience's attention away from relevant issues; and fallacies of language use that occur when words and grammar are used by an arguer to mislead or confuse the recipients. Before examining each of these types, however, it is important to pause briefly to discuss the nature of fallacies and consider how they function in argument.

The Nature of Fallacies

Fallacies are the dark side of arguments. Too often they are unrecognized and receive little attention either by argument critics or by audiences. This appendix is devoted to a discussion of fallacies because they are both deceptive and persuasive. In fact, they are sometimes so persuasive that what an audience does not know can hurt it, or at least affect it in adverse ways.

The ability to recognize faulty arguments and to understand why they are faulty is a difficult skill to develop, yet it is an important skill. Faulty arguments are often hard to recognize because they are both appealing and deceptive. Faulty arguments are particularly important objects of study because they attempt to persuade an audience to alter ideas, values, beliefs, attitudes, or actions on the basis of misleading premises or faulty reasoning. Precisely because the purpose of argument is to persuade audiences to accept sound, well-supported claims, we should avoid practices that lead them to base decisions on erroneous inferences and assumptions.

While fallacies represent a misuse of argument, someone who commits a fallacy is not necessarily evil or ethically corrupt. Arguers may commit fallacies unintentionally as well as intentionally. Unintentional fallacies occur when an arguer is unaware of proper argument construction or use and commits a fallacy without realizing it. In this sense, fallacies are not only deceptive to audiences, but to speakers and writers as well.

Some arguers, however, may intentionally commit a fallacy so as to persuade a listener rather than search out appropriate support for argument positions. Intentional fallacies represent a deliberate attempt to mislead an audience into taking some action based on false information. For example, an arguer might use a biased source, omit part of a quotation thereby misrepresenting what a source said, or attribute a statement to an opponent that was never made. Such intentional fallacies carry important ethical implications as discussed in Chapter 2.

Consider the argument that develops in the following paragraphs. It illustrates how fallacies find their way into arguments and how we can justify contradictory premises.

Lawrence West's career has focused on developing nuclear weapons at the Lawrence Livermore National Laboratory. When he began, he expressed reservations about working on weapons of mass destruction and his role in their manufacture. Over time, however, he was able to dismiss his concerns and argued:

> Nowadays I would be quite willing to go and do full-time weapons work because I see the vast possibilities. . . . A tremendous amount of creativity is needed, and there are very few scientists willing to do it. Nuclear weapons can devastate the world. I recognize that. But we are making anti-weapons. My primary interest is not trying to find better ways to kill people, but better ways to kill arms. . . . I don't think I fall in that category of working on weapons of death. We're working on weapons of life, ones that will save people from the weapons of death.[1]

West's argument that building weapons of mass destruction saves lives is interesting because it juxtaposes two seemingly irreconcilable premises. On the one hand, a recipient is faced with the premise that nuclear weapons can destroy the world, and on the other hand, with West's conclusion that such weapons made by the United States are not weapons of death but are instead weapons of salvation. The argument is almost Orwellian in the sense that "War is peace" and "Weapons of mass destruction save lives."

This is an example of a flawed argument because the arguer uses the way it is expressed to convince the audience to simultaneously hold two mutually exclusive beliefs. While its surface meaning may seem apparent, closer examination of the argument reveals a flaw in the argument. The way it is expressed may seem reasonable, but its development is not.

West's argument reasons from disassociation as discussed in Chapter 8. It places opposite terms together in an attempt to justify building nuclear weapons. For example, West says that bad weapons are weapons of death, which can result in world destruction. However, the weapons he helps build are weapons of life, weapon-killers, antiweapons, which preserve world peace. The problem with the argument is that it assumes the positive attributes through assertion without any justification for or evidence supporting his claims. Instead, West uses strong and emotion-laden language to focus attention away from his lack of evidence and support. The resulting argument is fallacious.

Theorists who study argument agree almost unanimously that fallacies are deceptive and consequently dangerous.[2] Even Aristotle observed that honest speakers needed to prepare for spurious arguments and arguments that look genuine but are no more than shams.[3] All recipients of argument, therefore, need to develop a critical capacity to understand and assess the arguments directed at them.

The development of the capacity to recognize and diagnose the errors in fallacies depends on skills this appendix is intended to help you develop. These fallacies have already been addressed in the body of the book; however, we wanted to put them all together in an appendix to help illustrate their interrelationships and function. In order to recognize errors in inferences, you need to recognize what type of argument is being used and what tests of evidence or reasoning should be applied to it. To decide whether a premise adequately supports a claim you must determine whether the premise is relevant to the claim and at the same time independent of it. If an argument's language seems misleading, you need to identify the way in which its author is manipulating word meanings so as to deceive the audience. If an argument's central issue is evaded by the use of emotional appeals, you must be able to identify what the central issue is and how it is being avoided.

While many theorists have identified countless types and variations of fallacies, our focus here is to help make you aware of how fallacies can infiltrate arguments and unsuspecting audiences and deceive them. The treatment of specific fallacies in this appendix will make you sensitive to the factors that make fallacies dangerous and enable you to identify and accurately criticize the fallacies you encounter. A final word of caution, however. Just because an argument is fallacious does not necessarily mean that the claim is incorrect. The claim may, in fact, be reasonable and valid, but not for the reasons and evidence expressed in the argument.

Types of Fallacies

Fallacies of Faulty Reasoning

Fallacies of faulty reasoning occur when arguers make errors in their inferences. Four types of faulty reasoning were discussed in Chapter 8: false analogy, hasty generalization, false cause, and slippery slope.

False Analogy
A false analogy compares two things that are not alike in significant respects or have critical points of difference.

Hasty Generalization
A hasty generalization draws a conclusion about a class based on too few or atypical examples.

False Cause
False-cause fallacies occur when the arguer offers a cause for a consequence that is not directly related to the consequence. Chapter 8 offered two examples of false causes: *post hoc* and single cause.

Post Hoc Ergo Propter Hoc
Post hoc ergo propter hoc fallacies mistake temporal succession for causal sequence.

Single Cause
Single-cause fallacies occur when an advocate attributes only one cause to a complex problem.

Slippery Slope
The slippery slope fallacy assumes, without evidence, that a given event is the first in a series of steps that will lead inevitably to some outcome.

Fallacies of Grounding

Fallacies of grounding are the result of arguments that either use poor evidence or no evidence whatsoever. Instead, poorly grounded arguments tend to confuse reasoning or claims with evidence. Chapter 7 examined two such fallacies: begging the question and *non sequitur*.

Begging the Question
The fallacy of begging the question assumes as a premise or as evidence for an argument the very claim or point that is in question.

Non Sequitur
The *non sequitur* fallacy contains a claim that is irrelevant to or unsupported by the evidence or premises purportedly supporting it.

Fallacies Related to the Audience

Fallacies related to the audience occur when arguers present arguments to direct a recipient's attention away from the central argument toward some other irrelevant argument. We discussed four types of audience-related fallacies: *ad hominem, ad populum*, appeal to tradition, and straw arguments.

Ad Hominem
Ad hominem fallacies launch an irrelevant attack on the person or source originating an argument instead of responding to substantial issues raised in the argument.

Ad Populum
Ad populum fallacies occur when the substance of an argument is avoided and the advocate appeals instead to popular opinion as a justification for the claim.

Appeal to Tradition
Appeal to tradition fallacies occur when someone claims that we should continue to do things the way we have always done them simply because we have always done them that way.

Straw Arguments
The straw argument fallacy attacks a weakened form of an opponent's argument or an argument the opponent did not advance.

Fallacies of Language Use

Language is the medium in which arguments are communicated, and it has an inevitable impact on the way in which they are perceived and interpreted. In Chapter 5 we discussed the influence language has on argument and explored three different fallacies related to language: equivocation, amphiboly, and emotive language.

Equivocation
The fallacy of equivocation exploits the fact that a word has more than one meaning so as to lead to a false conclusion.

Amphiboly
The fallacy of amphiboly exploits ambiguity in grammatical structure to lead to a false or questionable conclusion.

Emotive Language
The fallacy of emotive language manipulates the connotative meaning of words to establish a claim without proof.

NOTES

1. *New York Times* (January 31, 1984): C5.
2. Irving Copi, *Informal Logic* (New York: Macmillan, 1986): 69–97.
3. Copi, 114.

INDEX

Abstraction, in language use, 98–100
Access, as criterion for evidence, 157
Ad hominem, fallacy of, 83–84
Ad populum, fallacy of, 84–85
Ad verecundium, fallacy of, 162
Agent, in plans on policy propositions, 274
Amphiboly, fallacy of, 114–115
Analogical style of argument, 35–36
Analogy
    false, 205–207
    as form of reasoning, 192–194
    tests for, 193
Appeal to tradition, fallacy of, 85–86
Application, stock issue of, 230–232, 255
Arguer, intentions, 82–83, 113, *See also* Source credibility
Argument
    analysis of, 296–310
    audience adaptation and, 16–17
    cases, 20
    chains, 19, 150, 317–318, 304–305
    definition of, 8
    ethical context, 37–41
    fields, 52–56
    functions, 10–11
    model, 14–20
    occasion, 48–49, 56
    spheres, 49–52
    strength of, 73
    style of, 33
    type of interaction, 8–11. *See also* Criticism, of arguments; Fields
Argumentation
    and critical thinking, 5–7

definition of, 5
perspectives, 11–14
Aristotle, 75–76, 258
Artifacts
    definition of, 152
    as evidence, 152
Attention gaining, strategies for, 79–82
Attitudes, of audience, 74–75
Attitudinal blame, in policy analysis, 273, 283–284
Attractiveness of sources, and persuasiveness, 77–78
Audience
    analysis of, 73–75
    attitudes of, 16–17, 186, 228
    evidence and, 81, 149
    indifference to argument, 73, 78
    level of dispute and, 16–20
    misdirecting attention, 82–83
Authority
    as form of reasoning, 202–204
    tests of, 203

Backing, in Toulmin model, 312, 316–317
Balance, as criterion for proposition, 135–136
Beardsley, Monroe C., 297–298
Begging the question, fallacy of, 162
Beliefs, 247. *See also* Value
Benefits, in policy argument, 274–275
Biographical dictionaries, 169, 170, 172
Bitzer, Lloyd F., on the rhetorical situation, 56

Blame
    definition of, 272
    stock issue of, 272–273
Book reviews, 169
Books, as evidence, 169
Brockriede, Wayne, on ethics, 39–40
Burden of proof, 136–137, 226–228
Burden of rejoinder, 232
Burke, Kenneth, on language and terministic screens, 103–104

Cacioppo, John T., on expertise, 79
Case
    definition of, 223
    prima facie, 228, 276–278. *See also* Policy argument, Value hierarchy
Case level refutation, 7–8, 223–228, 232
Categorical syllogism, 187, 189
Causal argument
    false, 208–209
    as a form of reasoning, 198–201
    and relational and predictive claims, 138
    in slippery slope fallacy, 209–210
    tests of, 199–200
CD-ROM sources, 168–171
Chain argument, 304–307, 317–318
Challenge, as criterion for proposition, 136–137
Claim
    in analogy, 192–193
    in argument chains, 17–20, 149–150, 304–307
    as argument part, 17–20, 298–299, 308, 317
    characteristics of, 126–131

367

Claim, *continued*
  definition of, 8
  double-barreled, 134–135
  and evidence, 156
  explicit vs. implicit, 71
  implicit, 308, 317
  networks of, 129–130
  placement in argument, 128–129
  and proposition, 126–131
  relation of fact, value, and policy, 224–226
  in Toulmin model, 311
  types of, 137–140
Clarity
  as criterion for proposition, 132–135
  in language use, 109–115
Clark, Ruth Ann, 72
Coexistential argument, as form of reasoning, 201–204
Cognitive language, function of, 106
Cognitive processing
  and persuasion, 77–79
  versus noncognitive factors, 77
Comparative advantage case, 280–283
Compendiums, 172
Complex (Type II) argument, 302–304
Compliance, 77
Compound (Type IV) argument, 303, 305–306
Conclusion, *See* Claim
Conclusion indicators, 298–299
Concrete language, 98–100, 109–110
Connotative meaning, 100–102
Consistency, and credibility, 82, 155–156
Contradictions, as means of refutation, 233
Controversiality, as criterion for proposition, 131–132
Copi, Irving, 298
Correlation, 200–201
Cost, in policy argument, 274
Cost/Benefits, stock issue of, 274–275
Counteradvocacy, 233
Counterproposal, strategy of, 287–288
Credibility. *See* Source Credibility
Criteria
  definition of, 254
  stock issue of, 254
Critical thinking, 5–7, 82, 184–185, 222, 235, 256
Criticism, of arguments, 301–302, 309–310

Cross examination, 329, 337
Cross Examination Debate Association, 328–329
Culture
  characteristics of, 29–31
  definition of, 29
  and style of argument, 33–36
  subcultures in, 29–33
Cure, as stock issue, 273–274

Damer, Edward, on fallacies, 86
Data, in Toulmin model, 311, 316–317
Debate
  educational, 328–330
  formats for, 334–338
  propositions in, 330–331
Defense of the present policy, strategy of, 285–286
Defense of the present policy with minor repairs, strategy of, 286–287
Definition, stock issue of, 229
Definition of terms
  for clarity, 110–111
  for criticism, 299–300, 307–308
  in value debate, 252–253
Demographics of audiences, 75
Denotative meaning, 100–101
Derived credibility, 76
Descriptions, as evidence, 151
Diagrams
  of argument, 301–310
  of argument model, 14–20
  of argument structure, 301–303
Dialectical perspective, 11–13
Direct refutation, strategy of, 232, 278
Disjunctive syllogism, 187, 190
Dissociation, as form of reasoning, 203–205
Double-barreled claims, 134–135. *See also* Begging the Question fallacy

Effects of plans in policy proposals, 274
Ehninger, Douglas, on evidence consistency, 155
Emotive language
  fallacy of, 115–116
  function of, 105
Encyclopedias, as source for evidence, 168, 172
Equivocation, fallacy of, 114
ERIC, 165

Ethics
  and accuracy of citation, 158
  content and relational levels, 38–41
  definition of, 37
  and misdirection, 82–83
  and organization of arguments, 72
Ethos, 75
Euphemism, definition of, 102
Evidence
  accuracy of citation, 157–159
  as argument part, 9–10, 14–20
  characteristics of, 149–150
  consistency, 155
  credibility of, 80–82
  definition of, 9–10
  ethical requirements for, 159
  evaluating statistics, 159–161
  evaluation of, 153–161
  expertise, 154
  external consistency, 155
  fact, 150–151
  fallacies of faulty, 161–163
  internal consistency, 155–156
  and level of dispute, 18, 149–150
  locating, 163–173
  objectivity, 154
  opinion, 150–151
  primary source, 158
  recency, 156
  relevance, 156–157, 159
  reliability, 153–154
  secondary source, 158–159
  tests of, 153–161
  types of, 150–153
Examples
  in argument from generalization, 194–197
  as form of reasoning, 196
Exigence, 56
Expanded Academic Index, 165, 169
Expertise
  in argument from authority, 202
  as criterion for evidence, 154
  and source credibility, 75–76
  strategies for enhancing, 77–79
Extended arguments, 129
Extraneous material, in argument diagrams, 300

Fact, claims of, 137–139, 224–226
Fact books, 170, 172
Fallacy
  definition of, 82
  ethics of, 82–83

INDEX

False cause, fallacy of, 208–209
Farrell, Thomas B., 49–52
Field dependence, 55–56
Field invariance, 55–56
Fields
  characteristics of, 52–55
  definition of, 52
  and evaluating arguments, 55
  stock issue of, 253
Figurative analogy, 193–194
Flow sheet, in debate, 334–336
Formal logic, 185–188
Formats, for debate, 334–338

General model
  for argument analysis, 297–310
  Toulmin model, compared to, 318–319
General reference works, as evidence, 172–173
Generalization
  in debate, 333
  as form of reasoning, 194–196
  tests of, 196–197
Goals argument
  definition of, 283
  format for, 284–285
  identification of, 284
Goodnight, G. Thomas, 49–52
Government documents, as evidence, 171–172

Harm. *See* Ill.
Hass, R. Glen, on expertise, 76
Hastings, Arthur, on evidence, 148
Hasty generalization, fallacy of, 207–208
Hayakawa, S. I., on abstraction, 99
Hierarchies, stock issue of, 255–256
Historical claims, 138–139, 224

Identification, and source credibility, 77
Ill
  in counterproposal strategy, 287
  issue in policy refutation, 276–280
  in policy cases, 282–283
  stock issue of, 270–272
Incompatibilities, as form of reasoning, 189–190
Index to U. S. Government Periodicals, 171
Inference
  analogical, 192–194

in argument from authority, 202–203
in causal argument, 198–201
and claims of fact, 137–138
definition of, 10, 184–185, 188–205
in generalization, 194–197
in sign argument, 201–202
as statement of reasoning, 184–185
Information: novel and persuasiveness, 70–71
Initial credibility, 76
Inoculation effect, 71–73
Instrumental values, 247
Internalization, and source credibility, 78–79
Internet, 165
Interviews
  and audience analysis, 77–78
  as evidence, 172
Issues
  definition of, 126, 228
  relation to proposition, 223
  stock in fact arguments, 229–231
  stock in policy arguments, 269–275
  stock in value arguments, 252–256
Issues brief, definition, 235

Johannesen, Richard L., on ethics, 38
Johnstone, Barbara, on argument styles, 33–37
Jurisdiction, as argument in debate, 332–333

Language
  ambiguity in, 97, 109–114
  connotative, 100–102
  definition of, 95
  denotative, 100–101
  fallacies of, 113–116
  functions of, 105–109
  influence on perception, 103–105
  presence in, 111
  racist, 112–113
  sexist, 112
Legal Resource Index, 165
Level of dispute
  and argument chains, 304
  and claims, 129
  definition of, 16–17
  in fallacy of begging the question, 162
  and the proposition, 20
  role in argumentation, 16–19

Literal analogy, 192–193
Logic, formal, 185–188
Logical perspective, 12–13, 186
Logos, 75

Macro arguments, 20
Magazines, as source of evidence, 169–170
Makau, Josina, 234
Mandate, in policy plans, 274
Meaning, in language, 96–97
Metalingual, language function, 107
Metaphor, and figurative analogy, 193
Minnick, Wayne, 38
Minor repairs, strategy of, 286–287
Misunderstanding, of language 96–97
Model of argument, 14–20. *See also* Diagrams, General Model
Multilogic, 7

National Debate Tournament, 328–329
National Newspaper Index, 165, 171
Necessary condition, reasoning from, 199
Need. *See* Ill.
Needs analysis case, 275–276
Newman, Dale R.
  on accessibility of evidence, 157
  on reliability, 153
  on using statistics, 159–160
Newman, Robert P.
  on accessibility of evidence, 157
  on reliability, 153
  on using statistics, 159–160
Newspapers, as sources for evidence, 170–171
Non sequitur, fallacy of, 163–163
Nosich, Gerald M., 5–6

Objections, responding to, 72–73
Objectivity
  as criterion for evidence, 154–155
  and language use, 100–102
Occasion, argument, 56
Ogden, C. K.: *The Meaning of Meaning,* 97
Olbrechts-Tyteca, L.
  on inference making, 186–188
  on value hierarchies, 250–251
One-sided analysis, 71–72
Online, vs. hard copy sources, 165–168
Opinion
  as argument from authority, 202
  as evidence, 150–151

Order effects, 71–72
Organization of arguments, 71–73
Orwell, George, on language use, 104, 109

Parameter, 331
Pathos, 75
Paul, Richard W., 5–6, 256
Perelman, Chaim
  on inference making, 186–188
  on value hierarchies, 250–251
Periodicals, as source of evidence, 166, 169–170
Person/act argument, 202
Personal sphere of argument, 50
Persuasion, and language use, 100–102, 106–107
Persuasiveness
  and argumentation strategies, 67–73
  and credibility of sources, 75–79
  and organization of arguments, 71–73
Petty, Richard E., on expertise, 79
Phatic language, function of, 106
Plan of action, in policy arguments, 273
Poetic language, function of, 108
Policy argument
  comparative advantage format, 280–283
  future orientation, 266–267
  goals format, 283–285
  needs format, 275–276
  probability and, 267
Policy claims, 140
Post hoc ergo propter hoc, fallacy of, 208
Predictive claims, 138
Premise, major vs. minor, 187
Premise indicators, 298–299
Premises
  relation to claim, 303–306
  as starting points for argument, 149, 298
Presence, language use in argument, 111
Presentation of message, and source credibility, 79–80
Presentational style of argument, 35
Presumption
  and appeal to tradition, 85–86
  and burden of proof, 136–137, 226–228
  definition of, 136–137
Primacy-recency effect, 73

Proposition
  arena of, 223
  boundary, 127
  and claim, 126
  definition of, 126
  emergence, 128–129
  in extended arguments, 8
  and field of argument, 129
  formulating, 131–137
  issue relevance, 127
Public opinion, 84–85
Public sphere of argument, 50–51

Qualifier, in Toulmin model, 312
Qualitative significance, 271
Quasilogical, as form of reasoning, 189–191
Quasi-logical style of argument, 33–35

Racist language, 112–113
Reasoning
  as inference making, 188–204
  in argument model, 18
  definition of, 10
Recency, as criterion for evidence, 156
Recipients. *See also* Audience
  and emotive language, 115–116
  as evaluators of evidence, 67–70
  predisposition of, 255
Reciprocity, as form of reasoning, 190–191
Refutation
  definition of, 232
  direct, 232–234
  exploratory, 233
  specific, 232
  tests of evidence, 234
Relational claims, 138
Reliability, as criterion for evidence evaluation, 153
Reluctant testimony, 82
Reports, as evidence, 151
Rescher, Nicholas, on values, 249–250
Research, conducting, 163–173
Reservation, in Toulmin model, 312–313
Rhetorical language, function of, 107
Rhetorical perspective, 13–14, 186
Rhetorical situation, definition of, 56
Richards, I. A., *The Meaning of Meaning,* 97
Risk analysis, 225
Rokeach, Milton, on values, 247–248, 250

Sample, representative vs. unrepresentative, 160–161, 207–208
Sapir, Edward, on language, 103
Scriven, Michael, on argument analysis, 298
Sexist language, 112
Sign, as form of reasoning, 201–202
Simple argument, definition of, 298, 301–303
Simplicity, in language use, 109–110
Single cause, fallacy of, 209
Slippery slope, fallacy of, 209–210
Source credibility, 75
Sources
  citation of, 157–159
  objectivity of, 154–155
  primary, 158
  qualifications of, 154
  secondary, 158–159
Spheres of argument, 49–52
Statistical Abstract of the United States, 170
Statistics
  collection of, 151–152
  evaluation of, 159–161
  as evidence, 151–152
  poor method, 161
  pseudo, 160
  representative sample, 161
  unrepresentative sample, 160
Stock issues
  definition of, 252
  in policy arguments, 269–275
  in value arguments, 252–256
Strategies
  for persuasion, 67
  for refutation, 233–234
Straw argument, fallacy of, 86–87
Structural blame, in policy analysis, 272
Structures, definition of, 272
Style, argument, 33
Subclaims, 129
Subculture, 29–33
Sufficient condition, reasoning from, 199
Syllogism
  definition of, 185
  types, 187–188
Systems perspective, 268–269

Technical sphere, of argument, 50
Terminal values, 247
Terministic screens, 104

INDEX

Testimony
    reliability, 153–154
    reluctant, 82
Threshold, stock issue of, 229–230
Topicality, 331–332
Toulmin model
    parts of, 311–315
    usefulness of, 318–319
Toulmin, Stephen
    on argument fields, 52–56
    Uses of Argument, 52, 185, 186, 310
Tradition, appeal to, fallacy of, 85–86
Transitivity argument, as form of reasoning, 189
Tree diagrams, 310
Triangle of meaning, 97
Trustworthiness, 78
Two-sided analysis, 71–72

Validity, in informal logic, 186
Value
    claims of, 139
    cultural differences, 32
    definition of, 139
    personal, 247
    social, 227, 247–248
Value claims
    definition of, 139
    in fields, 140
Value emphasis, 249–250
Value hierarchy
    definition of, 204–205, 247
    the essence, 251
    the existent, 251
    the person, 251
    of quality, 251
    of quantity, 250–251

Value object, definition, 252
Value redistribution, 249
Value restandardization, 250
Value system, 247
Vividness of language use, 111
Vocabulary, size of, 104

Warrant, in Toulmin model, 311–318.
    See also Inference, Reasoning
Wenzel, Joseph W.
    on argument contexts, 28
    on argument fields, 62
    on argument perspectives, 11
    on value claims, 139
Whately, Richard, on challenge, 136–137
Whorf, Benjamin, on language, 103
Windes, Russel R., on evidence, 148
World Wide Web, 165–167